CANADIAN SOCIAL TRENDS

TRANSPARENCY MASTERS

A set of transparency masters of graphs and charts in this book may be obtained from the publisher.

CANADIAN SOCIAL TRENDS

**Edited by
Craig McKie and Keith Thompson**

Thompson Educational Publishing, Inc.

Additional copies of this publication may be obtained from:
Thompson Educational Publishing, Inc.,
11 Briarcroft Road, Toronto,
Ontario, Canada M6S 1H3
Telephone (416)766-2763 Fax: (416) 766-0398.

Canadian Cataloguing in Publication Data

Main entry under title:

Canadian social trends

ISBN 1-55077-009-8 (bound) ISBN 1-55077-010-1 (pbk.)

1. Canada - Social conditions. I. McKie, C. (Craig),
1944-   . II. Thompson, Keith, 1947-   .

HN103.C35 1990   971   C90-093689-4

ISBN 1-55077-009-8 Cloth
ISBN 1-55077-010-1 Paper

Printed in Canada.
1 2 3 4 5   94 93 92 91 90

TABLE OF CONTENTS

UNIT I: POPULATION, HUMAN GEOGRAPHY, AND HEALTH

Population

Human Geography

Health

UNIT 2: WOMEN, MARRIAGE, AND THE FAMILY

Women

Marriage

The Family

UNIT 3: WORK , LEISURE, AND SOCIAL PROBLEMS

PREFACE

Canadians live in a society in which a remarkable amount of change is occurring. We have grown accustomed to it. Perhaps we even take it for granted. This book contains a vast amount of information about Canada and Canadians, past and present. We hope it will be useful to anyone who wants to understand what is happening in Canada today, why it is happening, and what is likely to happen in the future.

To begin to understand the complexity of modern society, let alone change it, it is not sufficient to know only the current facts. We must also know the underlying dynamics of social change. The selections in this book examine current facts in the context of longer-term changes in population, health, family, work and leisure patterns. The over-riding goal is to leave the reader with a comprehensive picture of change and stability in Canadian society.

At no other time in history have citizens had access to so much information about their society. Indeed, the sheer volume of information can be a source of anxiety. How is it possible to grasp what is really going on? This book is a product of this information revolution. It distils thousands of volumes of published and unpublished material about Canada. The material has been prepared to the highest standards of accuracy and is presented in an interesting and colourful manner using photographs, charts, graphs and tables.

In selecting the material for this volume, we have tried to present a full picture while not losing important details. Readers should be able to get enough information on topics that interest them, while not losing sight of the significance of these facts. Each selection maintains an historical perspective. Current facts are contrasted with past trends, and implications for the future are explored.

This volume has three major units:

I: Population, Human Geography and Health

II. Women, Marriage and the Family

III. Work, Leisure and Social Problems

Unit I contains material on the underlying population shifts in Canada, urbanization and changes in the health of Canadians. The whole of **Unit II** is devoted to assessing the major and important changes that have occurred in the status of Canadian women, as well as in the institutions of marriage and the family. **Unit III** examines changes in our working lives, our leisure pastimes, and concludes with a look at some outstanding social problems in Canada today.

Our society has already undergone enormous changes. What will happen in our children's lifetime, not to mention our grandchildren's lifetime? It is of course impossible to know, at least to know precisely. In part, where we go from here will depend on what each of us does to shape our society. This volume begins to look at some of the issues we will face. We hope it will encourage you to play a part in making it a better place for present and future generations.

CM/KT

Acknowledgements

We would like to acknowledge the extensive editorial work which went into the preparation of articles for *Canadian Social Trends*. This work was carried principally by Mary Anne Burke, Mary Sue Devereaux, Colin Lindsay, and Jo-Anne Parliament. An editorial review committee at Statistics Canada, composed of John Coombs, Denis Desjardins, Ian Macredie, Doug Norris, Bruce Petrie, Gordon Priest, and Ed Pryor helped to oversee the selection of articles and provided support whenever required.

We must also acknowledge the essential production coordination activities of Cheryl Sarazin, the contributions of Griffe Design, Ove Design Group, the production staff of the Publications Division at Statistics Canada, the support staff of the Housing, Family and Social Statistics Division, and of course the numerous authors whose original work is represented here. Also to be thanked are the numerous undergraduate students from Carleton University, the University of Ottawa, Sir Wilfrid Laurier University, the University of Waterloo, and the University of Windsor who have worked as research assistants on the project over the past four years, and especially Cathy Shea and Carol Strike who stayed on for several terms.

Many other people have been associated with the *Canadian Social Trends* project at one time or another since its inception. There are too many to thank individually but their contributions are nevertheless remembered with thanks.

Illustration and photography sources:
Cover illustration: **Manitoba Party** by William Kurelek; oil on maisonite, 1964. Courtesy of The Issacs Gallery. National Gallery of Canada, Ottawa.
Text photographs: Canadian Social Trends, Ottawa Police Force, Alcoholism and Drug Addiction Research Foundation, Ontario Lottery Corporation, Health and Welfare Canada, Regional Industrial Expansion, Photo Centre, SSC, Daniel Boult, Cattroll/Ritcey Photo Associates, Gary Gellert, Tom Skudra, Douglas Walker/MASTERFILE (p.118), Al Harvey/MASTERFILE (p.75, 227), Ted Grant/MASTERFILE (p.225), Albert Prisner, Image Bank.
Illustrations: Les Ames, Bob Stephenson, Gordon Weber.

List of Contributors

Owen Adams is Chief of the Health Status Section of the Health Division at Statistics Canada.

Luc Albert is Chief of the Subject Matter Specifications Section of Census Operations at Statistics Canada.

Jane Badets is an Analyst with the Housing, Family, and Social Statistics Division, at Statistics Canada.

Renée Beneteau served two terms as a coop student research assistant with the Canadian Social Trends project .

Mary Blickstead did article research under contract for the Canadian Social Trends project.

Monica Boyd is a Professor in the Department of Sociology and Anthropology at Carleton University.

Mary Anne Burke is an Associate Editor with Canadian Social Trends project.

Peter Chisholm served one term as a coop student research assistant with the Canadian Centre for Justice Statistics at Statistics Canada.

Gary L. Cohen is an Analyst with the Labour and Household Surveys Analysis Division at Statistics Canada.

Mary Sue Devereaux is a Managing Editor with the Canadian Social Trends project.

Shelley Donald served one term as a coop student research assistant with the Canadian Social Trends project.

Doreen Duchesne is an Analyst with the Labour and Household Surveys Analysis Division at Statistics Canada.

Leslie Gaudette is an Analyst with the Health Division at Statistics Canada.

David Gower is an Analyst with the Labour and Household Surveys Analysis Division at Statistics Canada.

Janet Hagey is Director, Quantitative Analysis and Socio-demographic Research, Indian and Northern Affairs Canada.

Douglas J. Higgins is Chief, Projections and Analytic Systems in the Education, Culture, and Tourism Division at Statistics Canada.

Judith Hollands served a term as a coop student research assistant with the Canadian Social Trends project.

Holly Johnson is an Analyst with the Canadian Centre for Justice Statistics at Statistics Canada.

Réjean Lachapelle is Research Director, Language Studies, in the Social and Economic Studies Division at Statistics Canada.

Colin Lindsay is a Managing Editor with the Canadian Social Trends project.

Eugen Lupri is a Professor in the Department of Sociology at the University of Calgary.

Betsy MacKenzie did article research under contract for the Canadian Social Trends project.

Katherine Marshall is an Analyst with the General Social Survey project at Statistics Canada.

Jean-Pierre Maynard is Head, Unemployment Insurance Data in the Labour Division at Statistics Canada.

Laurie McDougall is an Analyst in the Education, Culture, and Tourism Division at Statistics Canada.

Nancy McLaughlin is an Analyst in the Labour and Household Surveys Analysis Division at Statistics Canada.

Susan McMillan was an officer with the Regional Office of Statistics Canada in Toronto.

Joanne Moloney is an Analyst in the Labour and Household Surveys Analysis Division at Statistics Canada.

Maureen Moore is a Senior Analyst with the Demography Division at Statistics Canada.

George A. Mori is a Senior Analyst in the Housing, Family and Social Statistics Division at Statistics Canada.

Dhruva Nagnur was a Senior Analyst with the Social and Economic Studies Division at Statistics Canada.

Michael Nagrodski is a technical officer with the Social and Economic Studies Division at Statistics Canada.

Atul Nanda served one term as a coop research student with the ethnicity unit of the Housing, Family, and Social Statistics Division at Statistics Canada.

Shirley Neill served one term as a coop research student with the Canadian Social Trends project.

Jo-Anne B. Parliament is an Associate Editor with the Canadian Social Trends project.

G. Picot is a Senior Analyst, Business and Labour Market Analysis, in the Social and Economic Studies Division at Statistics Canada.

J. Rick Ponting is a Professor in the Department of Sociology at the University of Calgary.

Gordon E. Priest is Director of the Housing, Family, and Social Statistics Division at Statistics Canada.

Edward T. Pryor is Director-General of the Census and Demographic Studies Branch at Statistics Canada.

Linda Robbins is a Research Home Economist, Food Markets Analysis Division at Agriculture Canada.

Georgia Roberts is an Analyst with the Health Division at Statistics Canada.

Horst Stiebert is Chief, Unemployment Statistics in the Labour Division at Statistics Canada.

Nat Stone is a Public Affairs officer with the Department of External Affairs.

Carol Strike is an Analyst with the General Social Survey project at Statistics Canada.

J. L. Swinamer is an Analyst in the Education, Culture, and Tourism Division at Statistics Canada.

Pierre Turcotte is an Analyst in the Housing, Family, and Social Statistics Division at Statistics Canada.

Ted Wannell is a Senior Analyst in the Social and Economic Statistics Division at Statistics Canada.

Pamela M. White is a Senior Analyst with the Housing, Family, and Social Statistics Division at Statistics Canada.

Anthony Young is an Analyst in the Education, Culture, and Tourism Division at Statistics Canada.

POPULATION, HUMAN GEOGRAPHY, AND HEALTH

Design concept for proposed mural for *First Ministers' Conference on Aboriginal Rights* by Cecil Youngfox.

Population

ETHNIC ORIGINS OF THE CANADIAN POPULATION

by Pamela M. White

At the turn of the century, the Canadian population was made up largely of people representing two major ethnic groupings: British and French. However, successive waves of immigrants from many different countries have resulted in a much more ethnically diverse country. During the first decades of this century and after the Second World War, large numbers of immigrants came to Canada from Western and Eastern Europe, as well as from Scandinavia. In the 1960s, a growing proportion of immigrants came from Southern Europe and the United States; in the 1970s and 1980s, immigrants have come primarily from Asia, Africa, the Caribbean, and Central and South America.

The current ethnic composition of the population represents a combination of the Canadian-born descendents of the various waves of immigrants, recent arrivals, and the Aboriginal population. By 1986, people with British or French backgrounds still made up the largest ethnic communities; however, neither group accounted for a majority of the population. At the same time, nearly one in four Canadians reported an ethnic background that did not include British or French origins.

Most Canadians British or French
In 1986, people with British and French ethnic backgrounds were the largest ethnic groupings in Canada. People with British backgrounds, that is, those who reported either English, Irish, Scottish, Welsh, or some combination of British origins, made up 34% of the population. Those who reported a French background made up 24% of all Canadians.

In addition, another 5% of people reported a combination of British and French ethnic backgrounds, while 13% reported some combination of British and/or French and other origins.

Many with non-British, non-French roots
People whose ethnic backgrounds do not include either British or French roots also make up a major component of the population. In 1986, 25% of all Canadians reported that they had neither British nor French ethnic origins.

People with European backgrounds have traditionally comprised the largest groups having neither British nor French

[1] Includes only those giving a single ethnic response.

origins. Overall, in 1986, people reporting a single European background other than British or French made up 16% of the total population. Those reporting German, Italian, and Ukrainian ancestry[1] were the largest of these groups, accounting for 3.6%, 2.8%, and 1.7%, respectively, of all Canadians.

However, as a result of increasing levels of non-European immigration in the 1970s and 1980s, a significant proportion of the population now reports non-European,

particularly Asian, backgrounds.

People reporting a single Asian background made up 4% of the overall Canadian population in 1986. Of these, 1.4% reported Chinese origins, while people with South Asian backgrounds, primarily Asian Indians, made up another 1.1%.

The largest single non-European ethnic group, however, are North American Aboriginals. In 1986, over 3/4 of a million people, 3% of the total population, reported some Indian, Inuit, or Métis

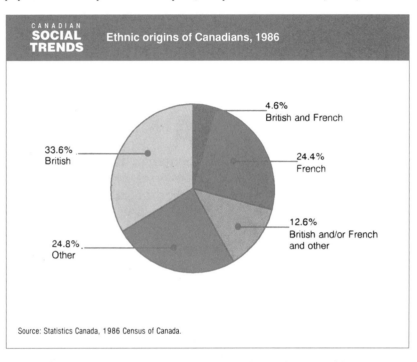

CANADIAN SOCIAL TRENDS
Ethnic origins of Canadians, 1986

33.6% British
4.6% British and French
24.4% French
12.6% British and/or French and other
24.8% Other

Source: Statistics Canada, 1986 Census of Canada.

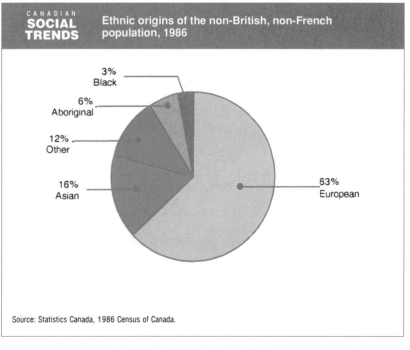

CANADIAN SOCIAL TRENDS
Ethnic origins of the non-British, non-French population, 1986

3% Black
6% Aboriginal
12% Other
16% Asian
63% European

Source: Statistics Canada, 1986 Census of Canada.

ancestry. Of these, about half reported a mix of Aboriginal and non-Aboriginal origins.

Wide regional variation in ethnicity

The ethnic make-up of the population varies considerably across Canada. While people with British origins made up the largest proportion of the population in all provinces except Quebec, the size of this group ranged from almost 90% of the population in Newfoundland to only 30% in Manitoba and Saskatchewan.

Not surprisingly, most of the population in Quebec, almost 80% in 1986, reported French as their ethnic origin. People with French ancestry also represented about a third of the population of New Brunswick. The proportion of the population reporting French origins was much smaller in the other provinces, ranging from 9% in Prince Edward Island to just 2% in British Columbia and Newfoundland.

There was also wide variation in the proportion of the provincial populations

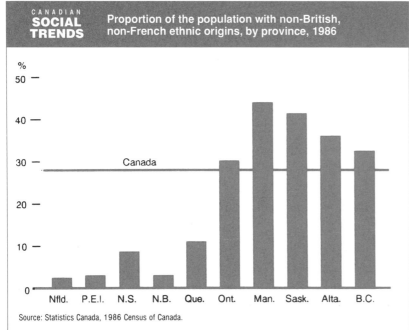

CANADIAN
SOCIAL TRENDS

Proportion of the population with non-British, non-French ethnic origins, by province, 1986

Source: Statistics Canada, 1986 Census of Canada.

with origins other than British or French. This grouping made up over 40% of the population in Manitoba and Saskatchewan, over 35% in Alberta, and over 30% in Ontario and British Columbia. By contrast, just 11% of people in Quebec, 9% in Nova Scotia, 3% in New Brunswick and Prince Edward Island, and 2% in Newfoundland reported other ethnic affiliation.

The composition of the population with neither British nor French ethnic origins also varies considerably by province. In the Prairie Provinces, people of German and Ukrainian ancestry were the largest of these ethnic groups. In fact, people giving a single ethnic origin of either German or Ukrainian represented 19% of the population in Saskatchewan, 17% in Manitoba, and 12% in Alberta.

People of German ancestry were also the second largest ethnic group in British Columbia. People of Asian descent, however, made up the next largest ethnic group in this province: 4.0% of British Columbia residents said they had Chinese roots and 2.4% were South Asian in origin.

The western provinces also have relatively large Aboriginal populations. People reporting native ancestry as their only ethnic origin made up 6% of Saskatchewan residents, 5% in Manitoba, and 2% in Alberta and British Columbia. People of Italian descent were the largest non-British, non-French ethnic group in both Ontario and Quebec. Those reporting Jewish ancestry and Aboriginals made up the next largest ethnic groups in Quebec, while in Ontario, people of German and Dutch ancestry were the next most numerous groups.

People giving German ancestry as a single ethnic response made up just under 3% of Nova Scotia residents, while those of Dutch descent represented about 1% of residents of both Nova Scotia and Prince Edward Island. As well, just under 1% of Nova Scotia residents reported they were black, the highest provincial figure for this group.

People of Aboriginal descent were the largest ethnic group other than British or French in both Newfoundland and New Brunswick. However, at just over 0.5% of the population, they made up only a small proportion of the residents in each province.

Ethnic origins of the population, by province, 1986

	British	French	British and French	British and/ or French and some other	Other	Total	Main other groups (single ethnic responses as a percentage of total population)	
				%				%
Newfoundland	89.0	2.0	4.3	2.4	2.3	100.0	Aboriginal	0.7
							German	0.2
Prince Edward Island	69.1	8.9	12.1	6.7	3.2	100.0	Dutch	1.0
							German	0.4
							Aboriginal	0.3
Nova Scotia	62.7	6.2	9.3	13.1	8.6	100.0	German	2.5
							Dutch	1.1
							Black	0.9
New Brunswick	46.9	33.3	10.0	6.6	3.2	100.0	Aboriginal	0.6
							German	0.5
							Dutch	0.4
Quebec	5.9	77.8	2.7	2.7	11.0	100.0	Italian	2.5
							Jewish	1.3
							Aboriginal	0.8
Ontario	43.8	5.9	5.7	14.3	30.2	100.0	Italian	5.1
							German	3.2
							Dutch	1.9
Manitoba	29.6	5.3	3.4	17.7	44.0	100.0	German	9.2
							Ukrainian	7.6
							Aboriginal	5.3
Saskatchewan	29.8	3.4	2.8	22.5	41.5	100.0	German	12.9
							Ukrainian	6.1
							Aboriginal	5.6
Alberta	34.4	3.3	3.9	22.3	36.1	100.0	German	7.8
							Ukrainian	4.6
							Dutch	2.4
British Columbia	41.8	2.4	3.7	19.6	32.5	100.0	German	5.2
							Chinese	4.0
							South Asian	2.4
Canada	33.6	24.4	4.6	12.6	24.9	100.0	German	3.6
							Italian	2.8
							Ukrainian	1.7

Source: Statistics Canada, 1986 Census of Canada.

CANADA'S IMMIGRANT POPULATION

by Jane Badets

Immigrants have always made up an important component of the Canadian population with each successive wave of immigrants leaving its own distinct mark on Canadian society. Over the years, they have provided labour, capital, and creativity for the development of the country. In addition, the importance of the immigrant population may grow in the future if the fertility rate in Canada continues to fall.

The share of the population made up of immigrants has remained relatively stable during the last several decades. Changes have occurred, however, in the numbers coming from different parts of the world. As well, because immigrants tend to settle in certain regions, their influence is felt unevenly across the country.

Overall, in 1986, 3.9 million immigrants were living in Canada.[1] They represented 16% of the total population, about the same proportion recorded in each census since 1951.

The relative stability in the immigrant component of the population in the last three decades represents a change from the first half of the century when the figure fluctuated. In 1901, for example, just 13% of the population were immigrants. However, as a result of the large influx of people into the country in the early 1900s, immigrants' share of the population jumped to 22% by 1911, and remained at that level through the 1931 census period.

When they arrived; where they come from
Canada's immigrant population is split evenly between those who arrived before and after 1967. Half (50%) of all immigrants living in Canada in 1986 arrived before 1967, while 31% came between 1967 and 1977, and 19% arrived during the last decade.

There have been major changes, though, in the distribution of immigrants from different parts of the globe. In particular, the proportions originating in Asia and other non-European areas has increased, while the share from Europe has declined.

People born in Asia make up the largest group of recent arrivals, accounting for 40% of all immigrants living in Canada who came to this country between 1978 and 1986. In contrast, Asians represented only 11% of those who arrived before 1978.

There were also substantial increases in the proportion of immigrants from several other non-European areas. For example, people from the Caribbean, and Central and South America made up 15% of immigrants living in Canada in 1986 who arrived in the last decade, whereas they represented only 7% of those who came before 1978. Similarly, the proportion of the immigrant population from Africa and the Middle East rose from 4% of pre-1978 arrivals to 8% of those who arrived between 1978 and 1986.

At the same time, the proportion of all immigrants who were born in Europe fell from 70% of those who arrived before 1978 to fewer than 30% of those who came during the last decade.

Europeans, though, still made up the largest share of all immigrants living in Canada in 1986, accounting for 10% of the total Canadian population. Immigrants from Asia represented another 3% of all Canadians, while people born in the Caribbean and Central and South America,

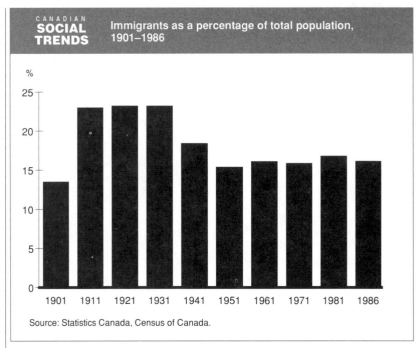

CANADIAN SOCIAL TRENDS
Immigrants as a percentage of total population, 1901–1986

Source: Statistics Canada, Census of Canada.

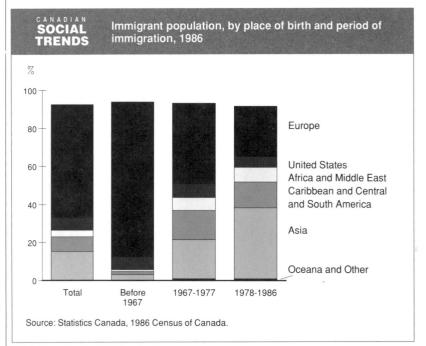

CANADIAN SOCIAL TRENDS
Immigrant population, by place of birth and period of immigration, 1986

Source: Statistics Canada, 1986 Census of Canada.

Africa and the Middle East, and the United States each accounted for about 1% of the overall population.

Provincial concentration
Over the years, immigrants have tended to settle in certain regions of the country. For example, in 1986, over nine out of ten immigrants lived in just four provinces: Ontario, Quebec, British Columbia, and Alberta.

There were particularly large concentrations of immigrants in Ontario and British Columbia; in each province, immigrants made up close to one of every four residents in 1986. Immigrants also made up 16% of the population in Alberta and 14% in Manitoba.

[1] The data in this article refer to the number of immigrants living in Canada at the time of the 1986 Census.

On the other hand, immigrants comprised only 8% of the population in Quebec, 7% in Saskatchewan, and fewer than 5% in each of the Atlantic provinces.

Most immigrants in major urban areas
Immigrants are also more likely than the overall population to live in large cities. While fewer than one-third of all Canadians lived in Toronto, Montreal, or Vancouver in 1986, more than half the immigrant population lived in one of these areas. In fact, almost a third (32%) of all immigrants lived in the Toronto metropolitan area.

Toronto had the largest immigrant population of any metropolitan area. In 1986, 36% of people living in Toronto were immigrants. Immigrants also made up almost 30% of Vancouver residents.

There were also relatively large immigrant populations in most major urban areas in southern Ontario and the Western provinces. On the other hand, immigrants generally made up smaller proportions of the population in cities in Quebec and the Atlantic provinces.

An older population
The age composition of the immigrant population differs markedly from that of non-immigrants. Specifically, the immigrant group has both a higher proportion of older people and a lower proportion of children than non-immigrants.

In 1986, 17% of immigrants, compared with 9% of non-immigrants, were aged 65 and over. The situation was reversed at the other end of the age scale where only 5% of immigrants, but 25% of non-immigrants, were younger than age 15.

More with university degrees
Immigrants are more likely than non-immigrants to have a university education. In 1986, 12% of immigrants aged 15 and over had a university degree, compared with 9% of non-immigrant adults.

At the same time, a greater proportion of immigrants had less than Grade 9 education. Nearly one-quarter (23%) of immigrants aged 15 and over living in Canada in 1986 had less than Grade 9, compared with 16% of non-immigrants.

Immigrant women were particularly likely to have relatively little formal education. Over a quarter (26%) of these women had less than Grade 9, compared with 16% of non-immigrant women and 20% of immigrant men.

Low levels of schooling were most common among immigrant women who came to Canada before 1967; almost a third (32%) of them had less than Grade 9.

Immigrants in the labour force
Overall, immigrants are somewhat less likely than non-immigrants to participate in the labour force. In 1986, 76.4% of all immigrant men, compared with 77.7% of non-immigrant men, were in the labour force. Immigrant women also had a lower overall participation rate than non-immigrant women: 53.5% compared with 56.5%.

However, the labour force participation of immigrants varies considerably depending on their age and length of residence in Canada. For example, among people aged 25-44, immigrants had a slightly higher labour force participation rate than

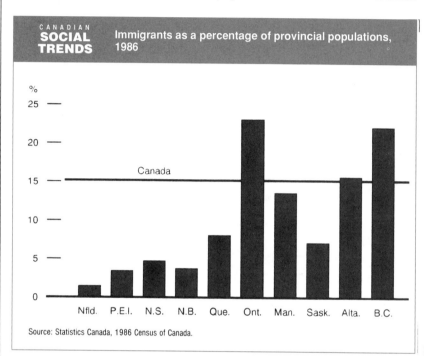

CANADIAN SOCIAL TRENDS — Immigrants as a percentage of provincial populations, 1986

Source: Statistics Canada, 1986 Census of Canada.

Occupational distribution of immigrants and non-immigrants, by sex, 1986

	Men		Women	
	Immigrants	Non-immigrants	Immigrants	Non-immigrants
	%			
Professional	16.1	12.4	18.9	21.3
Managerial	13.5	12.4	7.5	7.8
Clerical	5.9	7.0	28.2	34.7
Sales	7.4	9.1	8.5	9.6
Service	11.6	9.9	17.5	15.8
Primary	3.9	8.8	2.2	2.6
Processing	10.0	7.8	3.1	2.2
Product fabricating	12.4	9.4	10.1	2.9
Construction	10.0	10.1	0.3	0.3
Other	9.3	13.1	3.7	2.8
Total	**100.0**	**100.0**	**100.0**	**100.0**

Source: Statistics Canada, 1986 Census of Canada.

During the 1980s, the annual volume of immigration to Canada has fluctuated. The total number of immigrants fell from around 140,000 in 1980 to just over 84,000 in 1985, the lowest annual figure since the early 1960s. However, the number rose in each of the next three years, bringing the 1988 total to over 150,000, the highest level in more than a decade.

The largest group of 1988 immigrants (42%) came from Asia. Europe accounted for another 23%, while 14% came from North and Central America, 9% from the Caribbean, 7% from South America, and 5% from Africa.

During the 1980s, the proportion of immigrants claiming refugee status has generally been less than 20%. For example, in 1988, the figure was 17%.

non-immigrants. In 1986, 95.3% of immigrant men in this age group were in the labour force, compared with 94.8% for non-immigrant men. The rate for immigrant women in this age range was 75.1%, compared with 72.6% for non-immigrants.

Labour force participation rates of immigrants tend to increase with the length of residence in Canada. Of immigrant men aged 25-44, 96.3% of those who arrived more than 20 years ago were in the labour force, compared with just 87.1% of those who had lived in Canada three years or less. This trend was similar for immigrant women.

A different occupational profile

The occupational distribution of immigrants is different from that of non-immigrants.

Among men, the largest difference is in professional occupations. In 1986, 16% of immigrant men, compared with 12% of non-immigrant men, worked in professional jobs.

Immigrant men were also more likely than non-immigrants to be employed in managerial, product fabricating, processing, and service positions. On the other hand, comparatively few immigrant men worked in primary, clerical, or sales occupations.

There are also differences in the occupational distribution of immigrant and non-immigrant women. Immigrant women were three times more likely than their

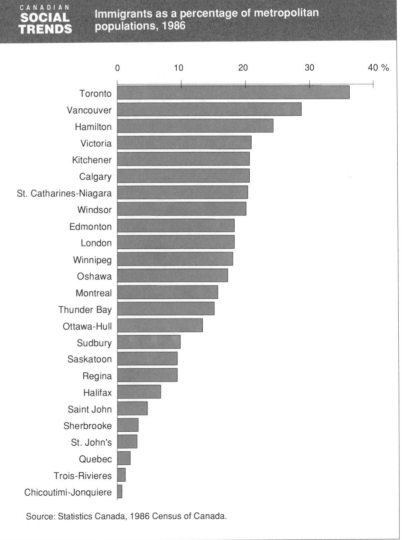

CANADIAN SOCIAL TRENDS

Immigrants as a percentage of metropolitan populations, 1986

Source: Statistics Canada, 1986 Census of Canada.

non-immigrant counterparts to be employed in product fabricating, mainly as garment workers and sewing machine operators. In 1986, 10% of immigrant women, compared with 3% of non-immigrants, were employed in these occupations.

Immigrant women were also more likely than non-immigrants to work in service occupations, while they were less likely to be employed in clerical, sales, or professional positions.

Employment income

Generally, immigrant men earn more than comparable non-immigrants, whereas the opposite is true for women. The average earned income of immigrant men who worked full time in 1985 was $31,800, compared with $30,200 for non-immigrant men. On the other hand, immigrant women working full time earned only $19,700, compared with $20,100 for similar non-immigrant women.

The trend was similar for those in the prime working ages. Immigrant men aged 25-44 employed full time in 1985 had an average employment income of $31,700, compared with $30,500 for non-immigrants. At the same time, immigrant women earned an average of $20,400 compared with $21,300 for non-immigrant women.

The income earned by immigrants varies according to their length of residence in Canada. For instance, men aged 25-44 who arrived before 1967 earned an average of $34,100 in 1985; this compared with an average of $22,900 earned by men who came to Canada between 1983 and 1986. Among women aged 25-44, those who immigrated before 1967 earned an average of $22,100 in 1985, compared with only $14,000 for those who had been in Canada three years or less.

LANGUAGE IN CANADA

by Luc Albert

Census data indicate that there have been several distinct trends in the linguistic make-up of Canada since 1971. Both the proportion of the population in provinces other than Quebec with English mother tongue,[1] and that with French mother tongue in Quebec have risen. As well, bilingualism has become more common, as a growing percentage of Canadians report they are able to conduct a conversation in both official languages.

English increasing outside Quebec

In the last decade and a half, the proportion of Canadians living outside Quebec with English mother tongue has increased. In 1986, 80.0% of people living in provinces other than Quebec reported English as their mother tongue; this was up from 78.4% in 1971 and 79.4% in 1981. During the same period, the proportion of this population with French mother tongue fell from 6.0% in 1971 to 5.0% in 1986.

Other than Quebec, New Brunswick has by far the largest share of its population with French mother tongue. In 1986, 33.5% of residents of this province had French as their mother tongue, down slightly from 34.0% in 1971.

The proportion of people with French mother tongue was much lower in the remaining provinces. The figure was around 5% in Ontario, Manitoba, and Prince Edward Island; 4% in Nova Scotia; 2% in Saskatchewan, Alberta, and British Columbia; and just 0.5% in New-foundland. As well, the percentage of the population with French mother tongue fell in all these provinces between 1971 and 1986.

The proportion of Canadians outside Quebec whose mother tongue was neither English nor French has also declined. In 1986, 14.9% of this population had a mother tongue other than an official language, down from 15.6% in 1971.

There is considerable provincial variation in the percentage of people with a mother tongue other than English or French. In 1986, 22% of Manitoba

[1] Mother tongue is the language first learned and still understood.

residents, along with between 15% and 17% of those in Ontario, British Columbia, Saskatchewan, and Alberta, had a mother tongue other than English or French. In comparison, only 2% of people in Nova Scotia and around 1% of those in the other Atlantic provinces had a mother tongue other than one of the official languages.

Francophone population increasing in Quebec

The proportion of Quebec residents with French as their mother tongue has increased steadily in the last decade and a half. In 1986, French was the mother tongue of 82.8% of the people living in this province, up from 80.7% in 1971 and 82.4% in 1981.

There has also been a slight increase in the proportion of Quebec residents reporting a mother tongue other than English or French, from 6.2% in 1971 to 6.8% in 1986. In contrast, the percentage of people in Quebec with English mother tongue fell from 13.1% in 1971 to 10.4% in 1986.

The actual number of people in Quebec with English mother tongue also

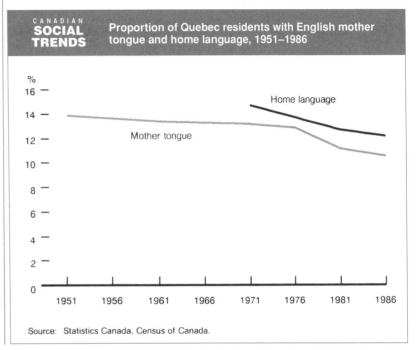

CANADIAN SOCIAL TRENDS

Proportion of Quebec residents with English mother tongue and home language, 1951–1986

Source: Statistics Canada, Census of Canada.

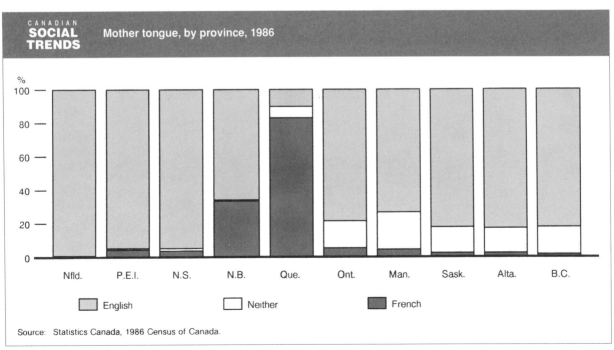

CANADIAN SOCIAL TRENDS

Mother tongue, by province, 1986

English   Neither   French

Source: Statistics Canada, 1986 Census of Canada.

continued to decrease between 1981 and 1986, although the decline was smaller than in the previous five-year period. The number of anglophones in Quebec fell 4% between 1981 and 1986, compared with a 12% decline between 1976 and 1981.

Much of the decline in Quebec's anglophone population is attributable to the fact that the number of these people leaving Quebec for elsewhere in Canada far exceeds the number entering the province from other regions. Between 1981 and 1986, 41,000 more anglophones left Quebec for other parts of Canada than came to Quebec from other provinces. This was down significantly from a net loss of 106,000 during the 1976-1981 period.

English increasing, French declining across Canada

When figures from Quebec and the other provinces are combined, the results show that the proportion of all Canadians with English mother tongue has risen, while the percentage whose mother tongue is French has fallen. Between 1971 and 1986, the percentage of people with English mother tongue rose from 60.2% to 62.1%, while the proportion with

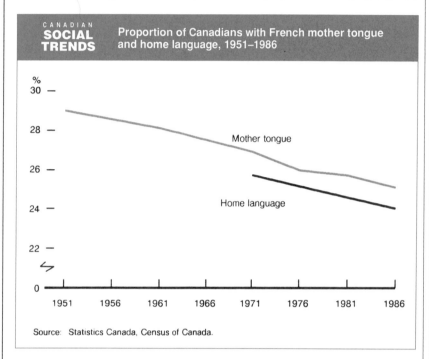

CANADIAN
SOCIAL TRENDS

Proportion of Canadians with French mother tongue and home language, 1951–1986

Source: Statistics Canada, Census of Canada.

Proportion of people in provinces outside Quebec with French mother tongue and home language, 1971 and 1986				
	French mother tongue		French home language	
	1971	**1986**	**1971**	**1986**
		%		
Newfoundland	0.7	0.5	0.4	0.4
Prince Edward Island	6.6	4.7	3.9	2.8
Nova Scotia	5.0	4.1	3.5	2.9
New Brunswick	34.0	33.5	31.4	31.3
Ontario	6.3	5.3	4.6	3.8
Manitoba	6.1	4.9	4.0	2.8
Saskatchewan	3.4	2.3	1.7	0.9
Alberta	2.9	2.4	1.4	1.1
British Columbia	1.7	1.6	0.5	0.6
Total	**6.0**	**5.0**	**4.3**	**3.6**

Source: Statistics Canada, Census of Canada.

Language transfers

For some Canadians, their mother tongue is not the language they speak most often at home. Such shifts, which are a major factor in determining the mother tongue of succeeding generations, have contributed to the growth of the English population in Canada. While 62.1% of Canadians reported English as their mother tongue in 1986, a considerably larger proportion, 68.9%, reported that this was the language they spoke most often at home.

Even in Quebec, more people spoke English in their home (12.3%) than learned it as their mother tongue (10.4%). This occurred largely because, in the past, most Quebec residents whose mother tongue was neither French nor English who made language shifts adopted English.[1]

The French-speaking community in Quebec has neither increased nor decreased as a result of language transfers. In fact, in 1986, the proportion of the Quebec population with French mother tongue (82.8%) was the same as that which spoke French most often at home.

Outside Quebec, though, the French-speaking community has declined as a result of language shifts. In 1986, French was the mother tongue of 5.0% of residents of provinces other than Quebec, but only 3.6% of this population reported it as the language they spoke most often at home.

The impact of language transfers in provinces outside Quebec has been greatest in the three western-most provinces. The francophone population in Saskatchewan, Alberta, and British Columbia has declined by over half as a result of language transfers. Such transfers also resulted in substantial proportional declines in the francophone populations in Manitoba, Prince Edward Island, Nova Scotia, and Ontario.

[1] A more comprehensive analysis of the 1986 Census is required to determine whether this process continued between 1981 and 1986.

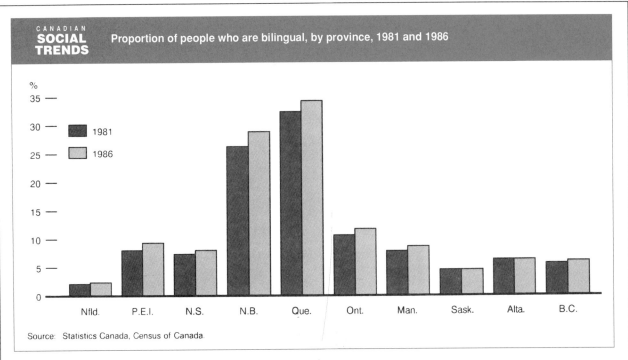

%

■ 1981

□ 1986

Nfld.　P.E.I.　N.S.　N.B.　Que.　Ont.　Man.　Sask.　Alta.　B.C.

Source: Statistics Canada, Census of Canada.

French mother tongue declined from 26.9% to 25.1%.

Several factors have contributed to the overall decline in the proportion of Canadians whose mother tongue is French. These factors include low fertility in Quebec, the small proportion of immigrants who speak French, as well as the linguistic assimilation of French-speaking minorities outside Quebec, and the tendency of people with mother tongues other than English or French to adopt the English language.

On the other hand, there has been little overall change in the proportion of Canadians with a mother tongue other than French or English. In the 1971-1986 period, the share of people with another mother tongue remained stable at around 13%.

However, there were changes in the proportion of people with different mother tongues. There was strong growth in the number of people reporting languages associated with the birthplaces of recent immigrants, notably Spanish, and Asiatic languages such as Chinese, Vietnamese, Persian (Farsi), and Tamil. On the other hand, the proportion of people with mother tongues such as German and Ukrainian has fallen.

More Canadians bilingual

In 1986, more than four million Canadians reported they could conduct a conversation in both English and French. That year, 16.2% of the population was bilingual, up from 13.4% in 1971 and 15.3% in 1981.

SCHOOL CROSSING

PASSAGE POUR ÉCOLIERS

Quebec has the highest proportion of population which is bilingual. In fact, slightly over half of all Canada's bilingual population in 1986 lived in this province. That year, 34.5% of Quebec residents reported they could conduct a conversation in either official language.

The most bilingual group within Quebec was anglophone. In 1986, more than half (54%) of these people were bilingual, as were almost half (47%) of Quebec residents whose mother tongue was neither English nor French. At the same time, about a third (30%) of Quebec francophones were bilingual.

In contrast, fewer than 6% of people residing outside Quebec with English, or a language other than English or French, as their mother tongue reported they were bilingual in 1986. However, the vast majority of people outside Quebec with French mother tongue were bilingual. In 1986, almost four of every five (79%) of them were able to conduct a conversation in both official languages.

Outside Quebec, the most bilingual province was New Brunswick, where 29.1% of the population reported themselves as able to conduct a conversation in both official languages. In the remaining provinces, the proportion of the population which was bilingual ranged from around 12% in Ontario to less than 3% in Newfoundland.

Between 1981 and 1986, bilingualism increased in all provinces except Alberta, where the proportion reporting they were able to converse in both official languages was unchanged.

Youth more bilingual

Young Canadians are generally more likely than older people to be bilingual. In 1986, 20.5% of the population aged 15-24 could conduct a conversation in either English or French; this compared with 19.9% of those aged 25-44, 16.8% of those aged 45-64, and 12.4% of people aged 65 and over. This suggests that French immersion programs in Canadian schools have contributed to the growth of bilingualism.

SOUTH ASIANS IN CANADA

by Pamela M. White and Atul Nanda

People who trace their ethnic origin to countries such as India, Pakistan, Sri Lanka, and Bangladesh account for a small but significant proportion of Canada's population. In 1986, these people, collectively identified as South Asians, numbered just over 314,000, and they made up 1.3% of the total Canadian population.

Most South Asians immigrants

The majority of Canada's South Asian community are immigrants. Over seven out of ten (71%) South Asians living in Canada in 1986 were foreign-born. The remaining 29% were born in Canada, the descendants of South Asian immigrants.

As well, most South Asian immigrants came to Canada in the last two decades. Of those living in Canada in 1986, 94% arrived after 1966; in comparison, only about half of all other immigrants arrived during the last two decades. As a result, South Asians made up 10% of all immigrants who arrived in Canada in the 1967-1986 period. In contrast, only 1% of the immigrant population which arrived before 1967 were South Asians.

The majority of South Asian immigrants have taken out Canadian citizenship. By 1986, 78% of all foreign-born South Asians who had been in Canada for more than three years were Canadian citizens.

Geographic concentration

The South Asian population tends to be concentrated in certain areas of the country. In 1986, 88% of all South Asians lived in just three provinces: the majority (51%) were in Ontario, while British Columbia was home to 25%, and 11% lived in Alberta.

As a result, South Asians made up 2.7% of the population in British Columbia, 1.8% in Ontario, and 1.5% in Alberta. In each of the remaining provinces, South

Asians represented less than 1% of the population.

South Asians also tend to live in major urban centres. Close to three-quarters of those in Ontario were in the metropolitan Toronto area, while 66% of British Columbia's South Asian population lived in Vancouver. As a result, South Asians made up 3.9% of the population in Vancouver and 3.8% in Toronto. They also made up 2.4% of people in Calgary and 2.1% in Edmonton.

South Asians were less well-represented in other major urban areas. In fact, their share of the population was either greater than or equal to the national average (1.3%) in only three other metropolitan areas: Kitchener (1.6%), Victoria (1.4%), and Winnipeg (1.3%).

A young population
The South Asian community is somewhat younger than the overall Canadian population. Because most South Asians immigrated to Canada as young adults after 1966, there is as yet no large elderly South Asian population. While the elderly constituted 10% of Canada's total population in 1986, just 3% of South Asians were aged 65 and over.

On the other hand, children make up a relatively large proportion of the South Asian population. In 1986, 30% of South Asians, compared with 22% of all Canadians, were younger than age 15.

A well-educated group
Canada's South Asians generally have higher levels of formal education than the overall population. This is partly attributable to Canadian immigration policy, which favours highly qualified applicants.

In 1986, 21% of South Asians aged 15 and over, compared with 10% of adult Canadians, were university graduates. At the same time, just 13% of South Asian adults, compared with 17% of the total adult population, had less than a Grade 9 education.

There are, however, considerable differences between the educational attainment of South Asian men and women. For example, while 25% of South Asian men were university graduates, the proportion among South Asian women was 17%. Nonetheless, both South Asian men and women were more than twice as likely as comparable Canadians to have a university degree. The corresponding figures for the Canadian population overall were 11% for men and 8% for women.

Much of the difference between the educational attainment of South Asian

men and women may be attributable to the different immigrant categories under which they are admitted to the country. Many South Asian men come as independent immigrants, and so are required to meet certain education and employment criteria. On the other hand, South Asian women are more likely to come to Canada as dependants sponsored by their husband or family, and so for them, educational qualifications may not be as important.

High labour force participation
South Asians are generally more likely than Canadians overall to be in the labour force. In 1986, 78.1% of South Asians aged 25 and over were in the labour force, compared with 66 1% of the total population.

This difference holds for both men and women. The labour force participation rate for South Asian men aged 25 and over in 1986 was 89.8%, about 10 percentage points above the rate (79.4%) for all

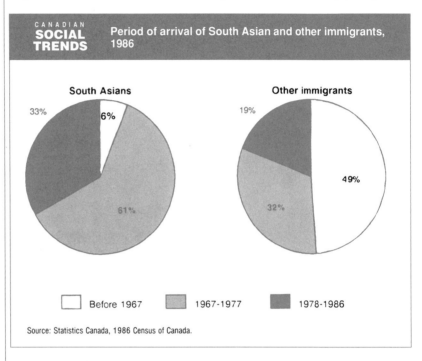

CANADIAN SOCIAL TRENDS Period of arrival of South Asian and other immigrants, 1986

South Asians

Other immigrants

☐ Before 1967   ▨ 1967-1977   ▧ 1978-1986

Source: Statistics Canada, 1986 Census of Canada.

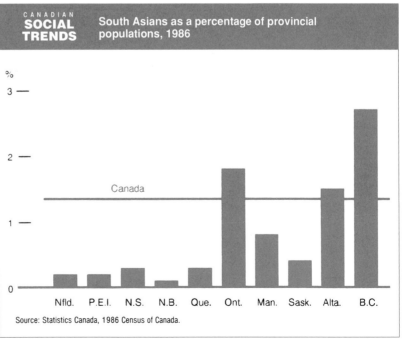

CANADIAN SOCIAL TRENDS South Asians as a percentage of provincial populations, 1986

Source: Statistics Canada, 1986 Census of Canada.

Canadian men. The corresponding rates for women were 65.6% among South Asians, and 53.6% for the total population.

Occupational differences

The occupational distribution of South Asians also differs from that of the total population.

Among men, South Asians are more likely than other Canadians to work in professional occupations. In 1986, 18% of South Asian men were in professional positions, compared with 13% of all Canadian men.

South Asian men were also more likely than other Canadian men to work in clerical, processing, and product fabricating occupations. In contrast, relatively small proportions of South Asian men worked in primary occupations and construction.

As was the case for all employed women, about one in three South Asian women working outside the home had a clerical job, and substantial proportions were employed in professional and service occupations. The representation of South Asian women in these areas, however, was lower than that for Canadian women overall. The percentages of South Asian women in managerial and sales jobs were also comparatively low. On the other hand, South Asian women were much more likely than other Canadian women to work in product fabricating.

Earned incomes similar

The earned incomes of South Asians are almost the same as those of Canadians overall. South Asian men who worked full time all year in 1985 had an average earned income of $30,100, slightly less than the $30,500 average for all Canadian men. At the same time, South Asian women who worked full time all year earned an average of $19,200, compared with $20,000 for their Canadian counterparts.

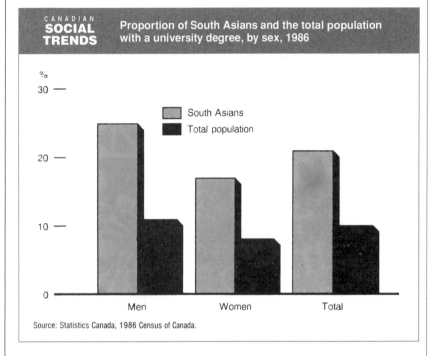

CANADIAN SOCIAL TRENDS

Proportion of South Asians and the total population with a university degree, by sex, 1986

South Asians
Total population

Source: Statistics Canada, 1986 Census of Canada.

Occupational distribution of South Asians and total population, by sex, 1986				
	Men		**Women**	
	South Asian	**Total Canadian**	**South Asian**	**Total Canadian**
		%		
Professional	17.8	13.1	15.9	20.9
Managerial	12.2	12.6	5.8	7.8
Clerical	9.6	6.8	32.2	33.5
Sales	8.2	8.8	6.9	9.4
Service	9.8	10.2	13.9	16.1
Primary	2.8	7.9	5.1	2.5
Processing	13.4	8.2	4.1	2.4
Product fabricating	12.0	9.9	10.4	4.2
Construction	2.9	10.1	0.1	0.3
Other	11.3	12.4	5.4	3.0
Total	**100.0**	**100.0**	**100.0**	**100.0**

Source: Statistics Canada, 1986 Census of Canada.

PUBLIC OPINION ON ABORIGINAL PEOPLES' ISSUES IN CANADA

by J. Rick Ponting

The Native Indian, Inuit, and Metis population has grown rapidly in recent decades to a position of increasing social, demographic, and constitutional prominence in Canadian society. In light of that growing stature, the attitudes of the larger non-Native society to Natives and contemporary Native issues are of general consequence. Those attitudes were the subject of a comprehensive survey undertaken for the University of Calgary by Decima Research Ltd. in 1986.

The survey results show that Canadians generally hold supportive attitudes toward Natives, although that support varies considerably from region to region and has eroded slightly since the mid-1970s.[1] Support drops significantly when Canadians perceive that special "privilege" is being conferred on Natives, with the exception of issues pertaining to land. Canadians seem to recognize Natives' special relationship with the land and up to a point, are willing to make accommodation for that.

While there is widespread support for the general notion of increased self-determination for Natives, levels of knowledge and awareness of aboriginal issues were found to be generally low.

Knowledge about Natives

From an estimated 225,000 Native persons living in what is now Canada just prior to the arrival of Europeans, the Native population declined to approximately half that number by the time of Confederation. However, by 1986, the Canadian Census found that the population reporting at least some Native origins had reached approximately three-quarters of a million or about 3% of the total population of Canada.

Despite the large number of people of Native origins, Canadians are not knowledgeable about the demographics of the Native population. For instance, in the 1986 survey, over one-third (37%), as compared to 46% in our similar survey in 1976, would not hazard a guess when asked what proportion of the total Canadian population is Native. An even greater proportion (41%) significantly over-estimated the size of the Native population in that they perceived it to be in excess of 8% of the total Canada population.

Using this and several other questions which tapped knowledge about certain rudimentary aspects of Native affairs, an Index of Knowledge about Native Affairs was constructed on which scores could range from a low of 3 to a high of 7.[2]

The national average score was low at 4.36. Most of the population congregated near the low end of the knowledge continuum both in the 1986 survey and on a comparable index in the 1976 study. In

---

[1] See Roger Gibbins, "The 1976 National Survey," in J.R. Ponting and R. Gibbins, *Out of Irrelevance: A Socio-Political Introduction to Indian Affairs in Canada,* Scarborough, Ontario: Butterworth, 1980, pp. 71-93.

[2] Other questions used in the Index of Knowledge about Native Affairs included those dealing with knowledge of the existence of the Indian Act, the difference between Status and non-Status Indians, and two other demographic measures — the percentage of the respondent's province which is Native and the percentage of Indians living on reserves.

both years, residents of Quebec exhibited particularly low levels of knowledge and westerners exhibited comparatively high levels of knowledge.

As in 1976, a majority was unaware of the difference between Status and non-Status Indians, although the size of that majority declined over the decade. These and other data indicate some small increase in Canadian levels of knowledge over the ten-year period.

An important area of knowledge measured was a respondent's understanding of the term "aboriginal people". Without prompting, only a tiny fraction of interviewees correctly identified this term as encompassing the Indian, Inuit, and Metis peoples.

Without assistance from the interviewer, almost a third of Canadians failed to indicate even an approximate understanding of the term. Significantly, even when explicitly asked, "Would you include the Metis people [as aboriginal people]?", only a slight majority said "yes." Even when explicitly asked, about one in five Canadian adults does not consider Indians and Inuits to be aboriginal people.

Familiarity with Native affairs

An Index of Familiarity with Native Events/Phenomena was also developed in both the 1976 and 1986 studies. The 1986 Familiarity Index was based on answers to a question in which respondents were given a list of seven events, organizations, or phenomena and were asked to indicate, on a three-point scale, how familiar they are with each one.[3] The national average score of 1.62 in 1986 was well below the mid-point (2.0) of the scale.

On all but two of the items a majority of respondents said they were "not at all familiar." Thus, a majority was unaware of such things as one of the most modern "treaties" (the James Bay and Northern Quebec Agreement of 1975), the existence of aboriginal rights in the constitution[4], and the Lyell Island controversy between

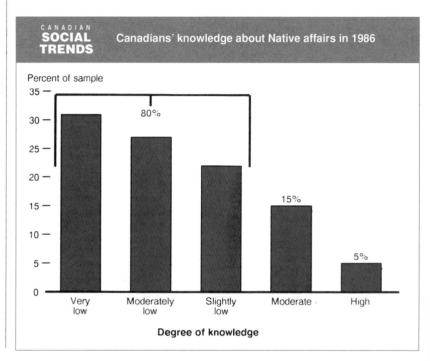

CANADIAN SOCIAL TRENDS
Canadians' knowledge about Native affairs in 1986

Percent of sample

Degree of knowledge

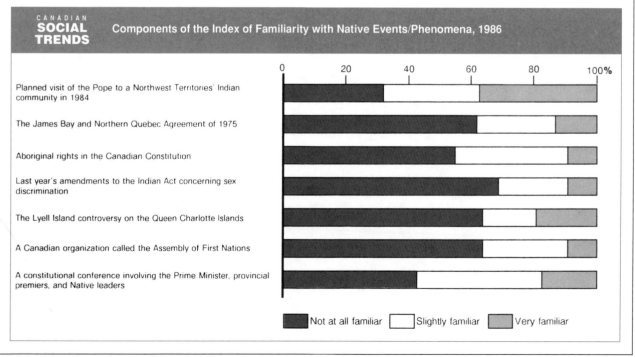

CANADIAN SOCIAL TRENDS
Components of the Index of Familiarity with Native Events/Phenomena, 1986

Planned visit of the Pope to a Northwest Territories' Indian community in 1984

The James Bay and Northern Quebec Agreement of 1975

Aboriginal rights in the Canadian Constitution

Last year's amendments to the Indian Act concerning sex discrimination

The Lyell Island controversy on the Queen Charlotte Islands

A Canadian organization called the Assembly of First Nations

A constitutional conference involving the Prime Minister, provincial premiers, and Native leaders

■ Not at all familiar   □ Slightly familiar   ▨ Very familiar

logging companies and Haida Indians in the Queen Charlotte Islands.

Only the two items involving well-known public figures received relatively high scores. These were "the planned visit of the Pope to a Northwest Territories' Indian community in 1984" and "a constitutional conference involving the Prime Minister, provincial premiers, and Native leaders."

Current measures of the Native population

According to the latest available data, the Native population of Canada can be described as follows:

The federal department of Indian and Northern Affairs Canada (INAC) 1987 register count of Status Indians stood at 415,898 individuals. As of July 15, 1988, figures for those people applying for reinstatement as registered Indians under Bill C31 were: reinstatement applications completed 61,008; applications in process 21,331; applications still to be reviewed 21,794, for a grand total of 104,133.

In the 1981 Census of Canada, the count of non-Status Indians was 75,110.

The 1986 Census of Canada showed the total population with aboriginal origins as follows:

• North American Indian	286,225	(40.22%)
• North American Indian and non-aboriginal	239,400	(33.64%)
• Metis	59,745	(8.39%)
• Metis and non-aboriginal	68,695	(9.65%)
• Inuit	27,290	(3.83%)
• Inuit and non-aboriginal	6,175	(0.87%)
• Other multiple responses with aboriginal origin(s)	23,995	(3.37%)
• Total population with aboriginal origins	711,720	(100%)

+ See also, Andrew Siggner, 'The Socio-demographic Conditions of Registered Indians,' *Canadian Social Trends*, Winter 1986, pp. 2-9.

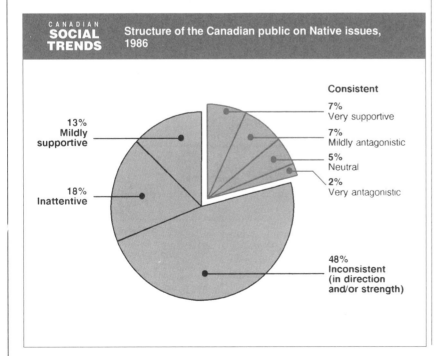

CANADIAN **SOCIAL TRENDS** Structure of the Canadian public on Native issues, 1986

13% Mildly supportive

18% Inattentive

Consistent

7% Very supportive

7% Mildly antagonistic

5% Neutral

2% Very antagonistic

48% Inconsistent (in direction and/or strength)

These findings parallel results on comparable questions in the 1976 study. For instance, over 55% in both studies reported virtually no familiarity (in 1976, vague familiarity at best) with the James Bay and Northern Quebec Agreement. Similarly, in 1976, two-thirds reported no familiarity or only vague familiarity with "the 1974 Supreme Court of Canada decision rejecting an Indian woman's argument that the Indian Act violated the Canadian Bill of Rights," while in 1986 the same proportion reported no familiarity with "last year's amendments to the Indian Act concerning sex discrimination." The latter was the government's legislative response to the issue raised in the 1974 court case.

Structure of the public

In light of the low levels of knowledge and familiarity with Native matters, it comes as no surprise that the Canadian population is not rigidly divided into opposing camps, each exhibiting consistency of opinion on Native issues. For instance, across two six-item Indexes of Sympathy for Natives/Indians, only a small fraction (2%) of the sample consistently falls at the very antagonistic end of the spectrum, while 7% consistently fall at the opposite extreme as very supportive.

Almost half of Canadians hold inconsistent views in the strength or the direction of their opinion on Natives and Native issues. A further one in five Canadians is almost totally inattentive to Native issues, although he or she will often render an opinion when asked by an interviewer.

Overall, considering those persons whose views are consistent and which fall not just in the extreme categories but also in the neutral, mildly antagonistic, and mildly supportive ranges, one finds that those with favourable views toward Natives outnumber those who hold antagonistic views by a margin of about

[3] In 1986, the categories were "very," "slightly," and "not at all" familiar. In 1976, the categories were "quite," "somewhat," "vaguely," and "not at all" familiar. A respondent's score on the 1986 index was his/her average score over the seven items, where scores could range from 1.0 ("not at all familiar") to 3.0 ("very familiar").

[4] For instance, Section 35.1 of the Constitution Act, 1982, states: "The existing aboriginal and treaty rights of the aboriginal peoples of Canada are hereby recognized and affirmed."

two to one. Nevertheless, those who do not show attitudinal consistency (48%) outnumber those who do.

The structure of the public varies considerably from one region of Canada to another. For instance, a clear majority in each of the western provinces falls into the "inconsistent" category, and in Quebec, an unusually large portion of the population (about 30%) falls in the "inattentive" category.

General orientations: changes since 1976

The findings from the 1986 survey taken together with comparable measures from 1976 suggest that there has been a slight erosion in support for Natives over the ten-year period, to the extent that six questionnaire items included in both surveys are indicative of the general tenor of public opinion towards Natives. A comparative Index of Sympathy (or general supportive attitudes) for Indians was formed by combining scores from six individual questions. Examination of the distribution of Canadians on this Sympathy Index reveals that, relative to the 1976 curve, the 1986 curve is shifted slightly toward the unsupportive end of the continuum.[5]

However, it is important to bear in mind that despite that slight erosion of attitudinal support, the average in 1986 is almost exactly at the mid-point on the continuum. On average, Canadians do not tend to be markedly hostile nor markedly supportive in their attitudes toward Indians. Nor does either year's curve exhibit two "humps" that would indicate a sharply divided public.

Several other items from 1976 were also repeated in 1986. Among these was one which revealed that Canadians continue to attach low priority to the improvement of the social and economic situation of Natives.

Self-government and special status

For several years, Native self-government has been the focus of the constitutional debate over Native rights. Significantly, "self-government" and "special status" for Natives elicit quite different responses from Canadians. Self-government is not viewed as a form of "special status" for Natives; instead, it is seen in a much more positive light.

There is a striking contrast between the curve depicting the distribution of the responses of Canadians on the Index of

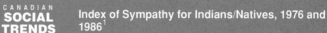

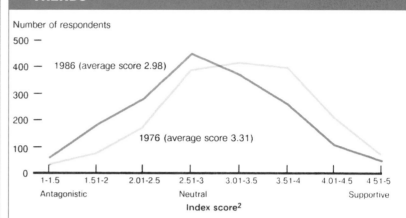

Index of Sympathy for Indians/Natives, 1976 and 1986[1]

[1] 1976 data are weighted by province alone. 1986 data are weighted simultaneously by province, age, sex, and language most often spoken at home.
[2] Scores range from 1 (antagonistic) through 3 (neutral) to 5 (supportive) across the items answered (minimum 3 items).

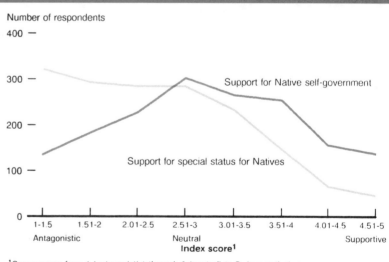

Support for special status for Natives and for Native self-government, 1986

[1] Scores range from 1 (antagonistic) through 3 (neutral) to 5 (supportive) across the items answered.

Support of Native Self-Government and the curve depicting the Index of Support for Special Status for Natives. Most Canadians fall on the unsupportive side of the mid-point (3.0) on the "special status" index, while the reverse is true on the "self-government" index.

The shapes of the two curves differ markedly. When the word "special" was

[5] The social science literature leads us to expect an even lower level of support for Natives than was found in the 1986 study. Thus, the significance of the changes between 1976 and 1986 should not be over-emphasized, for they may merely be a slower-than-normal appearance of the normal evolution of public opinion on numerous social issues in advanced industrial societies. See Anthony Downs, "Up and Down with Ecology — The 'Issue-Attention Cycle'," *The Public Interest*, XVIII: pp. 38-50.

actually incorporated in a question, responses were even more antagonistic.

For instance, respondents were asked to choose which of the following two statements comes closer to their own view: "For crimes committed by Indians on Indian reserves, there should be special courts with Indian judges"; or "Crimes committed by Indians on Indian reserves should be handled in the same way as crimes committed elsewhere." Almost two-thirds chose the latter statement, while only about one-quarter chose the former statement. An almost identical ratio appeared on two other questions dealing with "special" arrangements in other institutional spheres.

It would seem that self-government is not viewed as a special privilege, but instead, as implementation of a basic democratic right of self-determination. Support for this interpretation is to be found in respondents' answers to a question which asked them to complete the following sentence: "One of the best things that could happen to Indians would be if the federal government_____ ." By a wide margin, the most frequently cited types of response were those which called for the government to "grant" Indians greater autonomy, self-

About the survey

The national sample consisted of 1,834 non-aboriginal persons aged 18 and over living in the ten provinces, but excluding the very small populations of the Yukon and North-west Territories. Within each household, a single respondent who had the next birthday closest to the date of the interview was selected. Households were selected at random by computer using Statistics Canada enumeration areas as the primary sampling unit. Clusters of seven interviews were conducted in each enumeration area selected.

Probability of selection was disproportionate by province, and within each province the sample was stratified by community size. A weighting scheme was used to bring the sample back into the proper proportions vis-à-vis the 1981 non-Native Census population (in the ten provinces). It simultaneously took into account age, sex, province, and language most often spoken at home.

In 19 out of every 20 national samples of this size drawn in Canada, the results would fall within about plus or minus two percentage points of the results found here.

Data were collected through in-home, face-to-face interviews averaging seventy minutes in duration. The questionnaire contained two hundred questions, including sixty dealing explicitly with Native matters.

Sampling, translation, data collection, coding of closed-ended questions, and data entry were done under contract by Decima Research Ltd. The questionnaire was designed by the author.

A 1976 survey, comparative results of which are also presented here, was virtually identical in sample size and was very similar in sampling design. Roger Gibbins, a political scientist at the University of Calgary, was co-director of that study.

Components of the Index of Comparative Sympathy for Natives, 1976, 1986

Year	Phraseology of item	% Agreeing	% Disagreeing	National average[1]
1976	The federal Department of Indian Affairs tends to be more concerned with bureaucratic red tape than seeing to the needs of the Indian people.	65	12	3.96
1986	Same	55	15	3.69
1976	Indians deserve to be a lot better off economically than they are now.	72	12	4.05
1986	Same	48	29	2.32
1976	Indians, as the first Canadians, should have special cultural protection that other groups don't have.	44	36	3.09
1986	Same	38	46	2.82
1976	Most Indian leaders who criticize the federal Department of Indian Affairs are more interested in improving their own political position than they are interested in improving the lot of their people.	29	36	3.12
1986	Native leaders who call for self-government for Native people are more interested in promoting their own personal career than in helping Native people.	30	41	3.18
1976	Indian people themselves, not the provincial government, should decide what Indian children are taught in school.	35	49	2.78
1986	Native schools should not have to follow provincial guidelines on what is taught.	22	67	2.18
1976	Where Indian principles of land ownership conflict with the white man's law, Indian principles should be given priority.	30	35	2.91
1986	Same	33	44	2.81

[1] The average can range from 1.0 to 5.0. The mid-point (neutral) is 3.0. For all items, in calculating the average, a response which is strongly supportive of Indians/Natives is scored as 5, a strongly antagonistic response is scored as 1, etc. Thus, on the first item agreeing responses were scored as supportive (4 or 5, depending on whether "strongly agree" or "moderately agree"), and disagreeing responses were scored as antagonistic (1 or 2), while on the fourth item the reverse was true. A score of 3 was assigned to respondents who chose the "neither agree nor disagree" category; while those who said "don't know/no opinion" were not given a score.

Opinions on specific issues: "special status" and self-government, 1986							
Statement	Agree strongly	Agree moderately	Neutral	Disagree moderately	Disagree strongly	Don't know; no opinion	Total
				%			
Special status							
If Parliament and the elected leaders of the Native people agreed that some Canadian laws would not apply in Native communities, it would be all right with me.	15	23	10	19	25	9	101[1]
Native schools should not have to follow provincial guidelines on what is taught.	9	13	5	26	41	5	99[1]
Native governments should have powers equivalent to those of provincial governments.	13	18	10	24	27	8	100
Native governments should be responsible to elected Native politicians, rather than to Parliament, for the federal government money they receive.	11	17	15	19	25	13	100
Self-government							
It is important to the future well-being of Canadian society that the aspirations of Native people for self-government be met.	17	25	17	19	14	9	101[1]
Those provincial premiers who oppose putting the right to Native self-government in the Constitution are harming Native people.	17	21	17	21	13	12	101[1]
Most Native leaders who call for self-government for Native people are more interested in promoting their own personal career than in helping Native people.[2]	13	17	16	23	18	13	100
The Constitution of Canada should specifically recognize the right of Indians to self-government.	18	23	13	21	19	7	101[1]

[1] Totals may not add to 100% due to rounding.

[2] An agreeing response was treated in the analyses as indicative of an antagonistic toward self-government, and a disagreeing response was treated as supportive of self-government. For all other questions above, the respective interpretations were the reverse of those just cited.

determination, and responsibility over their own affairs.

Land claims

Noteworthy levels of support for Natives were also found on questions dealing with land claims and land use conflicts, particularly those involving natural resource development projects. For instance, the 1976 survey asked whether respondents regarded "all", "many", "few", or "no" Indian land claims as valid. A majority (61%) said "all" or "many," while about one-third (35%) said "few" or "none."

In 1986, on a different question concerning land claims, only about one-fifth (21%) of Canadians seemed to challenge the validity of Native land claims. A challenge was indicated by agreement with the position that the government should offer Natives neither land nor financial compensation when negotiating future land claim settlements with them. Fifteen percent favoured offering only more land, while 22% favoured offering "financial compensation for the lands lost," and 26% favoured offering both land and compensation.

Another important question on land claims in the 1986 survey asked respondents to choose which of three statements comes closest to their own view. The statements, with the percent choosing each, are: "Native land claims should **not** be allowed to delay natural resource projects at all" (19%); "Natural resources development companies should not be allowed to even set foot on land claimed by Natives until those Native land claims have been settled" (42%); and "I haven't given any thought to the matter of land claims and natural resource development" (30%).

Despite the high level of support for Native land claims found in the 1976 survey data, it was expected that the stark choice offered in the 1986 survey — with its implications of job creation — would produce a preponderance of opinion unfavourable to Natives. However, the reverse proved true, as support for Natives on land issues generally held firm over the ten years between the surveys.

Similarly, a slight majority agreed with the statement: "Where Natives' use of land conflicts with natural resource development, Native use should be given priority," while only about one-third of the sample disagreed.

However, there are limits to how far respondents are prepared to go in accommodating Natives on land matters. These limits are illustrated by responses to the statement: "Where Indian principles of land ownership conflict with the white man's law, Indian principles should be given priority." In both 1976 and 1986, those unwilling to make such a major compromise outnumbered those favouring such a compromise — 35% to 30% in 1976 and 44% to 33% in 1986. Average support on the question declined slightly from 2.91 to 2.81 (where scores could range from "1" to "5").

Regional variation

One of the main findings of the 1976 survey was that from one region of the

---

Glossary of terms

Native peoples: This term includes registered (also called Status) Indians, non-Status Indians, Metis and Inuit.

Native Indians: Usually refers to both Status and non-Status Indians.

The Indian Act: A piece of federal legislation first passed in 1876. The Act sets out the rules governing Indian reserves and outlining the powers held by Band Councils. The Act also sets out the criteria by which persons are or are not recognized as "Indians."

Indian Register: A list of all registered Indians (as defined in the Indian Act) which is kept by the federal department of Indian and Northern Affairs Canada (INAC). Information on this list concerning the demographic characteristics of the Indian population is updated regularly by band officials and published as of December 31 of each year. The Register is intended to list all persons legally entitled to be registered as Status Indians rather than just those who may be ethnically defined as Status Indians (e.g., a non-Indian woman who marries a Status Indian man is legally entitled to be registered as a Status Indian, even if she is not of North American Indian ethnic origin).

Registered Indian: A person who is "registered as an Indian in the Indian Register."

Metis: There are at least two different views about the meaning of the term Metis. Some maintain that the term refers to those of aboriginal ancestry who are descended from the historic Metis community of Western Canada. Others say that Metis refers to anyone of mixed aboriginal and non-aboriginal ancestry who identifies themselves as a Metis, as distinct from Indian or Inuit.

Inuit: Formerly known as Eskimo, these Native peoples have traditionally resided north of the tree line in the Northwest Territories, Labrador, and along the northern coast of Quebec.

Indian bands: Groups of registered Indians recognized by the federal government, for whose common benefit and use, land has been set aside and monies held by the government.

Indian reserve: Land, the legal title to which is held by the federal government, that has been set apart for the use and benefit of an Indian band and that is subject to the terms of the Indian Act.

Off-reserve Indian population: The Indian Register defines an Indian as residing off-reserve if he or she has lived off-reserve for at least 12 consecutive months.

James Bay Agreement of 1975: The first major agreement between the Crown and Native people in Canada since the treaties of the nineteenth and early twentieth centuries. This agreement was reached after four years of negotiations, court cases, and bargaining following the 1971 announcement of plans to build a system of hydroelectric dams on the east coast of James Bay in the province of Quebec.

Bill C31 and the 1985 Amendments to the Indian Act: Bill C31 was designed to end many of the discriminatory provisions of the Indian Act, especially those which discriminated against Indian women. The Bill changed the meaning of the term "Status" and for the first time allowed for the reinstatement of Indians who had lost or were denied Status and/or band membership in the past. It also allows bands to determine their own band membership criteria.

country to another, there was often striking variation in orientation to, and knowledge about, Indians. In the 1986 data, the same observation can be made for Native people in general, and not just Indians.

On both general and specific measures of support for Indians or Natives, there is a pattern to the regional variation. Respondents in Quebec tended to be most supportive, while those in Ontario and Manitoba ranked close behind. Those in the three most westerly provinces (each considered separately) were least supportive, while those in the Atlantic provinces (combined) fall into an intermediate position, which is usually closer to western Canada than to central Canada.

The distribution on the 1986 Index of Sympathy for Indians[6] illustrates this pattern well. On this scale, where scores can range from a low of "1" to a high of "5" and the mid-point is "3," the national average is 3.29, which is well to the sympathetic side of the mid-point. The average score for Quebec is 3.44, while Ontario and Manitoba are close behind at 3.40 and 3.39, respectively.[7] There is a large gap between these three provinces and the Atlantic region, whose average score is 3.08. Alberta, British Columbia, and Saskatchewan exhibit average scores of 3.08, 3.04 and 2.91, respectively.

Another illustration of regional variation is provided by a question which asked respondents which of three "things" Canadian Indians need most — more money from government, less control by government, or more rights in the Constitution. Nationally, 7%, 33%, and 45% chose these three, respectively, while the remaining 16% were undecided. The proportion choosing "more rights in the constitution" ranged from 33% in Vancouver (and 37% in the rest of British Columbia) to 52% in Toronto and Quebec-outside-Montreal. (Forty-three percent of Montrealers and 46% of Ontarians-outside-Toronto chose this option.) Support for "less control by government" ranged from about 21% in Quebec to about 46% in British Columbia.

Other determinants of opinions

Province of residence was not the only factor to show a significant effect in the formation of attitudes toward aboriginal people. As might be expected, there were numerous other factors which play contributing roles in the formation of public attitudes toward Native peoples and their concerns. Unfortunately, space does not allow an extended discussion of these other contributing factors, and they can only be mentioned in passing here.

For example, support for multiculturalism was found to be associated with many measures of support for Natives. Political party identification at the federal level, as well as strong adherence to the "small-c" conservative philosophy, were also related to views on Native matters. Language spoken was related to both levels of support and knowledge. Francophones tended to be more supportive of, but less knowledgeable about, Natives than were Anglophones.

Two other factors emerge with striking regularity as being particularly important in determining Canadians' orientations toward Natives. These factors were: a person's assessment of the competence of Native people in managing their own affairs and a person's perceptions of whether or not Natives are presently receiving an excessive or an inadequate amount of financial assistance from government.

[6] This Index is slightly different from the previously discussed comparative (1976-1986) Index of Sympathy, because that index excluded some items that form part of the 1986 sympathy scale only.

[7] On some indexes or individual questions, there is also considerable variation within Quebec and/or within Ontario, as between the dominant city and the rest of the provinces.

Canadians who perceive Natives to be receiving too much financial assistance from government are highly likely to be **unsupportive** of Natives on all four of the indexes examined here. In contrast, if a respondent holds the view that adequately funded Native governments are able to meet the needs of individual Natives better than governments can, then that person is highly likely to be **supportive** of Natives on all four indexes.

Among factors showing little effect on attitudes were: age, sex, level of formal education, family income, labour union membership, religious affiliation, size of community of residence, disposition to support underdogs, and having experienced a declining standard of living (or its opposite).

One final note on the determinants of attitudinal support for Natives is in order. Despite assessing over two dozen factors in attempting to explain why people hold supportive or unsupportive views, it did not prove possible to account for more than 40% of the variation observed. Thus, our current understanding of the factors leading to the formation of views on Native issues is at best modest.

Summary

When surveyed, Canadians tend to be generally supportive of Natives' aspirations for self-government and their land claims, but are wary of arrangements which connote special privileges. Over a ten-year period ending in 1986, attitudes and opinions toward Natives and Native issues changed very little from their generally supportive levels. This support was not based on extensive knowledge of Native issues; knowledge levels remained low.

Important also is the fact that the Canadian public is not rigidly divided into two opposing camps on Native issues. Canadians' views on Natives and Native issues are **not** tightly interwoven with larger philosophical views. However, in the absence of such linkages between Native issues and wider concerns, those Native issues remain on the periphery of Canadians' consciousness.

The assistance of Marion Jones in providing the "Glossary of terms" and "Current measures of the Native population" is gratefully acknowledged.

RELIGIOUS AFFILIATION IN CANADA

by George A. Mori

The vast majority of Canadians have reported some religious affiliation in response to the question "What is your religion?" on the Census going back to 1871.[1] There have, however, been several major changes in the religious affiliation of Canadians in the last few decades. There has been a significant increase in the percentage of the population affiliated with the Catholic Church,[2] while the proportion affiliated with the various Protestant denominations has declined. There has also been an increase in the proportion of the population reporting no religious preference. As well, while most Canadians have reported a religious affiliation on the Census, another survey has shown that much smaller numbers participate regularly in services or meetings.

Catholics and Protestants[3]

Historically, most Canadians have been either Protestant or Catholic. At the time of the 1871 Census, 98% of the population was affiliated with one of these two religious groups, and as recently as 1961, the figure was 96%. While this percentage has declined somewhat in recent years, 89% of the population was still either Protestant or Catholic in 1981.

A major change, however, has occurred in the distribution of the population between Protestant and Catholic. Through the late 1800s, and the first few decades of the century, Protestants clearly outnumbered Catholics. In the last several decades, though, this has been reversed. The percentage of the population affiliated with a Protestant denomination fell from 54% in 1931 to just over 40% in 1981. The proportion affiliated with the Catholic Church increased from 41% to 47% between 1931 and 1961, and remained at that level in both 1971 and 1981.

The drop in the percentage of the population affiliated with the Protestant denominations has been accounted for by declines in the mainline Protestant groups. In 1981, 35% of all Canadians were affiliated with either the Anglican, Baptist, Lutheran, Presbyterian or United Church denominations. This however, was down from 40% in 1971 and 49% in 1941. As well, with the ex-

ception of the Baptists, the total number of persons affiliated with each of these denominations actually declined between 1971 and 1981. In this period, the number of persons reporting themselves as Presbyterian fell 7%, while the number of Anglicans declined 4% and Lutherans 2%. The decline in the number affiliated with the United Church was less than 1%. In contrast, the number of persons reporting affiliation with the Baptist denomination increased 4% in this period.

On the other hand, the share of the population affiliated with Protestant denominations other than the mainline groups has increased. In 1981, these other Protestant denominations accounted for 6% of the Canadian population, up from 5% in 1971 and 3% in 1941. The fastest growing of these denominations has been the Pentecostal Church. In the 1971–1981 period, for example, the population affiliated with this denomination increased 54%, from 220,000 to 339,000.

At the same time, though, several other Protestant denominations have declined in numbers. These groups include the Unitarians, down 31% between 1971 and 1981, Doukhobors (-27%), and Jehovah's Witnesses (-17%). The decline in the number of Jehovah's Witnesses is particularly notable in that this group was among the fastest growing Christian denominations in Canada between 1941 and

1971. However, in the 1971–1981 period, the number of Canadians reporting affiliation with the Jehovah's Witnesses declined from 173,000 to 143,000.

The Growth of the Population Reporting No Religious Preference

As recently as 1961, almost all Canadians reported some religious affiliation. That year, less than 1% of the population said they had no religious preference. By 1981, however, the percentage of Canadians with no religious preference had climbed to 7%.[4] The number of Canadians reporting no religious preference increased from less than 100,000 in 1961 to 1.8 million in 1981. Of the 1981 total, however, only 11,000 reported themselves as agnostics, while just 4,500 said they were atheists.

Other Religious Groupings

The religious mosaic in Canada is completed by a number of diverse groups including the Eastern Orthodox denominations of the Christian faith, Eastern Non-Christian religions, and Judaism, as well as several small groups which do not fall into any of the conventional religious categories. Together, in 1981, these religious groupings accounted for almost one million Canadians, or about 4% of the total population. the overall percentage of the population affiliated with these groups has been relatively stable most of this century.

In 1981, there were 362,000 persons affiliated with the Christian Eastern Orthodox denominations. The vast majority of these, almost 90%, were Greek Orthodox. There were just over 300,000 persons affiliated with one of the Eastern Non-Christian religions in 1981. The largest of these groups in Canada were Islam, Hinduism, Sikhism, and Buddhism. Also, in 1981, there were 296,000 persons of Jewish faith in Canada. They represented 1.3% of the total population, down slightly from 1.5% in 1951.

There are several other small groups which cannot be classified into any of the conventional religious categories, but which are nonetheless oriented toward spiritual concerns. These include followers of Native Indian or Inuit religions, as well as New Thought-Unity-

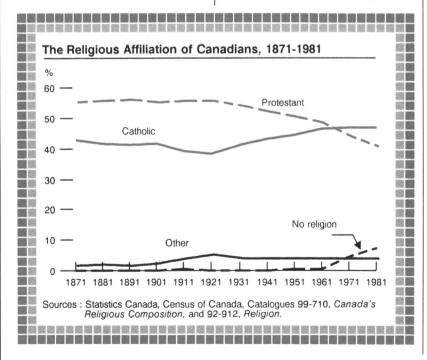

The Religious Affiliation of Canadians, 1871-1981

Sources : Statistics Canada, Census of Canada, Catalogues 99-710, *Canada's Religious Composition,* and 92-912, *Religion.*

Metaphysical, Pagan, Fourth Way, and Theosophical groups. There was, however, a total of only 13,450 people affiliated with these groups in 1981.

The number of followers of cult or sect religions in Canada appears to be very minimal compared to the overwhelming number of Canadians who subscribe to Christian, Judaic, or Eastern Non-Christian religions, or who subscribe to no religion at all.

Provincial Variation in Religious Affiliation

Considerable variation exists in the religious make-up of the provinces. The vast majority of people in Quebec — 88% in 1981 — was affiliated with the Catholic Church. The only other province with a Catholic majority was New Brunswick. Protestants made up over half the total population in all other provinces in 1981, ranging from 51% in Prince Edward Island to 63% in Newfoundland.

Recent Trends in Religious Affiliation

The General Social Survey conducted by Statistics Canada in the fall of 1985 provided more recent data on the religious affiliation of Canadians. Because of differences between the 1985 General Social Survey and the 1981 Census,[5] direct comparisons between data from these two sources must be made with caution. Nevertheless, several general trends are apparent.

The shift in the distribution of the population between Protestant and Catholic appears to have continued. In the 1981-1985 period, the Roman Catholic population increased 3.5%, while the number of persons affiliated with the mainline Protestant denominations declined 3.0%. Persons reporting "other" religions, a category which includes the smaller Protestant denominations and other

Catholics, increased 13.3%.

The secularization trend which first became evident in the 1971 Census also showed no sign of letting up in the early 1980s. Between 1981 and 1985, the number of Canadians aged 15 and over reporting no religious affiliation increased 57%, from 1.3 million to over 2.0 million. During the same period, there was no change in the number of adult Canadians reporting some religious affiliation. As a result, the percentage of the population aged 15 and over reporting no religious preference increased from 7% in 1981 to 10% in 1985.

[5] The religious questions asked on the General Social Survey and the Census were not identical. As well, while the Census covered the whole population, the General Social Survey included only the non-institutionalized population aged 15 and over living in the ten provinces.

British Columbia and Alberta had the largest percentage of their populations reporting no religious preference. In 1981, 21% of residents of British Columbia and 12% of those in Alberta reported no religious affiliation. In fact, these two provinces, with just over one-fifth of the total Canadian population, accounted for almost half (46%) of all those who reported no religious preference in 1981. In Ontario, Manitoba and Saskatchewan, the percentage of the population with no religious preference was similar to the national rate, while just 3% of the population in the Atlantic Provinces, and 2% of those in Quebec reported no religious preference.

Involvement in Religious Activities

While most Canadians still report a religious affiliation, a much smaller proportion regularly attends religious observances. According to the General Social Survey, in 1985, only 30% of Canadians with a stated religious preference attended a religious service or meeting on a weekly basis, while a further 17% did so at least once a month. On the other hand, more than one in five persons (21%) with a stated religion never attended a service or meeting.

There was considerable variation among religious groups in the frequency of attendance at services. Among both Baptists and Roman Catholics, around 40% attended a religious service at least once a week, while over half attended at least once a month. More than half of those affiliated with Eastern Orthodox denominations also attended a service at least monthly. In comparison, much smaller percentages of those affiliated with the Anglican and United Churches, as well as those of Jewish faith*, attended religious observances on a regular basis.

There has also been a decline in the frequency of attendance at religious services for some groups in the last decade. Between 1975 and 1985,[6] the percentage reporting weekly attendance at religious services or meetings declined from 25% to 15% for members of the United Church, from 45% to 36% for Roman Catholics, and from 24% to 17% for Anglicans. On the other hand, there was little or no change in the frequency of attendance for Presbyterians, Lutherans, Baptists, and among persons of Jewish faith*.

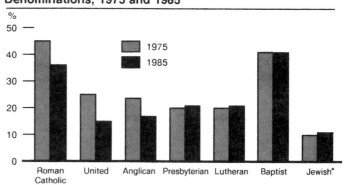

Weekly Attendance at Religious Services, by Selected Denominations, 1975 and 1985

* Figure should be used with caution because the sampling variability is high.
Sources: Statistics Canada, The General Social Survey, 1985, unpublished data; Bibby, R.W., "The State of Collective Religiosity in Canada: An Empirical Analysis", *Canadian Review of Sociology and Anthropology,* 16(1), 1979.

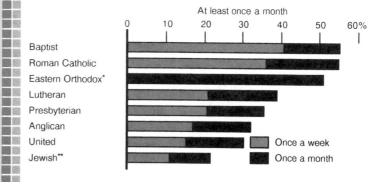

Frequency of Attendance at Religious Services, by Selected Denominations, 1985

* The weekly figure for Eastern Orthodox cannot be expressed because the sampling variability is too high.
**Figure should be used with caution because the sampling variability is high.
Source: Statistics Canada, The General Social Survey, 1985, unpublished data.

* Figure should be used with caution because the sampling variability is high.
[6] The 1975 figures are from Bibby, R.W., "The State of Collective Religiosity in Canada," *Canadian Review of Sociology and Arthropology* 16(1) 1979; the 1985 data are from the General Social Survey.

Religious affiliation of the population, by province, 1981

	Catholic	Protestant	Other religious groupings	No religious preference	Total
	%				
Newfoundland	36.3	62.6	0.1	1.0	100.0
Prince Edward Island	46.6	50.5	0.3	2.7	100.0
Nova Scotia	37.0	58.0	0.9	4.1	100.0
New Brunswick	53.9	42.9	0.4	2.9	100.0
Quebec	88.2	6.4	3.4	2.1	100.0
Ontario	35.6	51.8	5.4	7.2	100.0
Manitoba	31.5	56.6	4.4	7.5	100.0
Saskatchewan	32.4	58.3	3.1	6.3	100.0
Alberta	27.7	56.0	4.5	11.7	100.0
British Columbia	19.8	54.7	4.5	20.9	100.0
Canada	**47.3**	**41.2**	**4.1**	**7.4**	**100.0**

Source: Statistics Canada, Catalogue 92-912, *1981 Census of Canada, Population: Religion*.

Socio-demographic profile of selected religious groups, 1981

	Total population	Median age	Median years of schooling	Average income[1]	Unemployment rate[2]
	000s			$	%
Catholic	11,403	28.2	11.4	12,300	9.0
Protestant	9,915	31.6	12.0	13,200	5.8
Eastern Orthodox	362	33.8	10.8	12,400	5.7
Eastern Non-Christian	306	27.0	12.7	12,900	7.2
Jewish	296	35.1	13.3	19,500	5.3
Other groups	13	30.5	12.9	12,200	9.4
No religious preference	1,784	26.3	12.6	14,900	6.5
Total population[3]	**24,084**	**29.4**	**11.8**	**13,000**	**7.4**

[1] Weighted 1980 average total income of population aged 15 and over with income.
[2] Percentage of persons aged 15 and over in the labour force who were unemployed in the week prior to June 3, 1981.
[3] Includes 5,500 persons not classified elsewhere.
Source: Statistics Canada, 1981 Census of Canada, unpublished data.

The highest percentages of persons affiliated with other religious groupings were reported in Ontario (5.4%), Alberta (4.5%), British Columbia (4.5%) and Manitoba (4.4%). In contrast, less than 1% of the population in the Atlantic Provinces belonged to one of these groups.

Socio-demographic Profile of Religious Groups

Religious affiliation still reflects important underlying social differences among Canadians. For example, in 1981, Protestants were on average older, and had more median years of schooling, higher average incomes, and lower unemployment rates than did Catholics. In fact, the average income of Catholics was among the lowest of all religious groups, and their unemployment rate was among the highest.

Persons of Jewish faith had the highest median age, the most schooling, the highest average income, and the lowest unemployment rate of any religious group. The income figures for the Jewish group are most striking. In 1981, the average income of those affiliated with the Jewish faith was 50% higher than the national average. Their average income was also 31% higher than that of the population with no religious preference, the grouping with the second highest average income.

[1] This report refers only to the stated religious preference of Canadians, and not to their actual membership in a religious group. As such, these figures may differ significantly from membership figures reported by the various religious groups and denominations.

[2] Includes persons affiliated with the Roman, Polish National, and Ukrainian Catholic Churches. Roman Catholics, however, make up the vast majority of persons in this group — 98% in 1981.

[3] Persons belonging to Eastern Orthodox denominations are also Christians. For the purposes of this report, however, they are included in the category "Other Religious Groupings."

[4] Part of the increase in the reporting of no religious preference may be due to a change in the way census data are collected. In the 1961 and earlier Censuses, data were collected by interviewers; however, the 1971 and 1981 Censuses were conducted on a self-enumeration basis. There apparently is a greater tendency for respondents to indicate no religion in the latter context. The increases in the number of persons reporting no religious affiliation in the 1971 and 1981 Censuses and in the 1985 General Social Survey, however, are a fairly clear indicator of an overall trend.

Human Geography

URBAN CANADA

by Mary Anne Burke

Transformation of Canada from a predominantly rural society to an urban one has occurred in a little over one hundred years. The pace of urbanization has varied by province, as have the factors at work behind the process. While the growth rate of the Canadian population is slowing, concentration in a few urban areas continues to increase.

Urban life is now reality for the majority of Canadians. In 1986, three-quarters of the population lived in urban areas, primarily in Ontario, Quebec and British Columbia. Increasingly, this means living in large metropolitan areas. In 1986, 60% of Canadians lived in one of 25 census metropolitan areas (CMAs), up from 54% five years earlier. In fact, Toronto, Montreal and Vancouver together accounted for 31% of the Canadian population in 1986, up from 29% in 1981.

Urban Growth

The rate of urban growth varied by census period, province, and by city size. With the exception of 1981, the percentage of the Canadian population classified as urban has increased with every census since 1871, when 18.3% of the population was considered urban. By 1931, 50% of the Canadian population was urban, and by 1976 the figure had climbed to 76.1%. By 1981, however, the urban population had dropped half a percentage point to 75.6%. By 1986, the urban component again increased to 76.3%.

The decline of the urban population recorded in the 1981 Census reflected a short-term increase in the proportion of the population residing in rural non-farm areas and commuting to large urban areas to work, as well as a blurring of urban/suburban/rural borders around metropolitan areas such as Toronto. The recent resurgence of urban growth may signal a movement back to urban core areas. Preliminary 1986 Census data indicate, for example, that since the previous census, population had increased in the urban cores of the CMAs, Toronto, Montreal and Vancouver.

By Province

Except for Prince Edward Island and New Brunswick, each province was

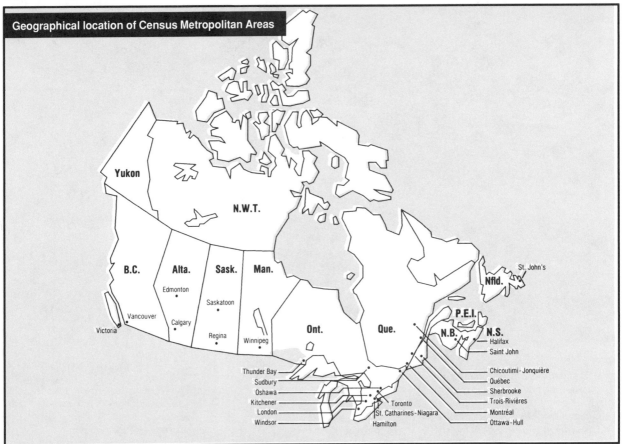

Geographical location of Census Metropolitan Areas

predominantly urban in 1986. That year, the urban proportion of the population stood at 82% in Ontario; 79% in British Columbia and Alberta; 78% in Quebec; 62% in Manitoba; 61% in Saskatchewan; 59% in Newfoundland; and 54% in Nova Scotia.

Prince Edward Island remained predominantly rural with only 38% of its population in urban areas. New Brunswick was the only other province in which a majority of the population did

not live in urban areas. In 1986, only 49% of the population of New Brunswick was urban; this was down from 57% in 1971.

Urbanization was most rapid in British Columbia, Ontario, Quebec and Alberta. Ontario and British Columbia met the urban criteria in 1911, Quebec in 1921, and Alberta 1956. By 1971, all the provinces except Prince Edward Island were more than 50% urban, with Ontario and Quebec as high as 80%, and British Columbia, 75%.

By City Size

The average growth rate for all urban areas has slowed considerably since 1971. In part, this reflects the overall decline in Canada's population growth. For the 1981-1986 period, the national growth rate was 4.2%, the lowest five-year growth rate in the last 25 years. As well, the urban population is now so large that even substantial absolute numbers of migrants seem small in comparison with the population already in urban areas. From 1981 to 1986, urban areas 10,000 and over had an average growth rate of 6.0% compared with 12.2% during the 1966-1971 period. The average growth of CMAs was 5.9% for the 1981-1986 period, far below the 27.6% increase from 1966 to 1971. The comparable figures for CMAs of 500,000 population and over were 6.2% for the period 1981-1986 and 19.2% for the earlier period.

Since CMAs were first defined, their number has increased from 15 in 1951 to 25 in 1986. CMAs have grown in size at a faster rate than urban areas under 100,000 population. In fact, since 1951, CMAs have accounted for 77% of Canada's total population growth.

During the 1981-1986 period, the three fastest growing CMAs were Saskatoon (which increased by 14.6% or 46,455 people), Ottawa–Hull (10.1% or 101,385), and Toronto (9.5% or 428,221). Calgary and Edmonton, the fastest growing CMAs during the previous five years, had much lower percentage increases during the 1981-1986 period, reflecting a downturn in local economic conditions (see accompanying article on Calgary). Calgary's population increased 7.2% (78,583) over the period 1981-1986 compared with 25.7% for 1976-1981. Over the same period, Edmonton's population growth rate fell to 6.0% (128,408) from 18.1%. During the 1981-1986 period, Montreal's population grew 2.1% (269,880), up from 0.9%, and Vancouver's by 8.9% (112,546), up from 8.7%. Sudbury was the only CMA to lose population, declining by 4.6% (1,046) between 1981 and 1986. Movement out of Sudbury had started during the 1971-1976 period, when the population fell 0.4%.

During the years 1981 to 1986, the CMAs Montreal, Toronto and Vancouver accounted for 69% of urban growth in Canada, up from 60% during the period 1966-1971. Calgary and Edmonton accounted for 22.5% of urban growth from 1981-1986.

Population Movement Key to Urban Growth

Urban growth in Canada has resulted from a combination of natural increase, internal migration, and immigration from outside the country. With the decline of fertility rates, internal migration and immigration have become increasingly more important factors in urban growth.

In general, in the earlier decades of this century, the main flow of internal migration was from rural to urban areas.

However, as the size of the rural farm population decreased to current levels, urban-bound migrants tended to be rural non-farm residents, or people moving from one urban area to a larger one.

Since the 1950s, the flow tended to be from smaller urban areas to large metropolitan areas. During the period 1956-1961, 75% of all urban migrants moved to another urban area, less than 20% moved to a rural non-farm area, and only 4% moved to a rural area. This pattern remained basically the same for the period 1976-1981.

During the period 1956-1961, 55% of rural migrants moved to urban areas, increasing to 70% for the period 1976-1981.

For the 1976-1981 period, CMAs were points of origin or destination for

Percentage of urban population, by province, 1851–1986

	1851	1861	1871	1881	1891	1901	1911	1921	1931	1941	1951	1961	1971	1981	1986
									%						
Nfld.	-	-	-	-	-	-	-	-	-	-	43	51	57	59	59
P.E.I.	-	9	9	11	13	15	16	19	20	22	25	32	38	37	38
N.S.	8	8	8	15	19	28	37	45	47	52	55	54	57	55	54
N.B.	14	13	18	18	20	23	27	35	35	39	43	47	57	51	50
Que.	15	17	20	24	29	36	45	52	59	61	67	74	81	78	78
Ont.	14	19	21	27	35	40	50	59	63	68	73	77	82	82	82
Man.	-	-	-	15	24	25	39	42	45	46	56	64	70	71	62
Sask.	-	-	-	-	-	6	16	17	20	21	30	43	53	58	61
Alta.	-	-	-	-	-	16	29	31	32	32	48	63	74	77	79
B.C.	-	-	9	18	43	46	51	51	62	64	69	73	76	78	79
Canada	13	14	18	23	30	35	42	47	53	56	62	70	76	76	76

Source: Statistics Canada, Census of Canada.

Percentage of Canadian population in Census Metropolitan Areas, 1951–1986

	1951	1956	1961	1966	1971	1976	1981	1986
				%				
Toronto	9.0	9.8	10.5	11.4	12.3	12.2	12.4	13.5
Montreal	11.0	11.4	12.2	12.9	12.7	12.2	11.6	11.5
Vancouver	4.2	4.3	4.5	4.7	5.0	5.1	5.2	5.5
Ottawa-Hull	2.2	2.3	2.5	2.6	2.8	2.9	2.8	3.2
Edmonton	1.4	1.7	2.0	2.1	2.3	2.4	2.7	3.1
Calgary	1.0	1.3	1.5	1.7	1.9	2.1	2.4	2.7
Winnipeg	2.6	2.6	2.6	2.5	2.5	2.5	2.3	2.5
Quebec	2.1	2.0	2.1	2.2	2.2	2.2	2.2	2.4
Hamilton	2.0	2.1	2.2	2.3	2.3	2.3	2.2	2.2
St. Catharines-Niagara	1.4	1.5	1.4	1.4	1.4	1.4	1.1	1.4
London	1.2	1.2	1.2	1.3	1.3	0.1	1.2	1.4
Kitchener	0.8	0.8	0.9	1.0	1.1	1.1	1.1	1.2
Halifax	1.0	1.1	1.1	1.1	1.0	1.0	1.0	1.2
Victoria	0.8	0.9	0.9	0.9	0.9	1.0	1.0	1.0
Windsor	1.3	1.3	1.2	1.2	1.2	1.1	1.1	1.0
Oshawa	0.3	0.3	0.3	0.4	0.4	0.5	0.5	0.8
Saskatoon	0.4	0.5	0.5	0.6	0.6	0.6	0.6	0.8
Regina	0.5	0.6	0.6	0.7	0.7	0.7	0.7	0.7
St. John's	0.6	0.6	0.6	0.6	0.6	0.6	0.6	0.6
Chicoutimi-Jonquiere	0.7	0.7	0.7	0.7	0.6	0.5	0.5	0.6
Sudbury	0.6	0.7	0.7	0.7	0.7	0.7	0.6	0.6
Sherbrooke	0.4	0.4	0.4	0.4	0.4	0.3	0.3	0.5
Trois-Rivieres	0.3	0.3	0.3	0.3	0.3	0.2	0.2	0.5
Thunder Bay	0.5	0.5	0.6	0.5	0.5	1.0	0.5	0.5
Saint John	0.6	0.6	0.5	0.5	0.5	0.5	0.5	0.5
Total - CMAs	**45.7**	**48.2**	**50.9**	**53.4**	**55.1**	**54.7**	**54.4**	**59.8**

Source: Statistics Canada, Census of Canada.

more than 2.5 million migrants, according to a recent study[1]. This movement of people profoundly affects the nature of Canadian metropolitan areas. Migration was clearly the major contributor to the growth of Calgary and Edmonton. Over the past thirty years, these two CMAs had annual growth rates of 4% to 5%, despite rates of natural increase of no more than 2% per year.

Other fast-growing CMAs like Saskatoon, Kitchener, Toronto, Regina, Ottawa–Hull, Vancouver, and Victoria also had positive net migration. In CMAs with below-average or negative growth rates during the 1976-1981 period — Chicoutimi–Jonquière, St. Catherines–Niagara, Saint John, Thunder Bay, Windsor, Winnipeg, and Montreal — net migration was negligible or negative.

Immigration can moderate the effects of internal migration. For example, without the addition of 64,000 immigrants between 1976 and 1981, Montreal's net out-migration would have been 105,000 instead of 41,000. In Toronto, the arrival of 153,000 immigrants during this period more than offset the loss of 9,000 residents to other parts of Canada and contributed to the overall growth of the CMA.

Heartland/Hinterland

Migration and immigration trends have reinforced and helped shape the disparate distribution of population in Canada. A Canadian heartland and hinterland have developed, reflecting the very uneven distribution of urban areas. Ontario, Quebec and the far western provinces dominate the other regions of Canada by sheer volume of population, number of CMAs, CMAs over 500,000, and in turn, economically.

In 1986, almost 70% of Canada's 165 urban areas with more than 10,000 residents were in Ontario, Quebec, and British Columbia. Ontario accounted for 30% of the total, Quebec for 22%, and British Columbia for 17%. The next largest concentrations of urban areas with at least 10,000 population were in Alberta (8%) and Saskatchewan (6%). The remainder were distributed relatively evenly among the other provinces.

The population is further concentrated in several large CMAs. Toronto, Montreal and Vancouver accounted for 31% of the Canadian population in 1986. In fact, most of the population is located in a corridor from Windsor to Quebec City. This area represents 5% of Canada's land surface and, in 1986, accounted for two-thirds of the Canadian population. The situation is similar in British Columbia, where most of the population is concentrated in and around Vancouver in the Fraser River Valley.

[1] Shaw, R. Paul, *Intermetropolitan Migration in Canada: Changing Determinants Over Three Decades*, Statistics Canada, Catalogue 89-504.

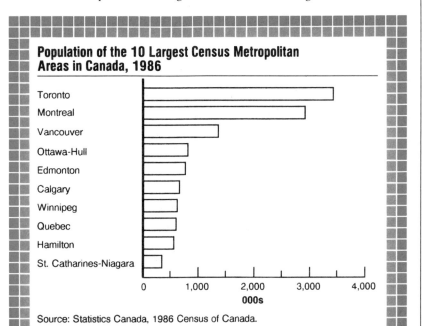

Population of the 10 Largest Census Metropolitan Areas in Canada, 1986

Source: Statistics Canada, 1986 Census of Canada.

Percentage population change of Census Metropolitan Areas, 1951–1986

	1951-1956	1956-1961	1961-1966	1966-1971	1971-1976	1976-1981	1981-1986
Toronto	21.1	21.4	18.3	14.8	7.7	7.0	9.5
Montreal	18.6	20.8	15.4	6.7	2.7	0.9	2.1
Vancouver	18.3	18.8	12.9	16.0	7.8	8.7	8.9
Ottawa-Hull	18.1	24.3	15.0	13.9	11.8	3.6	10.1
Edmonton	44.1	32.5	18.8	16.5	11.7	18.1	6.0
Calgary	41.2	38.8	18.4	22.0	16.5	25.7	7.2
Winnipeg	15.5	15.4	6.7	6.2	5.2	1.1	5.6
Quebec	12.8	14.7	15.6	10.0	8.1	6.3	3.3
Hamilton	20.6	16.8	13.6	9.0	5.2	2.4	2.8
St. Catharines-Niagara	26.3	12.4	14.9	6.3	5.6	0.8	0.2
London	19.7	17.3	14.4	12.7	6.9	4.9	4.7
Kitchener	19.7	20.3	24.1	18.0	14.1	5.7	8.1
Halifax	22.6	12.0	7.7	6.1	7.0	3.6	6.6
Victoria	18.2	15.1	12.5	11.7	11.0	7.0	5.8
Windsor	13.5	4.0	9.4	8.5	-0.5	-0.6	1.2
Oshawa	25.1	28.8	23.8	13.0	12.4	14.1	9.2
Saskatoon	36.7	31.1	23.7	9.1	5.8	15.3	14.6
Regina	25.8	24.9	16.8	6.3	7.4	8.7	7.7
St. John's	15.3	14.7	10.3	12.1	8.8	6.5	4.6
Chicoutimi-Jonquiere	19.6	15.4	3.5	0.6	1.8	5.1	0.2
Sudbury	32.6	13.0	5.6	13.7	-0.4	-4.5	-4.6
Sherbrooke	13.4	13.6	13.4	6.1	7.1	6.1	3.8
Trois-Rivieres	14.4	10.8	6.9	2.5	0.6	5.1	2.8
Thunder Bay	17.3	16.6	6.6	3.8	4.0	1.8	0.2
Saint John	9.8	11.1	5.8	2.4	5.8	0.9	0.2

Source: Statistics Canada, Census of Canada.

Immigration has reinforced the existing distribution of the urban population. Immigrants tend to go to Ontario, Quebec, British Columbia and Alberta. In 1986, half of all immigrants to Canada went to Ontario; 19% to Quebec; 13% to British Columbia; 10% to Alberta; 4% to Manitoba; 2% to Saskatchewan; and 2% to the Atlantic region. Most immigrants settle in large metropolitan areas. In 1986, Toronto received 30% (29,000) of the total; Montreal, 17% (17,000); Vancouver, 9% (8,700); Calgary, 4% (4,000); Edmonton, 4% (3,800); Winnipeg, 3% (3,300); and Ottawa–Hull, 3% (3,400).

Growth rate by size of urban area, 1951–1986

	Urban area 10,000+ and over	CMAs 100,000+ and over	CMAs 500,000+ and over
1951-1956	12.6	21.6	18.5
1956-1961	12.9	19.4	9.2
1961-1966	13.6	14.0	16.1
1966-1971	12.2	27.6	19.2
1971-1976	0.9	8.5	6.1
1976-1981	2.8	7.7	5.0
1981-1986	6.0	5.9	6.2

Source: Statistics Canada, Census of Canada.

Urban Issues

Present-day urban society in Canada is a reflection of past and present individual choices and policy decisions concerning the economy, technology, the environment, and population. For example, early decisions concerning investments in the exploitation of Canada's natural resources — fur, lumber, wheat, and minerals — influenced population growth, movement and distribution. Likewise, decisions concerning the development of technology (for example, the decisions made by entrepreneurs to invest in the development of the railways, and along specific routes) also contributed to current urban patterns. Decisions to develop and use the Great Lake Waterway System as a major transportation route have also had an impact on the configuration of present-day urban Canada. More recently, the point system, adopted to select immigrants to Canada, favours applicants with skills suited to a high-tech, urban environment, rather than those with skills geared to a rural environment.

Differences in the timing and nature of economic developments and policies

Distribution of urban areas by province, 1986

	Number of urban areas		% distribution of urban areas of 10,000 or more population
	1,000 or more population	10,000 or more population	
Newfoundland	57	7	4.2
Prince Edward Island	7	2	1.2
Nova Scotia	39	7	4.2
New Brunswick	39	6	3.6
Quebec	241	36	21.8
Ontario	250	49	29.7
Manitoba	41	5	3.0
Saskatchewan	68	10	6.1
Alberta	99	13	7.9
British Columbia	92	28	16.9
Northwest Territories	1	1	0.6
Yukon	6	1	0.6
Total	940	165	100.0

Source: Statistics Canada, 1986 Census of Canada.

Migration to and from Census Metropolitan Areas (CMAs), 1966–1971 and 1976–1981

		Other CMAs			Non-metropolitan areas			Immi-gration	Total net internal migration plus immi-gration
		In	Out	Net	In	Out	Net		
Calgary	1966-71	36,110	26,026	10,085	42,300	26,620	15,680	24,040	49,805
	1976-81	88,735	33,710	55,025	69,175	58,640	10,535	30,440	96,000
Chicoutimi-	1966-71	3,615	8,505	-4,890	6,920	7,215	-295	1,340	-3,845
Jonquiere	1976-81	3,335	6,430	-3,095	6,245	5,960	285	445	-2,365
Edmonton	1966-71	28,430	31,900	-3,470	52,020	34,165	17,885	21,510	35,895
	1976-81	63,085	35,760	27,325	72,390	65,930	6,460	27,735	61,520
Halifax	1966-71	10,755	15,785	-5,030	21,580	20,530	1,320	6,105	1,205
	1976-81	15,125	19,510	-4,385	24,455	24,720	-265	3,865	-785
Hamilton	1966-71	25,870	21,205	4,665	19,885	18,190	1,695	26,530	32,890
	1976-81	31,975	29,660	2,315	18,370	23,810	-4,810	10,730	8,235
Kitchener-	1966-71	15,210	10,880	4,330	17,680	14,390	3,290	15,125	22,745
Waterloo	1976-81	17,525	18,885	-1,330	18,675	18,730	-55	6,850	5,465
London	1966-71	21,565	17,060	4,505	21,000	18,010	2,990	15,055	22,550
	1976-81	20,340	23,525	-3,185	23,755	22,380	1,375	5,860	4,050
Montreal	1966-71	44,925	78,875	-33,950	115,465	88,780	26,685	115,345	108,080
	1976-81	41,925	120,115	-78,190	97,420	124,830	-27,410	64,495	-41,105
Ottawa-Hull	1966-71	41,480	30,060	11,420	44,080	27,580	16,500	27,605	55,525
	1976-81	58,380	66,530	-8,150	41,030	40,505	525	18,740	11,115
Quebec City	1966-71	15,265	17,145	-1,880	36,885	16,510	20,375	5,930	24,425
	1976-81	15,035	23,095	-8,060	32,430	25,755	6,675	4,425	3,040
Regina	1966-71	7,000	16,005	-9,005	18,465	11,590	6,875	3,080	950
	1976-81	10,630	11,755	-1,125	17,325	14,430	2,895	3,255	5,025
St. Catharines-	1966-71	12,330	14,700	-2,370	10,915	10,145	770	10,825	9,225
Niagara	1976-81	14,520	17,400	-2,880	10,015	12,290	-2,275	4,560	-595
St. John's	1966-71	2,730	6,595	-3,865	11,705	6,390	5,315	1,965	3,415
	1976-81	4,575	7,395	-2,820	9,640	9,820	-180	1,360	-1,640
Saint John	1966-71	3,220	3,775	-555	6,630	6,670	-40	1,400	805
	1976-81	4,405	5,020	-975	7,475	9,180	-1,705	1,095	-1,585
Saskatoon	1966-71	6,650	15,010	-8,360	20,590	13,060	7,530	3,370	2,540
	1976-81	12,110	11,180	930	23,005	16,180	6,825	3,765	11,520
Sudbury	1966-71	7,810	8,755	-965	15,015	10,375	4,640	4,410	8,085
	1976-81	4,070	10,990	-6,926	8,215	13,975	-5,760	850	-11,830
Thunder Bay	1966-71	4,605	5,650	-1,585	6,555	4,815	1,740	2,955	-370
	1976-81	4,685	7,260	-2,565	7,715	6,000	1,715	1,545	695
Toronto	1966-71	95,330	84,770	10,770	90,200	120,885	-30,685	262,280	242,280
	1976-81	127,435	109,095	18,340	96,350	123,660	-27,310	152,890	143,920
Vancouver	1966-71	69,220	28,625	40,595	62,335	56,475	5,860	71,670	118,125
	1976-81	78,575	40,245	38,330	65,320	85,365	-20,045	61,250	79,535
Victoria	1966-71	19,760	11,280	8,480	15,890	11,700	4,190	8,570	21,240
	1976-81	25,080	16,185	8,895	20,115	20,415	-300	6,560	15,155
Windsor	1966-71	9,895	10,390	-495	8,705	9,140	-435	13,250	12,320
	1976-81	7,060	14,250	-7,190	7,565	12,630	-5,065	5,780	-6,475
Winnipeg	1966-71	19,830	28,070	-18,260	38,760	29,380	9,380	23,780	14,920
	1976-81	22,005	42,295	-20,290	35,210	37,500	-2,290	19,135	-3,445

Source: Shaw, R. Paul, *Intermetropolitan Migration in Canada, Changing Determinants over Three Decades*, Statistics Canada, Catalogue 89-504.

Distribution of immigrants to Canada, by province and selected metropolitan areas, 1981–1986

	1981		1982		1983		1984		1985		1986[1]	
	Number	%	Number	%	Number	%	Number	%	Number	%	Number	%
Province												
Newfoundland	480	0.4	406	0.3	275	0.3	299	0.3	325	0.4	266	0.3
Prince Edward Island	126	0.1	165	0.1	105	0.1	109	0.1	113	0.1	164	0.2
Nova Scotia	1,403	1.1	1,254	1.0	833	0.9	1,034	1.2	974	1.2	1,082	1.1
New Brunswick	988	0.8	751	0.6	554	0.6	600	0.7	609	0.7	619	0.6
Quebec	21,118	16.4	21,331	17.6	16,374	18.4	14,641	16.6	14,884	17.7	18,826	19.3
Ontario	54,890	42.7	53,031	43.8	40,036	44.9	41,527	47.1	40,730	48.3	48,340	50.0
Manitoba	5,359	4.2	4,931	4.1	3,978	4.5	3,903	4.4	3,415	4.1	3,685	3.8
Saskatchewan	2,401	1.9	2,125	1.8	1,735	2.0	2,150	2.4	1,905	2.3	1,824	1.9
Alberta	19,294	1.5	17,948	14.8	10,688	12.0	10,670	12.1	9,001	10.7	9,478	9.7
British Columbia	22,007	17.0	18,996	15.7	14,447	16.2	13,190	15.0	12,239	14.5	12,227	12.5
Yukon	119	0.1	69	0.1	73	0.1	41	0.1	36	0.1	44	0.1
Northwest Territories	82	0.1	111	0.1	59	0.1	75	0.1	71	0.1	62	0.1
Total	**128,618**	**100.0**	**121,147**	**100.0**	**89,157**	**100.0**	**88,239**	**100.0**	**84,302**	**100.0**	**97,474**	**100.0**
Cities												
Toronto	29,338	22.8	28,163	23.3	22,216	24.9	27,197	30.8	23,622	28.0	28,603	29.3
Montreal	16,352	12.7	16,341	13.5	13,052	14.6	11,883	13.5	12,862	15.3	16,647	17.1
Vancouver	14,810	11.5	12,526	10.3	10,015	11.2	9,385	10.6	8,935	10.6	8,701	8.9
Ottawa-Hull	3,208	2.5	3,243	2.7	2,508	2.8	3,126	3.5	3,316	3.9	3,394	3.5
Edmonton	7,308	5.7	7,159	5.9	4,493	5.0	4,276	4.9	3,694	4.4	3,801	3.9
Calgary	8,389	6.5	7,694	6.4	4,360	4.9	4,540	5.2	3,669	4.4	4,071	4.2
Winnipeg	4,104	3.2	3,891	3.2	3,318	3.7	3,210	3.6	2,947	3.5	3,338	3.4

[1] Preliminary data.

Source: Department of Employment and Immigration, *Landed Immigrants: CLPR by Selected Areas of Destination and Province, 1981-1986*

cross the regions of the country have profoundly affected the economic potential of these regions and subsequent policy development. Regional disparities in income and economic opportunities, and the concentration of population in a few metropolitan centres have been some of the outcomes of these differences.

While urbanization has benefitted Canadian society in many ways, both urban growth and the concentration of the population in a handful of large metropolitan areas have not been without social costs. Rural depopulation and breakdown of local communities, escalating land and housing costs, fiscal burdens on regional governments, environmental pollution and decay, and traffic congestion, for example, have all accompanied the development of an urban society.

Awareness of the growth, movement and distribution of today's urban society will aid in the understanding of the role policy decisions play in the shaping of Canadian society.

AVERAGE EXPENDITURE OF URBAN CANADIANS

by Mary Anne Burke

Expenditure patterns of urban Canadians have been considerably transformed since the 1960s by a rise in the portion of average income taken by taxes. Taxes, rather than food, now account for the single largest expenditure of urban families and unattached individuals.

Expenditure on basic necessities such as shelter, food, and clothing, however, continues to account for a substantially larger proportion of expenditure of families in the lowest income quintile, compared to those in the highest quintile.

Overall Expenditure Patterns

In 1984, the average expenditure of urban Canadian families and unattached individuals was $32,680. This represented about 93% of before-tax income and other money receipts.

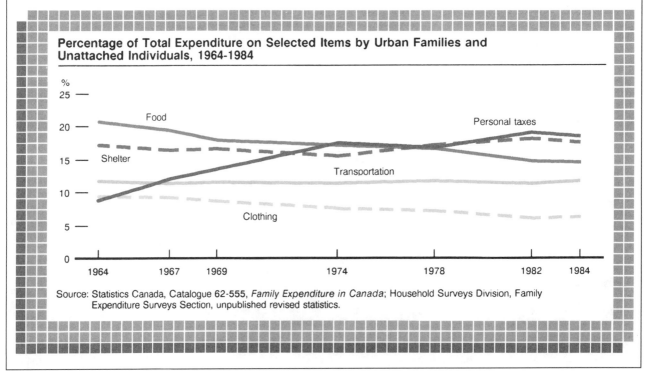

Percentage of Total Expenditure on Selected Items by Urban Families and Unattached Individuals, 1964-1984

Source: Statistics Canada, Catalogue 62-555, *Family Expenditure in Canada*; Household Surveys Division, Family Expenditure Surveys Section, unpublished revised statistics.

Personal income taxes accounted for nearly 19% of total expenditure in 1984, compared to 18% for shelter, 15% for food, 12% for transportation, and 6% for clothing. The percentage of expenditure on taxes remained around this level since the early 1970s, after a decade of steep incline. In 1964, for example, personal taxes accounted for 9% of all expenditure.

In the same period, the share of expenditure on shelter remained relatively constant. The proportion of all spending devoted to shelter dropped from 17% in 1964 to less than 16% in 1974, but increased to 18% by 1982. It remained at that level in 1984.

The percentage of expenditure on food declined steadily, from 21% of total spending in 1964 to 15% in 1984. Over the same period, the share of expenditure on clothing dropped from 10% to 6%. Spending on transportation remained relatively constant at around 12% of total expenditure over the past two decades.

Expenditures by Income Group

Generally, lower income groups spend proportionately more on food and shelter, and less on taxes, than do higher income groups. In 1984, for example, over 50% of all expenditure by the lowest income quintile was for food (22%) and shelter (31%). In comparison, just over a quarter of total expenditure by the highest income quintile was on food (12%) and shelter (14%). On the other hand, personal taxes accounted for only 2% of spending by those in the lowest income quintile compared to nearly 26% for those in the highest quintile. Between 1974 and 1984, tax expenditure dropped from 4% to 2% for the lowest quintile and increased slightly, from 24% to 26%, for the highest quintile.

As well, while all income quintiles experienced increased shelter expenditure between 1974 and 1984, the increase was highest in the lowest income quintile. In this period, the percentage of spending on shelter by the lowest income quintile increased by 4.9 percentage points compared to a 1.2 percentage point increase for those in the highest income quintile. The proportion of total expenditure on food, clothing, and transportation, on the other hand, declined by relatively similar amounts in all income groups during this period.

Percentage of Urban[1] Family Expenditure on Selected Items, by Income Quintiles, 1969–1984

	Food	Shelter	Clothing	Transpor-tation	Personal income taxes
Lowest Quintile			%		
1969	26.1	27.3	8.2	8.0	0.9
1974	26.4	25.6	7.3	7.7	3.6
1978	24.7	28.6	6.6	8.5	2.2
1982	22.6	29.6	5.9	8.8	2.5
1984	21.8	30.5	5.5	8.0	2.0
Second Quintile					
1969	20.7	18.8	8.5	11.7	8.8
1974	20.1	18.2	7.5	12.3	10.8
1978	19.6	20.1	7.0	12.4	10.2
1982	17.4	22.1	6.1	12.4	11.0
1984	17.7	21.7	6.1	12.8	9.9
Third Quintile					
1969	19.6	17.6	8.6	12.2	11.5
1974	18.6	16.0	7.6	12.3	15.0
1978	17.9	18.1	7.1	12.4	14.0
1982	16.0	19.1	5.9	12.3	16.3
1984	15.4	18.9	6.3	12.9	15.2
Fourth Quintile					
1969	17.7	15.8	9.1	12.4	13.5
1974	17.1	15.1	7.7	12.3	17.7
1978	16.0	16.4	7.2	12.3	17.8
1982	14.6	17.3	6.1	12.2	19.4
1984	14.4	17.0	6.1	12.3	19.0
Highest Quintile					
1969	14.1	13.9	8.9	11.2	20.6
1974	14.0	12.7	7.6	10.7	24.3
1978	13.9	14.3	7.4	11.3	23.3
1982	11.9	14.8	6.2	10.5	26.3
1984	12.1	13.9	6.6	11.1	25.8

[1] Covers 17 cities, except for 1974 when Charlottetown, Summerside and Victoria were not included.
Source: Statistics Canada, Catalogue 62–555, *Family Expenditure in Canada*, 1984; Household Surveys Division, Family Expenditure Surveys Section, unpublished revised statistics.

The average growth rate of Canada's 25 census metropolitan areas for the 1981–1986 period was 5.9%. This was well above the national average.

The biggest gainer among Canada's census metropolitan areas during the 1981–1986 period was Saskatoon with a population growth rate of 14.6%. Ottawa-Hull ranked second with a growth rate of 10.1%, followed by Toronto with 9.5%.

The metropolitan areas of Calgary and Edmonton, which experienced very substantial growth rates of 25.7% and 18.1% during the 1976–1981 period, grew by 7.2% and 6.0%, respectively, between 1981 and 1986.

Toronto, Montréal and Vancouver continue to be Canada's three largest metropolitan areas. Together they comprised 7.7 million people, or 30.5% of Canada's population in 1986. This was up from 29.1% in 1981.

A preliminary analysis of the growth in these three census metropolitan areas indicates a resurgence in the growth of their central cities.

Major centres getting larger

Rank 1986	Census Metropolitan Area	Population 1986	Percentage Change[1]		
			1971-1976	1976-1981	1981-1986
1	Toronto	3,427,168	7.7	7.0	9.5
2	Montréal	2,921,357[2]	2.7	0.9	2.1
3	Vancouver	1,380,729	7.8	8.7	8.9
4	Ottawa-Hull	819,263	11.8	3.6	10.1
5	Edmonton	785,465[2]	11.7	18.1	6.0
6	Calgary	671,326[2]	16.5	25.7	7.2
7	Winnipeg	625,304	5.2	1.1	5.6
8	Québec	603,267	8.1	6.3	3.3
9	Hamilton	557,029	5.2	2.4	2.8
10	St. Catharines-Niagara	343,258	5.6	0.8	0.2
11	London	342,302	6.9	4.9	4.7
12	Kitchener	311,195	14.1	5.7	8.1
13	Halifax	295,990	7.0	3.6	6.6
14	Victoria	255,547[2]	11.5	7.0	5.8
15	Windsor	253,988	−0.5	−0.6	1.2
16	Oshawa	203,543	12.4	14.1	9.2
17	Saskatoon	200,665	5.8	15.3	14.6
18	Regina	186,521	7.4	8.7	7.7
19	St. John's	161,901	8.8	6.5	4.6
20	Chicoutimi-Jonquière	158,468	1.8	5.1	0.2
21	Sudbury	148,877	−0.4	−4.5	−4.6
22	Sherbrooke	129,960	-	-	3.8
23	Trois-Rivières	128,888	-	5.1	2.8
24	Thunder Bay	122,217	4.0	1.8	0.2
25	Saint John	121,265	5.8	0.9	0.2

1986 POPULATION OF CENSUS METROPOLITAN AREAS AND PERCENTAGE CHANGE, 1971-1986

[1] For each period, percentage change is calculated using the boundaries at the end of the period.

[2] Excludes population of one or more incompletely enumerated Indian reserves or Indian settlements.

CALGARY: A STATISTICAL PROFILE

by Nat Stone

The long-term trend in Canada has been toward greater urbanization, but growth rates of different Census Metropolitan Areas (CMAs) have varied widely since 1971. Some experienced rapid growth; others increased, but at a much slower rate; still others have actually declined. Calgary is an example of a Census Metropolitan Area where growth has been particularly rapid.

A Growing Population

In 1986, Calgary was Canada's sixth largest Census Metropolitan Area; in 1971, it had ranked ninth. During the 1971-1986 period, the population of Calgary grew from 403,300 to 671,300, a 66% increase[1]. In the same period, Edmonton grew 58%, while the two largest Census Metropolitan Areas, Toronto and Montreal, increased 30% and 6%, respectively. The total population of Canada rose 17% in this period.

The overall increase in Calgary's population since 1971 masks several dramatic fluctuations in the rate of growth during this period; these were associated with the ups and downs of the oil and gas industry. In fact, the price of crude oil has been the most important factor in the city's growth and economic health. When oil prices skyrocketed in the 1970s, for example, so did the growth rate of Calgary's population, but as prices slumped in the 1980s, the rate of increase dropped precipitously.

During the late 1970s, when the oil and gas industry was booming, Calgary grew faster than any other metropolitan area in Canada. Between 1976 and 1981, Calgary's population rose 26%, from 469,900 to 592,700. Edmonton also grew at a substantial rate (18%), but Toronto increased just 7%, and Montreal only 1% in this period. The population of Canada as a whole rose 6%.

Population growth in Calgary slowed in the 1980s after the downturn in the oil and gas industry. Between 1981 and 1986, the population increased, but by just 7%. Although this was still above the national growth rate of 4%, Calgary fell to eighth place among Census Metropolitan Areas in terms of population growth during this period.

[1] Percentage changes are calculated using the boundaries at the end of the period.

Calgary Census Metropolitan Area Boundaries, 1971 and 1986

A Destination for Migrants

Migration has been the primary component of Calgary's growth. The net in-flow of migrants was particularly heavy during the late 1970s and early 1980s. Between 1976 and 1981, for example, almost three-quarters of the population increase was attributable to migration. In each of the three years from 1979 to 1981, net migration to Calgary totalled more than 20,000.

This massive influx ended in 1982. After a net gain of almost 24,000 migrants in 1981, Calgary suffered net losses of 6,300 in 1982, 12,300 in 1983, and 4,600 in 1984. Net migration returned to the positive side in 1985 when 5,200 more people moved to the city than left.

A Young City

Calgary has a relatively high concentration of young adults. In 1986, 23% of residents were aged 25-34, compared with 18% for Canada. Conversely, the proportion of elderly people was much lower in Calgary than in Canada as a whole. In 1986, only 7% of the population of Calgary, as opposed to 11% of all Canadians, were aged 65 and over. The percentage of Calgary residents under age 25 (39%) was slightly above the national figure (38%).

Family Patterns

The high proportion of young adults in Calgary is reflected in the marital status and family characteristics of the city's inhabitants. While the proportions of the population aged 15 and over who were married or single were similar to those for Canada as a whole in 1986, a somewhat

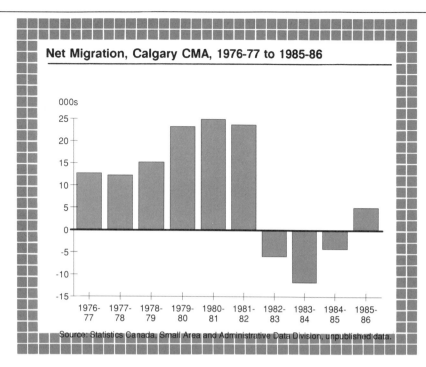

Net Migration, Calgary CMA, 1976-77 to 1985-86

000s

Source: Statistics Canada, Small Area and Administrative Data Division, unpublished data.

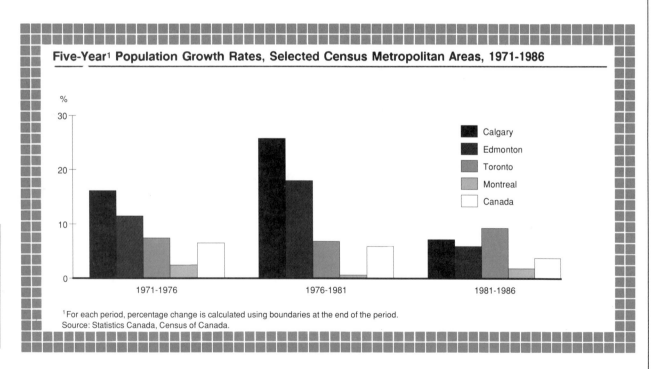

Five-Year[1] Population Growth Rates, Selected Census Metropolitan Areas, 1971-1986

%

Calgary
Edmonton
Toronto
Montreal
Canada

[1] For each period, percentage change is calculated using boundaries at the end of the period.
Source: Statistics Canada, Census of Canada.

higher proportion of the adult population in Calgary was divorced, and a smaller percentage was widowed. The proportion of Calgarians living alone was also slightly above the level for all Canada. As well, families in Calgary tended to have younger children than was the case for Canada overall.

Language, Ethnicity and Religion[2]

English was the mother tongue of 82% of Calgary's population in 1986; another 3% had learned both English and another language simultaneously. Chinese, German and French were each the mother tongue of about 2% of the population.

As the figures on language suggest, Calgary's ethnic composition was

[2] Mother tongue data are from the 1986 Census; ethnicity and religion data are available only from the 1981 Census.

Calgary was originally established as a North-West Mounted Police post in 1875; it was incorporated as a town in 1884, and as a city in 1893. The 1891 Census, the first to include Calgary, counted 4,000 residents.

Calgary's early growth was associated with development of the livestock industry and with the city's position as the chief transportation centre in Alberta. By 1911, the population had grown to 43,700.

The most crucial element in Calgary's growth has been the oil and natural gas industry. Oil was first discovered at Turner Valley, a few kilometres southwest of the

city, in 1914. Alberta's first oil refinery opened in Calgary in 1923. Subsequent discoveries at Turner Valley in 1924 and 1936, and especially the major find at Leduc in 1947, further established Calgary as the industry's administrative centre in Canada.

Growth in Calgary really took off after the Second World War. The oil industry attracted migrants in record numbers. Moreover, this was the baby-boom era when the annual number of births was climbing, not only in Calgary, but also in Canada generally. In both five-year intercensal periods between 1951 and 1961, Calgary's population grew about 40%; by 1961, the population totalled over a quarter of a million.

Population growth in Calgary slowed to around 20% in both five-year intercensal periods in the 1961-1971 decade. By 1971, the population was just over 400,000.

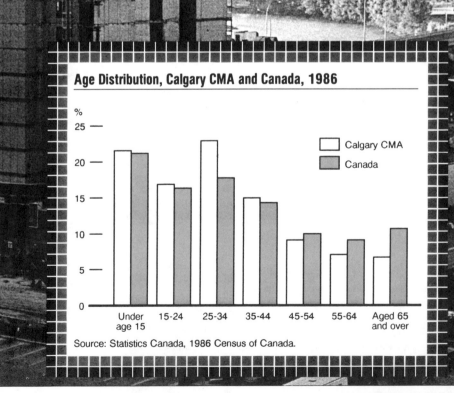

Age Distribution, Calgary CMA and Canada, 1986

Legend: Calgary CMA (white), Canada (grey)

Y-axis: % (0 to 25)

X-axis categories: Under age 15, 15-24, 25-34, 35-44, 45-54, 55-64, Aged 65 and over

Source: Statistics Canada, 1986 Census of Canada.

predominantly Anglo-Saxon. In 1981, 49% of the population claimed British roots, while 9% reported a combination of British and some other ethnic origin. The next largest ethnic groups were German (8%) and French (4%).

More than half of Calgary's population (55%) indicated religious affiliation with a Protestant denomination in 1981; another quarter were Roman Catholics. The proportion claiming no religious preference was 14%, double the percentage for all Canada.

Educational Attainment High

The population of Calgary is relatively well-educated. In 1981, 14% of the population aged 15 and over not attending school full-time were university graduates; the corresponding percentage for Canada was 8%. On the other hand, just 9% of adults in Calgary had less than a Grade 9 education, compared with 22% for Canada.

An Uncertain Labour Market

Labour force participation has grown significantly in Calgary since the mid-1970s. In 1986, 76% of the eligible population in Calgary was in the labour force, up from 67% in 1975. By comparison, the labour force participation rate for Canada as a whole rose from 61% to 66% during the same period.

Labour force participation in Calgary has been the highest of any Census Metropolitan Area since the late 1970s. The second highest participation rate in 1986 was 73% in Oshawa.

Unemployment has increased substantially in Calgary since the beginning of the economic recession in the early 1980s. In 1980, Calgary's unemployment rate was 3.6%, less than half the national level of 7.5%. But in both 1983 and 1984, over 12% of the city's labour force was unemployed; this was higher than the national rate. By 1986, Calgary's unemployment rate had fallen to 9.9%, though this was still slightly above the national rate of 9.6%.

Reflecting its position as the administrative centre of Canada's oil and gas industry, a relatively high proportion of the workforce in Calgary is engaged in managerial and administrative occupations, and in occupations related to the natural sciences, engineering and mathematics. In 1981, those employed in management and administration made up 12% of Calgary's labour force, compared with 9% for Canada. Occupations in scientific fields accounted for 8% of the Calgary workforce, compared with 3% for Canada.

Incomes Above the Norm

Over the last decade, incomes in Calgary have been well above those for Canada as a whole. The extent of the difference, however, has varied with fluctuations in the oil industry. The median income[3] of Calgary residents in 1976 was $9,200, about 10% above the median for all Canada. By 1982, the median income in Calgary had risen to $17,000, almost 24% above the national figure. The next year, however, the difference began to narrow. In 1985, the median income in Calgary of $17,900 was still higher than the median for all Canada, but only by 16%.

[3] Income data pertain to those who submitted income tax returns for the years in question. The median is the midway point: half the incomes are above the median, and half are below.

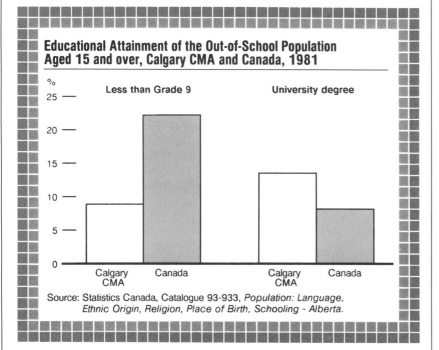

Educational Attainment of the Out-of-School Population Aged 15 and over, Calgary CMA and Canada, 1981

Source: Statistics Canada, Catalogue 93-933, *Population: Language, Ethnic Origin, Religion, Place of Birth, Schooling - Alberta.*

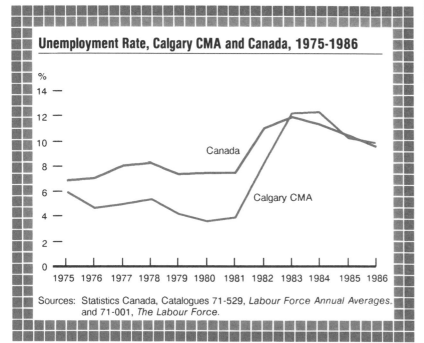

Unemployment Rate, Calgary CMA and Canada, 1975-1986

Sources: Statistics Canada, Catalogues 71-529, *Labour Force Annual Averages,* and 71-001, *The Labour Force.*

LOSS OF PRIME AGRICULTURAL LAND
THE EXAMPLE OF SOUTHERN ONTARIO

by Mary Anne Burke

The last 60 years have seen sweeping changes in Canadian agriculture. Both the rural population and total employment in agriculture have fallen sharply. Many smaller farms have been consolidated into larger ones. As well, agriculture's share of the Gross Domestic Product has dropped considerably, although the value of agricultural output has increased in absolute terms. At the same time, food imports have climbed.

In addition, the amount of land available for farming has declined. In 1986, farmland in Canada totalled 167.6 million acres, 6.5 million less than in 1951.

The loss of agricultural land is significant because, despite Canada's size, very little land — just 11% — is suitable for farming. Moreover, less than half of one percent of the total land base, an area slightly smaller than Nova Scotia, is prime agricultural land. Increasingly, conflicting demands are being placed on Canada's farmland, particularly the prime areas.

Prime agricultural land has been lost, partly as a result of the urbanization process. Early settlements were on prime farmland, and these communities set the pattern for later development. For example, as cities such as Toronto, Montreal and Vancouver have grown, the prime agricultural land base has been eroded in response to housing, transportation, and recreation pressures.

The net loss of farmland in Canada between 1951 and 1986 was a product of gains and losses in different regions. For example, some marginal land was gained on the northern edge of the Prairies; on the other hand, large amounts of prime land in Ontario were lost to agriculture.

Changes in Canadian agriculture

The shift from traditional labour-intensive farming to highly technical, mechanized methods resulted in fewer people farming larger areas. The percentage of the population living in rural areas has dropped, as has the proportion of the labour force employed in agriculture. In 1986, about a quarter (24%) of Canada's population was rural; this was down from more than half (53%) in 1921. During the same period, the proportion of the work force employed in agriculture fell from 33% to 4%. Meanwhile, average farm size rose from 198 acres in 1921 to 572 acres in 1986.

Agricultural output, as a percentage of Gross Domestic Product, fell from a high of 18% in 1926 to just 2% in 1986. This decrease, however, was uneven with major declines occurring in the late 1920s and again in the mid-1950s.

The dollar amount of imported foodstuffs has risen substantially. In 1986, Canada imported $6.7 billion worth of foodstuffs; allowing for inflation, this was a 264% increase from the 1946 total.

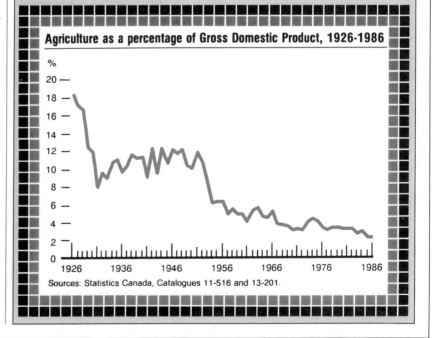

Agriculture as a percentage of Gross Domestic Product, 1926-1986

Sources: Statistics Canada, Catalogues 11-516 and 13-201.

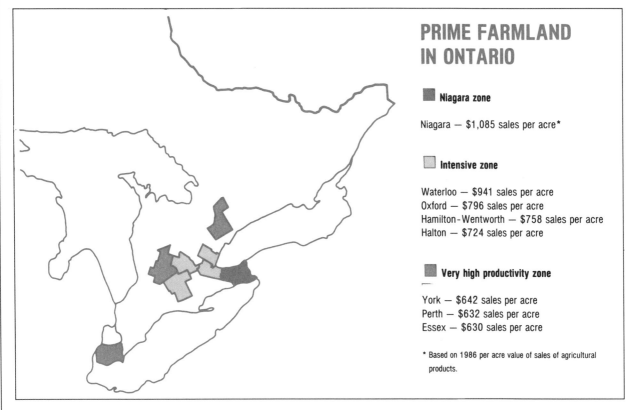

PRIME FARMLAND IN ONTARIO

■ **Niagara zone**

Niagara — $1,085 sales per acre*

□ **Intensive zone**

Waterloo — $941 sales per acre
Oxford — $796 sales per acre
Hamilton-Wentworth — $758 sales per acre
Halton — $724 sales per acre

■ **Very high productivity zone**

York — $642 sales per acre
Perth — $632 sales per acre
Essex — $630 sales per acre

* Based on 1986 per acre value of sales of agricultural products.

Loss of farmland in Ontario

The amount of agricultural land in Ontario has been falling since 1931. Between 1931 and 1986, the province experienced a net loss of 8.9 million acres of farmland, as total farm acreage dropped from 22.8 to 13.9 million acres. Of this decline, 5.7 million acres (64%) were unimproved land,[1] while the remaining 3.2 million acres (36%) were improved land.[2]

Of prime importance is the loss of agricultural land in southern Ontario. This region contains some of Canada's most productive farmland including the Niagara Peninsula, a unique tender fruit- and grape-growing area, and the Holland Marsh, north of Toronto. A high proportion of the land lost to farming in these areas was improved.

The number of farm acres in the prime agricultural zones of southern Ontario fell 26%, from 3.0 million to 2.2 million between 1931 and 1986. Of this decline, almost half a million acres, or 63% of the total, were improved land.

The greatest proportional loss of prime agricultural land in southern Ontario occurred in the Niagara zone, which had the highest per-acre dollar yield. In this zone, the amount of farmland fell by over a third (35%) from 366,000 to 237,000 acres. More than three-quarters (77%) of this loss was improved land.

During the same period, the other prime agricultural zones lost about a quarter of their farmland, again with improved land accounting for the largest proportion of the loss.

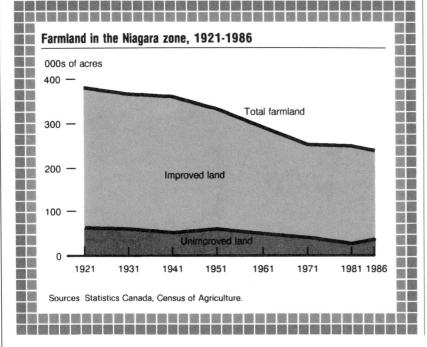

Farmland in the Niagara zone, 1921-1986

000s of acres

Total farmland

Improved land

Unimproved land

Sources Statistics Canada, Census of Agriculture.

[1] Unimproved land includes areas such as woodland, wood lots, Christmas tree lots, grazing or hay lands, bogs and marshes; it excludes large tracts of timber.
[2] Improved land includes all land under crops, as well as land such as summer fallow land and improved pasture land.

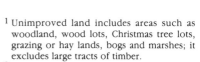

THE SERVICE SECTOR IN THE 1980s

by Colin Lindsay

The postwar period has been characterized by dramatic growth in the share of employment accounted for by service sector workers. While some Canadians regard service sector jobs as being inferior to those in the goods-producing sector, the service sector includes a wide variety of career-oriented occupations in the professions, education, business, and government.

Service sector growth in the 1980s

In 1987, 71% of all employment in Canada was in the service sector, up from 67% in 1980. This also represents a major change from the early 1950s, when less than half of all employment was in this sector.

The increase in the share of total employment in the service sector in the 1980s occurred because of significant growth in employment in this sector, combined with a small decline in employment in the goods-producing sector. Between 1980 and 1987, total service sector employment rose 18%, while the number of people employed in the goods-producing sector declined 1%.

The lack of growth in the goods-producing sector in the 1980s was attributable largely to the effect of the 1981-82 recession on employment, which was much greater in this sector than in the service industries. Between 1981 and 1983, service sector employment rose, albeit by only 1%, whereas employment in the goods-producing sector fell 10%.

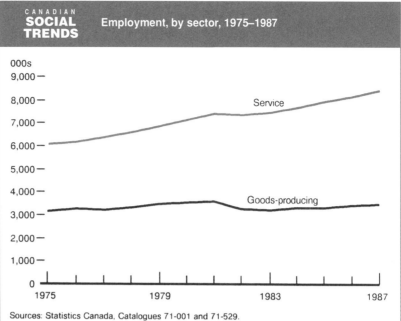

CANADIAN
**SOCIAL
TRENDS**

Employment, by sector, 1975–1987

000s

9,000 —

8,000 —

7,000 —

6,000 —

5,000 —

4,000 —

3,000 —

2,000 —

1,000 —

0 —

Service

Goods-producing

1975   1979   1983   1987

Sources: Statistics Canada, Catalogues 71-001 and 71-529.

Employment has grown in both sectors since the end of the recession, with service sector growth slightly outpacing that in the goods-producing sector. Between 1983 and 1987, employment rose 13% in the service sector and 9% in the goods-producing industries.

Service sector jobs changing

The majority of people working in the service sector are employed in clerical, sales, or service jobs. However, the proportion of service sector workers in these occupations has fallen in the 1980s, while that in managerial and professional positions has risen.

In 1987, 50% of all service workers were in clerical (20%), sales (13%), or service (18%) jobs. This was down, however, from 54% in 1980. Over the same period, the proportion of service workers in managerial or professional occupations rose from 29% to 35%.

Different industries growing

There was considerable variation in growth rates of different industries within the service sector. Increases were particularly large in the number of people providing services to business management and in employment in health and welfare services. Employment in services to business, such as accounting, engineering, and legal and management consulting, rose 38% between 1980 and 1987. In the same period, the number of people working in health and welfare services rose 33%.

Employment in consumer services, such as accommodation and food, amusement and recreation, and personal services, also rose substantially. The number of people working in each of these industries was up more than 20% over the 1980-1987 period.

Employment growth was somewhat slower in education, wholesale and retail trade, and finance, insurance and real estate. The number of people employed in these industries rose by around 15% between 1980 and 1987.

For the purpose of this review, the economy is divided into two main components, the **service sector** and the **goods-producing sector**.

The **service sector** includes distributive services such as transportation and storage, communications, utilities, and wholesale and retail trade; consumer services such as accommodation and food services, personal services, and amusement and recreational services; producer services such as services to business management, and finance, insurance and real estate; and non-commercial services such as education, health and welfare services, religious organizations, and public administration.

The **goods-producing sector** includes agriculture, manufacturing, construction, mining, forestry, and fishing.

On the other hand, there was only a 10% increase in the number of people working in public administration. Employment growth in federal public administration was particularly slow. Between 1980 and 1987, the number of people employed in federal public administration increased by just 5%. As a result of this slow growth, federal public administration's share of all employment in Canada declined from 2.5% in 1980 to 2.3% in 1987.

Employment in local and provincial administration grew at a somewhat faster rate than did federal public administration. However, at around 12% for each, growth in these industries was still below that for the service sector overall.

Women majority in service sector

Women make up the majority of service sector workers in Canada. In 1987, 51% of people employed in this sector were women; in contrast, women made up just 23% of goods-producing workers. A clear majority of both men and women, though, work in the service sector. In 1987, 84% of women with jobs outside the home and 61% of all male workers were employed in this sector.

There are significant differences in the types of service jobs held by men and women. In 1987, 63% of female service workers compared with 37% of men were in clerical, sales, or service occupations. In fact, almost one in three (31%) female service sector workers compared with just 8% of men was in a clerical position.

Overall, there was little difference in the proportion of male and female service sector workers with managerial and professional jobs. In 1987, 36% of men and 34% of women held such positions. However, within this category, a greater proportion of women than men were in professions such as nursing and teaching.

At the same time, men employed in the service sector were far more likely than women to be in other service industry jobs. In 1987, 27% of male service sector workers compared with just 3% of women were in occupations such as transportation, processing, and material handling.

Young most likely to have service sector jobs

Young adults are the most likely people to work in the service sector, although the majority of workers in all age groups are employed in this sector. Among 15-24-year-olds employed in 1987, 64% of men

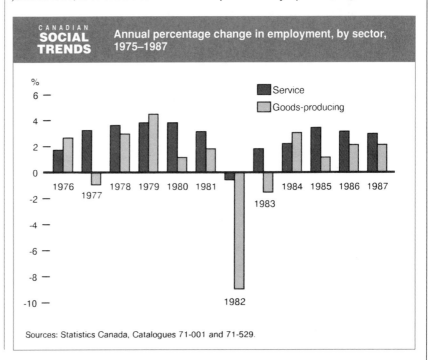

CANADIAN SOCIAL TRENDS Annual percentage change in employment, by sector, 1975–1987

Sources: Statistics Canada, Catalogues 71-001 and 71-529.

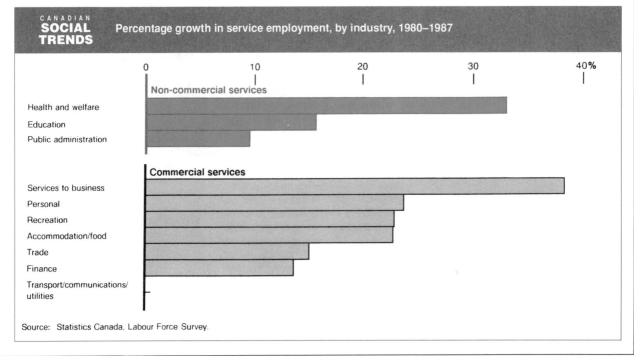

CANADIAN SOCIAL TRENDS Percentage growth in service employment, by industry, 1980–1987

Source: Statistics Canada, Labour Force Survey.

and 87% of women had service sector jobs. For men, the proportion employed in the this sector fell to around 60% for those aged 25 and over. For older women, the percentage ranged from 84% for those aged 25-44 to 78% for those aged 65 and over.

Growth industry in all regions
People employed in the service sector make up the majority of workers in all regions of Canada, though this sector's share of employment varies across the country.

The service sector's share of total employment was highest in British Columbia where it accounted for 76% of all employed people in 1987. Alberta and Atlantic Canada also have relatively large service sectors; 73% of workers in each of these areas had service jobs.

Ontario has the smallest proportion of its workforce employed in the service sector. In 1987, just 68% of people employed in this province were service workers. However, service sector growth has been much stronger in Ontario than in any other region in the 1980s. The number of people employed in Ontario's service sector rose 23% between 1980 and 1987 compared with an average of 15% in the other regions. As a result, Ontario accounted for almost half (47%) of all growth in service employment in Canada during the 1980s.

Part-time work a service phenomenon
In 1987, 89% of all part-time workers were in the service sector. That year, 19% of service sector workers were employed part-time compared with just 6% of goods-producing workers.

The incidence of part-time work varies widely in different service industries. Almost one-quarter of those employed in both community, business and personal services (24%), and wholesale and retail trade (23%) worked part-time in 1987. In comparison, the percentages working part-time in finance (11%), public administration (7%), and transportation, communications and utilities (6%) were much lower.

Female service sector workers are more likely than men to work part-time. In 1987, 28% of women employed in the service sector compared with 10% of men worked part-time. As well, part-time employment is relatively common among female service workers of all ages, whereas men aged 15-24 make up the vast majority of male part-time service workers.

In 1987, 73% of people employed part-time in the service sector worked part-time because they were going to school, had personal or family responsibilities, or did not want full-time work. Still, that year, 434,000 service sector workers, almost double the number in 1980, worked part-time because they could not find a full-time job.

Unemployment rate lower
The level of unemployment in the service sector is considerably below that in the goods-producing sector. The service sector had an unemployment rate of 7.5% in 1987 compared with 10.0% in the goods-producing industries.

Within the service sector, the unemployment rate ranged from just over 8% in community, business and personal services to less than 5% in finance.

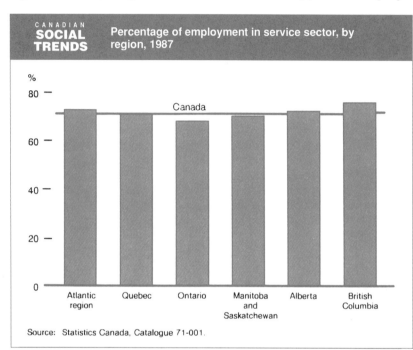

CANADIAN **SOCIAL TRENDS**

Percentage of employment in service sector, by region, 1987

Source: Statistics Canada, Catalogue 71-001.

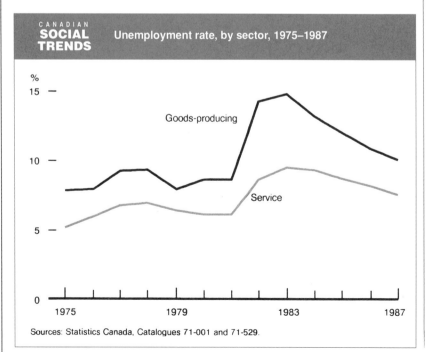

CANADIAN **SOCIAL TRENDS**

Unemployment rate, by sector, 1975–1987

Sources: Statistics Canada, Catalogues 71-001 and 71-529.

FORTY YEARS OF SOCIAL HOUSING IN TORONTO

by Susan McMillan

In an effort to improve the housing standards of the least well off, governments in Canada have constructed and currently operate housing developments of varying physical types. It has now been almost 40 years since the first of the massive low rental public housing projects was built in Canada. When it was constructed in the late 1940s, the initial development — Regent Park North in Toronto — was considered a progressive venture in social engineering. This and other public housing projects which soon followed held out the promise, not only of an urban renaissance for the decayed cores of Canadian cities, but also of a new and less impoverished life for residents. Although these initial goals have not been fully achieved, the quality of the housing stock has been improved.

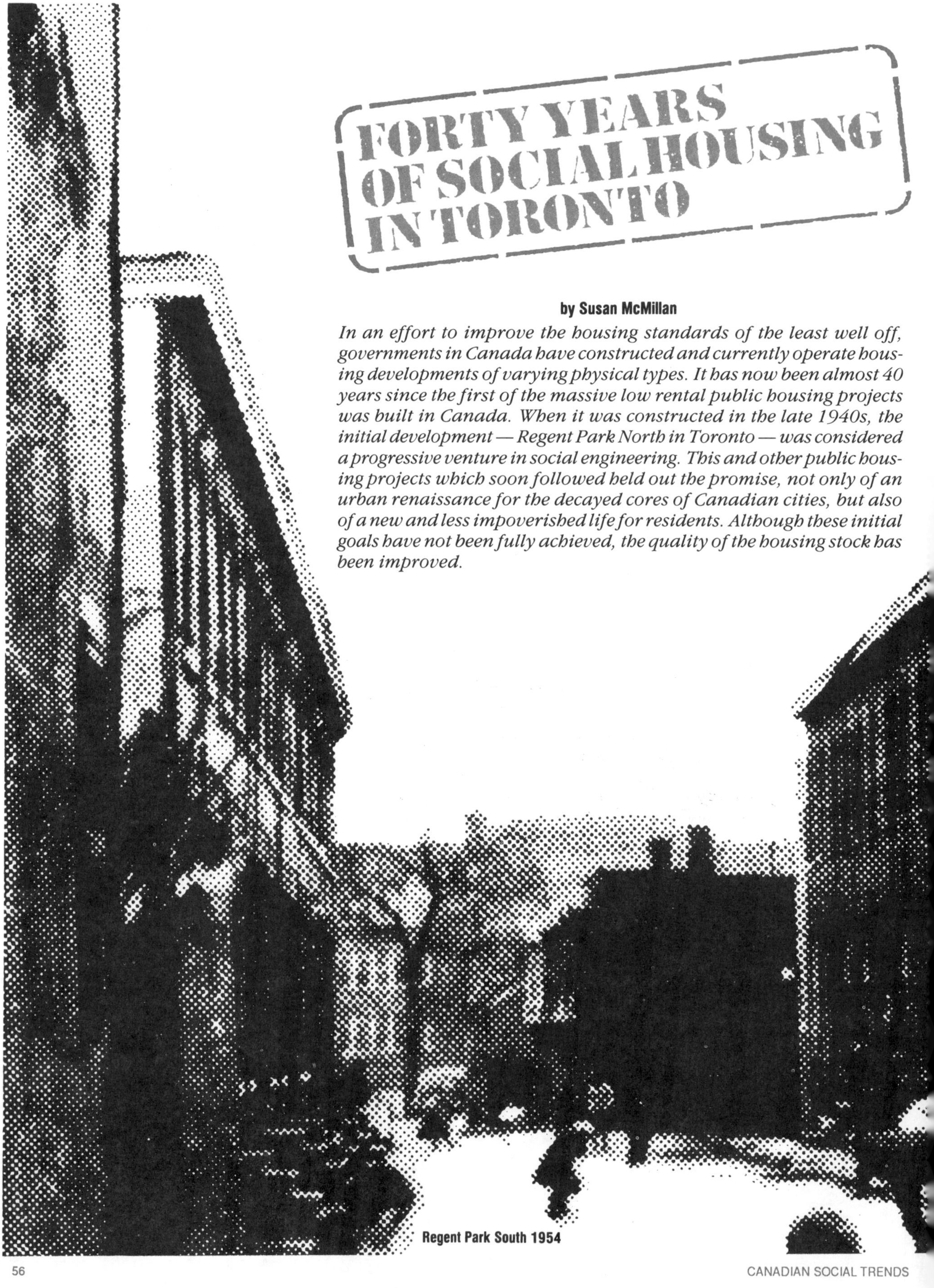

Regent Park South 1954

Regent Park North Pre-construction

Regent Park North Post-construction

The characteristics of today's public housing residents in Toronto not only differ from those of the city's residents in general, but they have also changed considerably since the first large-scale projects were built. In many instances, these changes reflect broader shifts occurring in Toronto or in Canadian society as a whole.

One feature that has consistently characterized these projects, and set them apart from the city as a whole since their construction, has been the persistent gap in employment and income levels between the residents of the projects and Toronto residents generally. In order to qualify as a project resident, an applicant must have a sufficiently low income. Projects thus tend to concentrate low-income persons in limited geographical areas. The outcome of such a process is that projects have higher-than-average numbers of female lone parents, dependent children and recent immigrants. They are also characterized by higher unemployment rates and lower-than-average labour force participation rates and incomes.

Nevertheless, the projects differ from each other in their physical characteristics (for example, urban or suburban location, and high-rise versus low-rise construction) and in the social characteristics of current groups of project residents. The four major projects described here were built in different time periods and take different physical shapes in distinctive Toronto locations. Each is unique.

Regent Park: The Original Slum Clearance Project, 1948

Regent Park has changed considerably since the days when it was first built. Some shifts in ethnic composition, age profile and family structure have followed patterns akin to those in the City of Toronto. However, other patterns, particularly the marked decline in the labour force participation rate for men between 1951 and 1981, are unique to Regent Park. In 1981, the percentage of Regent Park families headed by a lone parent was much higher than in Toronto as a whole. Also, that year, the percentage of Regent Park residents living below Statistics Canada's Low-Income Cut-Offs was considerably higher than for Toronto.

With few exceptions, the ethnic composition of Regent Park has reflected that of the city. In 1951, just over two-thirds of people in both the city and the project were of British origin. At the same time, a much larger percentage of Regent Park residents claimed French origin than did Toronto residents: 9% compared with 3%.

Thirty years later, the percentage of both Regent Park and Toronto residents claiming British origin had dropped significantly. In 1981, the percentage of those living in Regent Park claiming British origin had dropped to 52%, down from 67% in 1951. But for Toronto as a whole, the 1981 percentage was much lower at 42%, down from 69% in 1951. Visible minorities, on the other hand, had a much stronger presence in the project. In 1981, the percentage of Regent Park residents of the North and South American (including Caribbean) and African (including Black) origin was much higher than for the City of Toronto — 11% compared with 2%. Those of Chinese origin formed a significant minority in both the project (9%) and in the city as a whole (6%).

Despite the greater multicultural nature of Regent Park in 1981, the proportion of residents born outside Canada was smaller than in the City of Toronto (38% versus 43%), perhaps reflecting a large number of Canadian-born dependent children in the project. However, immigrants living in Regent Park tended to be more recent arrivals than those living in Toronto generally: 13% of Regent Park residents came to Canada between 1979 and 1981, compared with 9% of those in the city.

An aging trend, apparent in both Regent Park and Toronto between 1951 and 1981, was not as strong in the project as in the city as a whole. Over the three decades, the percentage of people aged 65 and over climbed from 6% to 8% in Regent Park. In Toronto, the percentage rose from 8% to 13%. In 1951, 12% of Regent Park residents were under age 5, compared with 10% of Toronto residents; by 1981, these percentages had dropped to 10% and 5%, respectively. Also in 1981, almost one-third of people living in Regent Park were under age 15, compared with only about one-sixth of Toronto residents.

Lone-parent families made up the majority of Regent Park families in 1981. Fully 53% of families were headed by a lone parent. The figure for Toronto was 15%.

In 1951, 30% of Regent Park households consisted of more than one family. The comparable figure for Toronto as a whole was 21%. But by 1981, multi-family households were a very small minority in both Regent Park and Toronto. Only 1% of Regent Park households consisted of more than one family, slightly lower than the 2% for Toronto. This decline signals a large reduction in overcrowding over the period in Toronto. By 1981, the average number of persons per room was 0.5 for the city of Toronto as a whole and no more than 0.7 in any of the four developments discussed here.

Male participation in the labour force dropped markedly in Regent Park between 1951 and 1981. By 1981, just over half (54%) of the men in Regent Park compared with 79% of men in Toronto were in the labour force. For both groups, the labour force participation rate had been 85% in 1951.

Over the same period, female labour force participation increased in Regent Park, although not as quickly as in the city as a whole. For female Regent Park residents, the labour force participation rate rose from 28% to 38%, compared with a rise of 23%, from 38% to 61%, for Toronto women.

Unemployment levels remained at least twice as high in Regent Park as in Toronto between 1951 and 1981. In 1981, 12% of the Regent Park labour force was unemployed, compared with 5% in Toronto.

Median household incomes in Regent Park were less than half those in the city of Toronto in 1980. Median household incomes were $9,400 in Regent Park South and just $5,900 in Regent Park North. The comparable income figure for Toronto was $19,900.

As well, in 1980, a much larger proportion of people in Regent Park were living below Statistics Canada's Low-Income Cut-Offs than was the case in the city as a whole. That year, 79% of unattached individuals in Regent Park were below the Low-Income Cut-Offs, compared with 34% in Toronto. The discrepancy among families was even wider: 69% of families in Regent Park lived below the Low-Income Cut-Offs, compared with 17% of Toronto families.

Lawrence Heights: Suburban High-Density, 1957

Lawrence Heights, a suburban development built as a compound of low-rise apartment buildings on 96 acres of farmland in North York, presents a slightly different pattern both architecturally and in terms of the characteristics of residents. Especially in terms of birth outside of Canada, Lawrence Heights residents were distinctive. About half the population of Lawrence Heights was born outside Canada, with most of these people immigrating between 1955 and 1977. Just over half of Lawrence Heights residents reported a non-British ethnic origin in 1981. A variety of origins made up this component: North and South American (including Caribbean), African (including Black), Greek, and Italian.

There was a smaller proportion of elderly persons in Lawrence Heights than in the City of Toronto. In 1981, 9% of Lawrence Heights residents were aged 65 and over, compared with 13% in Toronto. On the other hand, 30% of Lawrence Heights residents were under age 15, compared with 16% for Toronto. Families headed by a lone parent made up the majority of Lawrence Heights families in 1981: 55% compared with 15% for Toronto.

As in the case of Regent Park, labour force participation for both men and women was lower in Lawrence Heights than in Toronto. Fifty-nine percent of Lawrence Heights men were in the labour force in 1981, compared with 79% in Toronto. The percentage for Lawrence Heights women was 48%, compared with 61% for Toronto women. Unemployment rates were also higher in Lawrence Heights than in Toronto. In the public housing project, the unemployment rate was 7% for men and 8% for women. The comparable rate in Toronto for both men and women was 5%.

The median income of households in Lawrence Heights in 1980 is not available but in that year the average income was $12,900. The comparable figure for Toronto was $25,600. Thus, even when built in a suburban setting, public housing has tended to concentrate lone-parent families and visible minorities, as have the older downtown projects.

Moss Park: Downtown High Rise, 1960

Moss Park is a high-rise apartment complex. It is thus architectually less suited to the needs of families with young children. In 1981, Moss Park differed from Toronto as a whole as well as from other public housing projects, both in age and family structure. In Moss Park, there were proportionally fewer young children and many more elderly persons than in the other developments. The proportion of Moss Park's population under age 15 was 9%, less than Toronto with 16% and much less than other developments. The proportion of elderly aged 65 and over was 18% in Moss Park, compared with just 13% for Toronto.

In 1981, Moss Park had 29% of families headed by a lone parent, double the Toronto percentage of lone-parent families, but less than half the Regent Park proportion (69%).

The median household income in Moss Park, at $8,700, was less than half that for Toronto in 1980. However, Moss Park residents who did work had employment incomes similar to those in Toronto. For men, the Moss Park figure was lower than for Toronto — $12,000 compared with $14,500. But for women, employment income was actually higher

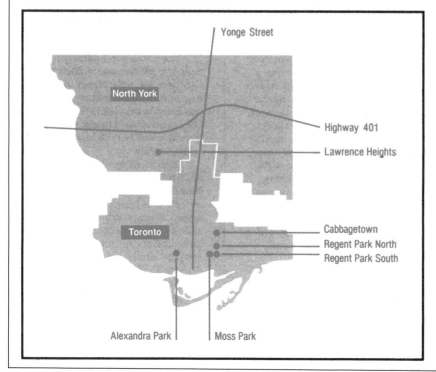

in Moss Park ($10,700) than for female workers in the city as a whole ($9,800).

The percentages of unattached individuals and families in Moss Park living below the Low-Income Cut-Offs were both considerably higher than those for Toronto as a whole. In 1981, 58% of unattached individuals and 37% of families in Moss Park were below the Low-Income Cut-Offs.

Alexandra Park: Mixed Renovation and Replacement, 1965

Alexandra Park is a downtown development in which total demolition did not occur. Rather, some old housing was renovated and new dwellings added to it. The 1981 profile of this project differed considerably from Toronto as a whole, as well as from Regent Park. The percentage of Alexandra Park residents claiming British origin was much lower than for Toronto in 1981. That year, only 28% of those living in Alexandra Park were of British origin compared with 20% in 1961. There were also large numbers of people living in Alexandra Park claiming Chinese and Portuguese origin — 23% and 16%, respectively.

As well, in 1981, 59% of Alexandra Park residents had been born outside Canada. Of those living in Alexandra Park who had immigrated to Canada, 12% had done so since 1979.

The project's multicultural nature is also reflected in the relatively high proportion of residents who speak a language other than English or French at home. In 1981, 41% spoke neither English nor French at home; in Toronto, the percentage was 25% and in Regent Park, only 15%.

The age profile of Alexandra Park is quite similar to that of Toronto. For example, in 1981, 14% of Alexandra Park residents were aged 65 and over, compared with 13% of those in Toronto. At the other end of the age range, 6% of the projects residents were under 5 years of age, compared with 5% for the city.

The proportion of lone-parent families in Alexandra Park was double that in Toronto as a whole. In 1981, 29% of families in this public housing project were headed by a lone parent.

The percentage of multi-family households in Alexandra Park dropped sharply between 1961 and 1981, yet remained higher than in Toronto. In 1981, 4% of the project's households contained more than one family, down from 21% in 1961 in the area where the development was subsequently built.

Regent Park 1987

Cabbagetown: Private Renovation Adjacent to Regent Park

Gerrard Street is the northern boundary of Regent Park North. North of that thoroughfare lies Cabbagetown, a stylish neighbourhood of renovated Victorian three-storey detached and semi-detached homes which, although run-down in the 1940s, were not included in the Regent Park demolition area. Although physically adjacent, the social profiles of Regent Park and Cabbagetown are substantially different.

Before the days of Regent Park, the two areas were more or less identical in dwelling conditions and characteristics of residents. But, as has been the case for three decades, the residents of Regent Park are now dissimilar, both economically and socially, from their near neighbours. Thus public housing of the Regent Park type, while offering better quality housing, has not fundamentally altered the social gulf which Gerrard Street has come to physically represent. Residents of the two communities still stand apart.

While Regent Park is a community of lone-parent families and many children, Cabbagetown residents tend to be childless couples. More than half the housing project families were headed by a lone parent in 1981, compared with

only about 18% north of the Gerrard Street boundary. Consistent with its lone-parent profile, Regent Park was characterized by considerably more adult women than men. In Cabbagetown, the opposite was true. In 1981, 30% of Regent Park residents were under the age of 15, while in Cabbagetown the young made up only about 12%. In fact, more than 40% of Cabbagetown families were childless, compared with 12% in Regent Park.

The labour force participation rates of both men and women in Cabbagetown were higher than in Regent Park and unemployment was much lower — less than 5%. Median household incomes in 1980 were at least $14,000[1] higher than in Regent Park.

In terms of ethnic origin, those of British extraction predominate in both communities. But with the exception of French and Chinese origins, no other ethnic group affiliations were recorded in significant numbers in Cabbagetown in 1981. By contrast, there were large Black and Asian communities in Regent Park at the time of the 1981 Census.

[1] Cabbagetown is divided into two areas: one had a median household income of $19,700; the other, $28,100.

Official recognition of inferior housing conditions in the Municipality of Toronto came in 1934 in an Ontario government report (the 'Bruce Report' — named after the then Lieutenant-Governor of Ontario). However, the Depression and wartime stringencies that followed precluded any immediate remedial action. But rapid urban population growth after World War II which reflected migration to the cities, high levels of immigration, and increased levels of child-bearing once again made the decayed state of the housing stock a public issue. Overcrowding, deterioration of inner-city dwellings, and suburban subdivision development each played a part in fostering demands for slum clearance and for low-cost rental housing.

To begin meeting these needs, the first major development project in Canada, *Regent Park North*, was initiated as a city-financed slum clearance and construction project. Between 1948 and 1957, existing housing was razed, and a complex of low-rise apartment blocks and rowhouses containing over 1,000 units was built.

The project was hailed as a milestone in slum clearance, and in 1958, the Toronto Board of Trade journal concluded optimistically that "experience in *Regent Park North* has now been sufficient to indicate very clearly that a new environment can do much to aid people in developing their individual strengths as well as their family ties".

Later projects were of a considerably higher density than *Regent Park North* in order to reduce costs. *Regent Park South,* for example, built in 1957-58 directly south of the first project, consists of high-rise apartment buildings containing almost 500 units. Another 253 units of row housing constructed nearby were intended primarily for families with young children.

Lawrence Heights, developed between 1957 and 1961 and owned by the Ontario Housing Corporation, differed from other public housing projects of the era. It was built in a newly developed suburban area, so no process of slum clearance preceded its construction. This project consists of just over 1,000 units

Moss Park 1964

in nineteen 3½-storey walk-ups and 66 blocks of rowhouses, as well as some semi-detached and detached homes. (An additional 127 senior citizen units in the area are owned by Metropolitan Toronto.) By design, *Lawrence Heights* was spatially and socially isolated from the surrounding neighbourhoods, a feature that drew criticism in its early stages.

Between 1960 and 1964, *Moss Park* was built just southwest of *Regent Park*. This high-density public housing project consists of three 15-storey buildings containing about 900 units in total. Before the project was constructed, the area it now occupies was a neighbourhood of private homes, rooming houses, and small industrial buildings. Residences in the area were, in the main, not structurally dilapidated. Nonetheless, clearance was seen as preferable to rehabilitation and maintenance.

Work began on *Alexandra Park* in southwest Toronto in 1965. Instead of removal and replacement of all dwellings, this project entailed both rehabilitation of some houses and complete replacement of others. Full demolition, a feature of early developments, had fallen from favour by 1965.

The original plan for *Alexandra Park* called for clearance of 39 of the total of 72 acres. Four hundred and ten housing units were eventually built in two high-rise buildings and a number of rowhouses. The remaining area was devoted to new and rehabilitated private dwellings, commercial buildings, new non-profit co-operative housing units, and senior citizen units. Other space was devoted to industrial and institutional uses. This mixture has given *Alexandra Park* a very different look from other public housing complexes.

During the 1960s, after several major public housing projects had

been completed, attitudes toward this type of housing began to shift, and criticism of major projects in principle became prevalent. Opponents pointed to the disruption imposed on communities for which clearance was being considered, as well as to the hardship of individual households whose homes were expropriated. This was particularly true for families not relocated in the new project. Some homeowners were unable to purchase a replacement home elsewhere with the proceeds of the expropriation. Other unattached residents and lodgers, not eligible to relocate, had to search for inexpensive accommodation outside the area. Many eligible families never relocated in the projects, but simply left the area, thereby contributing to the dissolution of an established community. The complexes also lacked social support systems such as community centres, daycare facilities, accessible parking, and playgrounds.

In the 1980s, public housing has taken on a new and broader meaning: mammoth public housing developments are no longer built. Such projects were primarily concentrated in Toronto, but public housing on a much smaller scale has been built throughout the country. Over 200,000 units have been built in Canada.

In Metropolitan Toronto today, emphasis is placed on 'assisted housing', particularly through mixed income programmes in which tenants pay rent according to their incomes, but with the majority paying market rents. There are a number of mixed income programmes; units may be leased by housing authorities in privately-owned buildings; non-profit building projects are also operated by some municipalities; and church, service, and other non-profit groups build and operate private non-profit housing. Such co-operative housing allows residents to participate in the management and maintenance of their own facilities, while subsidized housing in mixed buildings permits those with low incomes to blend in and live on an equal footing with unsubsidized tenants, thereby avoiding the stigma often attached to public housing residents.

	Developments					Adjacent private renovation
	City of Toronto	Regent Park (built 1948)	Lawrence Heights (built 1957)	Moss Park (built 1960)	Alexandra Park (built 1965)	Cabbagetown
Population						
Population	599,220	9,970	3,770	4,600	3,830	4,180
% under 5 years	5	10	8	4	6	4
% under 15 years	16	30	30	9	22	12
% 65 and over	13	8	9	18	14	5
Population 15 and over – % women	52	57	60	44	52	47
– % men	48	43	40	56	48	53
Households and Families						
Average persons per household	2.4	2.9	3.2	1.7	3.0	2.3
Average persons per room	0.5	0.7	0.7	0.5	0.7	0.4
% with more than one family	2.3	1.3	. . .	. . .	3.9	. . .
% of lone-parent families	15	69	55	29	29	18
Home Language						
Neither English nor French (%)	25	15	–	–	41	–
Labour Force						
Participation rate (%) – men	79	54	59	63	63	83
– women	61	39	48	45	47	66
Unemployment rate (%) – men	5	13	7	11	6	7
– women	5	12	8	4	2	2

Comparison of selected public housing projects, Cabbagetown and Toronto, 1981

Income (1980)	City of Toronto	North	South	Lawrence Heights	Moss Park	Alexandra Park	Cabbagetown
Median household income	19,900	5,900	9,400	12,800[1]	8,700	10,400	19,700/28,100[2]
Median employment income – men	14,500	6,400	7,800	–	12,000	10,200	15,700/17,000
– women	9,800	6,100	7,400	–	10,700	5,600	9,500/ 9,200
% living below the Low-Income Cut-Offs – families	17	69		–	37	47	12
– individuals	34	79		–	58	66	40

- Not available.
. . . Too small to report.
[1] Average household income.
[2] For median income, Cabbagetown is divided into two areas.
Source: Statistics Canada, 1981 Census of Canada.

Labour force participation dropped somewhat for men in Alexandra Park between 1961 and 1981, while for women, it remained stable. In 1981, 63% of adult male residents of Alexandra Park were in the labour force, compared with 79% in 1961. Throughout the same period, just under half of adult women living in this project participated in the labour force. At the same time, unemployment rates for both men and women dropped quite sharply.

Unemployment among men in Alexandra Park fell from 16% in 1961 to 6% in 1981. The comparable rate for men in Toronto in 1981 was lower, at 5%. The rate for female Alexandra Park residents also declined over the two decades, from 5% to 2%. In 1981, the unemployment rate of these women was actually lower than for women in Toronto as a whole (5%).

Median household income in Alexandra Park was just over half that in Toronto, at $10,400 in 1980. That year, two-thirds of unattached individuals and almost half of families lived below the Low-Income Cut-Offs, despite the relatively high levels of employment characteristic of this development.

Conclusion

While there is considerable variety in the social characteristics of the residents of these four public housing projects, there are underlying uniformities. All of the project residents taken together differ from Torontonians in general.

All four developments have a much higher percentage of both families and unattached individuals living below the Low-Income Cut-Offs; labour force participation for both men and women is

lower than in Toronto as a whole, and in most cases, unemployment is higher; and the percentage of project families headed by a lone parent is at least double that in Toronto. Thus, public housing projects continue to concentrate the less well off in specific geographic areas where significant redevelopment efforts were made in the 1950s and 1960s.

Health

INCREASED LIFE EXPECTANCY

by Jo-Anne Parliament

As in many developed countries, there has been a gradual decline in mortality rates in Canada over the past several decades. The improvement in mortality has occurred in all age groups, but particularly in the younger ones. Recently, though, there has also been a marked improvement in mortality among older age groups, especially older women.

The improvements in mortality have been accompanied by shifts in the distribution of the leading causes of death in Canada. While cardiovascular disease is the number one cause of death in Canada, deaths due to cardiovascular disease have declined as a percentage of all deaths in recent years. The percentage of deaths due to cancer, on the other hand, has increased. Some other diseases, such as tuberculosis, which were major causes of death in the past, are now rare as a cause of death.

Declining Death Rates

Age-standardized death rates have declined for both sexes, but particularly for women, over the past six decades. Between 1921 and 1981, the death rate among women dropped 65%, from 12.4 deaths per 1,000 female population to 4.3. For men, this rate declined 46%, from 13.3 deaths per 1,000 male population in 1921 to 7.2 in 1981.

Increased Life Expectancy

Women experienced greater increases in life expectancy than men in the last six decades, though there were improvements for both sexes. Between 1921 and 1981, life expectancy at birth increased by over 18 years for women, and by 13 years for men. Consequently, the life expectancy of girls born in 1981 (79 years) was seven years longer than that of boys born the same year. The gap between the life expectancy of men and women is most pronounced at birth. It subsequently declines with age such that at age 90 the difference is less than one year. More of the increases in life expectancy of both men and women occurred in 1921–1951 period than in the 1951–1981 period.

Life expectancies at birth have tended to be lower than the national average for both men and women in Quebec, Nova Scotia, and New Brunswick, and among men in Newfoundland, Ontario and the western

provinces — Saskatchewan in particular — have generally had higher life expectancies than the national average. However, since 1931, life expectancies

among all provinces have been converging. This holds for both men and women. In 1931, the difference in life expectancy at birth between the prov-

Contribution of Increases in Life Expectancy in Each Age Group to the Total Increase in Life Expectancy at Birth, 1921–1951 and 1951–1981

| | Men | | Women | |
	1921–51	1951–81	1921–51	1951–81
		%		
Under 1	44.8	41.5	27.8	24.6
1–4	17.6	7.3	12.7	4.6
5–24	21.7	7.3	20.0	5.9
25–44	15.1	9.5	20.2	9.6
45–64	-1.2	19.1	10.9	18.7
65 and over	2.0	15.2	8.4	36.6
Total	100.0	100.0	100.0	100.0
Total increase in life expectancy (in years)	7.6	5.5	10.3	8.1

Source: Nagnur, D., "Rectangularization of the Survival Curve and Entropy, the Canadian Experience, 1921–1981", *Canadian Studies in Population*, Vol. 13, No. 1, 1986.

Rectangularization of The Survival Curve

Between 1921 and 1981, there was a significant increase in the probability of survival in general, and of survival to successively older ages in particular. Because of this, survival curves, which show the number of survivors at different ages out of an initial cohort of 100,000 live births, have gradually flattened to form a more rectangular shape, hence the use of the term

rectangularization. The increase in the rectangularization of the survival curve was greater in the last three decades of the 1921–1981 period than in the first three. In 1981, the probability of survival was much greater for women than it was for men. As well, this difference was greater in 1981 than it had been in 1951; in 1921, there had been almost no difference.

The gap between the real and ideal (where theorectically everyone dies at about age 90) survival curves has narrowed significantly in recent years in Canada, as it has in many developed countries. In the United States, for example, 80% of the difference between the real curve, as it existed in 1900, and the ideal curve had been eliminated by 1980.

Number of Persons Out of an Initial Cohort of 100,000 Live Births Surviving to Different Ages, 1921, 1951 and 1981

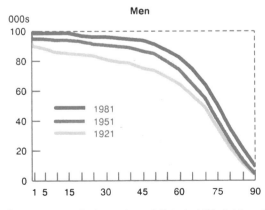

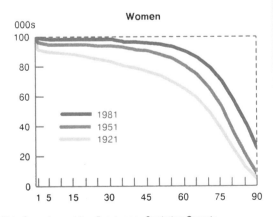

Source: Nagnur, D., *Longevity and Historical Life Tables, 1921-1981, Canada and the Provinces*, Statistics Canada, Catalogue 89-506.

ince with the highest life expectancy (Saskatchewan) and that with the lowest (New Brunswick) was 8 years for both men and women; by 1981, these gaps had closed to 2 years. As well, these gaps are expected to narrow still further in the future.

Reasons for Increased Life Expectancy

The main factor contributing to increased life expectancy in Canada between 1921 and 1981 was the reduction in infant mortality (deaths of children under age 1). In 1981, less than 1 baby in 100 died before its first birthday; in 1921, the ratio was almost 1 in 10. The decline in infant mortality made a greater difference to the overall increase in the life expectancy of men than that of women. Between 1921 and 1981, the reduction in infant mortality accounted for 43% of the increase in life expectancy at birth for men, compared to 26% of that for women.

Improvements in mortality among older age groups contributed more to the total increase in life expectancy at birth for both sexes during the second half of the 1921–1981 period than during the first half. Between 1951 and 1981, 55% of the total increase in life expectancy at birth for women, and 34% for men, was accounted for by improvements in mortality of those aged 45 and over. In the 1921–1951 period, the percentages were 19% for women and just 1% for men.

Leading Causes of Death

Increases in life expectancies, both at birth and for successively older age groups, have been accompanied by, and to some extent have been caused by, changes in the leading causes of death in Canada.

Between 1931 and 1981, there was a 90% decline in the death rate for children under age 5. In the same period, death rates for both children aged 5–14, and women aged 15–24, declined by around 80%. These were the largest declines in death rates of all age groups. Much of these declines resulted from the almost complete control of diseases such as polio, tuberculosis, diphtheria, whooping cough and the category of influenza, bronchitis and pneumonia, which were leading causes of death of young persons in earlier years.

In contrast to the decline in many causes of death among children and

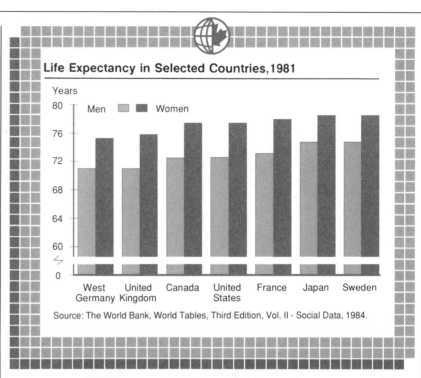

Life Expectancy in Selected Countries, 1981

Source: The World Bank, World Tables, Third Edition, Vol. II - Social Data, 1984.

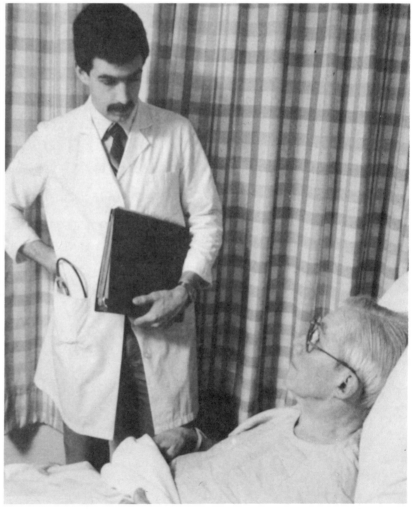

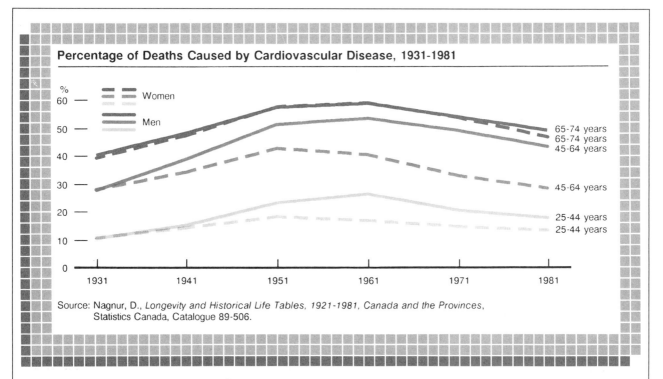

Percentage of Deaths Caused by Cardiovascular Disease, 1931-1981

Source: Nagnur, D., *Longevity and Historical Life Tables, 1921-1981, Canada and the Provinces*, Statistics Canada, Catalogue 89-506.

young adults, deaths due to accidents, poisonings and violence (including suicide) have increased substantially. Consequently, this category has been the leading cause of death for both men and women aged 5–24 since 1961.

Increases in deaths due to accidents, poisonings and violence have been particularly prevalent among men aged 15–24. As a result, the death rate for this group declined by only 50% between 1931 and 1981, a decline considerably smaller than that for other young persons.

The percentage of deaths caused by accidents, poisonings and violence also increased among the population aged 25–44 between 1961 and 1981. By 1981, this category accounted for 53% of all deaths for men in this age group, up from 42% in 1961. The percentage for women doubled over the same period, from 16% to 32%.

Among people aged 25–44, the percentage of deaths caused by cancer in 1981 was much higher for women (32%) than for men (13%). These percentages have been relatively stable since 1961. In the same period, the percentage of deaths due to cardiovascular disease, for both women and men aged 25–44, declined.

Cardiovascular disease was the leading cause of death for men aged 45–64, and for both men and women aged 65 and older in 1981. Deaths due to cardiovascular disease, however, declined as a percentage of all deaths for most of these older age groups in the last few decades. During the 1961–1981 period, the proportion of deaths among men aged 45–64 attributable to cardiovascular disease declined from 54% to 44%. The corresponding percentages for women were 41% and 29%. Cardiovascular disease accounted for almost half of all deaths of both men and women aged 65–74 in 1981, down from around 60% in 1961. The one exception to this trend was among men aged 75 and over. In 1981, 55% of deaths of men aged 75 and over were attributable to cardiovascular disease, the same as in 1961. The percentage of all deaths resulting from cardiovascular disease for women in this age group, however, dropped from 69% to 63% in this period.

The percentage of deaths resulting from cancer among those aged 45 and over increased in the last two decades. For women aged 45–64, the percentage of deaths due to cancer increased from 36% in 1961 to 45% in 1981. Consequently, cancer was the leading cause

of death for women in this age range in 1971 and 1981. The percentage of deaths due to cancer for men aged 45–64 increased from 21% to 30% over the same period. Cancer accounted for around 30% of deaths of both men and women aged 65–74 in 1981, up from around 21% in 1961. For those 75 years and older, the percentage of deaths caused by cancer doubled for both men and women over the 1961–1981 period.

■■■■

During the past six decades, life expectancy has increased considerably for both men and women, but especially for women. Increases in life expectancy have been due largely to reductions in infant and early childhood mortality. Further increases will have to come from two areas: reductions in diseases most characteristic of older age groups, such as cardiovascular disease and cancer; and the reduction of deaths due to accidents, poisonings and violence among younger age groups. These three categories are the leading causes of death in Canada, and are all heavily influenced by lifestyle and environmental factors.

AGING OF THE CANADIAN POPULATION

by Mary Sue Devereaux

1986 Census figures indicate that the rate of population growth in Canada continued to decline in the 1980s. Between 1981 and 1986, the population grew by only 4%, the lowest five-year increase in the last 25 years. Nevertheless, large-scale changes in the age distribution have continued. In particular, there has been considerable growth in the elderly segments of the population and in the proportion of people in their prime working years. On the other hand, the number of young adults has fallen dramatically.

These shifts in the age structure of the population reflect both increases in life expectancy and changing birth rates in the past, particularly the baby-boom of the 1950s and early 1960s and the baby-bust of the late 1960s and 1970s. As people born in those periods move through their life-cycle, they have had, or will have, profound effects on the school system, the labour force, family and housing services, health care institutions, and many other aspects of society.

The aging of the population is reflected in the median age, which in 1986 was the highest ever recorded. That year, the median age of Canadians was 31.6, up from 29.6 in 1981. Barring radical changes in fertility patterns or immigration levels, the median age is expected to continue to rise throughout the rest of the century.

Elderly Population Increasing

The population aged 65 and over has been the fastest-growing age group in Canada in the 1980s. The number of elderly Canadians rose 14% from 2.4 million in 1981 to 2.7 million in 1986, a rate of growth more than three times that of the population as a whole (4%). As a

consequence of this growth, the proportion of the population aged 65 and over rose from 9.7% in 1981 to 10.7% in 1986.

Growth in the number of Canadians aged 75 and over was particularly rapid. In 1986, more than one million people were at least age 75, an increase of almost 19% since 1981. During this period, the share of the population accounted for by those aged 75 and over rose from 3.6% to 4.1%.

In most age groups under 60, the number of men and women is roughly equal. Women, however, make up the majority of those aged 60 and over. As well, the predominance of women increases at successively older ages. In 1986, there were 138 women for every 100 men aged 65 and over, while among

those aged 85 and over, women outnumbered men by more than two to one. This imbalance is largely due to differences in longevity, with women outliving men an average of seven years.

The high growth rate of the population aged 65 and over is expected to continue well into the next century. In all probability, this will increase the demand for health and social services oriented to the elderly.

Working-Age Population Growing

The number of Canadians aged 25-44 has also increased substantially in the 1980s. Between 1981 and 1986, the population in this age group increased almost 14%. As a result, the proportion of all Cana-

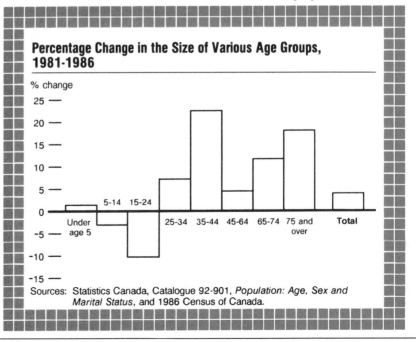

Percentage Change in the Size of Various Age Groups, 1981-1986

Sources: Statistics Canada, Catalogue 92-901, *Population: Age, Sex and Marital Status*, and 1986 Census of Canada.

Population distribution by age group, 1981 and 1986

	Age groups								
	Under age 5	5-14	15-24	25-34	35-44	45-64	65-74	75 and over	Total
Total population (000s)									
1981	1,783.4	3,697.7	4,658.7	4,216.2	2,968.2	4,658.1	1,477.7	883.2	24,343.2
1986	1,810.2	3,581.8	4,178.2	4,527.2	3,640.9	4,873.5	1,650.1	1,047.5	25,309.3
Percentage of total population									
1981	7.3	15.2	19.1	17.3	12.2	19.1	6.1	3.6	100.0
1986	7.1	14.2	16.5	17.9	14.4	19.3	6.6	4.1	100.0
Percentage change									
1981-1986	1.5	-3.1	-10.3	7.4	22.7	4.6	11.7	18.6	4.0

Sources: Statistics Canada, Catalogue 92-901, *Population: Age, Sex and Marital Status*, and 1986 Census of Canada.

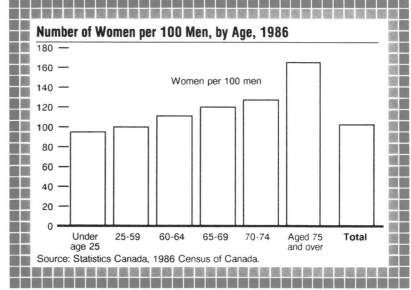

Number of Women per 100 Men, by Age, 1986

Women per 100 men

Under age 25 · 25-59 · 60-64 · 65-69 · 70-74 · Aged 75 and over · **Total**

Source: Statistics Canada, 1986 Census of Canada.

dians aged 25-44 rose from 29.5% in 1981 to 32.3% in 1986.

The size of the population aged 45-64 has been relatively stable. The number of Canadians in this age range rose by just under 5% in the 1981-1986 period. Their share of the total population remained almost unchanged at a little over 19%.

Young Adult Population Declining

There has been a marked decline in the population aged 15-24, most of whom were born during the so-called baby-bust of the late 1960s and 1970s. Between 1981 and 1986, the number of 15-24-year-olds fell 10%. Consequently, the share of the population accounted for by this age group declined from 19.1% to 16.5%.

One effect of the shrinking population aged 15-24 has been that the number of new labour market entrants has fallen dramatically. This contrasts sharply with the 1970s, when baby-boomers flooded into the labour force in record numbers.

Child Population Stable

Compared with the rapid growth in the number of children during the baby-boom, and the sharp decline during the subsequent baby-bust, the population aged 14 and under has been relatively stable in the 1980s.

From 1981 to 1986, the number of children under age 5 rose 2%, while the population aged 5-14 fell 3%. As a result, the overall share of the total population accounted for by these age groups dropped from 22.5% to 21.3%. The relative stability of this population suggests that enrolment in elementary and secondary schools should be stable into the early 1990s.

CARDIOVASCULAR DISEASE, CANCER AND LIFE EXPECTANCY

by Dhruva Nagnur and Michael Nagrodski

One way of measuring the effect of any specific disease is to estimate the number of years that would be added to life expectancy if deaths from that disease were deleted.[1] When these estimates are calculated for all causes of death in Canada, the deletion of deaths due to cardiovascular disease and cancer[2] result in, by far, the largest gains in life expectancy. In fact, the total gains to life expectancy that would result if deaths from these two diseases were deleted is much greater than that for all other diseases combined.

The deletion of deaths due to cardiovascular disease alone would result in the largest estimated gains in life expectancy of any disease. However, the number of years that would have been added to the average life expectancy of Canadians through the deletion of deaths due to this disease has declined slightly in recent years.

On the other hand, gains in life expectancy that would occur as a result of the deletion of deaths due to cancer have continued to increase, although they are still much smaller than those for cardiovascular disease.

Cardiovascular disease

The deletion of cardiovascular disease deaths would have added an estimated

[1] The assumption is made that all causes of death operate independently of one another.
[2] Cardiovascular disease refers to all diseases in Chapter VII of the 9th revision of *International Classification of Diseases*; cancer includes all diseases in Chapter II.

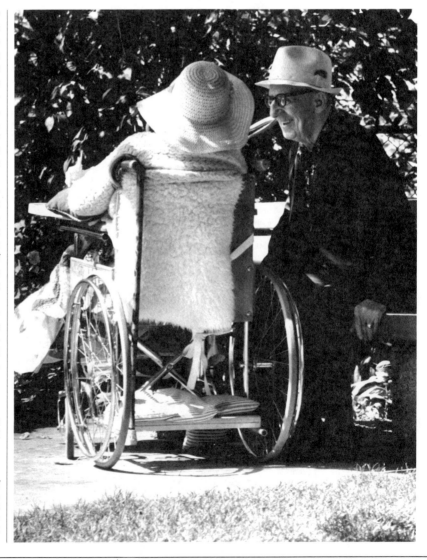

13.1 years to the life expectancy of women born in 1981 and 8.7 years to that of men. This would have raised the total life expectancy of women to 92 years, and that of men to 81 years.

The potential number of years of life that would be gained by the deletion of deaths due to cardiovascular disease, though, has fallen in recent decades. For example, the estimated increase for women was highest in 1971 when almost 15 years would have been added to female life expectancy. For men, the peak year was 1961, when over 11 years would have been added to their life expectancy.

Current estimates of gains in life expectancy that would occur if cardiovascular disease deaths were deleted, however, are still well above those recorded in the early part of the century. In 1921, the elimination of deaths due to cardiovascular disease would have added just 4 years to the life expectancy of both men and women.

Cancer

The deletion of deaths due to cancer would also add significantly to estimates of life expectancy in Canada, although these gains are considerably smaller than those for cardiovascular disease. But while gains in life expectancy attributable to the deletion of deaths due to cardiovascular disease have declined in recent decades, those for cancer have continued to increase.

Eliminating cancer deaths would have added 3.5 years to the life expectancy of women born in 1981, and 3.2 years to that of men. Ten years earlier, the gains would have been 3.1 years for women and 2.7 for

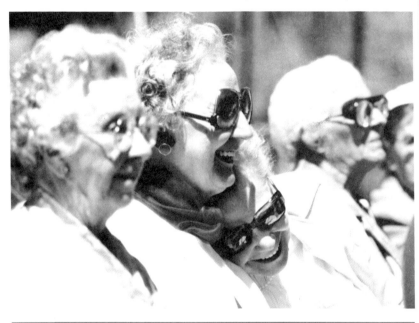

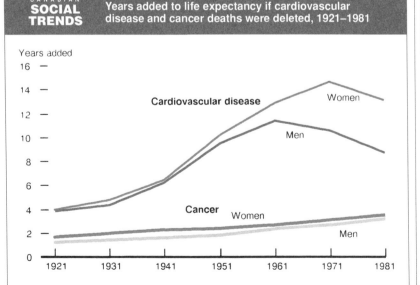

CANADIAN
SOCIAL TRENDS
Years added to life expectancy if cardiovascular disease and cancer deaths were deleted, 1921–1981

Years added

Cardiovascular disease — Women — Men

Cancer — Women — Men

Source: Nagnur, D. and M. Nagrodski, *Cause-deleted Life Tables for Canada (1921-1981)*, Statistics Canada, Analytical Studies Branch, Research Paper No. 13.

Cardiovascular disease and cancer: leading killers

There have been major shifts in the leading causes of death in Canada since the early 1920s. While cardiovascular disease has been the leading cause of death for both men and women since early in the century, the proportion of all deaths attributable to this cause was much larger in 1986 than in 1921.

In 1986, deaths from cardiovascular disease made up 45% of all deaths of women and 41% of those of men; this compared with fewer than 20% of deaths of both sexes in 1921. The percentage of deaths due to cardiovascular disease, however, has dropped in recent decades, from peaks of 51% for women in 1971 and 49% for men in 1961.

Cancer has been the second leading cause of death of women since 1931 and of men since 1941. In 1986, cancer accounted for 26% of all deaths of both men and women; this compared with 9% of female deaths and 7% of male deaths in 1921.

Unlike cardiovascular disease, though, the share of deaths attributable to cancer has continued to grow in recent years. For example, in 1971, 21% of all female deaths and 19% of those of men were due to this disease.

A number of other diseases which accounted for large shares of all deaths in the early part of the century are now almost unheard of as causes of death. Infectious and parasitic diseases, including tuberculosis, accounted for almost 15% of deaths in 1921; in 1986, however, only about half of one percent of all deaths were the result of these diseases. Similarly, certain diseases of infancy were responsible for almost 10% of deaths in 1921 compared with fewer than 1% in 1986.

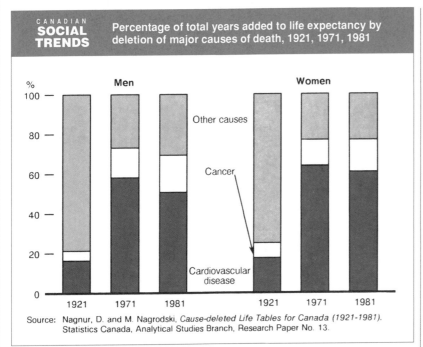

CANADIAN SOCIAL TRENDS | Percentage of total years added to life expectancy by deletion of major causes of death, 1921, 1971, 1981

%
100 —
80 —
60 —
40 —
20 —
0 —

Men   Women

Other causes

Cancer

Cardiovascular disease

1921   1971   1981   1921   1971   1981

Source: Nagnur, D. and M. Nagrodski, *Cause-deleted Life Tables for Canada (1921-1981)*. Statistics Canada, Analytical Studies Branch, Research Paper No. 13.

(11.9 years) was over twice that of all other causes of death combined (5.2 years.)

Of other causes of death, the elimination of accidental and violent deaths (excluding motor vehicle accidents) would have added the most to the life expectancy of both men and women. The elimination of this cause of death would have added 1.4 years to the life expectancy of men born in 1981 and 0.7 years to that of women. Increases to overall life expectancy of both men and women were very small for all other causes of death.

Conclusion

Cardiovascular disease and cancer far outweigh all other causes of death in their impact on life expectancy. As well, it is probable that this will be the case over the next several decades, particularly as the proportion of the population aged 65 and over continues to rise. Health care priorities will inevitably continue to be affected by these two diseases, especially the growing importance of cancer as a cause of death.

men, while in 1921, the gains would have been 1.7 years for women and 1.2 for men.

Cardiovascular disease, cancer and other diseases

The deletion of deaths due to cardiovascular disease and cancer would have added a total of 16.6 years to the life expectancy of women born in 1981, whereas the deletion of all other causes of death combined would have added just 4.9 years. The difference was not quite as large for men; still, the estimated gain in male life expectancy as a result of the deletion of cardiovascular disease and cancer

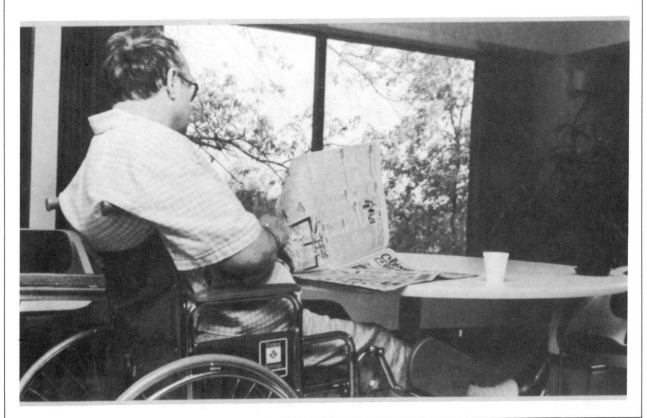

TRENDS IN CANCER SINCE 1970

by Leslie Gaudette and Georgina Roberts

Few Canadian families remain untouched by cancer[1]. Just over one in three Canadians will develop some form of this disease during their lifetime. Cancer is currently the second leading cause of death after heart disease, accounting for one in four deaths each year; in 1988, an estimated 50,800 Canadians will die from this disease. Also, because mortality due to heart disease has been falling, the percentage of all deaths attributable to cancer has risen. This trend is expected to continue as the number of older Canadians (the group most at risk from cancer) grows as a proportion of the overall population.

There has been considerable variation, though, in trends for the major types of cancer. For some types, such as lung cancer, rates have increased; for others, such as stomach cancer, rates have fallen. For still others, rates have been relatively stable.

The cost of caring for cancer patients is a major concern. Because the elderly population in Canada is growing rapidly, cancer care facilities can expect both caseloads and costs to increase. The introduction of new drugs and treatment technologies in the last decade has also meant rising costs for the care of cancer patients.

Incidence of cancer rising

The overall incidence rate for cancer (i.e., the number of new cases diagnosed each

---

[1] Cancer includes all invasive malignant neoplasms with the exception of non-melanoma skin cancer.

The cooperation of provincial cancer registries and vital statistics registrars in supplying the data used in this report is gratefully acknowledged.

Estimated new cases and deaths for major types of cancer,[1] 1988

	New cases			Deaths		
	Men	Women	Total	Men	Women	Total
Lung	11,200	4,200	15,400	9,300	4,100	13,400
Colorectal	7,100	6,900	14,000	2,900	2,800	5,700
Breast	. . .	11,500	11,500	. . .	4,600	4,600
Prostate	8,400	. . .	8,400	3,000	. . .	3,000
Uterine	. . .	4,300	4,300	. . .	900	900
Stomach	1,900	1,100	3,000	700	300	1,000
Other types	22,000	17,700	39,700	12,100	10,100	22,200
Total	**50,600**	**45,700**	**96,300**	**28,000**	**22,800**	**50,800**

[1] Excludes non-melanoma skin cancer.
. . . figures not applicable.
Source: Canadian Cancer Society, *Canadian Cancer Statistics, 1988*.

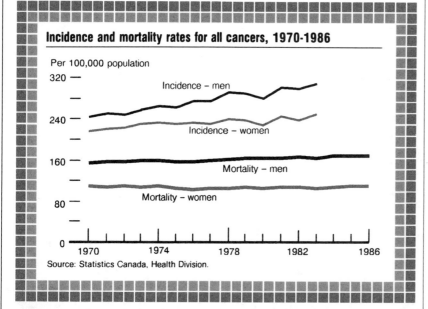

Incidence and mortality rates for all cancers, 1970-1986

Per 100,000 population

Incidence – men
Incidence – women
Mortality – men
Mortality – women

Source: Statistics Canada, Health Division.

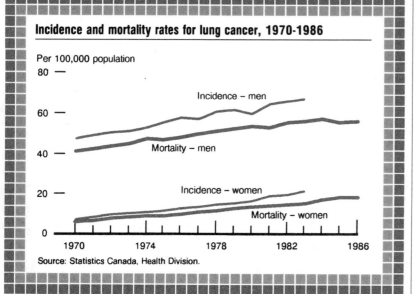

Incidence and mortality rates for lung cancer, 1970-1986

Per 100,000 population

Incidence – men
Mortality – men
Incidence – women
Mortality – women

Source: Statistics Canada, Health Division.

year per 100,000 population) has risen among both men and women, although the rate is higher and has increased more rapidly among men. Between 1970 and 1983, the age-standardized[2] incidence rate for men rose 27%, from 243 cases per 100,000 men to 309; for women, the cancer rate rose 16%, from 216 cases per 100,000 women to 250.

There has been considerably less change in mortality from cancer. The cancer mortality rate for women was stable between 1970 and 1986, while there was a small increase, about 8%, in the rate for men.

The cancer mortality rate is also higher among men than women. In 1986, there were 168 cancer deaths for every 100,000 men, compared to 111 for every 100,000 women.

The pattern of increasing incidence combined with stable mortality is not unique to Canada, but has occurred in other countries as well. Some of the increase in Canada's incidence rate, however, is attributable to more comprehensive registration, more thorough diagnostic procedures, and changes in the definition of an invasive malignancy. Nevertheless, it appears that better medical treatment, which has improved survival for some types of cancer, is at least partly responsible for differences in cancer incidence and mortality trends.

Different trends for different cancers
Trends for the most common types of cancer have differed. Since the early 1970s, rates for lung and prostate cancer have increased, while those for breast cancer have remained relatively stable. In the same period, rates for stomach and uterine cancer have declined, while colorectal cancer has been characterized by increasing incidence but declining mortality.

Lung cancer
The incidence of lung cancer, overall the most common type of cancer in Canada, has increased among both men and women since the early 1970s.

Lung cancer mortality among men, however, appears to have peaked in 1984. Because current levels of lung cancer mortality are closely related to past smoking rates, the decline in smoking first seen

[2] All rates are age-standardized, that is, they are calculated to show what they would have been if the age distribution was the same over time. The world population was used as a basis for the standardization. For more detail on the methodology and data, interested readers may refer to *Canadian Cancer Statistics, 1988*, produced jointly by Statistics Canada and the Canadian Cancer Society. Detailed data on cancer incidence, mortality, and hospital morbidity are available in *Cancer in Canada*, Statistics Canada, Catalogue 82-207.

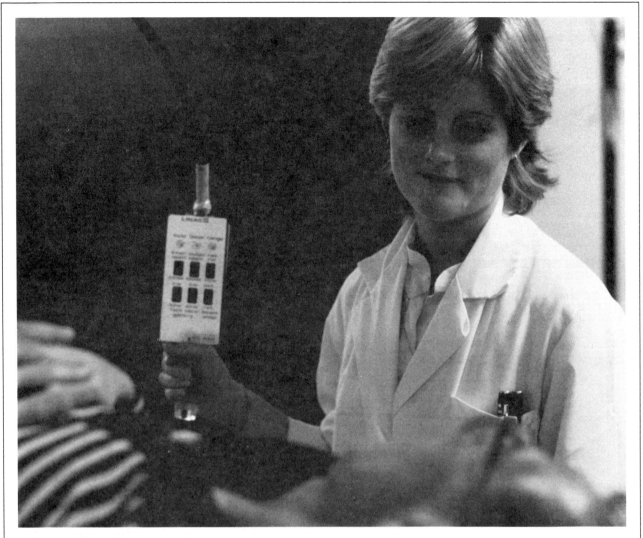

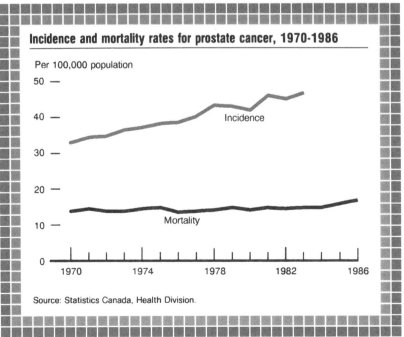

Incidence and mortality rates for prostate cancer, 1970-1986

Per 100,000 population

Incidence

Mortality

Source: Statistics Canada, Health Division.

among Canadian men 20 years ago is just beginning to result in reduced mortality from this disease. This pattern has already been observed in several other countries, most notably Denmark and Scotland, where actual declines in male lung cancer rates have occurred.

Both incidence and mortality rates for lung cancer have increased rapidly among women, although rates for women are still only about a third those of men. In addition, while lung cancer rates appear to have peaked for men, they are expected to continue to increase among women for the next several years, before they too are expected to decline. Thus, women's lung cancer rates are not expected to ever equal those currently experienced by men.

The difference between lung cancer trends of men and women are linked to smoking habits. Women began smoking in large numbers about 20 years after men. As well, smoking rates among women, particularly young women, are falling much more slowly than among men. Consequently, the full impact of smoking on female lung cancer rates has yet to be felt.

Prostate cancer

Rates for prostate cancer, the second most prevalent cancer in men, have also risen since the early 1970s. The incidence of this disease, however, has increased more rapidly than mortality.

Much of the increased incidence of prostate cancer, though, is generally attributed to improved diagnostic procedures and to more reporting of its discovery during an autopsy. Cancer of the prostate is very much a disease of elderly men, and it is common to find evidence of this cancer when an autopsy is conducted. As a result, less serious forms of this disease, which in the past may have remained undetected, are being identified and reported.

Breast cancer

Breast cancer, currently the most common type of cancer among women, accounts for about one out of every 20 deaths of women in Canada. As well, almost one Canadian woman in 10 will develop breast cancer during her lifetime.

Both incidence and mortality rates for breast cancer were approximately the same in the mid-1980s as in the early 1970s. The incidence rate for breast cancer, however, did fluctuate in this period. Although these fluctuations could have been random, they closely reflect patterns reported in the United States. In 1974, for example, the breast cancer incidence rate jumped suddenly in both countries. This has generally been attributed to increased detection of breast cancer following widespread publicity about the diagnosis of this condition in several prominent American women.

Despite intensive research, little has been discovered regarding risk factors for breast cancer which would be of use in planning preventive programs.

Stomach cancer

Stomach cancer rates have fallen since the early 1970s. The death rate due to this disease was nearly cut in half for both men and women between 1970 and 1986. Incidence rates also declined, though not as sharply. Both incidence and mortality rates for stomach cancer are more than twice as high for men as for women.

The decline in stomach cancer in Canada is similar to that reported in other industrial countries and is generally attributed to changes in diet.

Cancer of the uterine body and cervix

There have been sharp drops in both incidence and mortality rates for cervical cancer since the early 1970s. These declines are considered to be at least partially attributable to screening programs such as Pap smears, although some of the decline may be due to other factors.

Despite the overall drop in cervical cancer rates, the incidence rate for this disease has been stable in recent years. This levelling off reflects rising rates of cervical cancer among young women.

The mortality rate for cancer of the uterine body has also declined since the early 1970s. The incidence rate for this condition, however, was roughly the same in 1983 as in 1970, although there was a temporary increase in the incidence of this disease in the 1970s. This rise was also observed in other countries and has been related to use of replacement estrogen therapy at menopause.

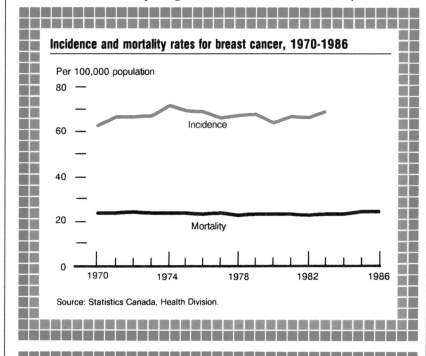

Incidence and mortality rates for breast cancer, 1970-1986

Per 100,000 population

Source: Statistics Canada, Health Division.

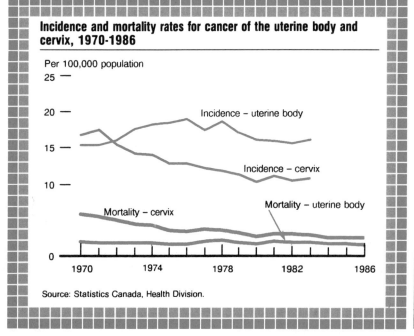

Incidence and mortality rates for cancer of the uterine body and cervix, 1970-1986

Per 100,000 population

Source: Statistics Canada, Health Division.

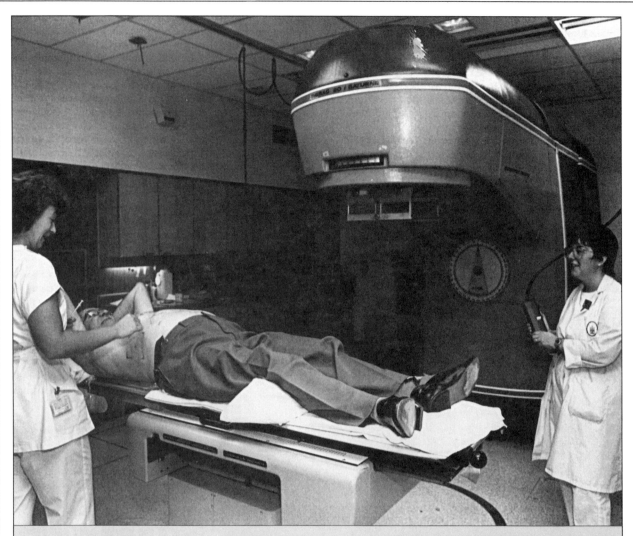

Cancer survival rates

Survival rates represent the percentage of cancer cases diagnosed between 1979 and 1981 who are still alive five years after the diagnosis. They are crude rates in that deaths may have resulted from other causes.

Survival rates for different types of cancer are available only for Alberta, but these are likely typical of current Canadian experience. There appear to be three distinct categories when survival from the major types of cancer is considered.

Breast and uterine cancer and melanoma are characterized by relatively high survival rates, while colorectal and prostate cancer show moderate survival levels. Survival rates for lung and stomach cancer, on the other hand, are very low.

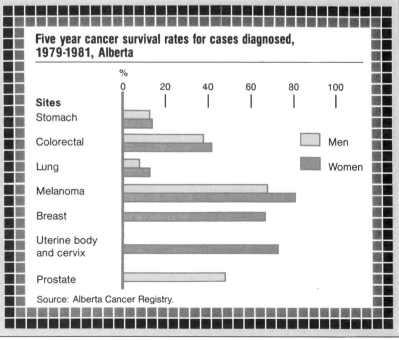

Five year cancer survival rates for cases diagnosed, 1979-1981, Alberta

Legend: Men, Women

Sites: Stomach, Colorectal, Lung, Melanoma, Breast, Uterine body and cervix, Prostate

Source: Alberta Cancer Registry.

Colorectal cancer

Trends for the incidence and mortality of colorectal cancer, which includes cancer of the large intestine and rectum, have diverged since the early 1970s. The incidence rate for this type of cancer has risen, while the mortality rate has fallen.

Both incidence and mortality rates for colorectal cancer are higher in men than in women. Moreover, incidence rates have increased faster in men, while mortality rates have declined more rapidly in women.

As with breast cancer, risk factors for this type of cancer are not well understood, although diet has been implicated.

Melanoma

While melanoma skin cancer is not one of the leading forms of cancer, it should be mentioned because the incidence of this

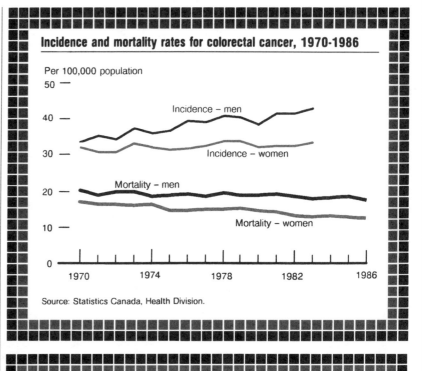

Incidence and mortality rates for colorectal cancer, 1970-1986

Per 100,000 population

Source: Statistics Canada, Health Division.

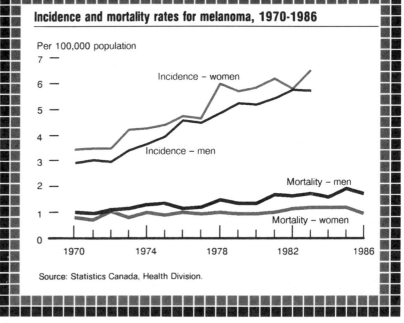

Incidence and mortality rates for melanoma, 1970-1986

Per 100,000 population

Source: Statistics Canada, Health Division.

disease nearly doubled among both men and women between 1970 and 1983. Mortality from melanoma also increased significantly among men, rising over 70% between 1970 and 1986. The mortality rate for this condition also rose for women in this period, but by a much smaller margin, just 20%.

The major risk factor for melanoma is exposure to sunlight, although the exact nature of the relationship is not well understood.

THE INCIDENCE OF SEXUALLY TRANSMITTED DISEASE IN CANADA

By Carol Strike

Sexually transmitted disease continues to be a major social concern in Canada. Although the incidence of gonorrhea and syphilis has declined, the prevalence of other sexually transmitted diseases has increased dramatically. AIDS (Acquired Immune Deficiency Syndrome) is the most serious of these newer diseases in that there is currently no cure and it is invariably fatal. The incidence of two non-life threatening sexually transmitted diseases, herpes and chlamydia, has also increased considerably in the 1980s.

The diagnosis, treatment, control and prevention of these increasingly more prevalent, sexually transmissible infections represents a formidable chal-

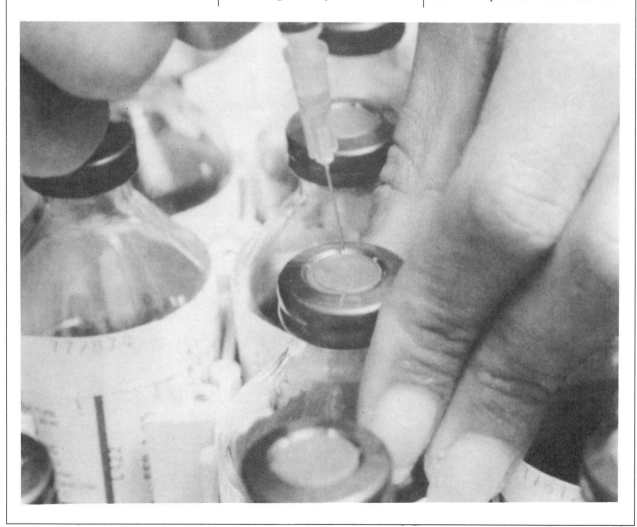

Sexually Transmitted Diseases

Sexually transmitted diseases (STDs) are transmitted through sexual contact with those infected with the condition. Although all STDs are passed in this manner, some may also be transmitted by other means such as sharing hypodermic needles, blood transfusions, and from a mother to an unborn child.

None of the STDs is gender specific, although some individuals are at higher risk of contracting one of these diseases because of their sex and sexual orientation.

AIDS, gonorrhea and syphilis are classified as notifiable diseases, that is, occurrences of these diseases must be reported to public health officials. Herpes and chlamydial infections are not notifiable diseases, and therefore the total number of cases reported is understated to some extent.

AIDS (Acquired Immune Deficiency Syndrome) causes a weakening of the body's ability to fight disease. People who contract AIDS become susceptible to other infections, to which healthy people are virtually immune. The impaired immune system of the AIDS victim,

however, cannot fight off these infections. Individuals can be carriers of the AIDS virus without developing the disease. It is not known, though, if, or when, these people will actually develop AIDS.

Herpes is a virus which results in skin eruptions in the genital area and other places on the body. While the virus remains with the infected person for life, the severity of the problem may vary over time. The condition is particularly prone to flareups when the body's resistance is weakened. Some victims experience numerous flareups, while others have only occasional bouts.

Chlamydia is a bacteria-like organism which causes a urethral discharge in men. Chlamydial infections in women often have no symptoms. However, this condition can result in pelvic inflammatory disease (PID), tubal pregnancies and infertility.

Gonorrhea is a bacterial disease which causes urethral discharge in men. As with chlamydia, women often do not experience overt symptoms, although gonorrhea can lead to PID and damage to the reproductive organs. Recently, several strains of gonorrhea resistant to tetracycline have emerged, making the control of this disease more difficult.

Syphilis is a bacterial disease which results in a painless sore at the point where the bacteria enters the body. Without treatment, the sore will eventually disappear, although the infection remains with the victim. If not treated with antibiotics, the condition is potentially fatal.

lenge for the health care disciplines, as well as for those involved in health education and promotion. Each sexually transmitted disease represents a distinct threat.

AIDS

The first AIDS case in Canada was reported in 1979, and through 1986, a total of 847 cases of AIDS had been reported. Of the total number of cases reported, 438 (or 52%) had resulted in death by the end of 1986. There was a particularly large increase in the number of cases reported in 1985. In that year, 305 new cases of AIDS were reported, a 120% increase from the number of new cases reported in 1984. The number of new cases (320) reported in 1986, however, was only 5% more than the number reported in 1985. As of May 18, 1987, 1,012 cases of AIDS had been reported in Canada; of these, 512 had resulted in death.

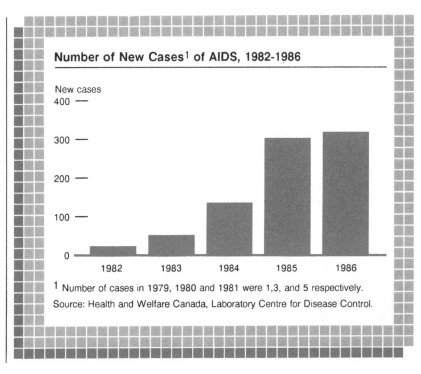

Number of New Cases[1] of AIDS, 1982-1986

New cases

[1] Number of cases in 1979, 1980 and 1981 were 1, 3, and 5 respectively.

Source: Health and Welfare Canada, Laboratory Centre for Disease Control.

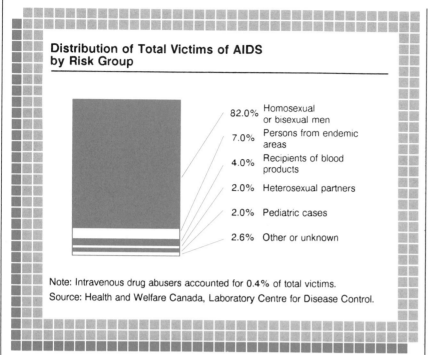

Distribution of Total Victims of AIDS by Risk Group

82.0% Homosexual or bisexual men

7.0% Persons from endemic areas

4.0% Recipients of blood products

2.0% Heterosexual partners

2.0% Pediatric cases

2.6% Other or unknown

Note: Intravenous drug abusers accounted for 0.4% of total victims.
Source: Health and Welfare Canada, Laboratory Centre for Disease Control.

Most AIDS victims have been adult males. Men accounted for 93% of all cases up to the end of 1986; adult women made up only 5% of the total, and children just 2%.

As well, most victims have been homosexual or bisexual men; this group accounted for 82% of the total number of cases through 1986. Other victims of this condition include persons from endemic or high risks areas such as Haiti (7%), recipients of blood or blood products (4%), heterosexual partners of persons in high-risk groups (2%), babies with high-risk parents (2%), and intravenous drug users (0.4%).

British Columbia has by far the highest incidence of AIDS in Canada. In 1986, there were 3.0 cases of AIDS per 100,000 population in British Columbia. This was over twice the next highest rate of 1.3 cases per 100,000 population reported in Ontario. Quebec was the only other region with at least one case of AIDS per 100,000 population. The lowest rate was in the Atlantic provinces — just 0.3 cases per 100,000 persons in 1986.

Although the current total of active cases of AIDS is low in comparison with other life-threatening illnesses, the number of Canadians known to be harbouring the virus in a latent state is much higher. Further unchecked spread of the virus is thus a major cause for concern.

Herpes

In 1985, there were 14,600 laboratory reports of herpes, 20% more than in 1984. Since 1978, there has been a tenfold increase in the number of laboratory reports of herpes.

The highest incidence of herpes occurs among the population aged 20–29. Persons in this age range accounted for almost half of all laboratory reports of herpes in 1985. The largest increase in the number of laboratory reports of herpes in 1985, though, occurred among persons aged 35–44. Women, especially younger women, experience a higher reported incidence of herpes than men. In 1985, almost two-thirds (64%) of all reports of herpes involved women. At the same time, women aged 15–19 had a rate almost five times that of men in the same age range.

Chlamydia

As with AIDS and herpes, the incidence of chlamydia has escalated dramatically in recent years. In 1985, there were 7,900 laboratory reports of chlamydia. This was twice the number of cases reported in 1984, and 5 times more than in 1983.

The vast majority of chlamydial infections occur to persons aged 15–29. As well, women experience higher rates of chlamydial infections than men. Women aged 20–29, for example, had a rate twice that of their male counterparts in 1985. For women aged 15–19, the number of laboratory reports of chlamydial infections was six times greater than that for men of the same age.

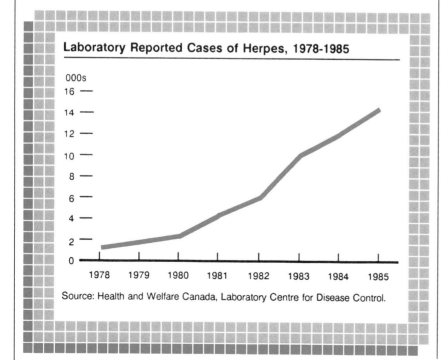

Laboratory Reported Cases of Herpes, 1978-1985

000s

Source: Health and Welfare Canada, Laboratory Centre for Disease Control.

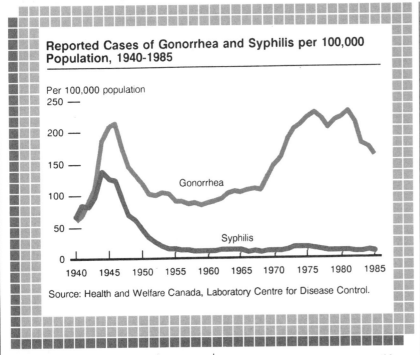

Reported Cases of Gonorrhea and Syphilis per 100,000 Population, 1940-1985

Per 100,000 population

Gonorrhea

Syphilis

Source: Health and Welfare Canada, Laboratory Centre for Disease Control.

Gonorrhea

The incidence of gonorrhea has declined in Canada in the 1980s. Still, almost 41,000 cases of gonorrhea — a rate of 161 cases per 100,000 population — were reported in 1985. The 1985 rate, however, was 8% lower than in 1984, and 30% lower than in 1980. The decline in the incidence of gonorrhea in 1985 was greater among men (down 11%) than women (down 4%). Men over age 20, however, had rates of gonorrhea twice that of women in the same age range. On the other hand, women aged 15–19, had a rate almost twice that of their male counterparts.

Gonorrhea is more common in the western provinces than in the east. In 1985, the number of cases of gonorrhea in the western provinces ranged from 298 per 100,000 population in Manitoba to 170 in British Columbia. Rates in the eastern provinces ranged from 164 in Ontario to 39 in Prince Edward Island.

Syphilis

The incidence of syphilis, once the most serious sexually transmitted disease, has been very low in Canada since the mid-1950s. Over this period, the number of cases of syphilis per 100,000 population fluctuated between 10 and 17. In 1985, 2,607 cases os syphilis were reported in Canada; this was 10.3 cases per 100,000 persons, down from 12.2 a year earlier.

Ontario and Alberta had the highest provincial rates of syphilis in 1985; there were 12.7 cases per 100,000 population in Ontario and 12.5 in Alberta. The Alberta figure, however, was just one-half that recorded in 1984. High rates of syphilis were also reported in British Columbia (10.8 cases per 100,000 population), Quebec (10.7), and Manitoba, (9.6). No other province had more than 2 cases per 100,000 persons.

AIDS IN CANADA

by Carol Strike

Acquired Immunodeficiency Syndrome, or AIDS, continues to represent a formidable challenge to Canadian society. AIDS is primarily a sexually transmitted disease caused by the Human Immunodeficiency Virus (HIV). This infection may result in development of life-threatening opportunistic infections and/or malignancies. While research for a cure or vaccine is ongoing, and education programs highlighting the dangers of this disease have been developed and introduced both to the public and in schools, the total number of cases of AIDS in Canada continues to increase.

AIDS cases and deaths

The first AIDS case in Canada was diagnosed in 1979; by the end of 1987, a total of 1,654 cases had been documented.[1]

A record number of new AIDS cases (615) were diagnosed in Canada in 1987. In fact, this figure was over 28% higher than the number of new cases diagnosed the previous year. As a result, the total number of AIDS cases in Canada rose 59% in 1987. This overall rate of growth, however, was down from 1986, when there had been an 86% increase. As well, by the end of 1987, 963 people in Canada had died from AIDS.

Individuals can carry the HIV for an indefinite period without developing either

[1] All data in this article are from the Federal Centre for AIDS, a branch of Health and Welfare Canada. In September 1987, the Federal Centre for AIDS accepted a revision proposed by the U.S. Center for Disease Control and broadened the criteria for an AIDS diagnosis. The new criteria will be applied to cases not previously identified as AIDS that occurred before this date. The resulting reclassification of some of these cases as AIDS may increase the total number of reported cases of this disease.

the illnesses characteristic of AIDS, or any of the symptoms of the infection. The Federal Centre for AIDS has estimated, for example, that about 30,000 people in Canada carry the HIV. Current evidence suggests that around 35% of carriers will develop AIDS within six years of infection. The Federal Centre for AIDS has projected that by the end of 1991, between 4,000 and 7,000 people in Canada will have been diagnosed as having AIDS.

Major risk factors for AIDS
The majority of AIDS patients have been homosexual or bisexual men. This group made up 80% of all cases through the end of 1987, as well as 84% of new patients in 1987.

People from countries where the HIV is widespread made up the second largest group of AIDS patients. Through 1987, 5% of all cases were in this category, with most likely acquiring the infection through sexual activity.

Intravenous (I.V.) drug abusers made up 3% of the total number of AIDS cases. Of these, 2.5% were also homosexuals or bisexuals, while the remaining 0.6% were people with no other risk factor.

Recipients of blood transfusions or other blood products made up another 5% of all AIDS patients, while heterosexuals who contracted the HIV infection through sexual contact with someone in a high risk group made up 2% of all cases. In another 3% of cases, risk factors were not identified.

In addition, 2% of AIDS patients have been children under age 15. Through 1987, 33 such cases had been reported. In 29 of these cases, transmission was from mother

to fetus; the others contracted the infection through transfusions received prior to the implementation of universal testing of blood donors.

Additional risk factors: age and sex
Men aged 20-49 make up the vast majority of AIDS patients. Through 1987, 83% of all those diagnosed with AIDS were men in this age range. Men aged 30-39 had the highest cumulative incidence of AIDS, with 38 cases per 100,000 men in this age group. Men aged 40-49 and 20-29 also had higher

than average rates: 24 and 13 cases per 100,000 population, respectively.

Men aged 50 and over had a cumulative AIDS rate of 5 cases per 100,000 population. In no other group did the AIDS rate exceed 1.5.

Most AIDS cases in three provinces
AIDS cases in Canada are concentrated in three provinces – Ontario, Quebec, and

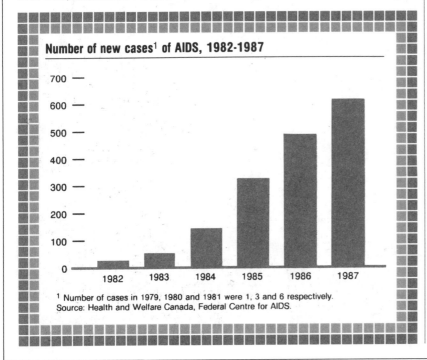

Number of new cases[1] of AIDS, 1982-1987

[1] Number of cases in 1979, 1980 and 1981 were 1, 3 and 6 respectively.
Source: Health and Welfare Canada, Federal Centre for AIDS.

Public perception of AIDS
Public awareness of AIDS in Canada was measured by Environics Research in a 1987 *Focus Canada Report* poll. Answers to the question, "Have you heard of the disease AIDS?" indicated that virtually all Canadians (99%) were aware of AIDS. In addition, the survey results suggested that most Canadians view AIDS as a serious problem. To the question, "Do you think that the disease AIDS is a very serious, somewhat serious, not very serious or not at all serious problem in Canada today?", almost 80% responded that it was a very serious problem. This was up from 1985, when only 56% of Canadians rated AIDS a very serious problem.

Perception of the seriousness of AIDS generally increases with age. For example, 85% of people aged 60 and over regarded AIDS as a very serious disease compared with 74% of those aged 20-29. Married people (81%) were also more likely than single people (74%) to regard AIDS as a very serious problem.

Concern about AIDS extends to specific issues. For example, the *Decima Quarterly Report* asked Canadians the following question in 1987:

"In determining the cost and availability of life insurance, life insurance companies might feel it is necessary for a person applying for life insurance to take medical tests for various diseases like AIDS. Would you strongly approve, approve, disapprove or strongly disapprove of life insurance companies requiring applicants to take such medical tests if they feel it was necessary?"

In response, 16% of those surveyed strongly approved testing, 57% approved, 20% disapproved, and 7% strongly disapproved. Only 1% had no opinion.

AIDS in Canada in an international perspective

The incidence of AIDS is much lower in Canada than in the United States. By the end of 1987, almost 50,000 cases had been reported in the United States. When expressed on a per capita basis, the incidence of AIDS was more than three times higher in the U.S. than in Canada.

For the most part, though, AIDS patients in Canada and the United States have similar characteristics. In both countries, most patients are men between the ages of 20 and 49, with those aged 30-39 having, by far, the highest cumulative rates.

Homosexual or bisexual men also account for the majority of AIDS cases in both countries, although their share is greater in Canada (80%) than in the United States (65%). Intravenous drug abusers, including homosexual or bisexual drug abusers, make up a much greater proportion of AIDS victims in the United States. Through 1987, 25% of American AIDS patients compared with just 3% of those in Canada were I.V. drug abusers.

As in Canada, AIDS in the United States is regionally concentrated. Just two states, California and New York, account for almost half of all U.S. cases.

On the other hand, the incidence of AIDS in Canada is roughly similar to that in European countries.

British Columbia. Through 1987, these provinces, representing about 73% of the Canadian population, accounted for 89% of all AIDS cases. As well, 87% of new cases diagnosed in 1987 occurred in these provinces.

British Columbia had the highest cumulative rate of AIDS of any province. Through 1987, 10.9 AIDS cases had been diagnosed in British Columbia for every 100,000 residents of that province.

Quebec and Ontario also had very high cumulative AIDS rates. Through 1987, there were 7.8 AIDS cases per 100,000 population in Quebec and 6.9 in Ontario. Trends in these two provinces, however, took different directions in 1987. The number of new cases rose 46% in Ontario; in contrast, the number of new cases in Quebec was almost the same in 1987 as in the previous year.

With a rate of 3.9, Alberta was the only other province in which the cumulative incidence of AIDS was over 3.5 cases per 100,000 population. Prince Edward Island and the Northwest Territories both reported their first AIDS case in 1987, while the Yukon had yet to report a case through the end of 1987.

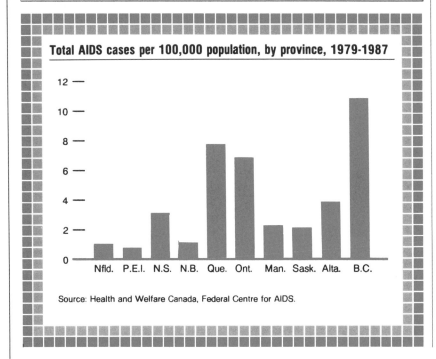

Total AIDS cases per 100,000 population, by province, 1979-1987

Source: Health and Welfare Canada, Federal Centre for AIDS.

AIDS Update
AIDS cases in Canada as of October 21, 1988.

Province	Number
British Columbia	416
Alberta	121
Saskatchewan	23
Manitoba	27
Ontario	805
Quebec	647
New Brunswick	10
Nova Scotia	32
Prince Edward Island	2
Newfoundland	10
North West Territories	1
Yukon	1
Total	**2,095**

Source: Federal Centre for AIDS, Health and Welfare Canada, published in *The New Facts of Life*, the AIDS newsletter of the Canadian Public Health Association., Vol 2., No. 3, November 1988.

LIFESTYLE RISKS:
Smoking and Drinking in Canada

by Craig McKie

Risks to the health of Canadians come in many forms. Some of these risks are infirmities which may afflict even those who follow rigourous preventive practices. But other risks are clearly more self-imposed in nature. These are best typified by the voluntary consumption of drugs, alcohol and tobacco. Though much has been written lately concerning the use of cocaine and other illicit drugs, tobacco and alcohol remain the most widely consumed, risk-associated products in Canadian society.

A recent overview of the smoking and drinking behaviour of Canadians is available from Statistics Canada's first annual General Social Survey, which was conducted in the fall of 1985. Data from this survey, combined with comparative figures from the 1978–79 Can-

Smoking Habits of Men and Women Aged 15 and Over, 1985

	Men	Women	Total
		%	
Regular cigarette smoker	33.1	27.8	30.4
Occasional cigarette smoker	4.4	4.3	4.3
Regular pipe or cigar smoker	2.6	--	1.3
Former cigarette smoker	25.0	16.4	20.6
Never smoked cigarettes regularly	33.9	50.3	42.3
Not stated	1.0	1.0*	1.0
Total	100.0	100.0	100.0

* Figure should be used with caution because the sampling variability is high.
-- Figure cannot be expressed because the sampling variability is too high.
Source: Statistics Canada, General Social Survey, 1985.

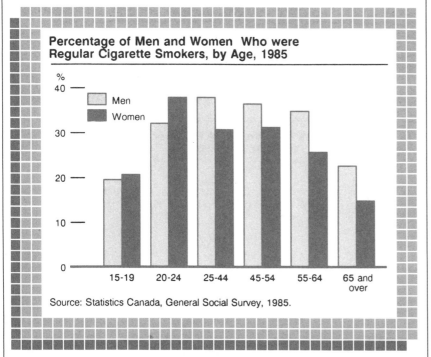

Percentage of Men and Women Who were Regular Cigarette Smokers, by Age, 1985

Source: Statistics Canada, General Social Survey, 1985.

ada Health Survey, provide a picture of widespread, but changing, use of tobacco and alcohol in Canada.

Canadians Who Smoke

Although a large proportion of Canadians still smoke tobacco products regularly, the level of smoking is declining. In 1985, 30% of the population 15 and over smoked cigarettes on a daily basis. This is down from the 37% estimated by the Canada Health Survey in 1978–79. In addition to regular cigarette smokers, in 1985, 4% of the adult population smoked occasionally and 1% smoked pipes or cigars daily. As well, 21% of the adult population were former smokers, while 42% had never smoked on a daily basis. There are considerable differences, however, in the smoking experience of Canadians depending on their age and sex.

Smoking Patterns of Men and Women

Overall, men were more likely than women to be regular smokers. In 1985, 33% of men compared with 28% of women were regular cigarette smokers. In the population under the age of 25, however, a greater percentage of women than men smoked regularly in 1985. Among those aged 20–24, 38% of women reported smoking cigarettes daily, compared to 32% of men. A greater percentage of women than men aged 15–19 also smoked regularly, although the difference was much smaller than that for the population aged 20–24.

The fact that more women than men aged 20–24 smoked regularly in 1985 represents a radical change from the

late 1970s, when more men than women in this age group smoked regularly. This shift occurred because the percentage of men aged 20–24 who smoked regularly declined much more dramatically than it did among women of the same age. Between the 1978–79 period and 1985, the percentage of men aged 20–24 who smoked regularly declined by almost 17 percentage points, while the decrease among women in this age group was just 7 percentage points.

There were also major declines in the incidence of smoking among men and women aged 15–19. The proportion of both these groups that smoked regularly declined by 13 percentage points between 1978–79 and 1985. Smoking also declined in this period among all other age groups, with the exception of women aged 65 and over. These decreases, however, were considerably smaller than those for men aged 20–24, and men and women aged 15–19.

Men were also heavier smokers than women. In 1985, 18% of men who smoked regularly, compared with 9% of female smokers, consumed 26 or more cigarettes a day. As well, men were heavier smokers in all age groups, even among those aged 15–24.

Men, however, were also more likely than women to have given up smoking, in part, because their initial smoking rates were much higher. In 1985, 25% of Canadian men aged 15 and over were former cigarette smokers, compared with 16% of adult women. As well, the proportion of men who were ex-smokers increased markedly with age. Among men aged 65 and over, for example, 49% were ex-smokers. The percentage of women who were ex-smokers, in contrast, was quite similar in all groups over the age of 25.

Education and Smoking

For both men and women, the higher the formal educational attainment, the lower the probability of smoking. Just over 25% of men who had either attended or graduated from a postsecondary institution were regular cigarette smokers, compared to close to 40% of men without any postsecondary experience. Among women, those with a postsecondary degree or diploma were characterized by the lowest incidence of regular cigarette smoking.

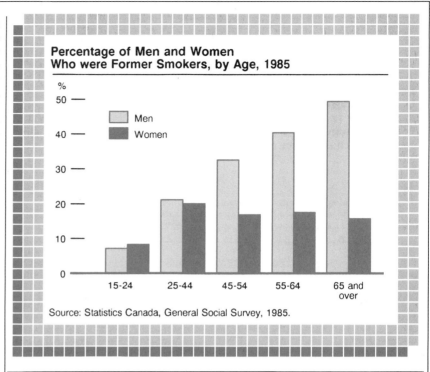

Percentage of Men and Women Who were Former Smokers, by Age, 1985

Source: Statistics Canada, General Social Survey, 1985.

Percentage of Men and Women Who Were Regular Cigarette Smokers, by Age, 1978-79 and 1985

	Men			Women	
	1978-79	1985		1978-79	1985
			%		
Age group					
15-19	32.3	19.6		33.9	20.8
20-24	48.9	32.2		45.2	37.9
25-44	44.6	38.0		37.2	30.7
45-64	42.2	35.6		32.0	28.6
65 and over	29.5	22.7		13.7	14.8
Total	41.3	33.1		33.5	27.8

Sources: Statistics Canada, Catalogue 82-538, *The Health of Canadians*; General Social Survey, 1985.

1978-79   1985

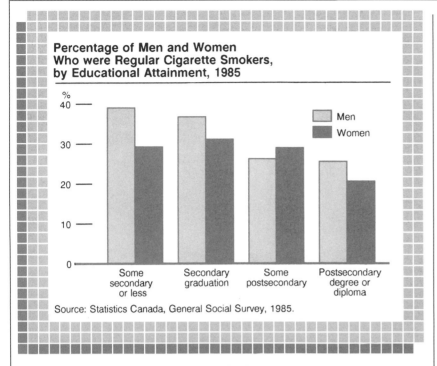

Percentage of Men and Women Who were Regular Cigarette Smokers, by Educational Attainment, 1985

%

Men
Women

Some secondary or less | Secondary graduation | Some postsecondary | Postsecondary degree or diploma

Source: Statistics Canada, General Social Survey, 1985.

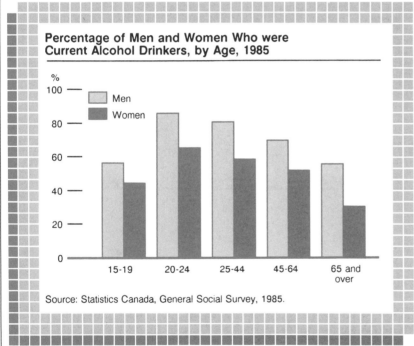

Percentage of Men and Women Who were Current Alcohol Drinkers, by Age, 1985

%

Men
Women

15-19 | 20-24 | 25-44 | 45-64 | 65 and over

Source: Statistics Canada, General Social Survey, 1985.

Changes in Drinking Patterns

Between the late 1970s and 1985, there was little overall change in the proportion of the population who reported themselves as current drinkers. However, for both sexes, and for all age groups, there was a shift towards more moderate drinking among current drinkers. Most significantly, there was a decline in the proportion of those consuming 14 or more drinks per week. The largest decline in heavy drinkers was among males aged 20–24. The percentage of men in this age group who reported consuming 14 or more drinks per week in 1985 was half of what it had been in 1978–79.

As with tobacco use, men were much more likely than women to drink alcoholic beverages regularly. In 1985, almost three out of four Canadian men were classified as current drinkers, in comparison with just over half of all women. Men were also much more likely than women to fall into the heavier drinking categories. In 1985, 28% of

Drinking Alcoholic Beverages

In 1985, nearly two out of every three Canadians aged 15 and over were current drinkers, that is, they drank an alcoholic beverage at least once a month. As well, close to half of adult Canadians drank at least once a week, and nearly one in five consumed at least 7 drinks per week. A further 18%

of the adult population described themselves as occasional drinkers, that is, they had less than one drink a month. The remaining 19% of the adult population either never drank or were former drinkers.

Sales of Tobacco and Alcohol

Recent shifts in the smoking and drinking habits of Canadians are also reflected in the sales of tobacco and alcohol. Cigarette sales in the month of August rose dramatically in the early 1970s to almost 9 million in 1983. In the next three years, however, cigarette sales plummetted to about half that amount. In August, 1986, just 4.6 million cigarettes were sold, fewer than the 1972 figure of 4.7 million.

Sales of alcoholic beverages have varied depending on the type of beverage. Between 1980 and 1984, the total volume of wine sales increased by 15%; however, sales of spirits decreased by 13% in the same period. The total volume of beer sold, on the other hand, has been stable, at just over 2 billion litres per year, since the late 1970s.

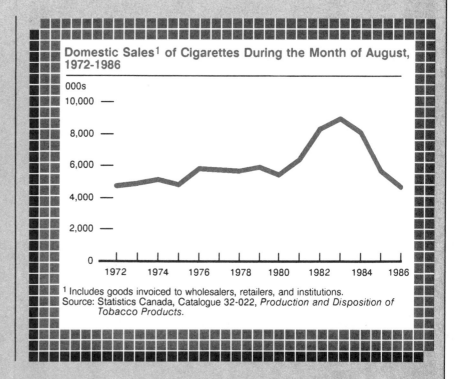

Domestic Sales[1] of Cigarettes During the Month of August, 1972-1986

000s

[1] Includes goods invoiced to wholesalers, retailers, and institutions.
Source: Statistics Canada, Catalogue 32-022, *Production and Disposition of Tobacco Products.*

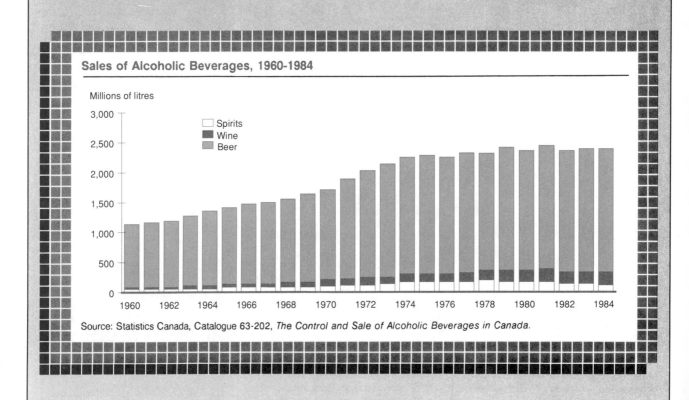

Sales of Alcoholic Beverages, 1960-1984

Millions of litres

☐ Spirits
■ Wine
■ Beer

Source: Statistics Canada, Catalogue 63-202, *The Control and Sale of Alcoholic Beverages in Canada.*

Alcohol Consumption by Men and Women Aged 15 and Over, 1985

	Men	Women	Total
		%	
Current drinkers (at least one drink per month)			
Less than one drink per week	13.8	15.7	14.8
1 – 6 drinks per week	31.6	27.5	29.5
7 – 13 drinks per week	14.9	6.4	10.6
14 or more drinks per week	13.0	2.6	7.7
Not known	0.5*	0.3*	0.4*
Total current drinkers	73.8	52.5	63.0
Occasional drinkers (less than one drink a month)	11.1	24.1	17.7
Never drank	8.1	16.9	12.6
Former drinker	6.5	6.3	6.4
Not known	0.5*	--	0.4*
Total	100.0	100.0	100.0

* Figure should be used with caution because the sampling variability is high.
-- Figure cannot be expressed because the sampling variability is too high.
Source: Statistics Canada, General Social Survey, 1985.

Alcohol Consumption, by Educational Attainment, 1985

	Some secondary or less		Secondary graduation		Some post-secondary		Postsecond-ary degree or diploma	
	Men	Women	Men	Women	Men	Women	Men	Women
				%				
Current drinkers								
Less than 7 drinks per week	38.4	31.6	48.3	47.7	49.5	53.2	52.0	54.3
7 or more drinks per week	23.3	6.1	34.0	9.6	31.5	12.5	29.5	11.1
Total current drinkers[1]	62.2	38.1	82.6	57.9	81.7	65.8	81.8	65.6
Occasional and non-drinkers	37.4	61.8	17.3	41.8	18.2	34.0	17.9	34.3
Total[2]	100.0	100.0	100.0	100.0	100.0	100.0	100.0	100.0

[1] Includes cases in which the volume of consumption was not known.
[2] Includes cases in which the drinking status was not stated.
Source: Statistics Canada, General Social Survey, 1985.

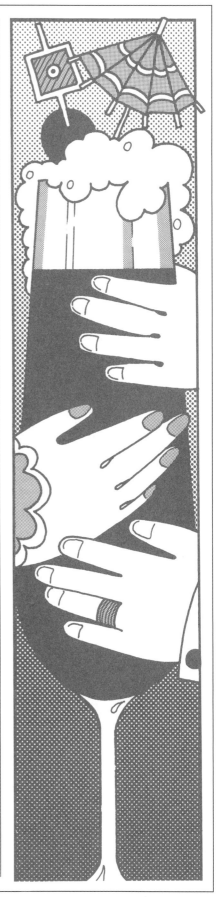

men consumed at least 7 drinks per week, and 13% consumed 14 or more drinks per week on average. In contrast, only 9% of women averaged more than 7 drinks per week, and less than 3% had 14 or more drinks per week.

For both men and women, those aged 20–24 were the most likely to report being current drinkers. In 1985, 86% of men and 64% of women in this age range were classified as current drinkers. This percentage declines with age among both men and women, such that only 56% of men aged 65 and over, and 31% of elderly women, were current drinkers.

Alcohol consumption is also fairly widespread in the population aged 15–19, even though individuals in this age range cannot legally buy alcoholic beverages, or consume them outside the home, in most Canadian jurisdictions. Nevertheless, in 1985, 57% of men aged 15–19, and 44% of women in this age range, were current drinkers. As well, an estimated 7% of men aged 15–19 consumed at least 2 drinks a day on average.

Drinking and Education

Alcohol use varies according to education levels, however, unlike smoking, the consumption of alcohol generally rises with education. Three out of four Canadians with some postsecondary education or more were current drinkers in 1985, compared with just half of those with some secondary education or less. For those with some secondary education or less, 62% of men and 38% of women were regular drinkers, whereas for those with at least some postsecondary experience, over 80% of men and over 65% of women were regular drinkers.

The relationship between alcohol use and education also holds for specific age groups. Among men aged 25–44, for example, 75% of those with secondary education or less were current drinkers, compared with 80–85% for other educational groupings. For women aged 25–44, 47% of those with secondary education or less were cur- rent drinkers, compared with 56% of high school graduates, and around 65% of those who had either attended, or graduated from a postsecondary institution.

TRENDS IN SUICIDE

by Renée Beneteau

A s a result of major increases in the Canadian suicide rate in the 1960s and 1970s, suicide rates during the 1980s have been the highest in history. During the last decade, the suicide rate has been about double what it was throughout most of the period from 1921 to 1961; as well, it has remained considerably above previous highs recorded during the Depression of the 1930s.

There were particularly large increases in the incidence of suicide among young adult men. By the mid-1980s, men in their twenties had one of the highest suicide rates of any age group. This is a change from the past when older men were generally the most likely to take their own lives. Suicide rates have also increased among women, although their rates remain well below those of men.

Increases in suicide

In 1986, the deaths of almost 3,700 Canadians were reported as suicides.[1] This represented 14.6 suicides for every 100,000 people, nearly double the rate that prevailed during most of the period from the early 1920s to the early 1960s. During the latter period, for example, there were around 7.5 suicides per 100,000 population. As well, the 1986 figure was well above the previous historical highs of just under 10 suicides per 100,000 population recorded in the early 1930s.

[1] The actual number of suicides in Canada may be underreported. A death is only certified as a suicide by medical and legal authorities when the victim's intent is clearly proven.

Almost all the increase in the suicide rate since 1960 occurred during the 1960s and 1970s. Between 1960 and 1978, the rate rose from 7.6 suicides per 100,000 population to 14.8. During the 1980s, the suicide rate has been relatively stable, ranging from a high of 15.1 suicides per 100,000 population in 1983, the highest rate ever recorded in Canada, to a low of 13.7 in 1984.

Suicide has accounted for roughly 2% of all deaths in Canada annually since the late 1970s. This proportion has risen over the last several decades from 1% in 1960 and 1.5% in 1970. In 1921, just 0.5% of all deaths were recorded as suicides.

Suicide largely a male phenomenon

The suicide rate for men is much higher than for women. In 1986, there were 22.8 suicides for every 100,000 men compared with 6.4 for every 100,000 women. Overall, almost 80% of all suicide victims in 1986 were men.

Suicide rates have nearly doubled for both men and women since the early 1960s; however, the growth patterns have varied. In particular, since the late 1970s, the rate for men has increased, while that for women has fallen.

Largest increases among young adult men

The largest increases in suicide have occurred among younger men. The suicide rate for men aged 15-19 rose from 5.3 per 100,000 population in 1960 to 20.2 in 1986. The rate for men in this age group, though, remains somewhat below rates for men aged 20 and over.

The suicide rate for men aged 20-24 also rose substantially from 12.3 in 1960 to 32.8 in 1986. In the same period, rates for men aged 25-44 nearly doubled. As a result, 1986 suicide rates for men aged 20-44 were generally either equal to, or greater than, those for older men. This is in sharp contrast to the early 1960s when rates for men aged 45 and over were considerably greater than those for men under age 45.

The suicide rate for men in their twenties is particularly high. In 1986, there were around 33 suicides per 100,000 men in this age range, the highest rate for any age group except men aged 70 and over.

Suicide rates, though, remain high for older men. In 1986, there were 34.9 suicides per 100,000 men aged 70 and over, the highest rate for any age group.

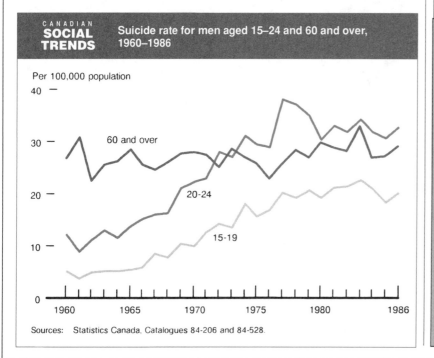

CANADIAN SOCIAL TRENDS — Suicide rate, by sex, 1921–1986

Per 100,000 population

Men
Total
Women

Sources: Statistics Canada, Catalogues 84-202, 84-206 and 84-528.

CANADIAN SOCIAL TRENDS — Suicide rate for men aged 15–24 and 60 and over, 1960–1986

Per 100,000 population

60 and over
20-24
15-19

Sources: Statistics Canada, Catalogues 84-206 and 84-528.

An international perspective

The suicide rate in Canada is similar to that in the United States. According to the World Health Organization, the age-standardized (to the world population) suicide rate in Canada in 1985 was 11.3 per 100,000 population. This was just slightly greater than the figure of 10.7 reported for the United States in 1984.

On the other hand, the Canadian suicide rate is generally below those in most European countries. For example, the Canadian rate was below those in Finland (22.6*), Austria (22.3*), Denmark (22.0), Switzerland (18.1*), France (17.5), Sweden (14.5), West Germany (14.0*), and Norway (12.5). The Canadian rate, though, was above those in England and Wales (7.1) and the Netherlands (9.3).

*Figure is for 1986; other figures are for 1985.

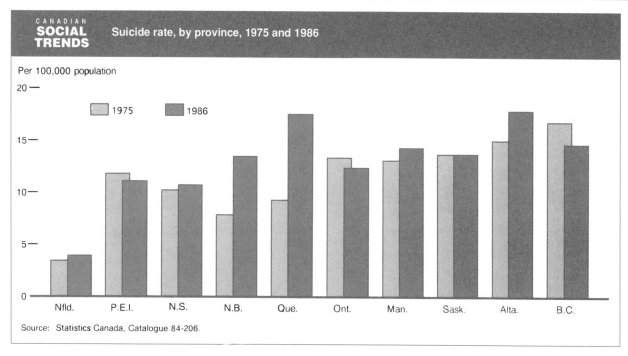

Per 100,000 population

☐ 1975   ■ 1986

Nfld. P.E.I. N.S. N.B. Que. Ont. Man. Sask. Alta. B.C.

Source: Statistics Canada, Catalogue 84-206.

The suicide rate for other male groups over age 45 ranged from 24.6 for men aged 65-69 to 30.0 for those aged 50-54.

There has, however, been little change in suicide rates among men aged 45 and over since the early 1960s. There were small increases in rates for men aged 45-54 and 70 and over, while rates for men aged 55-69 actually declined.

The age distribution of women who commit suicide differs from that of men, though for all age groups the female suicide rate is well below that for males.

The highest female suicide rate in 1986 occurred among women aged 50-54. That year, there were 12.9 suicides for every 100,000 women in this age range. Rates for other groups in the 30-69 age range varied from 7.9 for women aged 55-59 to around 10 for women aged 45-49 and 60-64.

In contrast to the situation with men, suicide rates among women aged 20-29 and 70 and over were relatively low. In 1986, there were fewer than 7 suicides per 100,000 women in these age ranges.

The suicide pattern among women aged 15-19 was similar to that for men of the same age. The incidence of suicide among women in this age group increased substantially in the 1960-1986 period, though their 1986 suicide rate was still below that for all groups of women aged 20 and over.

Male suicides more violent
Men generally employ more violent means than women to commit suicide. In 1986,

38% of male suicides involved firearms and another 27% were by hanging or strangulation. In contrast, only 12% of female victims used firearms, while 19% either hanged or strangled themselves.

Female suicide victims, on the other hand, were more likely than male victims to use drugs, pills, or other medication. In 1986, more than a third of all female victims (37%) compared with just 9% of men used these methods.

Another 13% of male and 10% of female suicides involved poisoning by gas, usually motor vehicle exhaust. The remaining 14% of male suicides and 23% of female suicides were committed by other methods such as drowning, jumping from high places, or stabbing.

Narrowing of provincial differences
Suicide rates have historically been higher in the west than in the eastern or central provinces. These differences, however, have diminished in recent years, primarily because of large increases in the incidence of suicide in Quebec and New Brunswick.

Alberta had the highest suicide rate in Canada in 1986 with 17.9 deaths per 100,000 population. The second-highest rate (17.6) was reported in Quebec. This was a major change from earlier years when Quebec's rate was among the lowest in Canada. For example, in 1975, there were just 9.3 suicides per 100,000 population in Quebec, the third lowest rate in the country.

The incidence of suicide also increased substantially in New Brunswick from 8.0

suicides per 100,000 population in 1975 to 13.5 in 1986.

Suicide rates in the remaining provinces were either stable or declined in the last decade. As a result, rates in Ontario and the other eastern provinces in 1986 were just below those in British Columbia, Saskatchewan, and Manitoba. The exception to this was Newfoundland, where there were only 4.0 suicides per 100,000 population.

Suicide high among Native Canadians
Suicide rates are especially high among Native people. In 1986, there were 56.3 suicides for every 100,000 Native men, almost 2.5 times the rate for all men (22.8). At the same time, the rate for Native women (11.8) was almost double the rate for all women (6.4).

The incidence of suicide is particularly high among young Native men. In 1986, there were more than 100 suicides for every 100,000 Native men aged 15-29.

Suicides in prisons
The suicide rate is also very high in federal penitentiaries and provincial prisons. In 1986, 17 inmates in these institutions committed suicide; this represented a rate of more than 60 suicides per 100,000 prison population.

WOMEN, MARRIAGE, AND THE FAMILY

Family and Rainstorm by Alex Colville.
© Alex Colville
Collection: The National Gallery of Canada, Ottawa.

Women

WOMEN EMPLOYED OUTSIDE THE HOME

by Jo-Anne B. Parliament

One of the major social trends in Canada in recent decades has been the increasing proportion of women employed outside the home. By 1988, for example, over half of all women had jobs. Working women, however, remain concentrated in traditional female occupations such as clerical work, and their earnings are still well below those of men.

The increase in the employment of women has also brought about a number of related social concerns such as the need for child care.

Growing proportion of women with jobs

The percentage of women employed outside the home has continued to increase sharply since the mid-1970s. Overall, 53% of women worked outside the home in 1988 compared with just 41% in 1975. In fact, women accounted for two-thirds of all employment growth in Canada between 1975 and 1988. Consequently, the number of women with jobs, as a percentage of all employed people, increased from 36% in 1975 to 44% in 1988.

The proportion of women with jobs did drop slightly during the recession in the early 1980s; however, by 1984, it was back up to the 1981 level. Since then, the percentage of women working has risen by over one percentage point each year.

Trends in the employment of men have differed from those of women. The proportion of men with jobs hovered around 73% from 1975 until the recession. The recession, however, had a much greater impact on men's than women's employment. Between 1981 and 1983, for example, the proportion of men with jobs fell 5.4 percentage points. While the proportion of men with jobs has climbed since then, the 1988 figure (71%) was still below the pre-recession level. Still, in 1988, the percentage of men with jobs was about 18 percentage points higher than that for women, although this was down from a 33 percentage-point gap in 1975.

Provincial differences

The proportion of women with jobs varies considerably by province. In 1988, this measure ranged from a high of 59% in Alberta to a low of 37% in Newfoundland. At least half of women were also employed in Ontario (58%), Manitoba (54%), Saskatchewan (53%), and British Columbia (50%). On the other hand, fewer than half of women in Quebec (48%), Prince Edward Island (47%), Nova Scotia (46%), and New Brunswick (44%) had jobs.

Largest gains at ages 25-54

Employment rates of women increased for all age groups under 65, with the largest gains among 25-54-year-olds. Between 1975 and 1988, the percentage of women aged 25-44 employed outside the home rose from just under 50% to about 70%; for women aged 45-54, the increase was from 44% to 62%.

The percentage of 15-24-year-old women working outside the home also grew, but not as dramatically as for women aged 25-54. The proportion of employed women in this age range rose from 50% in 1975 to 60% in 1988. On the other hand, there was only a small increase, from 29% to 33%, in the proportion of women aged 55-64 with jobs.

In contrast, employment rates dropped for most male age groups between 1975 and 1988. The decline among men aged 55-64, from 76% to 62%, was particularly sharp. In the same period, the share of men aged 25-54 with jobs fell between 2

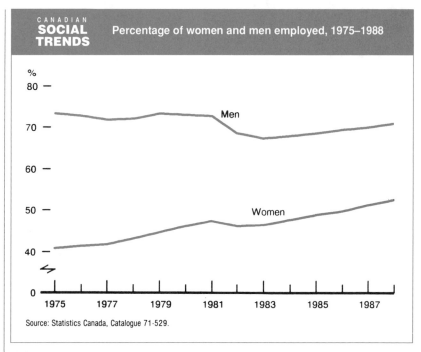

CANADIAN SOCIAL TRENDS

Percentage of women and men employed, 1975–1988

Source: Statistics Canada, Catalogue 71-529.

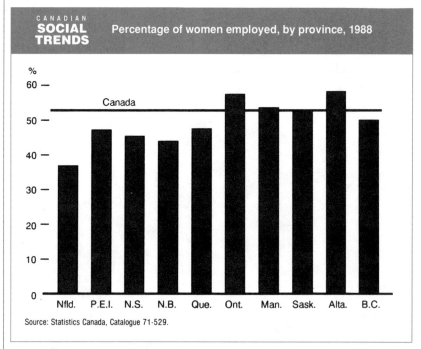

CANADIAN SOCIAL TRENDS

Percentage of women employed, by province, 1988

Source: Statistics Canada, Catalogue 71-529.

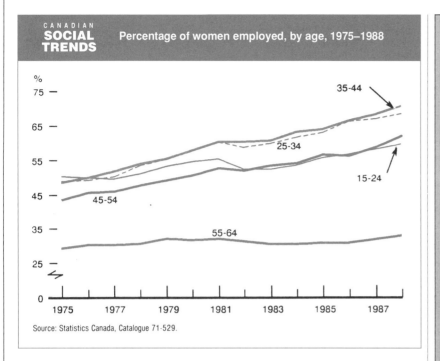

Percentage of women employed, by age, 1975–1988

CANADIAN SOCIAL TRENDS

%

75 —

65 —

55 —

45 —

35 —

25 —

0

35-44

25-34

45-54

15-24

55-64

1975   1977   1979   1981   1983   1985   1987

Source: Statistics Canada, Catalogue 71-529.

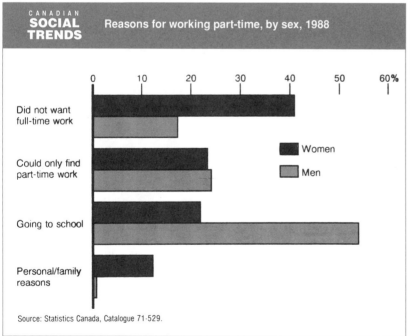

Reasons for working part-time, by sex, 1988

CANADIAN SOCIAL TRENDS

0   10   20   30   40   50   60%

Did not want full-time work

Could only find part-time work

Going to school

Personal/family reasons

■ Women
□ Men

Source: Statistics Canada, Catalogue 71-529.

Day care

The increase in the number of employed women has meant that a growing number of children live in families in which both parents are working. At the same time, the number of employed lone parents and the number of children in such families have also increased. The result has been a sharp upturn in need for non-parental care during the day or after school.

Between 1976 and 1986, the number of children under age 6 with either both parents working or an employed lone parent increased from just over 600,000 to 954,000. The majority of these children, about 90%, were in families in which both parents worked. The number of children aged 6-15 in families with both parents employed or with an employed lone parent also increased between 1976 and 1986, from 1.7 to 1.9 million. Over the same period, the total number of day-care spaces grew from 83,500 to 220,500.

with the situation among men. In 1988, for example, 75% of married men were working compared with 65% of single men.

Many more women with children working

There have also been major increases in the employment of women with children. In 1988, 57% of married women with children under age 6 whose husband was employed had jobs, up from 31% in 1976. In the same period, the proportion of married women with children aged 6-15 with jobs rose from 47% to 70%.

Female lone parents were somewhat less likely than mothers with employed husbands to have jobs outside the home. In 1988, just 42% of female lone parents with pre-school children and 63% of those with children aged 6-15 were employed. This is a reversal from the mid-1970s when a greater proportion of female lone parents than married women with children had been employed.

Rapid growth in female part-time employment

A considerable proportion of the increase in women's employment is attributable to part-time work. In fact, the increase in the

and 3 percentage points. Employment rates did rise among 15-24-year-old men; however, the increase was only about three percentage points.

More married women working

Employment growth was particularly substantial among married women. In 1988, 54% of these women had jobs com-

pared with 38% in 1975.

Nonetheless, married women are still less likely than their single counterparts to be employed outside the home. In 1988, 62% of single women had jobs, although this was up only modestly from 54% in 1975.

That single women are more likely than married women to be employed contrasts

number of women working part-time accounted for about one-third of all growth in the employment of women from 1975 to 1988. In this period, the number of women employed part-time doubled from 678,000 to 1.4 million. As a result, by 1988, 25% of employed women were working part-time, compared to just 8% of men. Overall, 72% of part-time workers in 1988 were women, up slightly from 70% in 1975.

Young women are the most likely to work part-time, although part-time employment is common among women of all ages. In 1988, 37% of employed women aged 15-24 had part-time jobs, while the corresponding figures were 20% for 25-44-year-olds and 26% for women aged 45 and over.

The incidence of part-time work among men is also highest for those aged 15-24. In contrast to women, though, part-time work is rare among men over age 25. In 1988, while 29% of employed men aged 15-24 worked part-time, just 2% of men aged 25-44 and 5% of those aged 45 and over did so.

Reasons for part-time employment
The primary reason women work part-time is that they do not want a full-time job. In 1988, 41% of women working part-time gave this as their reason for working part-time. Another 12% cited personal or family responsibilities, while 24% could only find part-time jobs, and 22% were going to school.

In comparison, the majority (54%) of men working part-time said they did so because they were going to school. Another 24% could only find part-time work, and 18% stated that they did not want full-time work. Just 1% gave personal or family responsibilities as their reason for working part-time.

Higher education, higher employment
Not surprisingly, women with the highest levels of education are the most likely to be employed. In 1988, 76% of women with a university degree, 69% with a postsecondary certificate or diploma, and 62% with some postsecondary training were employed. On the other hand, 52% of women with some high school education and just 22% with less than Grade 9 worked outside the home.

The pattern was the same among men; however, the gap between the proportions of women and men who are employed narrows at successively higher levels of education. For example, in 1988, there was a 10 percentage-point difference between the employment levels of women (76%) and men (86%) with a university degree. The difference was 15 percentage points for those with a postsecondary certificate or diploma; 20 percentage points for those with some high school; and 24 percentage points for those with less than Grade 9.

Most women still in traditional jobs
While the range of jobs held by women has grown in the last decade, [+] the majority of working women are still concentrated

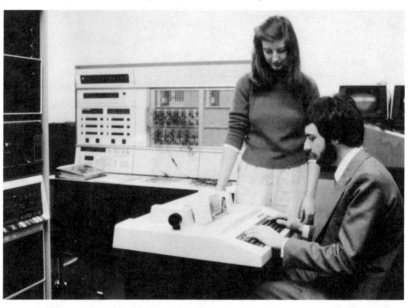

Employment statistics, 1975–1988

	Total employment		Percentage employed		Percentage employed part-time	
	Women	Men	Women	Men	Women	Men
	000s		%			
1975	3,381	5,903	40.8	73.5	20.3	5.1
1976	3,513	5,964	41.4	72.7	21.1	5.1
1977	3,619	6,032	41.7	72.0	22.1	5.4
1978	3,830	6,156	43.3	72.2	22.6	5.5
1979	4,033	6,362	44.7	73.3	23.3	5.7
1980	4,249	6,459	46.2	73.0	23.8	5.9
1981	4,445	6,556	47.4	72.9	24.2	6.3
1982	4,382	6,236	46.1	68.5	25.1	6.9
1983	4,472	6,203	46.5	67.5	26.1	7.6
1984	4,624	6,308	47.6	68.0	25.7	7.6
1985	4,794	6,429	48.8	68.7	26.0	7.6
1986	4,964	6,567	49.9	69.5	25.7	7.8
1987	5,152	6,708	51.2	70.1	25.1	7.6
1988	5,368	6,876	52.6	70.9	25.2	7.7

Source: Statistics Canada, Catalogue 71-529.

in a narrow range of traditional female occupations. In 1988, 73% of all working women were employed in either clerical, sales or service positions, teaching, or health services, mostly nursing. This figure was down only slightly from 78% in 1975, and it remains well above the proportion for men. In 1988, just 30% of men were employed in one of these occupations.

In terms of individual occupations, clerical postions still account for the largest share of working women. In 1988, almost 1 in 3 employed women (31%) had a clerical job, although this was down from 36% in 1975. Another 17% of employed women were in service positions; 10% were in sales; 9% were in health care occupations; and 6% were teachers.

Average earnings

The real average earnings of women employed full-time increased 8% between 1975 and 1987, while those of men actually declined slightly. Consequently, women's earnings as a percentage of men's rose from 60% in 1975 to 66% in 1987.

In 1987, women employed full-time earned an average of $21,000, up from $19,500 (in constant 1987 $) in 1975. Over the same period, average earnings of men dropped from $32,300 to $31,900.

The difference between the earnings of women and men persists at all educational levels. Even women with a university degree, the highest-paid group, made only 70% of the average earnings of male graduates. However, this may be changing, as the figure was 80% among university degree-holders aged 25-34.

There are some groups, though, in which the earnings of women and men are similar. For example, there is almost no difference between the average earnings of comparable, never-married women and men.

CANADIAN
SOCIAL TRENDS
Women's earnings as a percentage of men's, 1967–1987[1]

%

70 —

60 —

50 —

40 —

30 —

20 —

10 —

0

1967 1971 1973 1975 1977 1979 1981 1982 1984 1985 1986 1987

[1] Includes full-time, full-year workers.
Source: Statistics Canada, Catalogue 13-217.

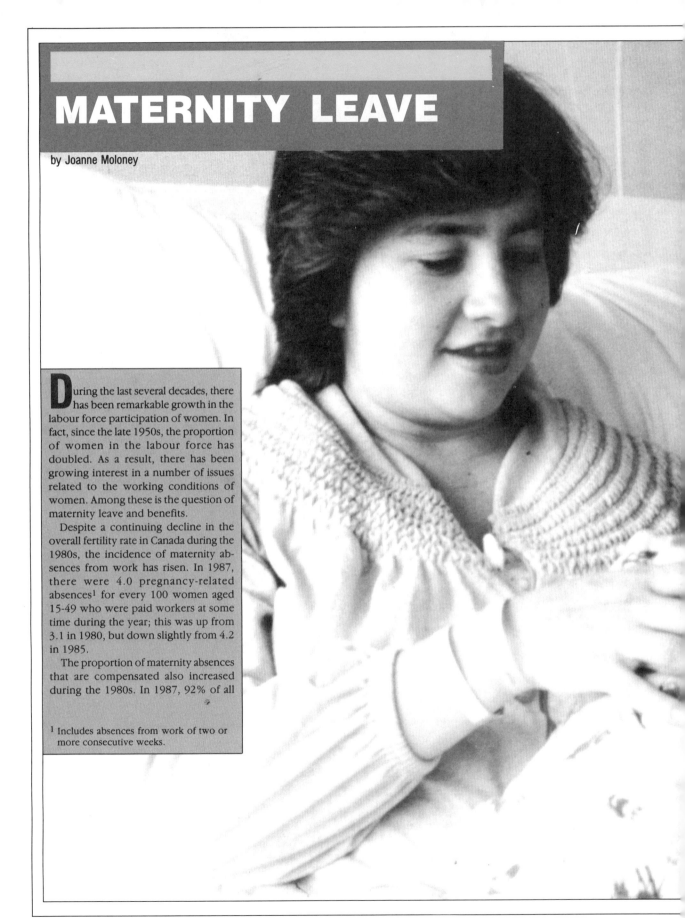

MATERNITY LEAVE

by Joanne Moloney

During the last several decades, there has been remarkable growth in the labour force participation of women. In fact, since the late 1950s, the proportion of women in the labour force has doubled. As a result, there has been growing interest in a number of issues related to the working conditions of women. Among these is the question of maternity leave and benefits.

Despite a continuing decline in the overall fertility rate in Canada during the 1980s, the incidence of maternity absences from work has risen. In 1987, there were 4.0 pregnancy-related absences[1] for every 100 women aged 15-49 who were paid workers at some time during the year; this was up from 3.1 in 1980, but down slightly from 4.2 in 1985.

The proportion of maternity absences that are compensated also increased during the 1980s. In 1987, 92% of all

[1] Includes absences from work of two or more consecutive weeks.

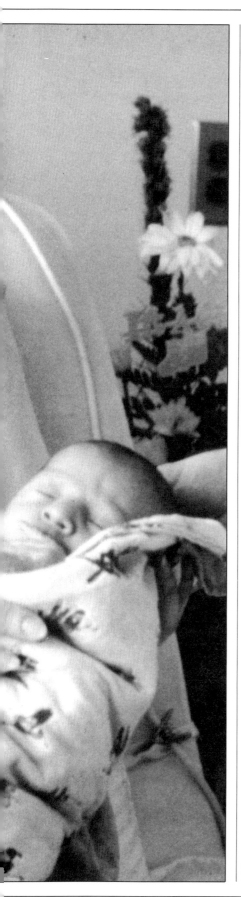

ended maternity leaves[2] were compensated, compared with 77% in 1980.

About two-thirds of the rise in the share of compensated maternity absences was accounted for by absences in which Unemployment Insurance benefits were the only compensation received. In 1987, these benefits were the only compensation received in 72% of cases, up from 62% in 1980.

The prevalence of other types of financial compensation, however, also increased. In 1987, 20% of women received other benefits such as full or partial pay from their employers or group insurance; this was up from 14% in 1980.

Because of the link between hours of work and the legal right to Unemployment Insurance benefits, there are marked differences in the proportions of full- and part-time workers receiving compensation for maternity leave. In 1984, 95% of women who were employed full time for at least 12 months before they stopped working and 90% of full-time part-year workers were compensated. By contrast, compensation rates were only 83% for those who worked part-time year-round and less than 60% for part-timers who had worked less than a full year prior to their absence.

Absence duration varies

The length of maternity absences varies considerably, although a substantial proportion last 17 weeks. Throughout the 1980s, for example, 14% of all ended absences were of this duration. Seventeen weeks was the single most common dura-

tion largely because statutory provisions entitle most women to 17 or 18 weeks, while the Unemployment Insurance program offers benefits for a maximum of 15 weeks following an initial two-week waiting period.

A high proportion of maternity absences, though, were relatively brief. For example, 11% of absences in the 1980-1987 period lasted just 2-6 weeks. However, some of these absences may have been sick leave taken for either illness or medical complications early in the pregnancy.

At the same time, close to 3 in 10 absences lasted more than 20 weeks: 15% were from 21-26 weeks and 14% were longer than 26 weeks.

The length of a maternity absence may be related to the financial compensation involved. From 1980 to 1987, compensated absences lasted an average of almost 19 weeks, compared with fewer than 15 weeks for non-compensated leaves.

Absences highest at ages 25-29

Maternity leave is most common among women aged 25-29. During the 1980s, there were an average of 9.1 pregnancy-related absences for every 100 working women in this age group, compared with 6.1 for women aged 30-34 and 4.3 for those aged 20-24. The incidence of maternity absences falls off sharply for women under age 20 and over age 34.

[2] Ended absences are those that had ended by the time of the survey in February following the reference year. These represented 71% of maternity absences from 1980 to 1987.

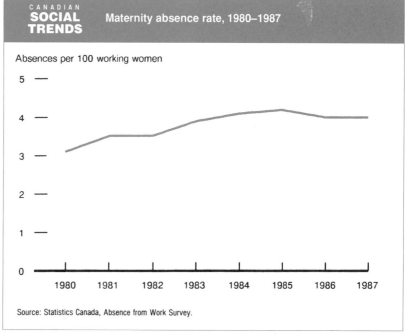

CANADIAN SOCIAL TRENDS Maternity absence rate, 1980–1987

Absences per 100 working women

Source: Statistics Canada, Absence from Work Survey.

It is not surprising that the incidence of maternity absence is highest among 25-29-year-olds, since their fertility rate is also the highest. However, the fact that maternity absences are more frequent among women in their early thirties than among those in their early twenties is somewhat surprising, as the fertility rate is higher among the younger group. The lower maternity absence rate among women aged 20-24 may occur because working women in this age range are more likely to postpone childbearing to establish a career, especially if they have completed a postsecondary education. The maternity absence rate among postsecondary graduates, for example, was just 2.5 for 20-24-year-olds, compared with 9.4 for women aged 30-34.

Absence rate highest in Quebec

The incidence of pregnancy-related absences varies considerably by province. During the 1980s, the number of these absences per 100 women aged 15-49 ranged from 3.0 in Newfoundland to 4.3 in Quebec.

The high incidence of pregnancy-related absences in Quebec is surprising, given that Quebec has the lowest fertility rate of any province. However, Quebec also has superior maternity leave provisions and benefits. As well as providing 18 weeks of regular maternity leave, Quebec legislation allows for other types of pregnancy-related leave. These include special maternity leave when there is a risk of miscarriage or a threat to the health of the mother and leave for legal or spon-

taneous abortion and stillbirths.

Quebec has also been a leader with respect to paid maternity leave. In the 1980-1987 period, 92% of all ended maternity absences in Quebec were compensated. Among the other provinces, the percentage of compensated maternity absences ranged from around 80% in Saskatchewan, Alberta, and British Columbia to 88% in New Brunswick, Ontario, and Manitoba.

The high compensation rate in Quebec is due mainly to the prevalence of maternity leave compensation other than Unemployment Insurance benefits. Other types of compensation were received in 35% of all ended maternity leaves in Quebec from 1980 to 1987, compared with just 19% in Canada as a whole.

Quebec also has the longest maternity absences. In the 1980s, absences in Quebec averaged over 20 weeks, while in the other provinces, they ranged from just over 15 weeks in Newfoundland to 19 weeks in Alberta.

Maternity leave and benefit entitlements

Working women in all provinces are entitled to a period of unpaid maternity leave. Provincial statutes and the Canada Labour Code allow 17 or 18 weeks of maternity leave, depending on the jurisdiction. Collective agreements negotiated by unions, or employers themselves, may offer maternity leave and benefits that exceed those in the applicable legislation.

For public servants, employment standards are set in public service acts. Many of these do not mention maternity leave; it is the collective agreements of public service unions that provide this leave. Entitlements for public servants range from four months in Prince Edward Island to 12 months in Saskatchewan.

In most jurisdictions, an employee must complete a minimum period of employment to be eligible for maternity leave. This qualifying period varies from 20 weeks in Quebec to one year plus 11 weeks in Ontario.

A large percentage of maternity absences are compensated, with Unemployment Insurance benefits the most widely available form of financial compensation. These benefits consist of 15 weeks of payments at 60% of the employee's regular wage, up to a maximum, which is increased each year. In 1989, the maximum weekly benefit was $363. As a rule, a woman must have worked 20 weeks within the last year to qualify for Unemployment Insurance maternity benefits.

A study for the Task Force on Child Care ranked Canada poorly compared with 22 industrialized countries in eastern and western Europe. Fifteen of these countries paid maternity benefits of 90-100% of the employee's usual earnings, up to a weekly maximum, for periods ranging from six weeks to nine months. The same study, however, showed that Canada's maternity leave provisions compared favourably with those in the United States.

Maternity leave by industry

The characteristics of maternity leave also vary by industry. During the 1980s, maternity absences were most common in public and regulated service industries.[3] There were 4.8 such absences for every 100 female paid workers aged 15-49 in these industries, compared with 4.0 absences in manufacturing, transportation, and storage industries, 3.2 in other service industries, and 2.1 in primary and construction industries.

Workers in public and regulated services also tend to take the longest maternity absences. From 1980 to 1987, ended absences for this group averaged 19.3 weeks, compared with 17.6 weeks in the other services, 17.0 weeks in manufacturing, transportation, and storage industries, and just 13.7 weeks in the primary and construction group.

There is less difference in the proportion of maternity absences compensated in the various industries, although the primary and construction sector does lag somewhat behind. In the 1980s, 89% of absences in the public and regulated services, 87% in manufacturing, transporta-

[3] Includes education, health, social, and government services, as well as the communication and utilities industries.

Maternity absence characteristics, by province, 1980–1987 average

	Maternity absences per 100 working women aged 15-49	Average duration of ended maternity absences[1]	Compensated ended maternity absences[1]
		Weeks	%
Newfoundland	3.0	15.4	86.2
Prince Edward Island	3.1	16.2	83.9
Nova Scotia	3.4	16.0	83.7
New Brunswick	3.3	16.8	88.0
Quebec	4.3	20.1	91.9
Ontario	3.8	17.3	88.4
Manitoba	3.2	17.0	87.8
Saskatchewan	4.2	17.5	80.6
Alberta	3.7	19.1	79.6
British Columbia	3.3	17.2	80.1
TOTAL	**3.8**	**18.2**	**87.3**

[1] Ended absences are those that had ended by the time of the survey in February following the reference year.
Source: Statistics Canada, Absence from Work Survey.

Maternity absence characteristics, by industry, 1980–1987 average

	Maternity absences per 100 working women aged 15-49	Average duration of ended maternity absences[1]	Compensated ended maternity absences[1]	Workers covered by collective agreement
		Weeks	%	%
Public/regulated services	4.8	19.3	88.9	60.2
Manufacturing/transportation/ storage	4.0	17.0	86.9	29.2
Primary/construction	2.1	13.7	77.3	5.2
Other services	3.2	17.6	86.3	9.6

[1] Ended absences are those that had ended by the time of the survey in February following the reference year.
Sources: Statistics Canada, Absence from Work Survey and Labour Market Activity Survey.

tion, and storage, and 86% in the other services were compensated. In comparison, the figure was 77% in the primary and construction industries.

Some of the variation in maternity leave characteristics in different industries may be attributable to differences in unionization rates. For example, 60% of women in paid jobs in public and regulated services were covered by a collective agreement, compared with 29% of those in manufacturing, transportation, and storage industries, 10% in other services, and just 5% in primary and construction industries.

Union membership, however, does not guarantee better maternity leave provisions and benefits than those stipulated by legislation. For example, in the early 1980s, just 49% of major collective agreements in Canada contained sections pertaining to maternity leave; and only 71% exceeded legislated limits. As recently as 1988, paid maternity leave was provided in just 26% of major collective agreements.

Other factors may also contribute to the differences in maternity absences in various industries, particularly those between the primary and construction industries and the other industry groups. The high rate of self-employment and the small average firm size characteristic of the primary and construction industries suggest that family businesses may be more common in this sector. And until July 1987, women employed by their spouse were not eligible for Unemployment Insurance maternity benefits.

Non-compensated and shorter absences in the primary and construction sector may also be related to the seasonal nature of the work in these industries. This could limit eligibility for maternity benefits, especially if regular benefits are received shortly before the maternity absence.

Finally, the generally lower profile of maternity absences in the primary and construction industries may also reflect the small number of women in these industries.

WOMEN IN PROFESSIONAL OCCUPATIONS: PROGRESS IN THE 1980s

by Katherine Marshall

One of the most fundamental changes in Canadian society over the past several decades has been the increased labour force participation of women. An important aspect of this trend has been the growing number of women employed in professional occupations.[1]

Women have made particularly substantial inroads into what have traditionally been male-dominated professions.[2] In fact, by 1986, the number of women employed in several of these occupations had grown such that the professions could no longer be considered male-dominated. Nonetheless, women continue to be significantly under-represented in most professions that have traditionally been male-dominated.

There are also differences in some of the employment characteristics of women and men in the professions. For example, the average income of women in professional occupations is considerably below that of comparable men, and there has been no reduction in the gap in recent years.

In addition, many of the family characteristics of women employed in professional occupations differ from those of other women and male professionals.

[1] Professional occupations are those in which 45% or more of people employed in that occupation in 1981 had at least a bachelor's degree. Overall, 46 occupational groups were classified as professional.
[2] A profession was considered male-dominated if 65% or more of the people employed in it in 1971 were men. Based on this criterion, 34 professions were classified as male-dominated.

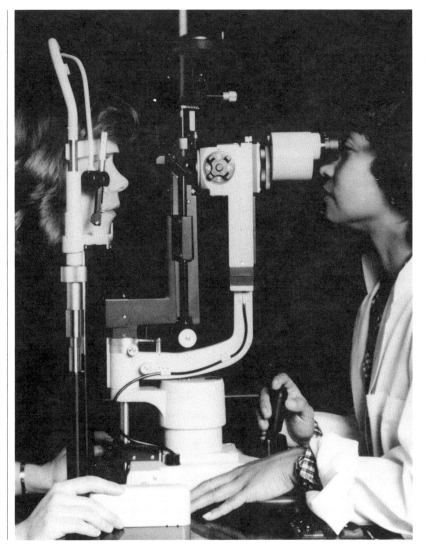

These differences are especially pronounced among women in male-dominated professions, who are less likely than others to be part of a family, or if married, to have children.

Most new professionals women

Women were responsible for slightly more than two-thirds of all employment growth in professional occupations between 1981 and 1986. In this period, the number of women employed in the professions rose 18%, from 383,000 to 453,000. In comparison, the number of male professionals increased just 6%. As a result, in 1986, 45.1% of all professionals were women, up from 42.5% in 1981.

Rapid growth in male-dominated professions

There has been a particularly large increase in women's participation in male-dominated professions in recent years. The number of women in these professions rose 42% between 1981 and 1986, from around 83,000 to just over 118,000. Meanwhile, the number of men in these professions increased just 9%. Still, in 1986, women made up only 23% of those employed in male-dominated professions, though this was up from 11% in 1971 and 19% in 1981.

Between 1981 and 1986, women's share of employment increased in all but one of the male-dominated professions. In fact, in more than half of these occupations, women accounted for the majority of employment growth, and in several, almost all growth was attributable to women.

Women were responsible for all employment growth among veterinarians between 1981 and 1986, as the number of women in this field increased about one and a half times, while the number of men actually declined slightly. Somewhat the same pattern occurred among sociologists and anthropologists. As well, women accounted for 91% of employment growth among pharmacists in this period, while the figure was 87% for optometrists, 86% for managers in the social sciences, 81% for biologists, and 77% for administrators in teaching.

As a result, women's share of employment in these professions increased dramatically. The percentage of veterinarians who were women doubled from 17% in 1981 to 35% in 1986, while the figure among optometrists rose from 18% to 32%. There were also increases from 48% to 58% for managers in the social sciences, from 39% to 48% for socio-

logists and anthropologists, from 42% to 50% for pharmacists, from 25% to 31% for administrators in teaching, and from 32% to 37% for biologists.

Women's share of employment also rose significantly among economists, chemists, and agriculturists in the 1981-1986 period.

Because of these trends, a number of professions can no longer be considered male-dominated. In 1986, women actually outnumbered men among both pharmacists and managers in the social sciences. As well, they made up over 35% of those employed in six other professional groups identified as male-dominated in 1971. These included sociologists and anthropologists, mathematicians and statisticians, veterinarians, biologists, community college teachers, and university instructors such as non-tenured professors and lecturers, and teaching and laboratory assistants.

Women also continued to make steady gains in the more high-profile professions such as medicine, dentistry, and law, accounting for close to half the employment growth in each between 1981 and 1986. As a result, women's share of

employment rose from 17% to 21% among doctors, from 8% to 14% among dentists, and from 16% to 22% among lawyers.

Women also made up almost half the increase in the number of university professors in the 1981-1986 period. However, because overall employment growth in this profession was relatively slow, the proportional representation of women in this field increased only slightly.

A number of professions continue to be heavily male-dominated, with women still representing less than 10% of total employment in ten of the 34 professions identified as male-dominated in 1971.

A particularly small proportion of people employed in engineering are women. In 1986, only 5% of all engineers were women, although this was up from 3% in 1981.

Women also made up only 9% of managers in the natural sciences and just 8% of physicists in 1986, though, as with engineering, these figures were up slightly from 1981. In addition, just over 10% of architects, meteorologists, geologists, ministers, and judges and magistrates in 1986 were women.

Women employed in professional occupations, 1971-1986

	Total number of women			Per-centage increase 1981-1986	Women as a % of total growth in profession 1981-1986	Women as a % of total employment in profession	
	1971	1981	1986			1981	1986
Male-dominated professions							
Management occupations, natural sciences and engineering	70	800	1,225	53.1	23.8	6.6	8.8
Management occupations, social sciences and related fields	760	3,805	6,090	60.1	85.9	48.2	57.7
Administrators in teaching and related fields	6,445	9,120	12,425	36.2	76.7	25.0	30.5
Chemists	895	1,975	3,080	55.9	63.5	20.4	27.0
Geologists	145	795	1,005	26.4	35.6	10.3	12.1
Physicists	45	65	95	46.2	*	5.0	7.9
Meteorologists	40	90	120	33.3	24.0	9.0	10.7
Agriculturists and related scientists	330	1,220	2,420	98.4	37.6	13.2	19.5
Biologists and related scientists	830	2,330	3,000	28.8	80.7	31.9	36.9
Architects	125	560	850	51.8	48.7	7.7	10.8
Chemical engineers	65	340	560	64.7	62.9	5.9	9.2
Civil engineers	235	980	1,490	52.0	*	3.0	4.6
Electrical engineers	205	1,000	1,655	65.5	14.4	3.7	5.2
Mechanical engineers	100	380	710	86.8	8.6	1.9	3.0
Metallurgical engineers	15	50	100	100.0	*	2.8	6.1
Mining engineers	20	105	155	47.6	*	2.9	4.3
Petroleum engineers	15	225	285	26.7	*	1.1	6.5
Nuclear engineers	--	40	70	75.0	*	4.8	9.5
Other architects and engineers	140	1,640	2,640	61.0	36.8	12.2	16.3
Mathematicians, statisticians, and actuaries	1,010	2,070	2,305	11.4	54.0	34.7	36.0
Economists	640	2,570	4,345	69.1	62.2	20.5	28.3
Sociologists, anthropologists, and related social scientists	170	540	685	26.9	290.0	39.0	47.7
Judges and magistrates	75	220	320	45.5	27.4	10.5	12.0
Lawyers and notaries	860	5,390	9,410	74.6	51.2	15.5	22.0
Ministers of religion	900	1,785	2,590	45.1	65.7	7.6	10.5
University teachers	5,190	9,785	11,470	17.2	48.7	26.5	28.4
Other university teaching and related occupations	1,525	6,170	8,640	40.0	44.1	45.8	45.3
Community college and vocational school teachers	3,280	13,770	16,945	23.1	57.1	41.6	43.8
Physicians and surgeons	3,150	7,255	10,175	40.2	47.3	17.4	21.2
Dentists	330	860	1,670	94.2	44.1	8.1	13.5
Veterinarians	75	605	1,510	149.6	114.6	17.2	35.1
Osteopaths and chiropractors	80	340	520	52.9	25.7	14.9	17.5
Pharmacists	2,540	6,090	8,755	43.8	91.1	41.8	50.1
Optometrists	105	365	840	130.1	87.2	17.7	32.2
Total male-dominated professions	**30,410**	**83,340**	**118,155**	**41.8**	**52.1**	**18.6**	**22.9**
Other professions							
Psychologists	2,035	4,600	7,075	53.8	79.6	52.6	59.7
Social workers	7,230	21,020	31,005	47.5	78.5	63.5	67.7
Supervisors in library, museum, and archival sciences	600	1,440	1,700	18.1	85.2	62.1	64.8
Librarians and archivists	6,120	13,575	15,315	12.8	80.6	80.9	80.9
Educational and vocational counsellors	1,690	3,050	4,285	40.5	84.0	49.3	55.9
Elementary and kindergarten teachers	140,500	152,335	163,505	7.3	79.0	81.5	81.3
Secondary school teachers	56,615	63,320	62,745	−0.9	*	43.8	45.7
Postsecondary school teachers	5,730	4,445	3,850	−13.4	*	63.9	74.1
Teachers of exceptional students	4,420	15,315	18,710	22.2	97.7	72.1	75.7
Physiotherapists, occupational and other therapists	5,895	12,525	16,855	34.6	86.0	85.0	85.2
Dietitians and nutritionists	2,010	3,280	4,250	29.6	100.0	94.3	95.5
Translators and interpreters	1,395	4,340	5,175	19.2	92.8	61.9	65.4
Total other professions	**234,240**	**299,250**	**334,470**	**11.8**	**9.7**	**66.2**	**68.6**
Total all professions	**264,650**	**382,590**	**452,610**	**18.3**	**68.5**	**42.5**	**45.1**

* Total employment in this profession declined between 1981 and 1986.
-- Amount too small to be expressed.
Source: Statistics Canada, Census of Canada.

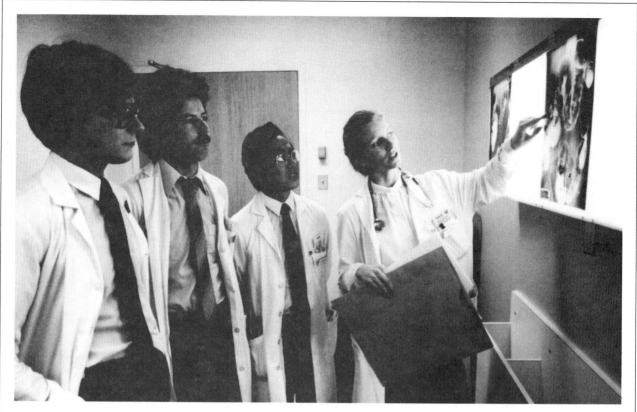

Women in other professions

Women's share of total employment in the 12 professions not classified as male-dominated also has risen. In 1986, 68.6% of people employed in these professions were women, up from 66.2% in 1981. This increase is a change from the 1971-1981 period when women's representation in these professions declined slightly.

However, the proportion of all female professionals working in the non-male-dominated sector has fallen. In 1986, 74% of professional women were in non-male-dominated occupations, down from 78% in 1981. This occurred largely because overall employment growth in these other professions was considerably slower than in the male-dominated sector. Between 1981 and 1986, total employment in the male-dominated professions increased 15%, compared with just an 8% rise in the other professions.

The slow overall employment growth in the non-male-dominated professions was largely attributable to slow growth in education. Between 1981 and 1986, the number of teachers increased only 2%, compared with a 29% rise in employment in other non-male-dominated professions.

As a result, the proportion of all female professionals in teaching-related professions has declined substantially, although teaching still accounts for more than half of all professional women. In 1986, 55%

of women in professional occupations were teachers, down significantly from 79% in 1971 and 62% in 1981.

Women make up well over half of those employed in all but one of the non-male-dominated professions. The exception was secondary school teachers, just under half (46%) of whom were women. In the remaining occupations, women's share of employment ranged from 56% of educational and vocational counsellors to 96% of dietitians and nutritionists.

Professional income: women still make less

Women in professional occupations have considerably higher employment incomes than other women. However, their average incomes remain well below those of comparable men, and the gap has not closed in recent years.

In 1986, the average employment income of women in male-dominated professions was almost $35,000, while those in the other professions made just over $30,000. In comparison, the figure for other women was under $20,000.

However, the average employment income of women working full-time in a male-dominated profession was just 71% of that of comparable men, while the figure was 83% in the other professions. As well, for both groups, the ratios were virtually unchanged from 1981.

Part of the difference in the employment income of women and men in professional occupations occurs because women tend to be younger, and as a result, have less seniority and lower earnings. Even so, women aged 25-34 in male-dominated professions had an average employment income that was only 81% that of their male counterparts in 1986.

Family and career

Working in the professions often involves considerable commitment and a demanding work schedule. As a result, many women entering these fields have different characteristics than other women and men in terms of blending family and career responsibilities. This is particularly true for women employed in male-dominated professions.

For example, in 1986, 24% of women aged 25 and over in male-dominated professions and 19% of those in other professions did not live in a family. In comparison, the figure was around 15% for both other women and men in the professions. Similarly, just 63% of married women in male-dominated professions had children, compared with over 70% of other women and male professionals.

WOMEN IN MALE DOMINATED PROFESSIONS

by Katherine Marshall

One of the most significant social trends in Canada over the past several decades has been the dramatic increase in the labour force participation of women. Concerns have been raised, however, that while the number of working women has increased, most are still employed in so-called women's occupations which are often characterized by poor pay and low status.

There is evidence, however, that in the period 1971-1981, women made substantial in-roads into what have traditionally been male-dominated professional occupations. These professions are of particular interest because they are generally among the best paid occupations in Canada, and most carry high levels of social status.

For the purposes of this report, professional occupations were those in which 45% or more of those employed in that occupation in 1981 had at least a bachelor's degree. For comparability, the same occupations were considered professional in 1971. A profession was classified as male-dominated if 65% or more of the people employed in it in 1971 were men. Overall, 46 occupational groups met the criterion for being professional; 34 of these were classified as male-dominated.

While women did make substantial gains in male-dominated professions in the 1970s, they were still significantly under-represented in these professions in 1981. As well, because these occupations often involve considerable commitment to the workforce and a demanding workload (elements not generally compatible with a woman's conventional family role), many women entering these fields had to adopt new patterns of behaviour. Women in male-dominated professions, for example, were more likely than women in other occupations to have never married, or if married, to have had fewer children or to be childless.

The total number of women employed in male-dominated professions in Canada rose from 30,410 in 1971 to 83,340 in 1981; this increase accounted for 29% of the overall growth in these occupations during this period. As a result, in 1981, women made up 19% of all those employed in male-

Women in non-male-dominated professions, 1971 and 1981

	Total number of women			Woman as a % of total growth in profession 1971-1981	Women as a % of total employment in profession	
	1971	1981	Percentage increase 1971-1981		1971	1981
Psychologists	2,035	4,600	126.0	56.1	48.7	52.6
Social workers	7,230	21,020	190.7	68.8	55.4	63.5
Supervisors in library, museum and archival sciences	600	1,440	140.0	79.2	47.4	62.1
Librarians and archivists	6,120	13,575	121.8	84.2	77.2	80.9
Educational and vocational counsellors	1,690	3,050	80.5	92.5	35.8	49.3
Elementary and kindergarten teachers	140,500	152,335	8.4	60.6	83.9	81.5
Secondary school teachers	56,615	63,320	11.8	27.3	47.2	43.8
Postsecondary school teachers	5,730	4,445	-22.4	27.6	49.4	63.9
Teachers of exceptional students	4,420	15,315	246.5	71.0	75.0	72.1
Physiotherapists, occupational and other therapists	5,895	12,525	112.5	86.9	82.9	85.0
Dieticians and nutritionists	2,010	3,280	63.2	91.7	95.9	94.3
Translators and interpreters	1,395	4,340	211.1	64.4	57.1	61.9
Total	**234,240**	**299,250**	**27.8**	**62.3**	**67.4**	**66.2**

Source: Statistics Canada, Census of Canada.

Women in Non-Male-Dominated Professions

By far, the vast majority of professional women work in the 12 occupational groups that were not male-dominated. In 1981, 78% of professional women, compared with just 30% of male professionals, were employed in one of these occupations. In fact, in 1981, 62% of all professional women were in teaching-related positions; however, this proportion was down from 79% in 1971. The female component of non-male-dominated professions ranged from 94% of dieticians and nutritionists, to 44% of secondary school teachers.

Between 1971 and 1981, the representation of women increased in 8 of the 12 non-male-dominated professions and declined in the others. Overall, while female representation dropped in only 5 of the 46 professions, because declines occured in the two largest female-dominated occupations, elementary and kindergarten, and secondary school teachers, the percentage of women in all professional occupations actually fell slightly from 43.1% in 1971 to 42.5% in 1981.

dominated professions, up from 11% in 1971.

During the 1971-1981 period, the proportional representation of women increased in all but 1 of the 34 professions identified as male-dominated. In addition, women accounted for the major share of the overall growth in employment in several of these occupations. In fact, women accounted for more than half of the total increase in employment in 6 of the 34 male-dominated professions. The largest increase occurred among pharmacists; women accounted for 78% of total employment growth in this profession over the 1971-1981 period.

The other professions in which women made up more than half of total employment growth were university teaching and related occupations[1] (55%), mathematicians, statisticians and actuaries (55%), management occupations in the social sciences and related fields (54%), optometrists (52%), and chemists (51%).

Women also accounted for more than 40% of the total increase in employment among community college and vocational school teachers (45%), university teachers[1] (44%), sociologists, anthropologists and other social scientists (43%), and administrators in teaching and related fields (41%).

As a result of this growth, the proportional representation of women in many of these professions also increased dramatically. The percentage of all pharmacists who were women, for example, rose from 25% in 1971 to 42% in 1981. In the same period, women as a proportion of all those employed in university teaching and related occupations increased from 30% to 46%, while for management positions in the social sciences and related fields, the increase was from 34% to 48%.

[1] University teachers include tenured professors. University teaching and related occupations include non-tenured professors and lecturers, teaching and laboratory assistants, and other instructors.

Women in male-dominated professions, 1971 and 1981

	Total number of women			Woman as a % of total growth in profession 1971-1981	Women as a % of total employment in profession	
	1971	1981	Percentage increase 1971-1981		1971	1981
Management occupations, natural sciences and engineering	70	800	1,042.9	7.6	2.7	6.6
Management occupations, social sciences and related fields	760	3,805	400.7	54.2	33.8	48.2
Administrators in teaching and related fields	6,445	9,120	41.5	41.2	21.5	25.0
Chemists	895	1,975	120.7	50.8	11.8	20.4
Geologists	145	795	448.3	23.2	2.9	10.3
Physicists	45	65	44.4	4.0	5.6	5.0
Meteorologists	40	90	125.0	27.0	4.9	9.0
Agriculturists and related scientists	330	1,220	269.7	31.8	5.1	13.2
Biologists and related scientists	830	2,330	180.7	36.4	26.1	31.9
Architects	125	560	348.0	14.0	3.0	7.7
Chemical engineers	65	340	423.1	12.9	1.8	5.9
Civil engineers	235	980	317.0	6.9	1.1	3.0
Electrical engineers	205	1,000	387.8	6.7	1.3	3.7
Mechanical engineers	100	380	280.0	4.5	0.8	1.9
Metallurgical engineers	15	50	233.3	3.8	1.7	2.8
Mining engineers	20	105	425.0	5.9	0.9	2.9
Petroleum engineers	15	225	1,400.0	6.7	1.1	4.9
Nuclear engineers	—	40	—	6.9	—	4.8
Other architects and engineers	140	1,640	1,071.4	15.0	4.0	12.2
Mathematicians, statisticians and actuaries	1,010	2,070	105.0	55.9	25.0	34.7
Economists	640	2,570	301.6	28.8	11.0	20.5
Sociologists, anthropologists and related social scientists	170	540	217.6	42.5	33.0	39.0
Judges and magistrates	75	220	193.3	18.6	5.7	10.5
Lawyers and notaries	860	5,390	526.7	24.9	5.2	15.5
Ministers of religion	900	1,785	98.3	26.9	4.5	7.6
University teachers	5,190	9,785	88.5	43.7	19.7	26.5
Other university teaching and related occupations	1,525	6,170	304.6	55.0	30.3	45.8
Community college and vocational school teachers	3,280	13,770	319.8	45.3	33.0	41.6
Physicians and surgeons	3,150	7,255	130.3	33.4	10.7	17.4
Dentists	330	860	160.6	13.6	4.9	8.1
Veterinarians	75	605	706.7	30.2	4.3	17.2
Osteopaths and chiropractors	80	340	325.0	22.0	7.3	14.9
Pharmacists	2,540	6,090	139.8	78.3	25.3	41.8
Optometrists	105	365	247.6	52.0	6.7	17.7
Total	**30,410**	**83,340**	**174.1**	**29.0**	**11.0**	**18.6**

Source: Statistics Canada, Census of Canada.

The proportional representation of women among optometrists, veterinarians, and lawyers and notaries also rose by 10 percentage points or more. However, even with these increases, women still made up fewer than one in five people employed in these professions in 1981.

Women also accounted for one-third of the total growth in the number of physicians and surgeons, the single, largest male-dominated professional group. As a result, the percentage of doctors who were women increased from 11% in 1971 to 17% in 1981.

On the other hand, women accounted for less than 10% of total employment growth in 9 of the 34 male-dominated professions during the 1971-1981 period. Women made up only 4% of the increase in the number of physicists, and just 8% of the increase in management occupations in engineering and the natural sciences. As well, about 8% of all employment growth in the various engineering professions in the 1971-1981 period was due to the increasing number of female engineers.

Because of these relatively slow growth rates, increases in the proportional representation of women in these professions were relatively small. In fact, the percentage of all physicists who were women actually fell slightly, from 6% in 1971 to 5% in 1981. This, however, was the only male-dominated profession in which the proportional representation of women declined.

The proportion of engineers who were women did increase; however, in 1981, only 4% of engineers, compared with 1% in 1971, were women. At the same time, the proportion of female managers in engineering and the natural sciences increased from 3% in 1971 to 7% in 1981.

Younger women were responsible for much of the increase in female participation in male-dominated professions. For example, women aged 25-34 accounted for almost half of the overall increase in female employment in these professions during the 1971-1981 period. In this period, the number of women aged 25-34 in male-dominated professions increased 274%. This compared with increases of 128% for women in all other ages groups and 57% for men aged 25-34.

The relative growth in employment of younger women in male-dominated professions was particularly strong in the prestigious categories of doctors, judges and lawyers, and university professors. Over the 1971-1981 period, the increase in the number of 25- to 34-year-old women in these professions was actually slightly greater than that for men in the same age group. Yet, despite this growth, women still made up just 20% of all doctors, judges, lawyers, and university teachers in 1981, and only 27% of those aged 25-34.

Socio-Economic Characteristics of Women in Male-Dominated Professions

Many of the social and economic characteristics of women employed in male-dominated professions differ from those of both men working in these professions and women employed in other occupations.

Compared with women in other occupations, those in male-dominated professions had the most education, the highest employment rate, and the greatest income. For example, women aged 25 and over employed full-time in male-dominated professions earned an average of $24,100 in 1980, compared with $21,100 for other professional women and $13,400 for women in non-professional occupations.

The average employment income of women in male-dominated professions, however, was considerably below that of

Selected family indicators, 1981				
	Women			Men in male-dominated professions
	Male-dominated professions	Other professions	Non-professionals	
% never married				
- 25-44 years	24.8	19.6	13.1	—
- 45 years and over	22.0	15.4	7.4	—
% who were spouses in husband-wife families	61.9	69.1	71.4	80.0
% of spouses in husband-wife families with children at home	59.8	67.9	69.0	69.9
% employed full-time				
- spouses in husband-wife families with children under 19 at home	50.8	46.2	47.8	93.2
- spouses in husband-wife families without children	73.6	70.3	62.6	82.0

— not available
Source: Statistics Canada, 1981 Census of Canada.

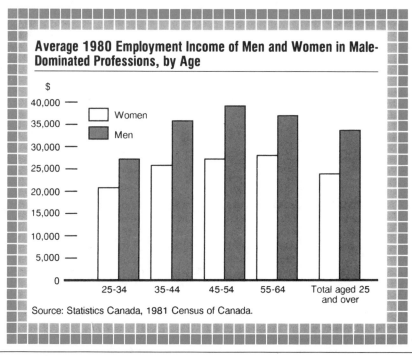

Average 1980 Employment Income of Men and Women in Male-Dominated Professions, by Age

Source: Statistics Canada, 1981 Census of Canada.

men in these occupations. The average earnings of women working full-time in male-dominated occupations were just 71% of those of comparable men in 1980. Part of this difference is explained by the relatively high proportion of women in these professions who were in the younger age groups; these women tend to have less seniority and lower average employment income than the older age groups. Also, women aged 25-34 in these professions had average employment incomes that were only 77% those of comparable men.

The family characteristics of women in male-dominated professions also differ from those of other groups. Women in these professions were the least likely of any occupational category, either male or female, to be in a husband-wife family. They were also more likely than other women to have never married. Among employed women aged 45 and over, for example, 22% of those in male-dominated professions had never married, compared with 15% of those in other professions and just 7% of non-professionals. As well, women in male-dominated professions had fewer children at home than other women and were more likely than other women not to have had children at all.

The differences in family characteristics also extend to a comparison of women and men in male-dominated professions. Women in these occupations were much less likely than men to be a spouse in a husband-wife family. In 1981, 62% of women in these occupations were married, compared with 80% of men. As well, those women in male-dominated professions who were in husband-wife families were less likely than comparable men to have children: 60% of married women, compared with 70% of married men, had children at home. In addition, only 51% of professional women in husband-wife families with children had full-time jobs, compared with 93% of similar men.

These figures indicate that it is still far easier for men to maintain both a professional career and a family. For many women, unlike men, the decision to pursue such a career may mean limiting marital or parental options.

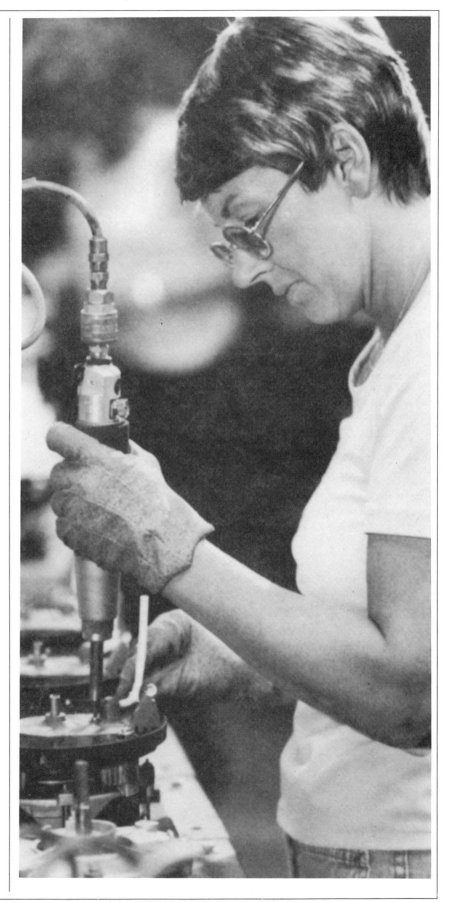

WOMEN TEACHING AT CANADIAN UNIVERSITIES

by Judith Hollands

Canadian universities have experienced phenomenal growth in the past twenty-five years. In this period, thousands of new teaching positions were created, many of which have been filled by women.[1] However, while women entered this profession at a more rapid rate than men, they remain a minority in Canadian university faculties. As well, they tend to be concentrated in the lower academic ranks, and at all ranks, are paid less than men.

Large proportional increases

The number of women teaching full-time in Canadian universities rose from fewer than 750 in 1960 to almost 6,000 in 1985. This was an increase of 713%. In the same period, the number of male university teachers rose 410%, from 5,700 to 29,200.

Most of the growth in the number of both male and female university teachers occurred between 1960 and 1975 when the baby-boom population flooded into Canadian universities. During this period, female faculty increased 487%, compared with 363% for male faculty.

The number of women teaching in Canadian universities continued to rise more rapidly than the number of men in the late 1970s and 1980s, although increases for both in this period were considerably below those of the previous decade and a half. Between 1975 and 1985, the number of women teaching at the university level rose 39% while the number of men increased just 10%.

Despite the relatively large proportional increases in the number of women teaching at Canadian universities, women remain a minority in this profession. In 1985, they made up just 17% of all full-time university

[1] This article refers only to full-time university teachers.

teachers; this was a gain of only 6 percentage points from 1960 when 11% of full-time faculty were women.

Women a minority in all disciplines

The majority of both male and female university teachers are employed in four broad fields of study: social sciences, health sciences, humanities, and education. A considerably higher proportion of female than male faculty, though, are concentrated in these disciplines. In 1985, 81% of all female faculty (compared with 64% of men) taught in one of these fields.

Women, however, are a minority in all disciplines. In 1985, their share of all full-time positions ranged from roughly one-quarter of those in education (26%), health sciences (24%), and fine and applied arts (24%) to just 6% of those in mathematics and physical sciences, and 2% of those in engineering and applied sciences. In addition, 21% of teachers in humanities, 17% of those in biological sciences, and 16% of those in social sciences were women.

The number of women as a percentage of all teachers has risen in each of these disciplines in the last decade. The largest increases, over four percentage points, were in social sciences, humanities, and fine and applied arts. The smallest increase, just one percentage point, occurred in biological sciences.

The wide range in the proportion of women teaching in various academic fields reflects, in part, that women are more likely to earn graduate degrees in some disciplines than in others. In 1986, for example, just over half (51%) of all doctoral degree recipients in education were women, as were more than a third of those in social sciences (37%), health professions (35%), and humanities (34%). Women's representation among doctoral graduates, however, was considerably lower in biological sciences (23%), mathematics and physical sciences (15%), and, especially, engineering and applied sciences (3%).

More women teachers in lower academic ranks

Generally, women teaching at Canadian universities make up a much greater proportion of all full-time faculty in the lower academic ranks than they do at higher levels. In 1985, women made up 44% of lecturers and instructors and 29% of assistant professors. In comparison, only 16% of associate professors and just 6% of full professors were women.

As well, women's share of full professorships in 1985 was just 2 percentage points higher than in 1960 when 4% of full pro-

fessors were women. In the same period, the proportion of associate professors who were women increased 6 percentage points, while the figure rose 17 points for assistant professors and 20 points for lecturers and instructors.

The slow movement of women into the higher academic ranks may be attributable, in part, to the generally long time lag between entry into university teaching and attainment of full or associate professor

status. Because the entry of large numbers of women into Canadian university faculties occurred only recently, a large proportion of them have not yet had time to acquire the seniority necessary to advance into the higher ranks.

Fewer female faculty with doctoral degrees

Another reason why women are concentrated in the lower academic ranks is that fewer female than male teachers have

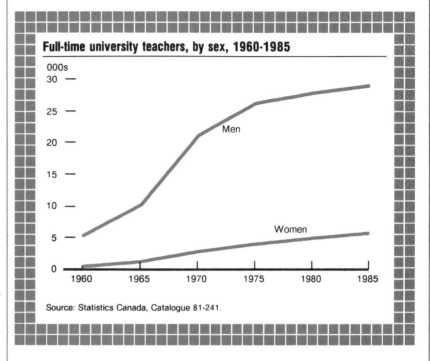

Full-time university teachers, by sex, 1960-1985

Source: Statistics Canada, Catalogue 81-241.

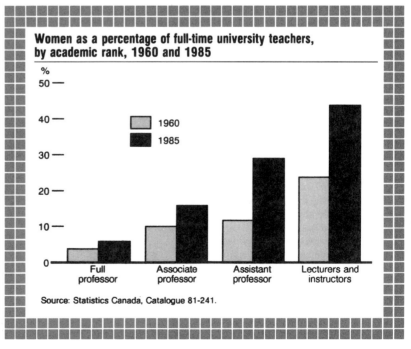

Women as a percentage of full-time university teachers, by academic rank, 1960 and 1985

Source: Statistics Canada, Catalogue 81-241.

doctoral degrees. In 1985, 47% of all female faculty compared with 69% of male teachers had doctorates. The difference in qualifications, however, has been closing. In 1975, 34% of female faculty members had doctoral degrees compared with 62% of male teachers.

A much smaller proportion of female than male university teachers with doctorates, though, are full professors. In 1985, just 20% of all female teachers with doctorates compared with 47% of similarly educated male teachers were full professors. Again, much of this difference may be attributable to differences in experience and senority.

Women's salaries lower

The concentration of female faculty in the lower academic ranks is reflected in lower median salaries for women teaching at Canadian universities. In 1985, the median salary of full-time female teachers was $41,300, about $10,000 less than the median salary for men ($51,400).

As well, the median salary of women university teachers has changed little in relation to that of their male counterparts in the last decade. In 1985, the median salary of female faculty was 81% that of men, down slightly from 82% in 1975.

While much of the overall difference in salary between male and female university teachers is attributable to differences in academic rank, median salaries of female faculty were also lower than those of men at each rank. As well, the higher the rank the larger was the difference. In 1985, the median salary of female full professors was $3,100 below that of male full professors. At the same time, female associate professors made about $1,900 less than men in this category, while the differences were $1,100 for assistant professors and $1,000 for lecturers and instructors.

The differences between the median salary of male and female university teachers at the various academic ranks remained when just faculty with doctoral degrees were compared. Female full professors with doctorates made $2,800 less than similarly educated male professors. For associate professors, the difference was $1,800 and for assistant professors it was $1,200. The comparison of the median salaries of lecturers and instructors with doctorates was not meaningful because of the small numbers of both men and women in this category.

As mentioned previously, the experience and seniority of men and women teaching in university differ, and these factors may explain some or all of the salary differences.

Female faculty also make less than their male counterparts in each of the major fields of study in which women are concentrated, although the size of the gap varies considerably. For example, the difference between the median salary of male and female full professors with doctorates was $3,800 in social sciences, $3,400 in health sciences, and $2,800 in education, but only $1,600 in humanities.

WOMEN PARENTING ALONE

by Maureen Moore

The number of lone-parent families, most of which are headed by women, has increased sharply in Canada in the last several decades. At the same time, the number of children being raised in these families has also risen dramatically. In fact, over one million Canadian children are currently living in families with just one parent.

Growth in the number of lone-parent families is of special concern because these families, particularly those headed by women, face a variety of economic disadvantages. For example, over half of lone-parent families headed by women, have incomes that fall below official Statistics Canada's Low-Income Cut-Off lines. As well, lone-parent families headed by women generally have less desirable living accommodations and fewer basic household facilities than other families.

The Growth of Lone-Parent Families

Between 1931 and 1986, the number of lone-parent families in Canada grew from 291,900 to 853,600. The increase, however, has been particularly rapid since the mid-1960s. Over the period 1966-1986, the number of lone-parent families rose 130%, while husband-wife families increased only 42%. As a result, by 1986, families headed by lone parents represented 13% of all families. This was up from 8% in 1966, but was still below the level recorded in 1931 (14%).

The percentage of all children under age 25 living in lone-parent families also increased substantially in the past two decades. In 1986, about 1.2 million children — more than 14% of all children in Canada — lived in lone-parent families.

In comparison, in 1966 fewer than 7% of all Canadian children lived in lone-parent families.

Lone-Parent Families Headed by Women

Most lone parents are women. In 1986, more than 700,000 lone-parent families, or 82% of the total, were headed by women. Women also constituted the majority of lone parents in every age group. The predominance of women as lone-parent family-heads was particularly great in younger age brackets.

Women made up 94% of all lone parents aged 15-24 in 1986, compared with 85% of those aged 25-44, and 77% of lone parents aged 45 and over.

Changing Paths to Lone Parenthood

The principal circumstances that result in women becoming lone parents have changed over the last few decades. Specifically, the percentage of female lone parents who are widowed has declined, while the proportions who are divorced or who have never married have increased.

In 1951, about two-thirds of female lone parents were widowed. By 1986, however, over half (57%) of female lone parents were either separated or divorced, while the percentage who were widowed had fallen to 28%.

The increase in the proportion of divorced female lone parents was especially sharp after the Divorce Act was passed in 1968. In fact, divorced mothers made up the largest single component of all lone-parent mothers (30%) in 1986; in comparison, in 1951 just 3% of lone-parent mothers had been divorced. In the same period, the percentage of female lone parents who were separated actually declined slightly, from 29% to 28%.

The proportion of lone-parent mothers who have never married has also increased substantially. Never-married women made up 15% of all female lone parents in 1986, up from just 1% in 1951. The marked growth in the proportion of never-married female lone parents reflects the overall rise in the number of out-of-wedlock births. These births more than quadrupled, from about 14,000 in 1951 to 59,600 in 1985. In this period, out-of-wedlock births as a percentage of total births increased from less than 4% to more than 16%.

The marital status of female lone parents is associated with their ages. Three-quarters of those who had never married, for example, were younger than age 35, while separated and divorced

Lone parents by age and sex, 1986

Age Group	Women Number	Women %	Men Number	Men %	Total Number	Total %
15-24	49,670	94	3,005	6	52,665	100
25-44	363,950	85	63,050	15	427,005	100
45-64	209,570	76	65,890	24	275,460	100
65 and over	78,715	80	19,800	20	98,510	100
Total	701,900	82	151,745	18	853,645	100

Source: Statistics Canada, 1986 Census of Canada.

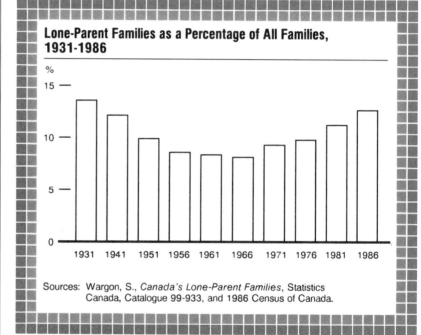

Lone-Parent Families as a Percentage of All Families, 1931-1986

Sources: Wargon, S., *Canada's Lone-Parent Families*, Statistics Canada, Catalogue 99-933, and 1986 Census of Canada.

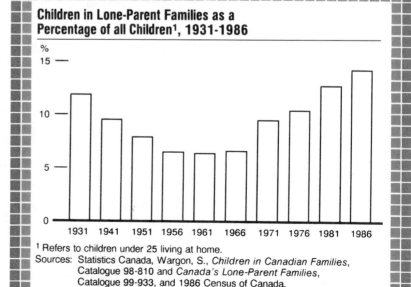

Children in Lone-Parent Families as a Percentage of all Children[1], 1931-1986

[1] Refers to children under 25 living at home.
Sources: Statistics Canada, Wargon, S., *Children in Canadian Families*, Catalogue 98-810 and *Canada's Lone-Parent Families*, Catalogue 99-933, and 1986 Census of Canada.

lone parents were clustered in their thirties and forties. Widows tended to be somewhat older; in 1986, about two-thirds of widowed lone parents were aged 55 or over.

Family Histories of Female Lone Parents and Wives[1]

The majority of female lone parents at one time were either married or lived in a common-law relationship. However, according to Statistics Canada's 1984 Family History Survey, their marital and childbearing patterns differed somewhat from those of women who were married or partners in a common-law relationship at the time of the survey.

Female lone parents tended to have entered their first marital or common-law union at a younger age than wives: 28% of lone parents had been in a union before they were 19, compared with 24% of wives. This difference was most noticeable among young women. Of women aged 20-24, 80% of lone parents had been in a union before they were 19, compared with 53% of wives.

Female lone parents were also more likely than wives to have lived common-law. Twenty-two percent of female lone parents had been in a common-law partnership, compared with 17% of wives.

As well, a higher percentage of female lone parents than wives entered a marital or common-law union around the time they gave birth. More than a quarter (26%) of female lone parents gave birth before or during the year they entered the union, compared with 16% of wives.

[1] Wives refers to women who are spouses or common-law partners with children.

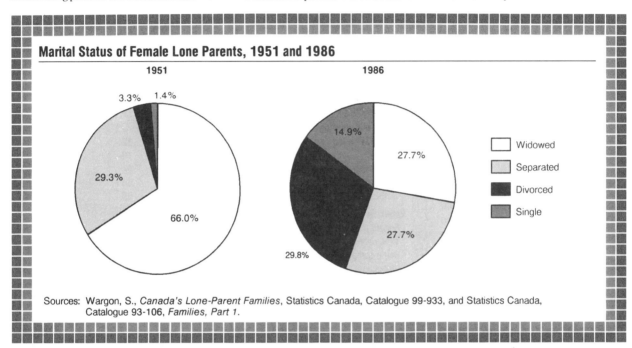

Marital Status of Female Lone Parents, 1951 and 1986

1951

3.3% 1.4%
29.3%
66.0%

1986

14.9%
27.7%
27.7%
29.8%

- Widowed
- Separated
- Divorced
- Single

Sources: Wargon, S., *Canada's Lone-Parent Families*, Statistics Canada, Catalogue 99-933, and Statistics Canada, Catalogue 93-106, *Families, Part 1*.

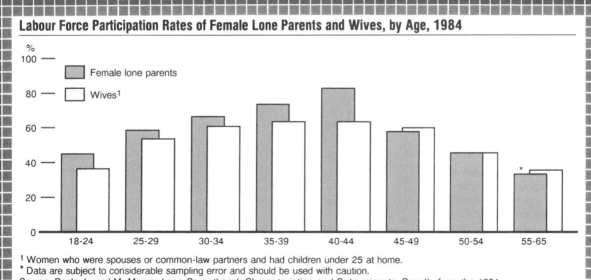

Labour Force Participation Rates of Female Lone Parents and Wives, by Age, 1984

%

- Female lone parents
- Wives[1]

18-24 25-29 30-34 35-39 40-44 45-49 50-54 55-65

[1] Women who were spouses or common-law partners and had children under 25 at home.
* Data are subject to considerable sampling error and should be used with caution.
Source: Poole, I., and M. Moore, *Lone Parenthood: Characteristics and Determinants, Results from the 1984 Family History Survey*, Statistics Canada, Catalogue 99-961.

Female lone parents also tended to have had a child earlier in life than did wives. Whereas 26% of female lone parents had their first child before they were 20, the comparable proportion for wives was 20%.

Education and Labour Force Characteristics of Female Lone Parents

Female lone parents generally had less formal education than wives. Just 24% of female lone parents, as opposed to 31% of wives, had at least some postsecondary training. In every age group, the percentage of wives who had attended a postsecondary institution exceeded the corresponding proportion for female lone parents.

On the other hand, a higher proportion of female lone parents than wives were in the labour force. For example, the 1984 labour force participation rate among women aged 18-24, was 45% for lone parents and 37% for wives. Labour force participation peaked for both groups among those aged 40-44, but at 83%, the participation rate for female lone parents was much greater than that for wives (64%). However, for women aged 45-64, the labour force participation rate for wives slightly exceeded that for lone parents.

A higher percentage of female lone parents began working only after the birth of their first child. Of those women who had ever worked, 30% of lone parents, compared with 17% of wives, started working after they first gave birth. As well, once in the labour force, female lone parents were more likely than wives to work continuously.

Income

The average income of female-headed lone-parent families was less than half that of husband-wife families with children. In 1985, lone-parent families headed by women had an average income of just over $20,000, compared with almost $44,000 for husband-wife families with children.

The sources of income of lone-parent families and husband-wife families with children also differ significantly. While earnings were the main source of income for both, female lone-parent families derived only 64% of their total income from earnings, compared with 87% for husband-wife families. On the other hand, government assistance, including family and youth allowances, unemployment insurance, social assistance, and pension benefits, made

	Female lone-parent households	Husband-wife households with children under age 18
	%	
Accommodations		
Renting	72	27
Single-detached dwelling	30	66
Built 1960 or before	40	35
Vehicles		
Automobiles		
—One	49	55
—Two or more	6	31
Vans and trucks	5	29
Comfort and safety		
Air conditioner	11	17
Smoke detector	63	80
Portable fire extinguisher	18	43
Cooking and cleaning		
Microwave oven	22	43
Freezer	40	70
Dishwasher	24	50
Automatic washing machine	64	86
Clothes dryer	60	84
Entertainment		
Record player	71	84
Tape recorder	60	72
Home computer	9	17
Videocassette recorder	22	49
Pay television	9	11
Black and white television only	8	3

Living accommodations and household facilities of female lone-parent households and husband-wife households with children, 1986

Sources: Statistics Canada, Catalogue 13-218, *Household Facilities by Income and Other Characteristics*, and Household Surveys Division, unpublished data.

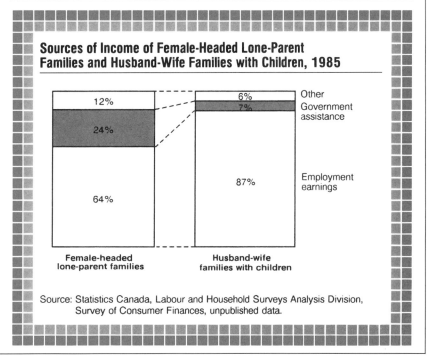

Sources of Income of Female-Headed Lone-Parent Families and Husband-Wife Families with Children, 1985

Female-headed lone-parent families: Other 12%, Government assistance 24%, Employment earnings 64%

Husband-wife families with children: Other 6%, Government assistance 7%, Employment earnings 87%

Source: Statistics Canada, Labour and Household Surveys Analysis Division, Survey of Consumer Finances, unpublished data.

up almost one-quarter of the total income of lone-parent families headed by women. In comparison, government transfers accounted for only 7% of the income of husband-wife families with children.

Lone-parent families headed by women had the highest incidence of low income of all family types. As well, the percentage of these families with low incomes increased in the early 1980s. In 1985, 60% of all lone-parent families headed by women had incomes that fell below Statistics Canada's Low-Income Cut-Offs. This was up from 53% in 1981. In contrast, just 11% of husband-wife families with children had incomes below the Low-Income Cut-Offs in 1985.

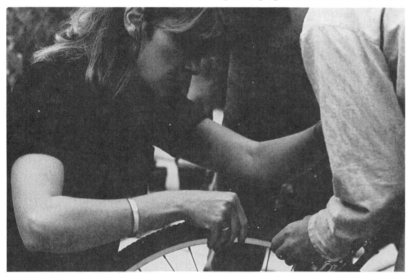

Family Expenditures

A survey of 17 major Canadian cities showed that in 1984, female-headed lone-parent families spent almost half (48%) of their before-tax income on basic necessities such as food, shelter and household operations. For husband-wife families with children, these expenditures accounted for just over a third (34%) of pre-tax income.

Relative income levels were also reflected in differences between the living accommodations and household facilities of lone-parent and other families. In 1986, just 30% of female-headed lone-parent families were living in single-detached houses; the corresponding figure for other families with children was 66%. As well, 72% of female-headed lone-parent families were renters, compared with 27% of other families. The dwellings of lone-parent families were also somewhat older than those of other families.

Virtually every household in Canada, whether lone-parent or not, had major household appliances and communications equipment such as refrigerators, telephones, radios and television sets. Lone-parent families headed by women, however, were less likely than other families with children to have appliances such as freezers, dishwashers and clothes dryers. Only 40% of lone-parent households, compared with 70% of other family households, for example, had a freezer. The proportions with a dishwasher were 24% for lone-parent families and 50% for other families.

This article combines information from several Statistics Canada sources. Long-term trends in both the number of lone-parent families and the number of children in these families are from the Census. Details on lone parents' marital and childbearing histories, as well as their education and labour force experience, are from the 1984 Family History Survey. Information about spending patterns is derived from the Survey of Family Expenditures. Data on dwelling characteristics and household facilities are from the Survey of Household Facilities and Equipment, and income figures are from the Survey of Consumer Finances.

Because these sources use different methodologies and definitions, the results are not strictly comparable. All sources define lone parents as people who do not live with a spouse or common-law partner, but who have at least one child still at home. However, the 1984 Family History Survey included only lone parents aged 18-65, while the other sources included lone parents of all ages. In the Census, children at home included those of any age (unless otherwise specified) provided they were unmarried. The Family History Survey, however, had an upper age limit of 24 on children at home, while the Survey of Household Facilities and Equipment and the Survey of Consumer Finances included only children under age 18.

Selected characteristics of female lone parents and wives, 1984		
	Female lone parents	Wives[1]
	%	
Less than age 19 at first union	28	4
Ever in a common-law union	22	17
Less than age 20 at birth of first child	26	20
Union before or in same year as birth of first child	26	16
At least some postsecondary education	24	31
Less than age 20 at labour force entry[2]	57	59
Started working only after birth of first child[2]	30	17
Labour force participation rate	61	57
Work interruptions lasting at least one year[2] (number)	0.8	1.0

[1] Women who were spouses or common-law partners, and had children younger than 25 at home.
[2] Includes only those who ever worked.
Source: Poole, I., and Moore, M., *Lone Parenthood: Characteristics and Determinants, Results from the 1984 Family History Survey*, Statistics Canada, Catalogue 99-961.

Conveniences and entertainment equipment such as microwave ovens, home computers and videocassette recorders, were also found less frequently in the homes of female lone parents than in other family households with children. While just 22% of lone-parent homes were equipped with a microwave oven, the proportion for other homes was 43%. Nine percent of lone-parent households had a home computer, and 22% had a videocassette recorder. The proportions for other family households were 17% and 49%, respectively.

Safety devices were also not as common in lone-parent homes as in households occupied by other families. Smoke detectors were installed in 63% of lone-parent homes, compared with 80% of other homes. The proportions with a fire extinguisher were 18% for lone-parent families and 43% for other households.

Lone-parent families headed by women were also less likely than other families to have an automobile. In 1984, 55% of female-headed lone-parent families had a car; the corresponding figure for other families with children was 86%.

Conclusion

Women of all ages are lone parents. While the characteristics of these women and the circumstances that produced their situations differ, it is possible to outline a general profile of female lone parents. Typically, the majority are either separated or divorced women who entered unions and started childbearing at relatively young ages. They also tend to have less education, but are more likely to be in the labour force than are wives. Thus, lone-parent mothers must raise children while facing a double disadvantage: they lack support from a spouse, yet have fewer job skills by which to gain an income appropriate to the task.

The income of lone-parent families headed by women is substantially below that of other families. This is reflected in the high percentage of such families with incomes below official Low-Income Cut-Offs and with living accommodations and household resources that are inferior to those of other families.

BIRTHS TO UNMARRIED WOMEN

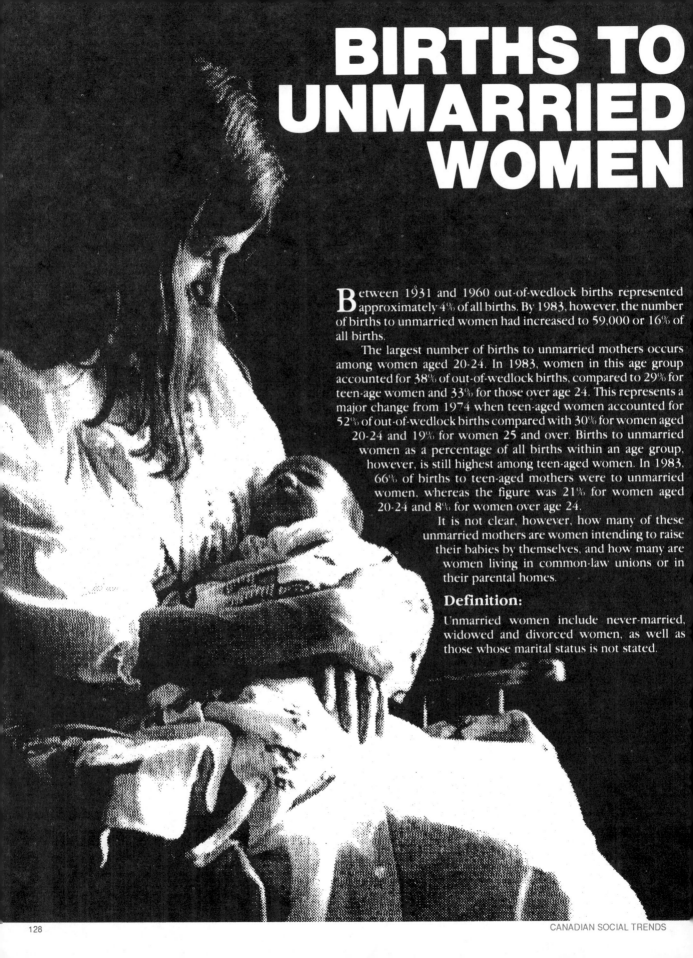

Between 1931 and 1960 out-of-wedlock births represented approximately 4% of all births. By 1983, however, the number of births to unmarried women had increased to 59,000 or 16% of all births.

The largest number of births to unmarried mothers occurs among women aged 20-24. In 1983, women in this age group accounted for 38% of out-of-wedlock births, compared to 29% for teen-age women and 33% for those over age 24. This represents a major change from 1974 when teen-aged women accounted for 52% of out-of-wedlock births compared with 30% for women aged 20-24 and 19% for women 25 and over. Births to unmarried women as a percentage of all births within an age group, however, is still highest among teen-aged women. In 1983, 66% of births to teen-aged mothers were to unmarried women, whereas the figure was 21% for women aged 20-24 and 8% for women over age 24.

It is not clear, however, how many of these unmarried mothers are women intending to raise their babies by themselves, and how many are women living in common-law unions or in their parental homes.

Definition:

Unmarried women include never-married, widowed and divorced women, as well as those whose marital status is not stated.

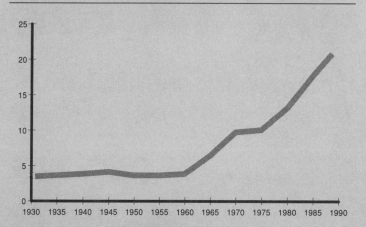

Live Births to Unmarried Mothers as a Percentage of Total Live Births, 1931–1987

Source: Statistics Canada, Catalogue No. 84–204, *Vital Statistics, Volume 1, Births and Deaths*; and unpublished data from *Vital Statistics*.

Out-of-Wedlock Births to Indian Mothers

Approximately 10% of births to unmarried mothers are births to Canadian Registered Indians. The number of births outside marriage has been increasing as a proportion of total Registered Indian births. It is estimated that in 1968 approximately 33% of Registered Indian births were outside marriage, a proportion which increased to 60%, or approximately 5,800 births by 1981.

Until recently Registered Indian women have lost their legal Indian status when they married someone who was not a Registered Indian. As a result, Registered Indian women may have chosen to live common-law to avoid losing their legal status for themselves or their children.

Live Births to Unmarried Women by Age Group, 1974–1987

	Age Groups		
	Under 20	20–24	25 and over[1]
	Numbers of births		
1974[2]	10,569	6,096	3,790
1975[3]	13,159	7,640	4,936
1976[3]	13,420	8,105	5,004
1977	17,554	12,857	9,296
1978	17,507	13,782	9,581
1979	17,349	15,225	10,918
1980	17,777	16,981	12,866
1981	17,745	18,798	14,672
1982	18,311	21,193	16,782
1983	16,889	22,682	19,401
1984[4]	16,445	23,773	21,544
1985[4]	15,975	25,008	24,525
1986[4]	16,194	25,922	26,586
1987[4]	16,297	26,473	29,943
	As a % of total out-of-wedlock births		
1974[2]	51.7	29.8	18.5
1975[3]	51.1	29.7	19.2
1976[3]	50.6	30.6	18.9
1977	44.2	32.4	23.4
1978	42.8	33.7	23.4
1979	39.9	35.0	25.1
1980	37.3	35.7	27.0
1981	34.7	36.7	28.7
1982	32.5	37.7	29.8
1983	28.6	38.5	32.9
1984[4]	26.6	38.5	34.9
1985[4]	24.4	38.2	37.4
1986[4]	23.6	37.7	38.7
1987[4]	22.4	36.4	41.2

Source: Statistics Canada, Catalogue 84–204, *Vital Statistics, Volume I, Births and Deaths*, and Health Division, Unpublished Data.
[1] Includes "not stated" ages.
[2] Excludes Quebec and Alberta.
[3] Excludes Quebec.
[4] Excludes Newfoundland.

Live Births to Unmarried Women as a Percentage of Births in Her Age Group, 1974-1987

	Age Groups			
	Under 20	20-24	25 and over[1]	All ages
1974[2]	36.3	8.2	3.2	9.3
1975[3]	39.9	8.8	3.7	10.1
1976[3]	43.0	9.5	3.7	10.5
1977	48.4	11.1	4.6	11.3
1978	51.4	12.2	4.7	11.7
1979	54.3	13.5	5.2	12.2
1980	56.8	15.1	5.9	13.2
1981	60.5	17.0	6.6	14.2
1982	64.2	19.3	7.4	15.5
1983	66.0	21.2	8.4	16.2
1984[4]	68.9	23.0	8.9	16.8
1985[4]	71.6	25.4	10.0	17.8
1986[4]	74.8	27.9	10.6	18.8
1987[4]	76.8	30.6	11.8	20.1

Source: Statistics Canada, Catalogue 84-204, *Vital Statistics, Volume I, Births and Deaths*, and unpublished data from *Vital Statistics*.
[1] Includes "not stated" ages.
[2] Excludes Quebec and Ontario.
[3] Excludes Quebec.
[4] Excludes Newfoundland.

THERAPEUTIC ABORTION IN CANADA

by Betsy MacKenzie

Editorial Note: In January 1988, a Supreme Court decision found that the abortion provisions of the Criminal Code were in violation of the Charter of Rights and Freedoms and were accordingly struck down.

The therapeutic abortion rate in Canada increased throughout the 1970s and peaked in 1979. A steady decline thereafter brought the 1985 rate down to the level of a decade earlier. In general, the rate of legal abortions in Canada has been lower than in most other industrialized countries.

Therapeutic abortion rates varied considerably across Canada, with residents of the Northwest Territories and British Columbia experiencing the highest levels in 1985, and residents of Prince Edward Island and New Brunswick, the lowest. During the 1975-1985 period, therapeutic abortion rates for women under age 25 were higher than for women aged 25 and over. A rising majority of women obtaining therapeutic abortions were single. The trend was toward earlier abortions with most occurring before 13 weeks' gestation.

Canadian Hospitals Performing Therapeutic Abortions

Therapeutic abortion committees were established at 250 Canadian hospitals in 1985, down from 274 in 1975.

In each province, the hospitals that provided the majority of abortions are in major cities or metropolitan areas. During 1985, three-quarters (74%) of therapeutic abortions were performed in just 15% of the hospitals with committees. In addition to women in the immediate vicinity, hospitals with committees served women coming from rural areas with no hospital, and those from centres without committees. In 1985, 15% of Canadian hospitals with committees performed no therapeutic abortions.

Trends in Therapeutic Abortion

The therapeutic abortion rate per 1,000 women aged 15-44 rose from 9.6 in 1975 to a high of 11.6 in 1979. By 1985, the rate had fallen to 9.9, close to what it had been in 1975.

Expressed per 100 live births, therapeutic abortions went from 13.7 in 1975 to almost 18 in the late seventies and early eighties, but by 1985, had dropped to 16.2.

The annual number of therapeutic abortions performed in Canadian hospitals with therapeutic abortion committees rose from 49,390 in 1975 to 66,319 in 1982. Numbers then declined to 60,956 in 1985.

Provincial Differences

Therapeutic abortion rates varied widely among the provinces and territories. Between 1975 and 1985, rates were highest for residents of British Columbia, the two territories, Alberta, and Ontario. Residents of Prince Edward Island, New Brunswick, and Newfoundland had the lowest rates.

Most provinces and territories mirrored the rise and fall in national therapeutic abortion rates between 1975 and 1985. The exceptions were Manitoba and the Northwest Territories, where 1985 rates were higher than in any other year since 1975, and Prince Edward Island, which experienced an almost steady decline.

Provincial distribution of hospitals with therapeutic abortion committees, 1975 and 1985		
	1975	**1985**
Canada	**274**	**250**
Newfoundland	6	5
Prince Edward Island	2	1
Nova Scotia	13	11
New Brunswick	8	8
Quebec	35	38
Ontario	110	95
Manitoba	9	8
Saskatchewan	10	8
Alberta	25	22
British Columbia	54	52
Yukon	1	1
Northwest Territories	1	1

Source: Statistics Canada, Catalogue 82-211.

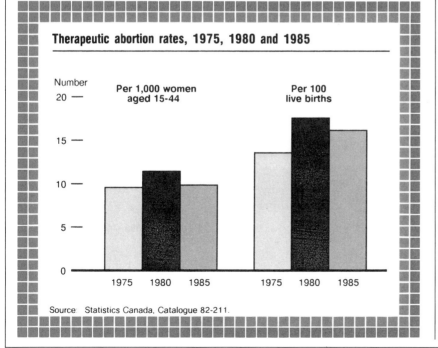

Therapeutic abortion rates, 1975, 1980 and 1985

Number

Per 1,000 women aged 15-44

Per 100 live births

20 —

15 —

10 —

5 —

0 —

1975 1980 1985   1975 1980 1985

Source: Statistics Canada, Catalogue 82-211.

Canada's Abortion Law, 1969-1988

This article refers to therapeutic (legal) abortions authorized under Section 18 of the Criminal Law Amendment Act, 1969, which came into force on August 26, 1969. This law permitted pregnancy termination only in accredited and/or approved hospitals and only if a hospital therapeutic abortion committee of not fewer than three physicians, appointed by the hospital board, certified by a majority of its members that continuation of the pregnancy "would or would be likely" to endanger the life or health of the pregnant woman.

Age Differences

Throughout the 1975-1985 period, the incidence of therapeutic abortion was higher among women younger than age 25. The 1985 rates per 1,000 women were 14.5 and 17.3 among 15-19-year-olds and 20-24-year-olds, respectively. Rates declined in each successive age group. For example, the rate for women aged 25-29 was 11.2, but for the 40-44 age group, just 1.6.

Abortion rates for each age group under 35 followed the rise and fall of the national trend between 1975 and 1985, and ended the period at a somewhat higher level than at the beginning. The rate for 20-24-year-olds showed the greatest overall increase: from 13.8 to 17.3 per 1,000 women. In contrast, rates for the 35 and over age group dropped almost steadily and were lower in 1985 than in 1975.

Higher Percentage of Single Women

Single women accounted for a rising percentage of therapeutic abortions during the 1975-1985 period. The percentage of all therapeutic abortions that were obtained by single women rose from 58% to 67%. At the same time, the proportion of married women fell from 31% to 22%, and those performed on women who were divorced, separated, widowed

Interpretation of Canadian Therapeutic Abortion Data

Information on therapeutic abortions in this article was collected in hospitals and transmitted to Statistics Canada mostly through provincial health departments. These numbers exclude abortions obtained by Canadian women in non-hospital settings or in other countries. Nevertheless, Statistics Canada also collects similar information from border states in the U.S.A., which showed that 2,798 Canadians obtained legal abortions there in 1985. Pregnancies terminated by methods such as the "morning after pill" are excluded.

Discrepancies in the definition of abortion affect data collection. While the Criminal Code did not stipulate a gestational time limit, provincial regulations required that terminations after 20 weeks be recorded as a stillbirth. Consequently, therapeutic abortions were under-reported.

Therapeutic abortions performed by Canadian hospitals with therapeutic abortion committees, 1985

	Percent of 250 hospitals	Percent of 60,956[1] therapeutic abortions
Abortion range	%	
0 abortions	14.6	–
1- 20 abortions	23.3	0.9
21- 50 abortions	10.3	1.4
51-100 abortions	10.3	3.1
101-200 abortions	10.7	6.6
201-400 abortions	11.9	13.6
400+ abortions	15.4	74.4
Not reported	3.6	–

[1] Includes foreign residents and residence not reported.
– nil or zero
Source: Statistics Canada, Catalogue 82-211.

Therapeutic abortions, 1975–1985

Year	Number of therapeutic abortions[1]	Therapeutic abortions per 1,000 women aged 15-44[2]	Therapeutic abortions per 100 live births[2]
1975	49,390	9.6	13.7
1976	54,536	10.3	15.1
1977	57,620	10.6	15.9
1978	62,351	11.3	17.4
1979	65,135	11.6	17.8
1980	65,855	11.5	17.7
1981	65,127	11.1	17.5
1982	66,319	11.1	17.8
1983	61,800	10.2	16.5
1984	62,291	10.2	16.5
1985	60,956	9.9	16.2

[1] Includes foreign residents and residence not reported, together totalling 0.2% or less of all therapeutic abortions.
[2] Based on Canadian residents only.
Source: Statistics Canada, Catalogue 82-211.

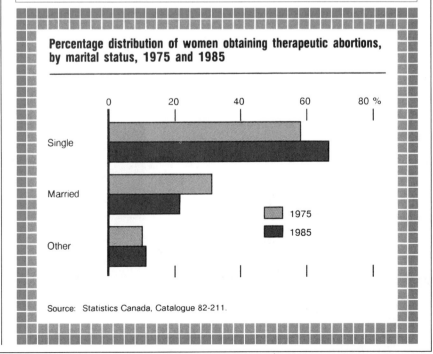

Percentage distribution of women obtaining therapeutic abortions, by marital status, 1975 and 1985

Source: Statistics Canada, Catalogue 82-211.

Therapeutic abortion rate, by age, 1975 to 1985

Per 1,000 women

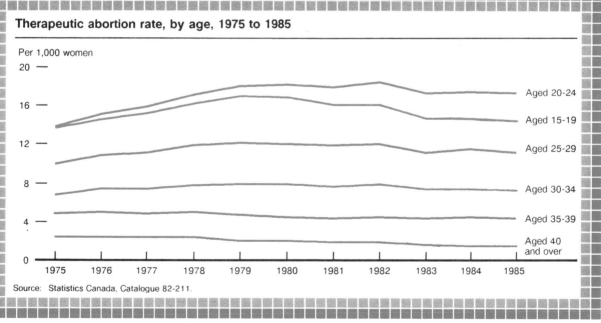

Aged 20-24

Aged 15-19

Aged 25-29

Aged 30-34

Aged 35-39

Aged 40
and over

1975 1976 1977 1978 1979 1980 1981 1982 1983 1984 1985

Source: Statistics Canada, Catalogue 82-211.

or living common-law remained almost unchanged, increasing slightly from 10% to 11%.

A Trend Toward Earlier Therapeutic Abortions

While the majority of therapeutic abortions continued to be performed between 9 and 12 weeks' gestation, the trend between 1975 and 1985 was toward earlier pregnancy terminations. The proportion occurring before 9 weeks rose from 22% in 1975 to 32% in 1985. Those performed between 9 and 12 weeks declined slightly from 59% to 57% of the total, while those performed after 12 weeks fell more sharply from 19% to 11%.

Marriage

CHANGES IN LIVING ARRANGEMENTS

by Mary Sue Devereaux

While the majority of the population still lives in families, results from the 1986 Census show ongoing changes in the living arrangements of Canadians. For example, increases in the number of lone-parent families, common-law couples, and one-person households have been particularly large. At the same time, average family size continues to decline.

Smaller proportion in families

In 1986, 84% of Canadians lived in families. This was down slightly from 85% in 1981 and continued a decline that began in 1966, when more than 88% of the population lived in families.

Although the proportion of Canadians living in families has dropped, the actual number of families rose 6% from 6.3 million in 1981 to 6.7 million in 1986. This increase, however, was much smaller than those of earlier years. For example, the number of families grew 13% between 1971 and 1976, and 10% between 1976 and 1981.

Varying growth rates

Over the 1981-1986 period, the number of lone-parent families and common-law unions increased much faster than traditional husband-wife families. During these five years, the number of lone-parent families rose 20% from 714,000 to 854,000, and common-law unions grew 37% from 357,000 to 487,000. In comparison, the number of traditional husband-wife families increased only 3% from 5.3 million to just under 5.4 million.

Consequently, lone parents and common-law couples accounted for a larger proportion of all families in 1986 than in 1981. Lone-parent families represented 13% of the total in 1986, up from 11% in 1981. At the same time, common-law unions as a percentage of all families rose from less than 6% to more than 7%. In contrast, the proportion accounted for by traditional husband-wife families fell from 83% to 80%.

Lone-parent families

The majority of lone-parent families (eight out of ten) were headed by women in 1986. More than half (57%) of these women were separated or divorced; 28% were widows; and 15% were unmarried mothers. This distribution was almost unchanged from 1981, but differed substantially from 1961, when 63% of female lone parents were widowed; 35% were separated or divorced; and just 2% were single mothers.

The relatively rapid growth in the number of lone-parent families is of concern because these families, particularly those headed by women, are likely to face a variety of social and economic difficulties. For instance, in 1986, 44% of all female-headed lone-parent families had incomes that fell below Statistics Canada's low income cut-offs.

Also, a growing proportion of Canadian children are living in lone-parent families.

In 1986, about 1.2 million children, or over 14% of all children in Canada, were members of lone-parent families; the corresponding proportion in 1961 was 6%.

Family size dropping

The average size of Canadian families is falling. In 1986, there were an average of 3.1 people in each family, down from 3.3 in 1981, and 3.9 in 1961.

Most of the decrease in family size is a result of the drop in the number of children per family, which is attributed largely to declines in fertility. The average number of children in each family fell from 1.9 in 1961 to 1.3 in 1986.

The increasing number of lone-parent families has also contributed to smaller family size. Lone-parent families averaged 2.6 people in 1986, compared with 3.2 for husband-wife families.

As well, the number of families with no children at home has grown. In 1986, the 2.2 million families that were either

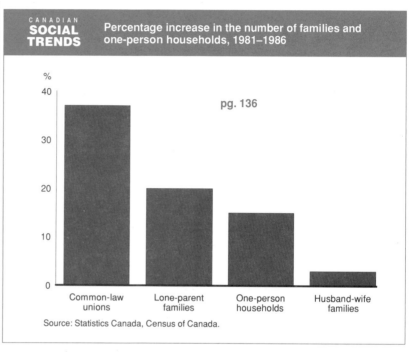

CANADIAN SOCIAL TRENDS
Percentage increase in the number of families and one-person households, 1981–1986

pg. 136

Source: Statistics Canada, Census of Canada.

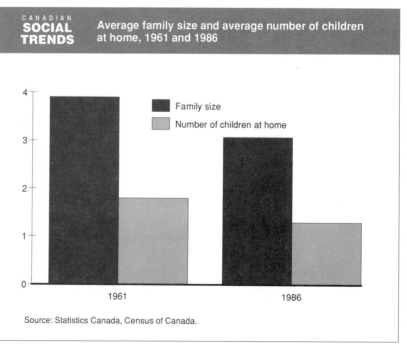

CANADIAN SOCIAL TRENDS
Average family size and average number of children at home, 1961 and 1986

Source: Statistics Canada, Census of Canada.

childless or whose children had left home represented 33% of all families, up slightly from 32% in 1981 and 29% in 1961.

Despite the increase in the number of families without children, close to 70% of Canadian families, a total of 4.5 million, had children at home in 1986. Also, about 1.5 million of these families had at least one child under age 6.

Solitary living

One of the fastest-growing groups of Canadians consists of people who live alone. Between 1981 and 1986, the number of one-person households rose 15%. By 1986, the 1.9 million Canadians living alone accounted for 10% of the population aged 15 and over, an increase from 9% in 1981, and from 4% in 1961.

The age distribution and marital status of people in one-person households differ substantially from those of the total adult population, with the elderly, particularly elderly widowed women, the most likely to live alone.

In 1986, 25% of people aged 65 and over were living alone; however, more than three-quarters (77%) of them were women. In fact, 34% of all elderly women were living alone. Most of these women, about eight out of ten, were widows. By contrast, just 14% of elderly men, half of them widowed, lived alone.

Differences in life expectancy, with women living longer than men, combined with the tendency for men to marry women somewhat younger than themselves, result in the large number of elderly widows left on their own.

At younger ages, the proportions of people in one-person households are comparatively small. Also, younger people living alone tend to be single, divorced, or separated rather than widowed. Fewer than 4% of 15-24-year-olds lived alone in 1986, and virtually all of them (96%) were unmarried. At ages 25-44, almost 8% of the population were living alone, and again, the majority (70%) were single. By ages 45-64, close to 10% of people were living alone. The most common marital status for this group was divorced or separated (43%), although single (29%) and widowed (28%) people made up substantial proportions.

MARITAL STATUS

by Mary Sue Devereaux

Although five years is a relatively short time for substantial population changes to occur, results from the 1986 Census show continuing shifts in the marital status of Canadians since the last count in 1981. The numbers who were divorced, separated, or widowed increased at a faster pace than did the married and single populations.

Census figures refer only to marital status when the count was taken. Therefore, these statistics do not indicate how many people have ever been divorced, separated, or widowed at some time in the past. For instance, since most divorced people eventually remarry, the number ever divorced would be much larger. The same applies to the separated and widowed populations, many of whom find new partners.

The currently divorced population, relatively small but fast-growing, increased 38% from 500,000 in 1981 to 690,000 in 1986. The separated and widowed populations ranked next in terms of growth, but with increases of 10% and 8%, were well below the rate for divorced people. The number in the separated category rose from 470,000 to 518,000, and the number of widows and widowers went from 1.16 million to 1.25 million.

The slowest-growing marital category was the single (never married) group, which rose just 3.2% from 5.3 million to 5.4 million. The increase in the number of married people was not much greater: a 4.8% rise from 11.5 million to 12.0 million.

Marital status reflects age and life cycle stage. For example, divorce and separation are most prevalent in the 35-44 and 45-54 age groups, both of which increased at a relatively fast rate and thereby contributed to the rapid growth of these two marital categories. Single people, on the other hand, are most likely to be in the 15-24 age group. The 10% decline in the size of this age group from 1981 to 1986 meant that slow growth of the single population was not surprising.

The differences in rates of growth between 1981 and 1986 were not large enough to significantly alter the proportion of the total population in each marital status. The 1986 Census recorded that 60.4% of adults were married; 27.2% single; 6.3% widowed; 3.5% divorced; and 2.6% separated. Slight increases in

the proportions who were divorced, separated, or widowed were made at the expense of the single and married categories.

A rising number of Canadians are living as husband and wife outside formal marriage. Since 1981, the number of reported common-law unions increased 38%. In 1986, 8% of all couples (about 487,000) reported their union was not based on a legal marriage, up from 6% or about 352,000 couples in 1981.

Overall, larger proportions of men than women were single or married; smaller proportions were divorced, separated, or widowed. The most obvious differences between men and women were the percentages who were single or widowed. Almost a third (31%) of men were single compared with fewer than a quarter (24%) of women. On the other hand, more than 10% of women were widowed, but just 2% of men.

While shifts in the marital status of the total population between 1981 and 1986 were relatively minor, changes in individual age groups signal continuing trends in marriage patterns and family life.

Single

The proportion of single people increased in all age groups under 45, particularly among young adults who are tending to marry at later ages. For example, more than 82% of 15-24-year-olds were single in 1986, a rise from about 79% in 1981. For 25-34-year-olds, the increase was from around 20% to 25%.

By contrast, among age groups 45 and over, the proportion of single people declined slightly between 1981 and 1986.

The percentage of single men exceeded the percentage of single women in all age groups up to 65. The disparity was greatest in the youngest age range, 15-24. Close to nine out of ten (88%) men

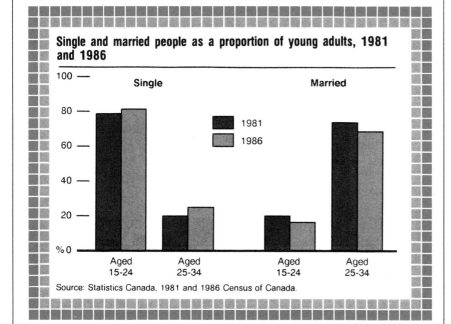

Population aged 15 and over, by marital status, 1981 and 1986			
Marital status	1981	1986	% change 1981-1986
Total population aged 15 and over	18,862,085	19,917,365	5.6
Single	5,255,110	5,425,290	3.2
Married	11,478,715	12,033,670	4.8
Separated	470,455	517,530	10.0
Divorced	500,135	690,490	38.1
Widowed	1,157,670	1,250,395	8.0

Source: Statistics Canada, 1981 and 1986 Census of Canada.

Single and married people as a proportion of young adults, 1981 and 1986

Source: Statistics Canada, 1981 and 1986 Census of Canada.

in this age group were single compared with about three-quarters (76%) of the women. The difference narrowed in each succeeding age group. By age 65 and over, the proportion of women who were single (8.6%) surpassed the corresponding proportion of men (7.6%).

Married

In all age groups except the elderly (65 and over), the proportion of people who were married dropped between 1981 and 1986. Declines were greatest among the young. In 1981, 20% of 15-24-year-olds were married; by 1986, the proportion was about 17%. The decrease among 25-34-year-olds was from 74% to 69%.

Under age 35, women are more likely than men to be married. This was particularly noticeable in the 15-24 age group. The proportion of these women who were married in 1986 (22%) was double the proportion for their male contemporaries (11%). By ages 35-44, men were slightly more likely than women to be married, and by age 65 and over, the gap widened so that the percentage of married men far exceeded the percentage of married women: 74% versus 40%.

Widowed

The proportion of each age group that was widowed either remained the same or declined slightly in the five years from 1981 to 1986.

Widowhood is rare among young people (fewer than half of one percent of those under 35), but becomes increasingly prevalent at older ages. By age 65,

about a third of the population is widowed. However, the proportions of elderly men and women who are widowed differ sharply. Almost half (48%) of women aged 65 and over were widows in 1986, compared with fewer than 14% of men. This disparity results from women's longer life expectancy and their tendency to marry men several years older than themselves. Women, therefore, frequently outlive their husbands. The large number of widows constitutes a sizable pool of potential spouses for the relatively few elderly men

who are widowed. In fact, the 1986 Census showed that 74% of elderly men were married.

Divorced

Divorced marital status is most common in the 35-54 age range, although even at these ages, in 1986 only a small minority of people were divorced. These are also the ages with the greatest increases in the proportions who were divorced. In 1986, over 6% of 35-54-year-olds were divorced, up from about 4.5% five years earlier. The proportions of

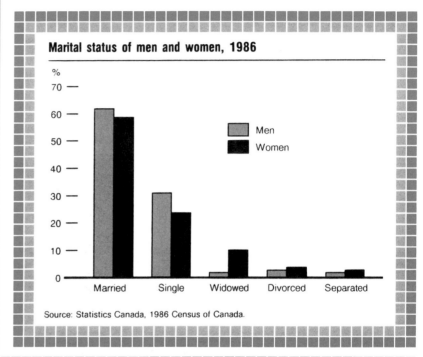

Marital status of men and women, 1986

Source: Statistics Canada, 1986 Census of Canada.

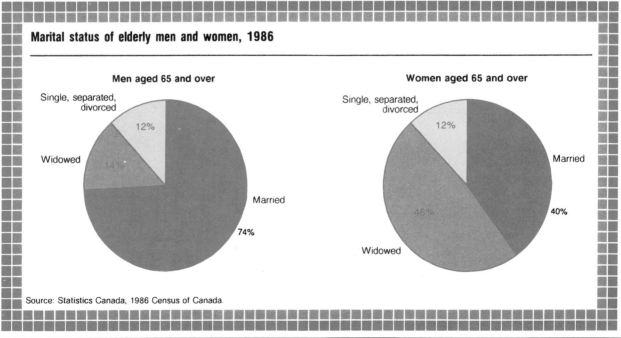

Marital status of elderly men and women, 1986

Men aged 65 and over

Women aged 65 and over

Source: Statistics Canada, 1986 Census of Canada.

divorced people aged 35 and under remained low between 1981 and 1986. Just 0.2% of 15-24-year-olds and 3.1% of 25-34-year-olds were divorced in 1986.

Among age groups 55 and over, divorced marital status was less frequent than among 35-54-year-olds, although the percentages have also increased. However, statistics from other sources indicate that by age 54, about one-third of adult Canadians have been divorced at least once.

Because women's remarriage rate is somewhat lower, at most ages they are more likely than men to be divorced. Overall, when the Census was taken in 1986, 4.1% of women were divorced compared with 2.8% of men. In the 35-54 age group, over 7% of women and about 5% of men were divorced. In older age groups, proportions dropped, and among the elderly, the percentages of men and women who were divorced were almost equal.

Separated

The only age group in which the proportion of separated people increased between 1981 and 1986 was 35-44. This was also the group most likely to report separated marital status: 3.6% in 1981; 3.9% in 1986.

Up to age 55, women were more likely than men to be separated. Percentages were equal among 55-64-year-olds, and by age 65 and over, the percentage of separated men surpassed that of women: 2.2% compared with 1.5%.

Conclusion

Between 1981 and 1986, divorced people constituted the fastest-growing marital category, followed by those who were separated. Although both groups are small, together numbering just over one million, they represent increasing proportions of the population. Moreover, since most divorced people eventually remarry, the numbers who have ever been divorced are much higher than Census figures indicate.

The proportion of young adults staying single is rising, while the percentage who are married has declined. This suggests that young people are postponing marriage and family formation.

Despite an increase in the number of widows and widowers, the proportion of the population who were widowed was almost unchanged between 1981 and 1986.

MARRYING AND DIVORCING: A STATUS REPORT FOR CANADA

by Owen Adams and Dhruva Nagnur

Throughout the 1970s and 1980s, patterns of marriage and divorce in Canada have changed. During this period, the number of marriages has declined, while the number of divorces has risen. In addition, Canadians are now older when they first marry and are less likely to remarry after divorce or widowhood. As well, the tendency to live common-law is increasing. In 1986, for example, 8% of all people in couples were in common-law relationships.[1]

As a result of these trends, Canadians now spend a smaller proportion of their lives in a marriage than was the case just a decade ago. The vast majority of adults, however, still marry and most Canadians continue to live in some kind of family setting.

[1] People living common-law were not included among those who were married.

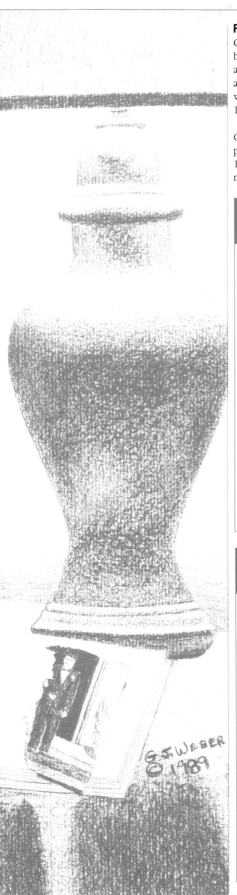

Fewer, later marriages

Generally, Canadians are waiting longer before they marry. In 1986, the average age at first marriage was 28 years for men and 26 years for women. For both, this was an increase of 3 years since the early 1970s.

In addition, a growing proportion of Canadians never marry. An analysis completed in 1985 suggested that, at that time, 17% of men and 14% of women would never marry. These figures were up from 10% and 8%, respectively, in 1971.

Nonetheless, the vast majority of Canadians still get married. It was projected in 1985 that about 85% of the population would marry sometime during their lives; this was down, however, from 91% in 1971.

Overall, the annual number of marriages fell from 200,000 in 1972 to 176,000 in 1986. This decline occurred despite the coming of age of the postwar baby boom generation.

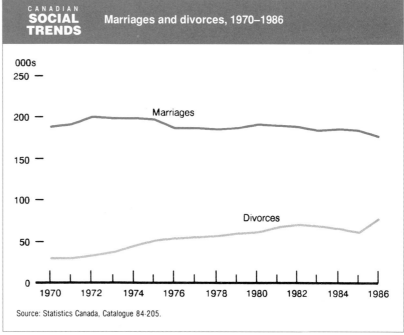

CANADIAN SOCIAL TRENDS

Marriages and divorces, 1970–1986

Source: Statistics Canada, Catalogue 84-205.

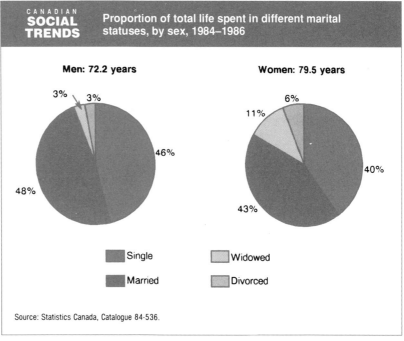

CANADIAN SOCIAL TRENDS

Proportion of total life spent in different marital statuses, by sex, 1984–1986

Men: 72.2 years

Women: 79.5 years

Single Widowed
Married Divorced

Source: Statistics Canada, Catalogue 84-536.

As well, marriages do not last as long as they did in the past. In 1985, the average length of marriage was 31 years, down from 35 years in 1971.

When second and subsequent marriages are included, Canadians spend about 45% of their lives in a marital relationship, a drop from an estimated 55% in the early 1970s.

The average proportion of life spent married differs for men and women. Men can expect to be married for close to half (48%) their lives, compared with 43% for women. This discrepancy occurs largely because women tend to outlive men by a considerable margin, and as a result, spend more years alone after their husbands have died.

Divorce and remarriage

Although marriage has traditionally been perceived as a lifelong commitment, a growing proportion of married couples divorce. In 1971, about one in five marriages was expected to end in divorce; by the mid-1980s, this figure was nearly one in three. In 1986, there were over 78,000 divorces in Canada, up from 30,000 in 1971.

Although divorce is more frequent than in the past, many divorced people remarry. In 1985, for example, at least one partner in 27% of all marriages was divorced.

However, remarriage after divorce is now less likely than in the early 1970s. An estimated 76% of divorced men in 1985 could expect to remarry, down from 85% in 1971. For women, the figure fell from 79% to 64% in the same period.

The increasing proportion of marriages ending in divorce and the decline in the likelihood of remarriage mean that people spend more years divorced. It was estimated in the mid-1980s that women would be divorced for an average of 5 years and men for 3 years. For both, the estimated average length of divorce has increased since 1971, when the figures were just over 2 years for women and 1 year for men.

Till death do us part

While 30% of couples eventually divorce, 70% remain married until one partner dies. Given that women are usually younger than their husbands and because women's life expectancy is longer than that for men, it is the husbands that most often die first. As a result, women tend to be widowed for considerably longer periods than men. As of 1985, women spent an average of 8 years, or 11% of their lives widowed compared to an average of just 2 years, or 3% of their lives, for men.

Both widows and widowers are now less likely to remarry than in the past. In 1985, 5% of widows could expect to remarry, compared with 9% in 1971. For widowers, the corresponding proportions were 14% in 1985 and 24% in 1971.

Moreover, widows and widowers who remarry tend to be relatively young. On average, widows who remarry are 11 years younger than all widows, while for widowers the difference is 9 years.

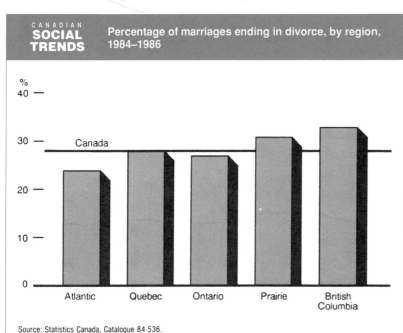

CANADIAN SOCIAL TRENDS

Percentage of marriages ending in divorce, by region, 1984–1986

Source: Statistics Canada, Catalogue 84-536.

Marriage and divorce in Canada and the United States

Although Canada and the United States share many cultural influences, marriage and divorce statistics in the two countries differ significantly. While roughly the same percentage of Canadians and Americans marry, a much higher proportion of American marriages, 44% compared with 28% in Canada, end in divorce. As well, the average length of marriage in the United States is 24 years compared with 31 years in Canada.

Nevertheless, Americans can expect to live in a marriage almost as long as Canadians, although they will marry more often to do so. Remarriage rates for both men and women are higher in the United States than in Canada.

Marriage and divorce trends in Canada (1984-1986) and the United States (1983)

	Men		Women	
	Canada	United States	Canada	United States
	%			
Population ever marrying	83	84	86	88
Marriages ending in divorce	28	44	28	44
Widowed persons remarrying	14	19	5	7
Divorced persons remarrying	76	85	64	76

Source: Statistics Canada, Catalogue 84-536.

Regional variations

Trends in marriage, divorce, and remarriage are fairly uniform across the country, although there are some notable exceptions. In particular, there are several sharp differences between Quebec and the rest of Canada. For example, while an estimated 15% of all Canadians will never marry, the figure exceeds 23% in Quebec. As well, Quebec residents tend to wait longer than people in the rest of the country before marrying; both men and women remain single nearly five years longer in Quebec than in any other region.

As well, people in Quebec are considerably less likely to remarry after divorce than are residents of other regions. For Quebec, 62% of divorced men and 47% of divorced women could expect to remarry, whereas the figures for Canada overall were 76% for men and 64% for women.

The incidence of divorce also varies by region. Estimates of the proportion of marriages that would end in divorce ranged from fewer than a quarter in the Atlantic provinces to almost a third in British Columbia.

DIVORCE RATES IN CANADA

by Owen Adams

The annual divorce rate in Canada has increased dramatically over the last two decades. This occurred largely because of the easing of legal restrictions on marital dissolution as a result of the 1968 Divorce Act and the Divorce Act, 1985.

The most recent legislation, the Divorce Act, 1985, was followed by a sharp increase in the divorce rate, which reversed a three-year downward trend.

The number of divorces per 100,000 married women rose 25% in 1986, to an all-time high of 1,255. In comparison, the rate had fallen 14% between 1982 and 1985, from 1,164 to 1,004.

Most of the period since the 1968 Divorce Act was passed, however, has been characterized by steadily increasing divorce rates. Shortly after passage of the Act, the rate more than doubled, rising from 235 divorces per 100,000 married

women in 1966 to 557 in 1969. Then, during the 1970s, the rate almost doubled again.

Divorce rates highest in Alberta and British Columbia

Divorce rates vary widely across the country. In 1986, there were 1,646 divorces per 100,000 married women in Alberta and 1,514 in British Columbia. This contrasted with 469 in Newfoundland and 637 in Prince Edward Island. Divorce rates in the other provinces ranged from just under 1,000 in New Brunswick and Saskatchewan, to around 1,100 in Manitoba, and 1,200 in Nova Scotia, Quebec, and Ontario.

The divorce rate rose in all provinces except Prince Edward Island in 1986. The largest increases occurred in Ontario and British Columbia, where rates rose 35% and 33%, respectively. Increases in Manitoba (25%), Saskatchewan (25%) and New Brunswick (24%) were similar to the national average, while there were somewhat smaller increases in Quebec (16%), Alberta (15%), Newfoundland (9%), and Nova Scotia (8%). On the other hand, the divorce rate fell 12% in Prince Edward Island.

Shorter duration of marriage

The duration of marriage before divorce has become shorter, particularly for people divorcing under the new Act.

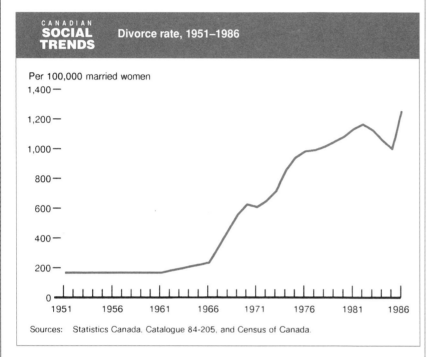

CANADIAN SOCIAL TRENDS Divorce rate, 1951–1986

Per 100,000 married women

Sources: Statistics Canada. Catalogue 84-205, and Census of Canada.

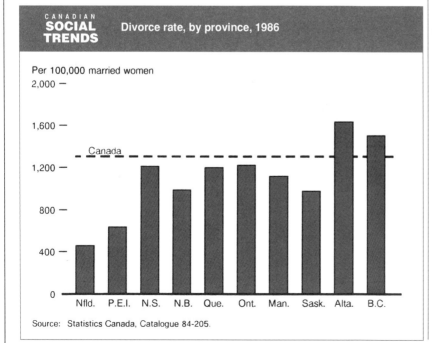

CANADIAN SOCIAL TRENDS Divorce rate, by province, 1986

Per 100,000 married women

Canada

Nfld. P.E.I. N.S. N.B. Que. Ont. Man. Sask. Alta. B.C.

Source: Statistics Canada, Catalogue 84-205.

Legislative changes

Before 1968, a divorce was difficult to obtain in Canada. Divorces were granted only if one of the spouses was proven to have committed adultery. Under the 1968 Divorce Act, however, divorce was permitted for either of two main reasons, or a combination of both. The first was that one of the spouses had committed a matrimonial offence, such as adultery or physical or mental cruelty. The second reason was that permanent marriage breakdown had occurred because of desertion or imprisonment, or because the spouses had lived apart for at least three years.

The Divorce Act, 1985, made marriage breakdown the sole ground for divorce. Under this Act, there are four reasons for marriage breakdown: separation for not less than one year, adultery, physical cruelty, and mental cruelty. Separation for at least one year was cited in 91% of divorces obtained under the new law in 1986.

Couples who divorced in 1986 under the new law had been married a median of 9.1 years, while the figure was 11.2 years for those who divorced that year under the old law. By contrast, in 1969, the median duration of marriage before divorce was almost 15 years.

Fewer children involved

Divorces granted under the new law in 1986 were also less likely to involve children than those granted under the old law. Of divorces obtained in 1986, children were involved in just one-third (34%) granted under the new Act, compared with more than half (52%) obtained under the old Act.

Under the new Act, as was the case under the old Act, wives are most likely to be awarded custody of the children after divorce. Wives received custody of 75% of the children in divorces granted under the new Act for which there was a custody order. The husband won custody of 12% of the children, while joint custody was ordered for 11%. For the remaining 2%, custody was awarded to someone other than the husband or wife.

COMMON-LAW UNIONS
NEARLY HALF A MILLION IN 1986

by Pierre Turcotte

A growing number of Canadians are living together without being married. In the five years between 1981 and 1986, the number of common-law unions increased sharply, while the number of married couples rose by only a small amount. As a result, not only the number but also the proportion of couples who were in common-law partnerships increased.

The characteristics of people in common-law relationships differ from those of people who are married. While common-law partners were older in 1986 than in 1981, they remained a much younger group than married people. Regardless of their age, people in common-law relationships were also less likely than married couples to have children at home.

Sharp increase in common-law unions

According to Census results, 487,000 couples (or 974,000 individuals) were living in common-law partnerships in 1986, a 37% gain over 1981, far outpacing the 2.7% rise in the number of married couples. Consequently, common-law unions accounted for 8% of all couples in 1986, up from 6% in 1981.

Common-law upswing offsets marriage downturn

The percentage of people aged 15 and over who were living in a union, either a common-law partnership or a legal marriage, decreased slightly between 1981 and 1986 from 61.1% to 60.6%. This small decline, however, masked a noticeable drop in the married compo-

nent and an almost compensating rise in the common-law share.

The proportion of people in common-law partnerships rose 1.1 percentage points from 3.9% in 1981 to 5.0% in 1986, nearly offsetting the 1.7 percentage-point decline from 57.3% to 55.6% in the proportion who were married.

Alternative for young couples

At young ages, relatively few people live as couples. In fact, at ages 15-19, less than 3% of the population lived as couples in 1986. By comparison, at ages 30-34, the proportion was 75%.

However, the younger the partners, the more likely is their union to be common-law. In 1986, six out of 10 partners aged 15-19 were in a common-law union. By ages 20-24, just over three out of 10 partners were living common-law, and among 25-29-year-olds, the figure was less than two in 10. At successively older ages, common-law partners represented a small and declining share of all people living in unions. But regardless of the age of the partners, proportionately more unions were common-law in 1986 than five years earlier.

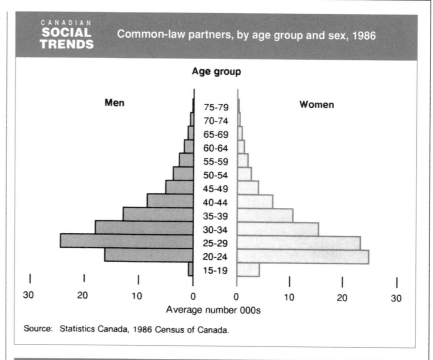

CANADIAN SOCIAL TRENDS — Common-law partners, by age group and sex, 1986

Age group

Men — Women

75-79, 70-74, 65-69, 60-64, 55-59, 50-54, 45-49, 40-44, 35-39, 30-34, 25-29, 20-24, 15-19

30 20 10 0   0 10 20 30

Average number 000s

Source: Statistics Canada, 1986 Census of Canada.

Common-law partners as a percentage of all persons living as couples, by age group, 1981 and 1986

Age group	1981	1986
15-19	49.5	59.6
20-24	23.1	32.9
25-29	11.3	16.6
30-34	6.8	10.3
35-39	5.1	7.4
40-44	3.9	5.9
45-49	3.0	4.5
50-54	2.4	3.5
55-59	1.8	2.6
60-64	1.5	2.1
65 and over	1.0	1.5
Total	**6.4**	**8.3**

Source: Statistics Canada, Census of Canada.

Cohabitation rates, by age group and sex, Canada, 1981 and 1986

Age group	Men		Women	
	1981	1986	1981	1986
15-19	0.7	0.5	3.0	2.4
20-24	9.1	8.5	14.9	15.1
25-29	18.7	20.0	20.8	23.4
30-34	22.5	24.7	19.1	22.9
35-39	22.7	25.1	16.5	19.6
40-44	19.2	23.3	13.4	16.6
45-49	15.5	19.5	10.0	13.3
50-54	11.9	15.8	7.1	9.5
55-59	9.0	11.9	4.5	6.1
60-64	7.0	9.1	2.7	3.8
65 and over	3.0	4.3	0.7	1.1
Total	**9.5**	**11.9**	**8.7**	**10.7**

Source: Statistics Canada, Census of Canada.

Most common-law partners young adults

People in common-law unions are relatively young. More than half the women and 43% of the men who lived common-law in 1986 were younger than age 30.

But while young adults continued to account for a large proportion of people living common-law, the median age of

common-law partners was about two years older in 1986 than in 1981. The median age of men rose from 28.9 to 30.7 years; for women, the increase was from 26.1 to 28.1 years.

Nonetheless, common-law partners remained considerably younger than married people. In 1986, the median age of married men was 43.8 years, while that of married women was 40.8 years.

Cohabitation rates rise

The likelihood that people of various ages will live in a common-law partnership can also be indicated by the cohabitation rate.

This rate expresses the number of common-law partners as a proportion of the total population "eligible" to live common-law, that is, people who are single, separated, divorced, or widowed.

Overall, the cohabitation rates of both men and women rose between 1981 and 1986. For men, the rate went from 9.5% to 11.9%, and for women, the increase was from 8.7% to 10.7%.

There was, however, a drop in the rate among 15-19-year-olds. This drop does not mean that more young people were marrying. There was simply a trend in the 15-19 age group away from living in

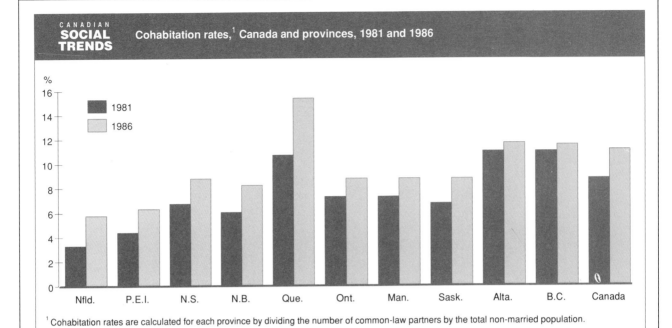

CANADIAN
**SOCIAL
TRENDS**

Cohabitation rates,[1] Canada and provinces, 1981 and 1986

%

■ 1981
☐ 1986

16
14
12
10
8
6
4
2
0

Nfld. P.E.I. N.S. N.B. Que. Ont. Man. Sask. Alta. B.C. Canada

[1] Cohabitation rates are calculated for each province by dividing the number of common-law partners by the total non-married population.
Source: Statistics Canada, Census of Canada.

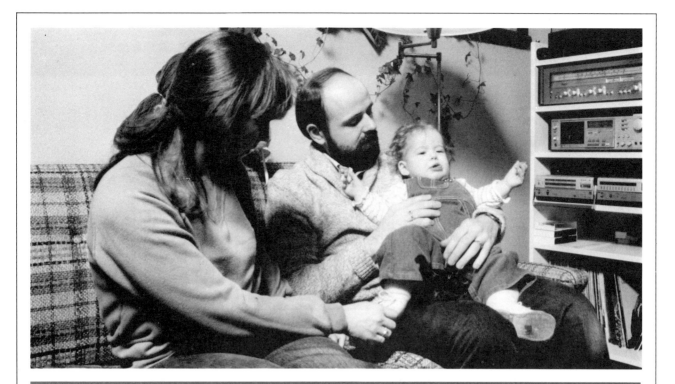

	Common-law		Married		Total population	
	1981	**1986**	**1981**	**1986**	**1981**	**1986**
Men						
15-19	8,340	4,655	6,060	2,585	1,150,185	965,280
20-24	83,080	81,630	223,065	133,325	1,137,555	1,095,400
25-29	88,120	122,670	588,505	525,565	1,058,940	1,138,670
30-34	61,160	90,335	730,165	699,385	1,002,510	1,065,220
35-39	38,715	65,005	639,110	737,880	809,375	996,965
40-44	24,230	42,395	537,410	617,685	663,420	799,710
45-49	17,630	26,525	509,025	514,255	622,935	649,960
50-54	13,315	19,210	497,350	484,815	609,385	606,090
55-59	9,080	13,705	455,545	467,525	556,100	582,885
60-64	5,740	9,245	369,300	417,875	450,870	519,410
65 and over	7,200	11,555	698,825	793,495	939,080	1,059,760
Total	**356,605**	**486,940**	**5,254,355**	**5,394,390**	**9,000,350**	**9,479,350**
Women						
15-19	32,450	21,535	35,555	15,155	1,114,660	926,805
20-24	109,625	123,505	416,685	284,620	1,153,110	1,104,015
25-29	77,675	116,085	708,420	670,485	1,082,080	1,165,550
30-34	47,865	76,735	756,430	758,415	1,007,580	1,093,095
35-39	29,325	52,670	622,640	739,240	800,695	1,007,695
40-44	18,715	33,950	516,655	593,330	656,785	797,365
45-49	13,275	21,110	480,915	490,235	613,370	649,455
50-54	10,290	14,430	467,950	453,670	613,480	606,145
55-59	7,450	10,410	435,940	430,590	601,905	601,245
60-64	4,770	7,625	330,055	384,980	506,260	584,535
65 and over	5,170	8,895	483,105	573,685	1,202,310	1,396,940
Total	**356,605**	**486,940**	**5,254,355**	**5,394,390**	**9,352,235**	**9,932,845**

Population aged 15 and over, by nature of marital union, age and sex, Canada, 1981 and 1986

Source: Statistics Canada, Census of Canada.

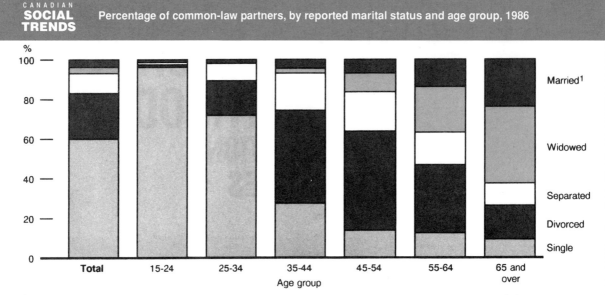

CANADIAN
**SOCIAL
TRENDS**

Percentage of common-law partners, by reported marital status and age group, 1986

%

100 —

80 —

60 —

40 —

20 —

0 —

Total   15-24   25-34   35-44   45-54   55-64   65 and over

Age group

Married[1]

Widowed

Separated

Divorced

Single

[1] It is not clear from Census data why some respondents who were living in common-law unions recorded themselves as married.
Source: Statistics Canada, 1986 Census of Canada.

couples, as the proportion staying in their parental home increased. The same pattern was apparent among men aged 20-24. At older ages, cohabitation rates of both sexes rose between 1981 and 1986.

Although the largest number of male common-law partners in 1986 were aged 25-29, male cohabitation rates peaked at 25.1% among 35-39-year-olds. This compares with rates of 20.0% for men aged 25-29, and just 8.5% for those in the 20-24 age group.

Among women, a similar pattern emerged, but their ages were somewhat younger. While the largest number of female common-law partners were aged 20-24, cohabitation rates peaked at 23.4% among 25-29-year-olds. The cohabitation rate for women aged 20-24 was much lower: 15.1%.

Wide provincial variations
Between 1981 and 1986, Quebec's cohabitation rate rose markedly from 10.8% to 15.5%. This was consistent with smaller proportions of people marrying in that province. As a result, in 1986, Quebec had the highest cohabitation rate in Canada. Alberta and British Columbia were also above the national average (11.3%), with 1986 rates of 11.9% and 11.6%, respectively.

By contrast, 1981 cohabitation rates had been highest in British Columbia and Alberta, while Quebec had ranked third. However, the increase in Quebec (4.7 percentage points), combined with gains of less than one percentage point in Alberta

and British Columbia, meant a change in the rank order of these three provinces by 1986.

On the other hand, in 1986 as in 1981, Newfoundland (5.9%) and Prince Edward Island (6.4%) had the lowest cohabitation rates. In the other provinces, 1986 rates varied between 8.4% and 9.0%.

Common-law unions not limited to single persons
In 1986, the majority (59%) of common-law partners were single. More than a third (37%) of the people living common-law, however, had been married previously. The remaining 4% identified themselves as "married".

As would be expected, almost all common-law partners aged 15-24 were single; in successively older age groups, the proportion of previously married partners increased.

Common-law couples less likely to have children at home
Regardless of their age, common-law couples are less likely than married couples to have children at home. In 1986, common-law couples had an average of 0.6 children at home, compared with 1.3 for married couples.

But between 1981 and 1986, the proportion of common-law couples with children increased, while the proportion for married couples fell slightly. In 1986, 37.8% of common-law couples had children at home, up from 34.2% in 1981. For married couples, the percentage

was 64.8% in 1986, down from 66.2% in 1981.

The number and/or presence of children at home should not be used as a measure of childbearing while in a common-law relationship. For example, these children may well have been born in a previous union.

Four in ten eventually marry
Living common-law does not preclude marriage. In fact, a 1984 survey[1] showed that 46% of men and 43% of women who lived in a common-law union later married their partner. Cohabitation, then, is not always a permanent alternative to marriage; it is frequently a prelude to marriage.

[1] Statistics Canada, Catalogue 99-955.

CHANGES IN FERTILITY AMONG CANADA'S LINGUISTIC GROUPS

by Réjean Lachapelle

Fertility depends on biological, cultural, economic and social factors. While it is difficult to determine the effect of any one of these factors, it is relatively easy to assess the consequences of differences in fertility, especially on the size and proportion of linguistic groups.

Despite heavy immigration and the linguistic assimilation of most of these immigrants into the group for which English is the mother tongue, the proportion of Francophones in the Canadian population held at 30% between 1850 and 1950, owing to a high fertility rate among French Canadian women. The fertility of Francophones then decreased, dropping below the Canadian average toward the mid-1960s. This change has contributed to a decrease in the proportion of the total Canadian population speaking French as a mother tongue — from 29% in 1951 to 25% in 1986.

Differences between Quebec and the rest of the country[1]

Vital statistics show that the fertility of Quebec women was approximately 40% greater than that of other Canadian women in the late 1920s. This gap narrowed, then disappeared around 1960. Over the past 25 years, the fertility of Quebec women has always been lower than that of women in the other provinces.

When Quebec joined the national vital statistics collection system in 1926, the

---

[1] This section uses vital statistics to compare fertility rates of women in Quebec with women in the other provinces, **regardless of their mother tongue**.

province's total fertility rate[2] — that is, the average number of children per woman — was 4.3. It was 45% higher than that of other Canadian women, who had an average of 3.0 children. After 1926, the fertility of Quebec women decreased, bottoming out during the depression of the 1930s. The total rate dropped to 3.2 in Quebec (in 1939) and as low as 2.4 elsewhere in the country (in 1937), a level slightly higher than the national average of 2.3 children per woman needed at that time (due to a higher mortality rate than today) to replace the population. During World War II, the fertility of Quebec women posted regular growth, and by 1947, it had risen to 3.9. It then varied between 3.8 and 4.1 until 1960. The war had more of an effect on fertility in the rest of the country. A pause from 1942 to 1945 (2.7 to 2.8 children per woman) was followed by recovery in 1946 and 1947 (3.5). Then, except during a short interruption between 1948 and 1950 (3.3), the fertility rate rose until 1960 (4.0).

During the 1950s, the fertility of Quebec women went back up to the level seen in the years preceding the Great Depression. In the rest of Canada, the fertility rate in the 1950s and early 1960s was approximately one third higher than the rate observed in the late 1920s. It was this remarkable increase that made the baby boom so big. The baby boom had less of an effect in Quebec.

Between 1926 and 1960, the fertility rate of women in Quebec moved gradually closer to that of other Canadian women. In effect, the ratio of the fertility rate of Quebec women to other Canadian women dropped from 1.45 in 1926 to 1.30 around 1940 and 1.15 around 1950. By the beginning of the Quiet Revolution in 1960, the level of fertility in Quebec was nearly equal to that in the other provinces.

Between 1960 and 1970, fertility declined very rapidly. The total fertility rate of women in Quebec dropped from 3.9 to 2.1, a decrease of nearly 50% in 10 years, while the fertility of other Canadian women fell but not so dramatically, from 4.0 to 2.5. Consequently, in 1970, the fertility of women in Quebec was 15% lower than that of women in the rest of the country.

By 1974, fertility in Quebec had dropped to 1.8 children per woman. Then, until 1979, it varied between 1.7 and 1.8, levels much lower than those needed to replace the population at the time (2.1). The decrease was more regular in the other provinces between 1970 (2.5) and 1980 (1.8). The differences were therefore less pronounced.

By 1986, the fertility rate of Quebec women had fallen still further to 1.4; that of other Canadian women held at between 1.7 and 1.8. The result was a new widening of the gap. In 1986, the fertility rate was 20% lower in Quebec than in the other provinces. Put another way, fertility in the rest of Canada was 25% higher than in Quebec.

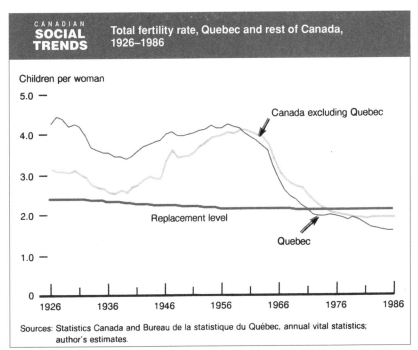

CANADIAN SOCIAL TRENDS
Total fertility rate, Quebec and rest of Canada, 1926–1986

Children per woman

Canada excluding Quebec

Replacement level

Quebec

Sources: Statistics Canada and Bureau de la statistique du Québec, annual vital statistics; author's estimates.

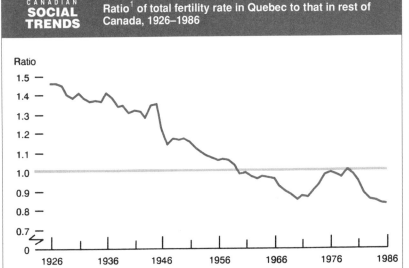

CANADIAN SOCIAL TRENDS
Ratio[1] of total fertility rate in Quebec to that in rest of Canada, 1926–1986

Ratio

[1] A ratio of 1.2 means that fertility in Quebec is 20% higher than that in the rest of the country. A ratio of 0.85 indicates that fertility in Quebec is 15% lower than that in the other provinces.
Sources: Statistics Canada, and Bureau de la statistique du Québec, annual vital statistics; author's estimates

[2] Total fertility rate is the average number of children that a group of women would have in their lifetimes if the age-specific rates observed for them in a given year continued until they had had all their children.

These differences in fertility between Quebec and the other provinces have significantly affected the demographic situation. For example, 85,000 births were recorded in Quebec in 1986. If the fertility rate for women in Quebec had been equal to that of other Canadian women (1.75 children per woman), there would have been 106,000 births, or 25% more. Note that births recorded in Quebec in 1986 accounted for 23% of the births recorded in the country (Newfoundland not included), and that Quebec women accounted for 27% of Canadian women of childbearing age. The reduction in Quebec's demographic weight with respect to births is a result of the low fertility observed in that province.

Since Francophones make up 80% of the Quebec population, and Anglophones make up at least 75% of the population in the rest of Canada, the changes in fertility between Quebec women and other Canadian women allow us to conclude that, in the country as a whole, the fertility rate of Francophones was higher than Anglophones until about 1955. However, between 1966 and 1974 and again after 1980, Anglophones registered the higher rate. For the other years, without additional information on fertility by mother tongue, it is difficult to know which group had the highest fertility, since the differences between Quebec and the other provinces were too small.

Completed fertility of cohorts, 1896-1951[3]

Census data have shown that the completed fertility[4] of Francophones was 80% higher than that of Anglophones for women born at the turn of the century.

This gap narrowed rapidly over the years and disappeared for women born between 1931 and 1936. For more recent cohorts, the completed fertility of Francophones has been lower than that of Anglophones.

Women born between 1901 and 1916 were between 15 and 30 years old in 1931. The Depression hit when they were at those ages when they would normally have had the highest marriage and fertility rates. In

[3] The sections that follow use census data to compare directly the fertility of Francophones with Anglophones.
[4] **Completed fertility** is the average number of children that the women born in a given year (**cohort**) had in their childbearing years.

these cohorts, and even in cohorts back to 1896, the completed fertility of Anglophones (2.3 to 2.6 children per woman) was below the level needed to replace the population. This narrowly defined "replacement level" depends on the mortality of women (estimated here for Canadian women as a whole) between birth and

the average age at childbirth. But, if one estimates instead a general replacement level that takes into account the improvements in mortality between the mothers' generation and the daughters' generation, it does seem that, despite their lower fertility, Anglophone women born between 1896 and 1916 were able to "replace" themselves.

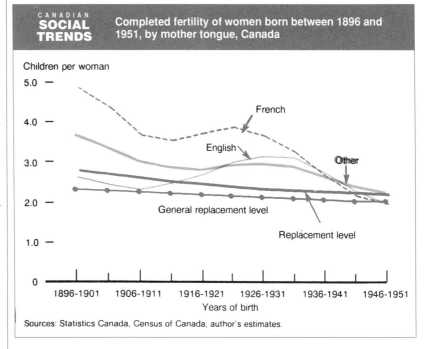

CANADIAN SOCIAL TRENDS

Completed fertility of women born between 1896 and 1951, by mother tongue, Canada

Children per woman

French

English

Other

General replacement level

Replacement level

Years of birth

Sources: Statistics Canada, Census of Canada; author's estimates.

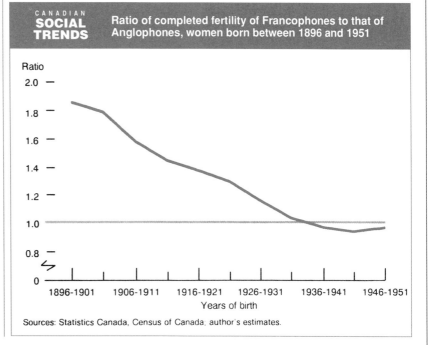

CANADIAN SOCIAL TRENDS

Ratio of completed fertility of Francophones to that of Anglophones, women born between 1896 and 1951

Ratio

Years of birth

Sources: Statistics Canada, Census of Canada; author's estimates.

For the Anglophone population, the high fertility rates that characterized the period following the depression of the 1930s and World War II resulted in an increase in the completed fertility of cohorts born after 1910. In effect, the average number of children rose from 2.3 for women born between 1906 and 1911 to 3.1 for women born between 1926 and 1936, a rise of one third. This increase was attributable to the rise in the proportion of women who married, the drop in the proportion of married women who remained childless and the increased average family size. This recovery in fertility resulted not only in an increase in the proportion of three-, four- and five-children families, but also in a not inconsiderable rise in the proportion of women having six or more children (12% in cohorts born between 1926 and 1931, compared to 9% in cohorts born between 1906 and 1911). However, the downward trend in the proportion of families having 10 children or more continued.

Among Francophones, no doubt because of their already high level of fertility, the increase in completed fertility was less pronounced and involved fewer cohorts. From a low of 3.5 children per woman in cohorts born between 1911 and 1916, completed fertility rose to 3.8 in cohorts born between 1921 and 1926. Although completed fertility was the same in the cohorts born between 1906 and 1911 and those born between 1926 and 1931 (3.6 children per woman), there were significant differences between the two groups — namely, an increase in the proportion of married women, a decrease in the proportion of married women without children and an increase in the proportion of women with two to five children. These changes were offset by a decrease in the proportion of larger families. The proportion of women with six or more children dropped from 26% in cohorts born between 1906 and 1911 to 21% in those born between 1926 and 1931.

The completed fertility of Anglophones differed little from that of Francophones in the cohorts born between 1931 and 1936. However, the proportion of married Anglophone women was higher than that of married Francophone women; those who were married remained childless or had only one child a little less frequently and a greater proportion of them had two to four children. Francophones still held their traditional advantage in the number of families with five or more children, and this offset their lower proportion of families with two, three or four children.

For women born after 1935, the completed fertility of Anglophones is higher than that of Francophones. The average number of children of Francophone women in the cohorts born between 1946 and 1951 (1.9) is, moreover, below the replacement level, even when one takes into account the probable reductions in mortality that will enable the daughters to live longer than their mothers. In these cohorts, the fertility of Francophones is lower than that of Anglophones except for

Years of birth	Children per woman			
	All languages	English	French	Other
Canada				
1896-1901	3.30	2.60	4.76	3.68
1901-1906	3.06	2.41	4.25	3.35
1906-1911	2.75	2.31	3.57	3.01
1911-1916	2.77	2.44	3.46	2.86
1916-1921	2.94	2.68	3.63	2.79
1921-1926	3.17	2.98	3.78	2.93
1926-1931	3.21	3.13	3.56	2.96
1931-1936	3.08	3.10	3.17	2.89
1936-1941	2.68	2.74	2.59	2.64
1941-1946	2.23	2.26	2.07	2.40
1946-1951	1.97	1.97	1.88	2.23
Quebec				
1896-1901	4.14	2.22	4.73	2.66
1901-1906	3.78	2.04	4.24	2.39
1906-1911	3.16	1.94	3.48	2.48
1911-1916	3.12	2.03	3.38	2.43
1916-1921	3.28	2.29	3.55	2.28
1921-1926	3.46	2.67	3.69	2.52
1926-1931	3.30	2.71	3.45	2.57
1931-1936	2.98	2.68	3.07	2.52
1936-1941	2.49	2.36	2.50	2.45
1941-1946	2.03	1.95	2.01	2.27
1946-1951	1.79	1.73	1.77	2.19
Rest of country				
1896-1901	3.00	2.63	4.94	3.81
1901-1906	2.79	2.44	4.42	3.46
1906-1911	2.59	2.34	4.00	3.08
1911-1916	2.64	2.47	3.82	2.91
1916-1921	2.82	2.71	4.03	2.86
1921-1926	3.07	3.00	4.26	2.98
1926-1931	3.17	3.15	4.12	3.01
1931-1936	3.12	3.12	3.72	2.94
1936-1941	2.76	2.76	3.03	2.67
1941-1946	2.30	2.28	2.36	2.41
1946-1951	2.01	1.99	2.04	2.24

Completed fertility by mother tongue, for women born between 1896 and 1951 (all marital statuses), Canada, Quebec and rest of country

Note: To calculate completed fertility for the three most recent groups of cohorts, the figure was increased for the number of children per woman estimated using the 1981 Census on the basis of observed fertility between 1981 and 1986.

Sources: Statistics Canada, Census of Canada; and author's estimates.

the first child, where the difference is negligible. In both groups, except perhaps in the case of first births, fertility has decreased for all birth order — particularly from the third child up — from the cohorts born between 1931 and 1936 to those born between 1946 and 1951. In other words, the recent decrease in completed fertility is affecting not only large families, but also three-children families, and perhaps even two-children families.

At first glance, it is interesting to note that the overall lower completed fertility of Francophones relative to Anglophones is not the case if we look separately at Quebec or at the rest of the country. The lower fertility of Francophones in the country as a whole is the result of the fact that, for cohorts born after 1935, the completed fertility of Francophones in Quebec is lower than that of Anglophones living outside Quebec.

In Quebec, as in the rest of Canada, the higher fertility of Francophones has decreased considerably and, for cohorts born after 1940, the completed fertility of women with neither English nor French as a mother tongue now exceeds that of Francophones. In addition, in the more recent cohorts — that is, those born between 1946 and 1951 — the higher fertility of Francophones relative to Anglophones is very small, even negligible, both in Quebec and in the rest of the country. Finally, for all the cohorts, the fertility of Quebec women is still lower than that of other Canadian women, regardless of mother tongue. This is no doubt a result of the higher proportion of Quebec women in all linguistic groups who live in major urban areas such as Montreal and Quebec City, which have always been associated with lower fertility.

Fertility since 1956

Between 1956 and 1961, the fertility of Francophones was still nearly 15% higher than that of Anglophones. The gap quickly narrowed and disappeared around the mid-1960s. Subsequently, except between 1976 and 1981, Francophone fertility has been lower than Anglophone fertility. From 1981 to 1986, Anglophone fertility exceeded Francophone fertility by more than 10%.

Analysis of the changes in completed fertility for women who were 30 years of age or older in 1981 does not allow us to describe the recent changes in fertility differences. To extend the study, we have to estimate the total fertility rates by

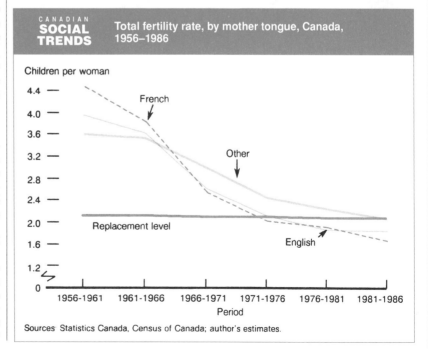

CANADIAN
SOCIAL TRENDS

Total fertility rate, by mother tongue, Canada, 1956–1986

Children per woman

French

Other

Replacement level

English

1956-1961 1961-1966 1966-1971 1971-1976 1976-1981 1981-1986
Period

Sources: Statistics Canada, Census of Canada; author's estimates.

Fertility rate by mother tongue, Canada, Quebec, and rest of country, 1956–86

Five-year period	Children per woman			
	All languages	English	French	Other
Canada				
1956-1961	3.88	3.80	4.31	3.48
1961-1966	3.51	3.48	3.66	3.40
1966-1971	2.49	2.46	2.36	2.85
1971-1976	1.98	1.95	1.85	2.32
1976-1981	1.75	1.68	1.72	2.11
1981-1986	1.66	1.67	1.49	1.94
Quebec				
1956-1961	3.99	3.26	4.22	2.79
1961-1966	3.43	3.04	3.54	2.93
1966-1971	2.26	2.09	2.27	2.58
1971-1976	1.82	1.62	1.81	2.26
1976-1981	1.71	1.46	1.71	2.04
1981-1986	1.49	1.46	1.47	1.79
Rest of country				
1956-1961	3.84	3.82	4.95	3.57
1961-1966	3.55	3.50	4.34	3.46
1966-1971	2.58	2.48	2.87	2.89
1971-1976	2.04	1.96	2.12	2.33
1976-1981	1.76	1.69	1.76	2.12
1981-1986	1.72	1.68	1.60	1.96

Sources: Statistics Canada, Census of Canada; and author's estimates.

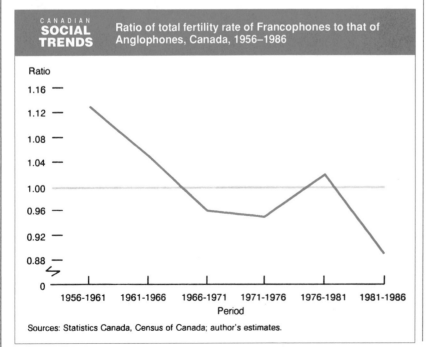

CANADIAN SOCIAL TRENDS Ratio of total fertility rate of Francophones to that of Anglophones, Canada, 1956–1986

Sources: Statistics Canada, Census of Canada; author's estimates.

mother tongue for the last few five-year periods. The results confirm the conclusions reached in the preceding analyses and add some useful details.

In Canada as a whole, Francophone fertility exceeded that of Anglophones not only until 1956, but also until 1966. After 1966 and until 1976, the fertility of Francophones was slightly lower than that of Anglophones. Between 1976 and 1981, Francophone fertility was once again higher than that of Anglophones, but only slightly. Finally, between 1981 and 1986, the gap widened as Francophone fertility decreased considerably from the previous five-year period while Anglophone fertility showed little change. The fertility of all the linguistic groups, including the group made up of women with mother tongues other than French or English, is now below the replacement level.

Until 1981, in Quebec as in all the other provinces, Francophone fertility was always higher than that of Anglophones. But a remarkable change took place between 1981 and 1986. In Quebec, Francophone fertility was then as low as that of Anglophones (1.5 children per woman); elsewhere in Canada, Francophone fertility was actually lower (1.6) than that of Anglophones (1.7). This change occurred despite the weaker concentration of Francophones in metropolitan areas, both in Quebec and elsewhere in Canada.

To discover whether Francophone fertility is now lower than Anglophone fertility in the Montreal area, total fertility rates were estimated for the three linguistic groups for the 1981-1986 period.[5] The Francophone rate was 1.33, that of Anglophones was 1.39, and that of the population for which neither official language was the mother tongue was 1.63. For the population as a whole, the total rate was 1.37. Thus, the fertility of all language groups in greater Montreal was very low, well below the replacement level. And as was to be expected, Francophone fertility was lower than that of Anglophones.

The recent lower fertility of Francophones outside Quebec was also

[5] For a description of how the Montreal area was delineated, see: Lachapelle, Réjean. ''The Strengthening of Majority Positions: Recent Developments in the Language Situation'', in Dumas, Jean. *Report on the Demographic Situation in Canada, 1986,* Ottawa, Statistics Canada, Catalogue 91-209E, 1987, p. 129.

observed between 1981 and 1986 in the two provinces in which most of them live. In Ontario, the total fertility rate for Francophones was 1.54, compared to 1.61 for Anglophones and 1.75 for the other groups. (The rate for the population as a whole was 1.63.) In New Brunswick, the rate was 1.67 for the overall population: 1.61 for Francophones and 1.68 for Anglophones.

These differences in fertility have had a significant effect on the linguistic composition of the population. Thus, in 1986, women for whom French was the mother tongue made up 26.5% of the Canadian population of childbearing age; however, only 23.8% of the children under five years of age had a mother for whom French was the mother tongue, owing to the lower fertility of this group. Mothers do not always pass their mother tongue on to their children; consequently, 23.1% of young Canadian children speak French as their mother tongue. In the country as a whole, then, the decrease has resulted mainly from differences in fertility, rather than from a change in mother tongue from one generation to the next.

Summary

The high fertility rates of French Canadian women are now a thing of the past. Since 1960, the fertility of all Quebec women has been lower than that of other Canadian women. In the country as a whole, the fertility of Anglophones has exceeded that of Francophones since 1966, except between 1976 and 1981.

Both in Quebec and in the rest of Canada, Francophone fertility had long been at least slightly higher than Anglophone fertility. This ceased to be the case between 1981 and 1986. The lower fertility of Francophones can be seen as much in the Montreal area as in Ontario and New Brunswick. It may be difficult to explain why Francophone fertility is lower in such different environments, but it is easy to estimate the effect this situation is having on changes in the number and proportion of Francophones in Canada.

Estimating fertility

Vital statistics provide an annual estimate of the total fertility rate for each province (except Newfoundland). To measure the approximate total fertility rate for Canada, Quebec excluded, we used these rates for Quebec and Canada and the proportion of Quebec women aged 20 to 34 in the total population of Canadian women belonging to the same age group. The total fertility rate for Quebec between 1951 and 1980 was then corrected to take into account late registration of births. The correction factor is small before 1965 and negligible after 1980.

The completed fertility of the cohorts by mother tongue is estimated using census results, which provide data on the number of live births experienced by non-single women. This approach results in an underestimation of the average number of children per woman, since it is based on the assumption that single women have no children. Of course, this introduces a margin of error, but it is no doubt fairly small since single women who have had a child may marry later on. Also in recent censuses, women living common-law have been included among married women.

The replacement levels were estimated using period life tables[1] and cohort mortality estimates.[2]

These estimates were extended for recent cohorts.

Unpublished census data were used to estimate the total fertility rates by mother tongue from 1956 to 1986. The estimation method makes use of the fact that approximately 95% of children under 15 years of age live with their mother or a woman who plays that role. The results obtained for all women differ very little from those provided by vital statistics. Moreover, the slight differences observed for the periods 1966-1971 and 1971-1976 between the estimates presented in a book by Réjean Lachapelle and Jacques Henripin[3] and those which appear in the second table are attributable to the fact that here data were used not only on children living in husband-wife families, but also on those living in lone-parent families in which a woman is head of the household.

[1] Nagnur, Dhruva. *Longevity and Historical Life Tables,* Ottawa, Statistics Canada, Catalogue 89-506, 1986.
[2] Bourbeau, Robert and Légaré, Jacques. *Évolution de la mortalité au Canada et au Québec, 1831-1931: essai de mesure par génération,* Montréal, Les Presses de l'Université de Montréal, 1982.
[3] *The Demolinguistic Situation in Canada: Past Trends and Future Prospects,* Montréal, Institute for Research on Public Policy, 1980, p. 114.

The Family

DUAL-EARNER FAMILIES: THE NEW NORM

by Maureen Moore

As a growing proportion of women have entered the paid labour force, the number of families in which both husband and wife have wage and salary incomes has increased.[1] Between 1967 and 1986, the number of dual-earner families rose from about 1.3 million to around 3.4 million. In fact, by 1986, they made up the majority of husband-wife families in Canada.

Traditional pattern replaced

In 1986, both spouses had earned incomes in 62% of all husband-wife families, up sharply from 34% in 1967. By contrast, the percentage of traditional families, those in which the husband was the sole earner, declined from 61% to 27%.

Families in which the wife was the sole earner or in which neither spouse had earnings have also increased over the last two decades, the former from 1% to close to 4%, and the latter from 4% to 7%. The

[1] This article refers only to husband-wife families in which at least one spouse was under age 65. Total figures include the earnings of family members other than husbands and wives, which amounted to 5% of dual-earner family income and 8% for traditional families.

majority of spouses in these families, particularly the husbands, were aged 55 or over.

Staying on top

A second income has become an important element in the maintenance of family income. The average income of dual-earner families was almost $50,000 in 1986, compared with just under $40,000 for families in which the husband was the sole earner. That year, the earnings of wives in dual-earner families averaged $14,000, about 29% of their families' total income.

The importance of the second paycheque is magnified when income quintile and low-income data are examined. In 1986, 81% of families in the upper fifth of the income distribution were dual earners, in contrast to just 35% of those in the bottom fifth.

The share of dual-earner family income provided by wives, however, is relatively the same for all income quintile groups. In 1986, wives' earnings amounted to 29% of the income of dual-earner families in the top fifth of the income scale, just slightly more than that (26%) for dual-earner families in the bottom fifth.

At the same time, only 4% of dual-earner families, compared with 13% of traditional families, had incomes below Statistics Canada's low-income cut-offs. Without wives' earnings, however, about the same proportion of dual-earner (14%) families would have been classified as having low incomes.

Social characteristics

Several characteristics of dual-earner families set them apart from couples in which the husband alone has an earned income. Spouses in dual-earner families are relatively young. They tend to have more formal education than other couples, and as a result, a higher proportion are employed in managerial or professional occupations. They are also less likely than traditional families to have children at home.

Dual earning is most common among young families. In 1986, 74% of families in which the husband was under age 45 had two earners, compared with 48% of families in which the husband was aged 45 and over.

In addition, wives' contribution to total family income was higher among young dual-earner couples than among older ones. Wives' earnings made up nearly a third (31%) of the total income of dual-earner families in which the husband was under age 45; this compared with about a quarter (26%) of the income of dual-earner families where the husband was older than 45.

Spouses in dual-earner families, particularly the wives, tend to have more education than those in traditional families. This is not surprising, since women with high educational attainment are more likely than others to be in the labour force. In 1986, 14% of wives in dual-earner families had a university degree, compared with 6% of those in traditional families. The gap between husbands' education was not as wide: 18% of husbands in dual-earner families were university graduates, compared with 14% of husbands in traditional families.

The percentage of income provided by wives in dual-earner families is also related to their education. Women who had a university degree provided the largest share: in 1986, it represented 35% of their families' total income. On the other hand, the proportion provided by dual-earner

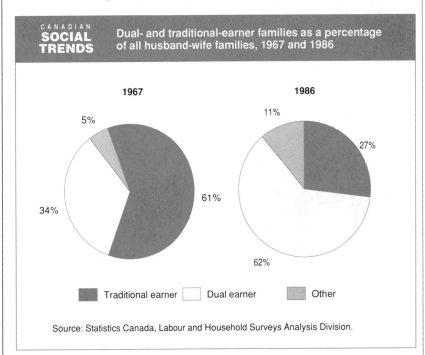

Dual- and traditional-earner families as a percentage of all husband-wife families, 1967 and 1986

Source: Statistics Canada, Labour and Household Surveys Analysis Division.

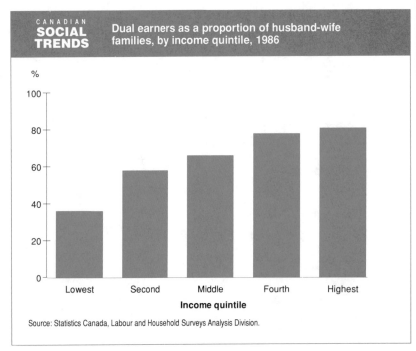

Dual earners as a proportion of husband-wife families, by income quintile, 1986

Source: Statistics Canada, Labour and Household Surveys Analysis Division.

wives with less than eight years of formal education was 23%.

Largely as a result of their higher level of education, spouses in dual-earner families are more likely than those in traditional families to have managerial or professional jobs. Whereas around 30% of both husbands and wives in dual-earner families worked in managerial or professional occupations, the proportion was just 24% for husbands in traditional families.

Spouses are more likely to be dual earners if the husband works full-time. While 71% of families in which the husband had a full-time job were dual earners in 1986, the figure was only 61%, if the husband had been unemployed sometime during the year.

However, wives' contribution to total dual-earner family income was greater if their husbands did not work full-time. For example, women whose husbands were unemployed for more than 27 weeks provided 37% of family income, while their share was 33% if the husband was unemployed 13-27 weeks, and 30% if he was out of work for less than 13 weeks. By contrast, wives' earnings amounted to 28% of total family income in dual-earner families where the husband worked full-time.

Overall, dual-earner families are slightly less likely than traditional families to have children at home. In 1986, 68% of dual-earner families had children, compared with 72% of traditional families.

The difference, however, was much sharper among young families. Only 32% of dual-earner families in which the wife was under age 25 had children, whereas the figure was 77% for traditional families. Among families in which the wife was aged 25-34, 70% of dual earners had children, compared with 95% for families in which the husband was the sole earner.

Regional differences

Dual-earner families are most common in the Prairies and Ontario. In 1986, 68% of husband-wife families in the Prairie provinces were dual earners, as were 66% of those in Ontario. By contrast, fewer than 60% of families in both Quebec (57%) and the Atlantic region (58%) had two earners, while the figure in British Columbia was 62%.

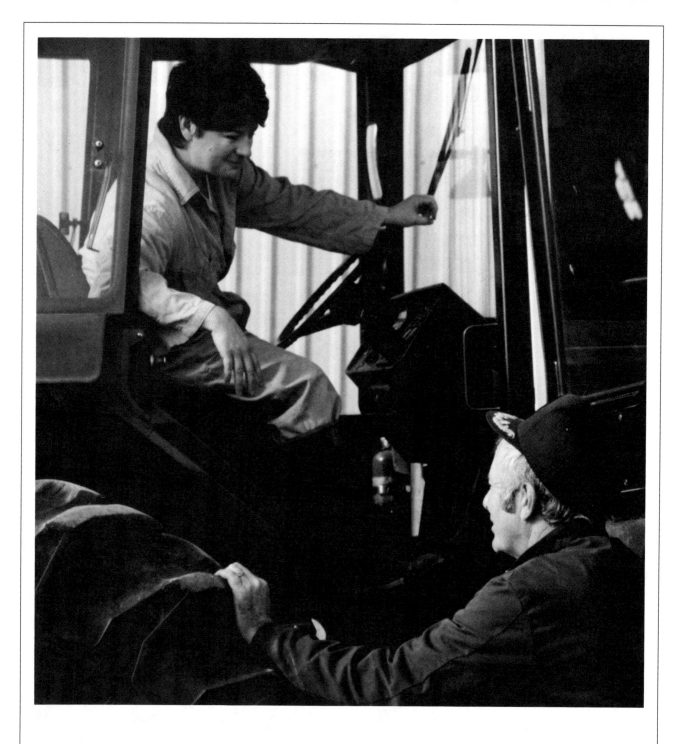

THE DECLINE OF UNPAID FAMILY WORK

by Doreen Duchesne

At the turn of the century, when Canadian society was mostly rural, unpaid family workers were an important part of the Canadian workforce. Their numbers, however, declined sharply as the economy industrialized and they now make up only a small fraction of total employment in Canada.

In 1987, for example, only 93,000 people were employed as unpaid family workers and they made up just 0.8% of all Canadians with jobs. These figures are down from 1975, when 132,000 unpaid workers made up 1.4% of total employment.

> An **unpaid family worker** is a person who works without pay on a family farm or in a business or professional practice owned and operated by a related member of the same household. Although this type of worker does not receive a formal wage or salary, he or she is considered to benefit financially from the family enterprise.

Most in agriculture

The majority of unpaid family workers are employed in agriculture. In 1987, 59,000 unpaid family workers, 64% of the total, worked in this industry. Their numbers have declined from 92,000 in 1975.

Unpaid family workers continue to be an important source of labour in agriculture, accounting for 12% of all people employed in this industry in 1987. This was down, though, from 19% in 1975.

The remaining third of unpaid family workers are employed in non-agricultural industries. In 1987, there were 34,000 such workers, 14% fewer than in 1975. Most of these workers are employed in retail trade or in community, business and personal service industries.

Married women the main source of unpaid family work

Most unpaid family workers are married women aged 25 and over. In 1987, these women made up 70% of the unpaid family work force. A further 18% of these workers were single 15-19-years-olds.

The number of unpaid family workers in each of these groups has declined. Between 1975 and 1987, the number of married women fell 23% from 84,000 to 64,000, while the number of teenagers dropped 51% from 34,000 to 17,000.

Much of the decline among married women occurred in agriculture. Between 1975 and 1987, the number of married women aged 25 and over working without pay in agriculture dropped 25% from 53,000 to 39,000.

Many of these women, however, were not moving out of agriculture. Rather, they were shifting into paid work and self-employment in this industry. For example, between 1975 and 1987, the number of wives aged 25 and over employed as paid workers in agriculture doubled to 35,000, while the number who were self-employed almost quadrupled to 34,000.

The shift from unpaid to self-employment possibly resulted from recent developments in matrimonial property law. These changes may have played a role in encouraging women to enter formal partnerships with their husbands in order to gain legal recognition for the value of the labour they contribute to the family business.

Changes in taxation law may have encouraged the shift to paid work. Since 1980, owners of unincorporated businesses have been allowed to claim a spousal employee's income as a tax deduction.

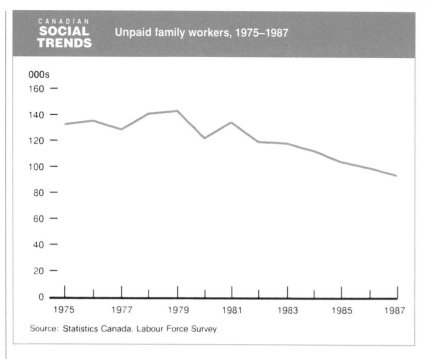

CANADIAN **SOCIAL TRENDS**

Unpaid family workers, 1975–1987

Source: Statistics Canada. Labour Force Survey

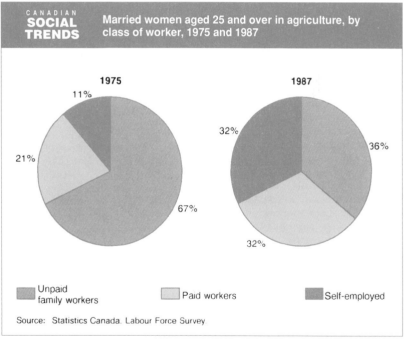

CANADIAN **SOCIAL TRENDS**

Married women aged 25 and over in agriculture, by class of worker, 1975 and 1987

■ Unpaid family workers　　■ Paid workers　　■ Self-employed

Source: Statistics Canada. Labour Force Survey.

THE VALUE OF HOUSEHOLD WORK IN CANADA

Adapted from article by J.L. Swinamer

Proposals to include the contribution of a woman's household work in the value of a family estate, or to make the value of such work pensionable under universal public pension plans, or even to pay wages to housewives, all require some basic agreement around the extent and worth of the work performed.

The value of household work in Canada for 1981 was estimated at between $121 billion and $139 billion.[1] To provide a perspective on this form of activity, these estimates represented 35.7% and 41.0% of GNP that year. The 1981 estimates of the value of household work as a percentage of GNP, however, are lower than estimates for 1971. Using the methodology that produced the lower estimate above, the value of household work declined from 40.9% of GNP in 1971 to 35.7% in 1981. This decline is due to the combined effect of increased labour force participation by women and lower time contributions to household work by women in the labour force versus those not in the labour force.

There are significant regional variations subsumed in the national average. The value of household work is higher where more hours are spent at it, which inevitably means in those regions where labour force participation by women is low. Again using the methodology which produced the lower national estimate, the value of household work in 1981 was calculated at more than half of provincial gross domestic product (GDP) in Newfoundland (55%), Prince Edward Island (66%) and Nova Scotia (50%), and close to half in New Brunswick (47%). At the other extreme, household work was valued at just 25% of provincial GDP in Alberta in 1981.

The estimated value of household work in Canada is consistent with earlier findings in other countries, which generally put the worth of household work around a third of GNP. Though the findings have been arrived at by various methods, and are not included in official estimates of GNP, they are seen as an important and necessary response to social pressure to place a dollar value on the household work done, most of it by women.

Detailed calculation and explanations of the value of household work may be found in a paper by J.L. Swinamer, "The Value of Household Work in Canada, 1981;" in the *Canadian Statistical Review*, Statistics Canada, Catalogue 11–003E, Volume 60, No. 3.

---

[1] These two figures are based on different methods of estimation. The first, which produced the lower estimate of the value of household work, calculated what it would cost to hire different persons to perform household activities such as child care, food preparation, cleaning, clothing care, marketing and household management. The higher estimate was derived by estimating what household workers would have earned had they participated in labour market activities.

CHILD CARE

by Mary Anne Burke

Shifting family behaviour, particularly the increase in the number of mothers working outside the home, has created a need for alternatives to the "stay-at-home" mother form of child care.

Statistics Canada's 1981 Survey of Child Care Arrangements found that more than half (52%) of all children under the age of six were cared for by someone other than their parents on a regular basis. Child care can be provided in many forms, from licensed day care centres and licensed family day care to private care by a nanny, neighbour or relative. In 1988, only 16% of preschool children with mothers in the labour force were in licensed family or centre day care on a full-time basis.

In 1988, there were more than 1.3 million preschoolers (under age 6) and 1.6 million school age children (aged 6–12) whose mothers were in the labour force. Thus, as many as 2.9 million children may have been in need of

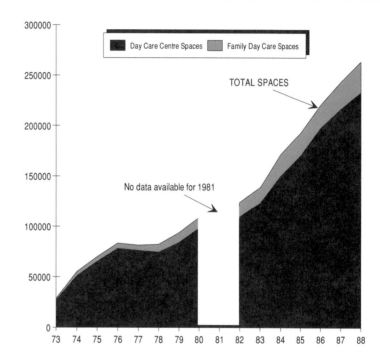

Licensed Day Care Spaces, 1973–1988

Day Care Centre Spaces Family Day Care Spaces

TOTAL SPACES

No data available for 1981

Source: Health and Welfare Canada, National Day Care Information Centre.
No data available for 1981.

DEFINITIONS

DAY CARE FACILITY: a licensed or provincially approved centre or private home which cares for children outside their home for eight to ten hours per day.

CENTRE CARE: a licensed day care centre caring for groups of children.

FAMILY DAY CARE: a program involving the selection and supervision by a government or authorized private agency of private families who care for children during the day.

For the purposes of this document, these last two forms are referred to as "licensed child care". All other forms of care are referred to as "informal" or "private" day care arrangements.

some form of alternate child care arrangements.

Most parents in need of child care services turn to informal, privately arranged types of care. The charges for such unlicensed care may sometimes fall outside of normal business practices and form part of the so-called "underground economy".

There were 264,000 day care spaces in 1988, up from 244,000 in 1987.* About 53,000 day care spaces in 1988 were reserved for children under three years of age. Care for children under three represents a high-cost, labour-intensive care which can cost parents as much as one-third more than the cost for an older child.

The majority of licensed spaces are in day care centres rather than in family day care. Of the day care centres, 62% are non-profit and 38% are commercial.

The continuing movement of women into the labour force, and the increase in lone-parent families will provide a growing demand for a variety of forms of child care. Some employers in the private and public sectors are responding to this demand by offering their employees child care associated with the work-place. However, privately arranged, unlicensed child care predominates at present.

---

* The actual growth rate (17%) between 1987 and 1988 was double that indicated by these figures. Prior to 1988 the number of spaces for Ontario was overstated because data on enrolment rather than number of spaces were reported. For the past few years enrolment was 122% of licensed spaces.

FAMILY HOMICIDE

by Holly Johnson and Peter Chisholm

Between 1974 and 1987, homicides involving people related to one another through marriage, common-law union, or kinship accounted for 39% of the total of 7,582 solved homicide offences in Canada. Domestic homicides decreased from 45% of the total solved in 1974 to a low of 33% in 1980, but then rose to 40% between 1985 and 1987.[1] The average annual number of family homicides over the 14-year period was 212.

Men who killed their wives or common-law partners were the single largest group of offenders (37%) in family homicides between 1974 and 1987. Wives and common-law wives were responsible in 12% of cases, fathers in 11%, and mothers in 9%. The remaining offenders were: a child of the victim (9%), a brother or sister (7%), an aunt, uncle, or cousin (7%), an in-law (3%), or another relative (5%).

Native offenders and victims

Native people[2] are greatly over-represented in homicide offences in general, and in family-related homicide in particular.

While Native people make up about 3% of the total population, they accounted for 23% of suspects and 22% of victims in family homicides in the 1974-1987 period. In fact, almost half (49%) of solved homicides involving Native victims were family-related. A quarter of these were committed by husbands, wives, or common-law partners.

Murder-suicide

Persons who commit domestic homicides often take their own lives immediately after the incident. Men who killed their spouse or child were more likely than any other group of suspects to commit suicide immediately following the incident. Over the 1974-1987 period, 31% of men who killed their wives, 19% of those who killed their common-law partners, and 24% of those who killed their children

later took their own lives. Much lower percentages of mothers (10%), wives (5%), and other family members (4%) killed themselves after the incident.

The rate of post-homicide suicide among Native suspects was much lower than among non-Natives. Native suspects committed suicide in only 5% of cases in contrast to 20% for non-Native suspects.

Location

Eight of ten family-related homicides occurred in the home of either the victim or the suspect. Remaining offences occurred in other private places (8%), in public places (6%), or in other or unknown locations (7%).

Alcohol and drugs

Between 1974 and 1987, police recorded either alcohol or drug consumption as a contributing factor in about 30% of domestic homicides. But the percentage of incidents involving alcohol alone

declined from about 47% of cases in 1975 to 21% in 1987. Evidence of drug consumption as a contributing factor remained at 5% over the 14-year period. Alcohol was likely to be a factor when women killed their partners, especially when the victim was a common-law spouse (69%) as opposed to a legally married partner (45%).

Alcohol was less likely to be involved when men killed their wives or common-law partners—just 21% and 39% of cases, respectively. Alcohol was a factor in 38% of offences involving other family members as victims and in 14% of cases of homicide by mothers.

[1] The homicide rate in Canada has declined over the past 14 years, from a high of 3.1 per 100,000 population in 1975 and 1977 to a low of 2.2 in 1986. The 1987 rate was 2.5.

[2] Includes status and non-status Native Indians, Métis, and Inuit.

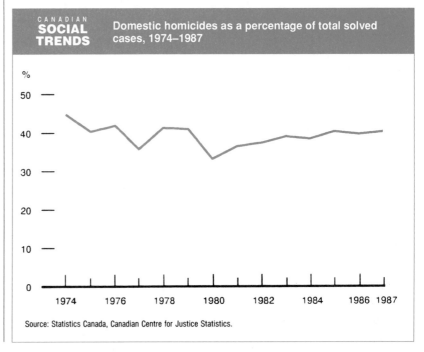

CANADIAN SOCIAL TRENDS — Domestic homicides as a percentage of total solved cases, 1974–1987

Source: Statistics Canada, Canadian Centre for Justice Statistics.

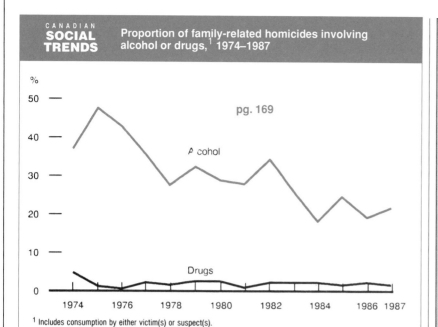

CANADIAN SOCIAL TRENDS

Proportion of family-related homicides involving alcohol or drugs,[1] 1974–1987

pg. 169

Alcohol

Drugs

[1] Includes consumption by either victim(s) or suspect(s).
Source: Statistics Canada, Canadian Centre for Justice Statistics.

Fully 65% of domestic homicides with Native victims between 1974 and 1987 involved alcohol consumption by either the victim or suspect or both, triple the rate for non-Natives (21%).

Method of killing

Between 1974 and 1987, shooting was the most frequent way that family members were killed, accounting for 37% of victims. Stabbing was the second most common method (23%), followed by beating (21%), and strangulation or suffocation (10%). All other methods, including drowning and arson, made up only 9%.

The use of firearms varied over the 14-year period, reaching a high of over 40% of all domestic homicides in 1974, 1980 and 1986 and a low of fewer than 30% in 1985. Stabbing, on the other hand, increased steadily as a proportion of the total from 13% to 30%.

Shooting was the most common way that men killed their wives. Half of these suspects used a firearm. Men who killed their common-law spouses, on the other hand, chose guns (34%) and beating (30%) in almost equal proportions. Guns were also used in 33% of cases of fathers killing their children.

The predominant method used by women killing their spouse or common-law partner was stabbing (45% and 65%, respectively). Women most often killed their children by strangulation or suffoca-tion (31%) or by other methods not involving firearms (31%). Fully one-fifth (22%) of mothers who killed their children were themselves teenagers at the time of the offence.

Assaults on wives: Results from the 1988 General Social Survey

The General Social Survey conducted by Statistics Canada in January and February of 1988 asked questions about criminal incidents that occurred in 1987 in which respondents were victims. All the estimates have high sampling variability and should be used with caution.

On the basis of this survey, the estimated number of wife assaults[1] for Canada in 1987 was 157,000 or about 1,500 per 100,000 women. However, this estimate is conservative in that the number of incidents per respondent was limited to a maximum of 3. The actual number of incidents per respondent ranged as high as 26.

The rate was highest for women aged 25-44 at 2,200 per 100,000, while the rate for those aged 15-24 was 1,900. The rate for those 45 or more years could not be calculated reliably.

About two-thirds (62%) of incidents involved being hit, slapped, kicked, or knocked down. Other attacks were incidents in which the victim was grabbed, held, tripped, jumped on, or pushed, while a small number were rapes, shootings, knifings, or assaults with objects. More than one in five (21%) of the assaulted wives later received attention from a doctor or nurse.

The majority (68%) of reported incidents occurred at night between 6 PM and 8 AM, while the remainder took place during the day or at an unspecified time. Almost three-quarters (73%) of incidents occurred in an urban setting, with the balance taking place in a town, village, or rural area, or in an unstated location.

[1] Assaults or sexual assaults against a female victim by her spouse or ex-spouse.

MALE VIOLENCE IN THE HOME

by Eugen Lupri

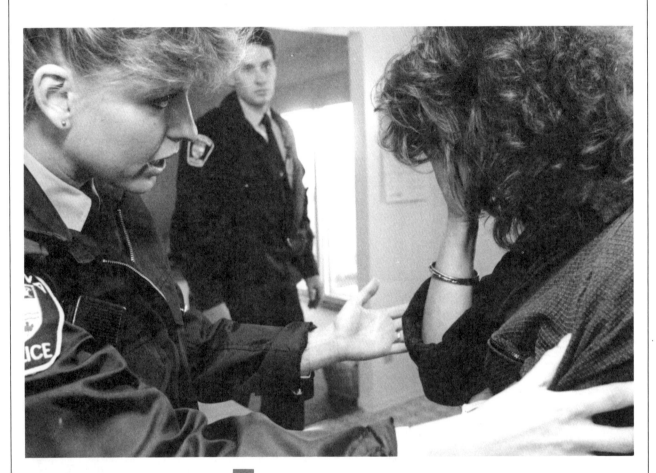

Eugen Lupri

The family can provide a private setting for the development of love and companionship. But the very privacy that fosters emotional attachments between partners also allows the expression of violent antagonism.

When surveyed under circumstances guaranteeing anonymity, Canadian men aged 18 and over reported that they had committed significant amounts of violence against their partners. In many instances, the violence was not an isolated incident, but had occurred several times during the previous year.

Overall, 12% of men reported that they had pushed, grabbed, or shoved their mates at least once during the previous year, and in two-thirds of these cases, the incidents had occurred more than once. Another 9% reported they had thrown an object at a mate.

Rates of more serious types of violence were lower: 6% reported kicking, biting, or hitting with a fist, 5% reported slapping, and 5% said they had hit with an object or had attempted to do so. Fewer than 3% reported beating their mates, while less than 1% claimed to have either threatened to use or actually used a knife or gun.

Almost one in five (18%) married or cohabiting men had committed at least one of eight listed violent acts.[1] The figure rose to about 30% among divorced or separated respondents. Considering only the five most serious acts, each of which carries a high risk of serious injury, about 10% of married and cohabiting men reported at least one such incident.

Characteristics of men who report assaulting their mates

While abuse of a female partner was reported by men in all income groups, it was more common among those with low incomes. The rate for men with annual incomes less than $20,000 was 26%, double the rate for men with incomes of $65,000 or over (13%).

More than half the male respondents

About the survey

These data were collected as part of a national survey of 1,834 men and women aged 18 and over, conducted by Decima Research Ltd. during November and December 1986. The findings presented here are based on the responses of the men.

The information was gathered by self-administered questionnaires, which interviewers left behind after personal interviews together with a return envelope to be completed by ever-married or cohabiting respondents.

Households were selected at random by computer using Statistics Canada enumeration areas as the primary sampling unit. Probability of selection was disproportionate by province, and within each province the sample was stratified by community size. A weighting scheme was used to bring the sample back into the proper proportions vis-à-vis the 1981 Census. In 19 out of every 20 national samples of this size, the results would fall within about plus or minus two percentage points of the results found here.

Eight questions on spousal violence appeared on the questionnaire after a series of less delicate questions on family life. A short written introduction presented the topic in terms of disagreements and conflicts that nearly all couples experience. If respondents were members of an ongoing marital or common-law relationship, the acts of violence referred to occurred in 1986. If respondents were separated, divorced, or widowed at the time of the survey, the questions referred to their last year of marriage.

Levels of violence ranged from throwing objects at a partner through pushing and shoving, slapping, kicking, hitting, beating, to the threatened or actual use of potentially deadly weapons such as guns or knives.

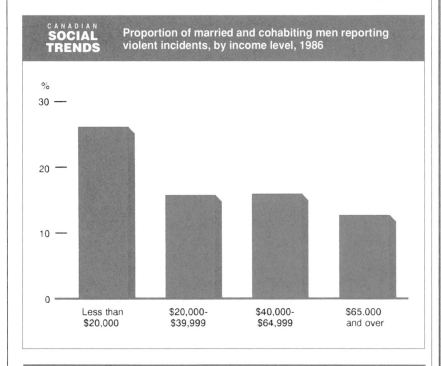

CANADIAN SOCIAL TRENDS — Proportion of married and cohabiting men reporting violent incidents, by income level, 1986

%

30 —

20 —

10 —

0

Less than $20,000 — $20,000-$39,999 — $40,000-$64,999 — $65.000 and over

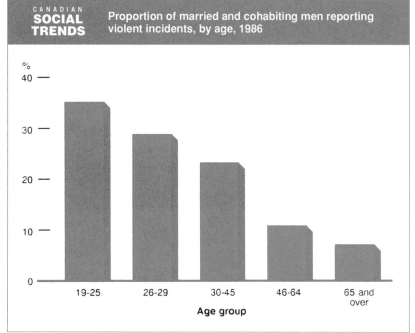

CANADIAN SOCIAL TRENDS — Proportion of married and cohabiting men reporting violent incidents, by age, 1986

%

40 —

30 —

20 —

10 —

0

19-25 — 26-29 — 30-45 — 46-64 — 65 and over

Age group

[1] Using the same Conflict Tactics Scales employed here, Michael Smith reported an annual incidence rate of 14.4% among a sample of 604 Toronto women in "The Incidence and Prevalence of Woman Abuse in Toronto" in *Violence and Victims*, Vol. 2, No. 3, 1987.

reporting violent incidents were aged 29 or younger. Although the rate was lower for older men, wife abuse occurs at all ages. In fact, 7% of men aged 65 and older reported such incidents.

Among younger men, those with the least education tended to report more incidents. For example, among those aged 18-44 with an incomplete high school education, 28% reported assaults as opposed to 17% with a graduate or professional degree. Among men 45 years and older, the highest rate found was for men with an incomplete university education (31%).

Geographic differences

Spousal assault rates were highest in the Western provinces and in the Atlantic region. British Columbia had the highest overall violence rate (26%), while the figure was 24% in the Atlantic provinces. Quebec (13%) had the lowest overall provincial rate, while Ontario's rate (17%) was close to the national average of 18%.

Wife abuse occurred more frequently in urban than in rural areas. Rates for men who lived in rural areas or in towns with fewer than 5,000 inhabitants were lowest (12%). Spousal assault rates were over 20% in medium-sized towns and cities (23%), and in metropolitan areas (21%).

Stress and violence

There is a strong relationship between stressful life events and reported male spousal violence. The interview schedule contained a checklist of 12 stressful events that respondents might have experienced in the previous five years:

• Unemployment for more than one month
• Personal bankruptcy
• A drop in wage or salary
• Taking an additional job to make ends meet
• Working more overtime than he wishes to make ends meet
• Child support or alimony payments that he did not have before
• A move to less expensive accommodations
• Taking in a boarder to help make ends meet
• One or more demotions
• Loss of income due to a return to school
• Some other important career setback
• Some other significant negative change in economic circumstances

Just 8% of men who reported none or only one of the listed stressful events also reported an instance of violence between themselves and their mates. But the proportion rose to 18% of those reporting two or three sources of stress, to 19% for those reporting 4 or 5 stressful events, and to 33% for those registering 6 or 7 such sources.

WIFE ABUSE

by Holly Johnson

Until recently, little has been known about the extent of wife abuse in Canada. A 1982 survey, however, gives an outline of the circumstances surrounding incidents of abuse and a profile of victims.

The Canadian Urban Victimization Survey estimated that in 1981 about 4 of every 1,000 women (aged 16 and over) in seven cities were assaulted or sexually assaulted by a spouse or former spouse.[1] Separated women were much more likely to be abused than married or divorced women. The abuse was often recurrent. Although weapons were rarely used, most abuse resulted in injury. Yet the evidence suggests that many assaults, even those involving serious injury, were not reported to the police.

Not an Isolated Event

The survey identified an estimated 11,000 incidents of abuse. Half the incidents involved women who were assaulted more than once. An additional 6% of the incidents involved a series of five or more assaults so similar that victims could not recall the details of each episode.

Rates Highest for Separated Women

The risk of assault was highest for women who were separated: the rate was 55 per 1,000 separated women, compared with 18 per 1,000 divorced women, and 2 per 1,000 married women. It is unclear from the survey the extent to which the abuse precipitated the separation or the separation precipitated the abuse.

Women in low-income households experienced the highest rate of assault. The survey recorded assault rates of 8.2 per 1,000 women in households with annual incomes of less than $9,000; 7.7 per 1,000 women in households with incomes from $9,000 to $20,000; and 2.3 per 1,000 women in households with incomes more than $20,000.

---

[1] Excludes assaults by male friends or partners not described by victims as a spouse or former spouse.

Injury Usually Results

An estimated 75% of the incidents involved physical violence or sexual assault; the remaining 25% were described as threats of violence. Most of the actual physical assaults resulted in injury to the woman, and a substantial proportion of these injuries were serious enough to require medical attention.

The presence of weapons, however, was relatively rare, occurring in 18% of all cases of wife abuse. About 12% of assaults involved bottles, blunt instruments, or other objects not usually considered weapons. Very few incidents (6%) involved guns or knives.[2]

At Home, at Night, on the Weekend

Wife abuse almost always happens in the home: 83% of incidents took place in the victim's residence, and 9% in the residence of another person. An estimated 75% of the assaults occurred in the evening or at night, and almost half (45%) happened on the weekend. About 50%

of the assailants were reported to be under the influence of alcohol at the time of the incident.

Fewer than Half Reported to Police

The police were called in fewer than half (44%) of the wife abuse incidents estimated in the survey. Outsiders were unlikely to summon the police; only 9% of abuse cases were reported by someone other than the victim, while 35% were reported by victims themselves.

Injury to the victim did not increase the likelihood that the abuse would be reported to the police. However, the presence of a weapon did: assaults involving weapons were almost twice as likely to be reported (64%) as those not involving weapons (39%).

Lower income women were most likely to call the police. Reporting rates were 44% for victims with household incomes under $9,000 and 53% for those in the $9,000 to $20,000 range, but fell to 26%[2] in the over $20,000 category.

The Canadian Urban Victimization Survey (CUVS) was conducted in 1982 by the Ministry of the Solicitor General and Statistics Canada. Approximately 61,000 residents of seven cities (Vancouver, Edmonton, Winnipeg, Toronto, Montreal, Halifax-Dartmouth, and St. John's) were interviewed by telephone about their experiences of crime and with the criminal justice system.

The survey included questions about sexual and non-sexual assault and the victim's relationship to the offender. Sexual assault refers to rape,

attempted rape, and molesting. Non-sexual assault ranges from verbal threats to an attack causing extensive injuries.

From the interviews, estimates were made for the population aged 16 and over in the seven cities. The sensitive nature of wife abuse means that the true incidence of this crime is likely to be undercounted, even in the CUVS. Nevertheless, the CUVS provides information not available from police records by counting incidents that were not reported, as well as those that were.

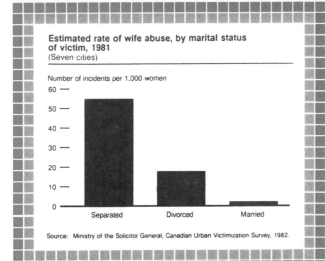

Estimated rate of wife abuse, by marital status of victim, 1981
(Seven cities)

Number of incidents per 1,000 women

Source: Ministry of the Solicitor General, Canadian Urban Victimization Survey, 1982.

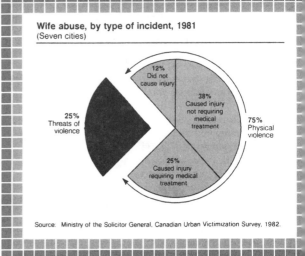

Wife abuse, by type of incident, 1981
(Seven cities)

12% Did not cause injury
38% Caused injury not requiring medical treatment
75% Physical violence
25% Threats of violence
25% Caused injury requiring medical treatment

Source: Ministry of the Solicitor General, Canadian Urban Victimization Survey, 1982.

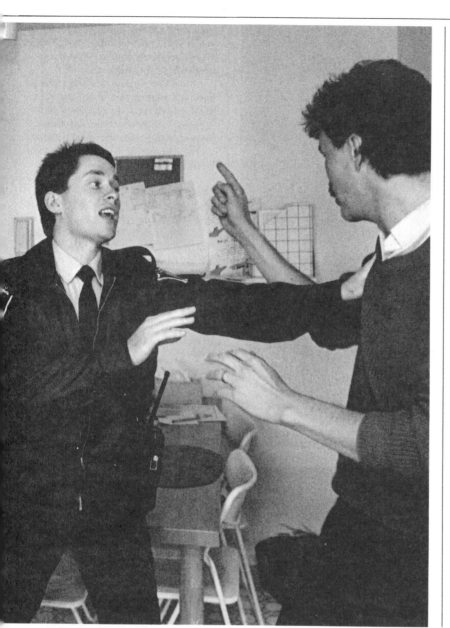

Reasons for Not Reporting

Responses to the survey indicate the main reasons why most wife abuse victims did not call the police.[3] Six out of ten (59%) who did not report the assault viewed the incident as a "personal matter and of no concern to the police," and a similar proportion (58%) believed that "the police couldn't do anything about it." Half (52%) cited "fear of revenge" by the offender. Fear of revenge was twice as likely to be a factor for women who were victimized more than once in the year than for those victimized on a single occasion. One-third (35%) did not report the incident because they wanted to protect the offender.

Police Performance

Of the abused women who did report the incident, most (63%) rated the overall performance of the police favourably. Three-quarters (73%) gave the police good or average ratings on being courteous, and 68% rated the police

[2] Because the estimates are based on very small samples, caution should be used when interpreting these data.

[3] Victims could state more than one reason for not reporting.

Emergency Shelters

The number of emergency shelters across Canada for abused women and their children continues to grow, increasing fourfold from 71 to 267 between 1979 and 1987. The provinces with the most shelters are Ontario (98), Quebec (70), British Columbia (39), and Alberta (18). Prince Edward Island and the Yukon each have one, and the Northwest Territories has two.

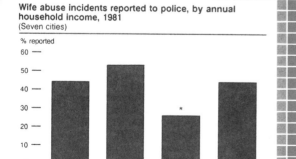

Wife abuse incidents reported to police, by annual household income, 1981
(Seven cities)

% reported

* Because estimates are based on very small samples, caution should be used when interpreting these data.
Source: Ministry of the Solicitor General. Canadian Urban Victimization Survey. 1982.

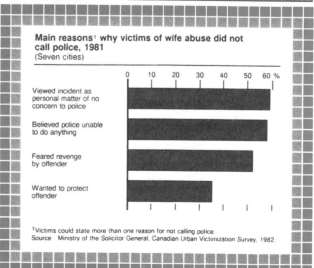

Main reasons[1] why victims of wife abuse did not call police, 1981
(Seven cities)

Viewed incident as personal matter of no concern to police

Believed police unable to do anything

Feared revenge by offender

Wanted to protect offender

[1] Victims could state more than one reason for not calling police.
Source: Ministry of the Solicitor General. Canadian Urban Victimization Survey. 1982.

positively on responding promptly. A much lower proportion (52%) felt they were adequately informed on the progress of the investigation.

Thirty-four percent of abused women received information about their legal rights and the services available to them. Victims who received such information were more likely than those who had not to rate the police favourably on their handling of the incident.

Other Sources of Support

Many women sought support outside the criminal justice system: 37% turned to friends and neighbours, and 20% sought out a family member.[4] One in four received assistance from a lawyer. Although 80% of victims thought counselling should be available, only 20% received support from a social service agency.

[4] Victims could list more than one source of assistance.

HELP AROUND THE HOUSE: SUPPORT FOR OLDER CANADIANS

by Janet Hagey

The majority of Canadians aged 55 and over[1] can perform most household chores on their own, according to Statistics Canada's 1985 General Social Survey. With advancing age and deteriorating health, however, the need for assistance increases, particularly for tasks involving some physical effort such as heavy housework, grocery shopping, and yardwork. Nonetheless, for all activities, the percentage of older people getting help exceeds the proportion who actually need it, although it is likely that many of those who require considerable support are already in institutions.

Need for help depends on task

Older Canadians are generally more likely to need help with tasks involving some physical exertion. For example, in 1985, 21% of people aged 55 and over required assistance with heavy housework, and 12%, with grocery shopping. In addition, 33% of those who did not live in an apartment needed help with yardwork. On the other hand, fewer than one out of ten people required aid with less strenuous tasks such as meal preparation (7%), money management (4%), light housework (3%), and personal care (2%).

Need rises with age

Not surprisingly, the need for household help increases with age. In 1985, nearly half (46%) of people aged 75 and over required assistance with heavy house-

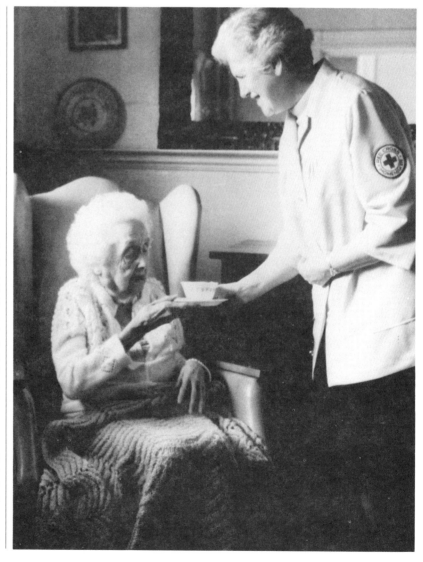

[1] Excludes people in residential care institutions.

work, and a third (33%), with grocery shopping. In comparison, only 22% of those aged 65-74 needed help with heavy housework, and 12%, with grocery shopping; for those aged 55-64, the figures were 10% and 5%, respectively.

Women aged 75 and over require the most support. In 1985, half of these women needed help with heavy housework, and 39% required assistance with grocery shopping. Among men, the figures were 43% for heavy housework and 23% for grocery shopping.

The proportions of people aged 75 and over needing help with chores involving less exertion were also higher than among those aged 55-74. Nonetheless, even at ages 75 and over, more than eight out of ten people could handle meal preparation, money management, light housework, and personal care without assistance.

Poor health increases need
As might be expected, people in poor health were more likely than others to require aid in performing daily household tasks. For example, of those who rated their health poor, 26% needed help with meals, 20% with light housework, 12% with money management, and 11% with personal care. In comparison, virtually all who rated their health excellent or good could manage these chores.

Grocery shopping was a problem for only 3% of older people in excellent health and 6% in good health; on the other hand, 43% of those in poor health required help buying groceries. In fact, people aged 75 and over who reported good or excellent health had less need for help with grocery shopping than did 55-64-year-olds whose health was poor.

Most older people who rated their health excellent or good could handle even such tasks as heavy housework and yardwork. By contrast, among those in poor health, two-thirds needed assistance with heavy housework, and three-quarters required help with yardwork.

Living arrangements related to need
People living alone or with their spouse are less likely to require help around the house than are those sharing accommodations with someone other than their spouse. However, the last group may have adopted this housing arrangement expressly because they need support.

Close to four out of ten (38%) older people living with others required help with heavy housework, compared with only 16% living alone and 20% living with their spouse. Similarly, 24% of those

living with others needed help grocery shopping, while the proportion was 11% for people living alone or with their spouse.

Even tasks that most older people can handle by themselves are troublesome for many of those who live with others. For instance, 11% of people living with others needed help with money management, and 9% required help with light housekeeping. By contrast, fewer than 5% of older people living alone or with their spouse required such support.

Much support for elderly
Regardless of the task, the proportion of older people who received help exceeded the percentage who claimed that they needed it. Not surprisingly, levels of support were particularly high among people living with their spouse or with others, as these companions undoubtedly shared in household chores. However, even people who lived alone received a considerable amount of help.

While 16% of older people living alone needed assistance with housework, 21%

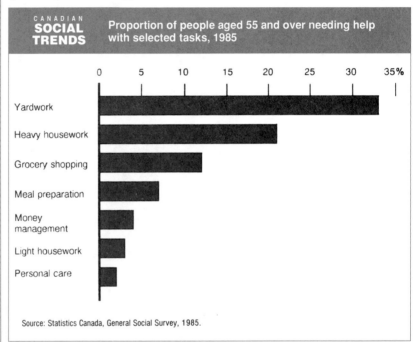

CANADIAN SOCIAL TRENDS

Proportion of people aged 55 and over needing help with selected tasks, 1985

Source: Statistics Canada, General Social Survey, 1985.

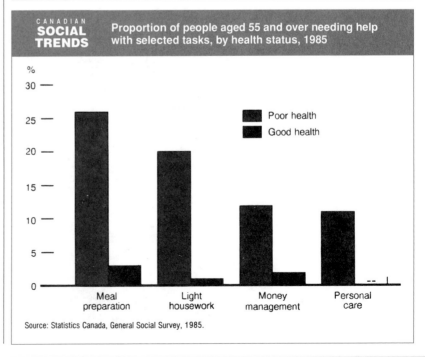

CANADIAN SOCIAL TRENDS

Proportion of people aged 55 and over needing help with selected tasks, by health status, 1985

Poor health
Good health

Source: Statistics Canada, General Social Survey, 1985.

received such help. The corresponding figures for grocery shopping were 11% and 20%. The pattern was similar for yardwork: 39% of older people living alone required help, but 57% of them actually received some assistance.

Sources of support

Support for older people comes from a variety of sources including spouses, children and other relatives, friends and neighbours, and formal support systems such as homemaker services and seniors' centres.

For men living alone, friends and neighbours were the main source of assistance with yardwork and grocery shopping. As well, friends and neighbours were their primary source of help with meal preparation, although formal organizations were also important. In addition, formal organizations were the major source of help with housework for men who lived alone.

Formal support was also important to older women who lived alone. Visiting homemakers and similar services were their most common source of help with housework and meal preparation. For yardwork, women living alone were more likely to be aided by friends and neighbours, while help in grocery shopping was most often provided by their children, particularly daughters.

Support for older people living with someone other than their spouse came largely from their children and other relatives. However, in many cases, the relatives providing support were probably the "others" with whom the older people shared their accommodations.

Because older married couples can usually rely on each other, they tend to receive much less assistance from other sources. For instance, a spouse was the sole source of assistance for nine out of ten married people who got help with grocery shopping and meal preparation. Such highly concentrated support, however, makes them vulnerable if that support is lost.

The additional help that older couples do get is likely to be provided by their children. Daughters aid with housework, meal preparation, and groceries; sons, with yardwork.

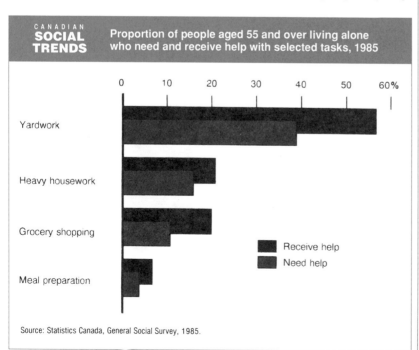

CANADIAN
SOCIAL TRENDS
Proportion of people aged 55 and over living alone who need and receive help with selected tasks, 1985

Source: Statistics Canada, General Social Survey, 1985.

RESIDENTIAL CARE

by Carol Strike

Residential care facilities are an important component of Canada's health care system. Occupants of these facilities receive nursing and counselling services, as opposed to the active medical treatment available in hospitals. While most residential care facilities are homes for the aged, they also include residences for psychiatrically disabled or developmentally delayed people, substance abusers, and emotionally disabled children.

In 1986-87, an estimated daily average of 226,000 people were in residential care facilities.[1] By comparison, an average of around 150,000 people were in hospitals each day.

Most in homes for the aged

Homes for the aged account for about seven out of ten people in residential care. In 1986-87, there were an estimated

[1] Includes facilities with four or more beds, which are funded, licensed, or approved by provincial/territorial departments of health/ social services.

158,000 residents per day in homes for the aged, a 24% increase from 1979-80. This rise reflects both the growing number of elderly people and the diminishing tendency for them to live with their adult children.

Most people in homes for the aged are women. In 1986-87, women made up 70% of residents in these facilities. As well, many residents are "older elderly" people. Over three-quarters (77%) of people in these facilities in 1986-87 were at least 75 years of age, and 40% were aged 85 and over.

Changes in other institutions
In 1986-87, 9% of the total estimated number of people in residential care were in homes for the psychiatrically disabled; 8% were in facilities for the developmentally delayed; 4% were in homes for emotionally disturbed children; 2% were in substance abuse facilities; and 5% were in other types of institutions.

This distribution reflects several shifts since the late 1970s. Between 1979-80 and 1986-87, the number of residents in substance abuse facilities increased 44%, while the number in facilities for the developmentally delayed rose about 15%.

On the other hand, the number of residents in facilities for the physically disabled decreased sharply. An estimated 11,000 people were in these facilities on a daily basis in 1979-80; by 1986-87, there were only 2,700. This decline occurred largely because of the movement of physically disabled people from institutions to either group homes with fewer than four beds or independent home care arrangements.

The estimated daily number of residents in facilities for emotionally disturbed children also declined between 1979-80 and 1986-87.

In contrast to homes for the aged, most people in other residential care facilities are male. In 1986-87, men made up the majority of residents in facilities for substance abusers (81%), the psychiatrically disabled (60%), the developmentally delayed (57%), and the physically handicapped (55%). As well, boys made up 63% of the estimated number of residents in facilities for emotionally disturbed children.

High occupancy rates
The number of people in residential care is related to the number of spaces available. In fact, during the 1980s, these facilities were filled close to capacity, with an overall occupancy rate of more than 95%.

Homes for the aged and facilities for the developmentally delayed had the highest occupancy rates, as residents represented 97% of the number of approved beds in both types of institutions in 1986-87.

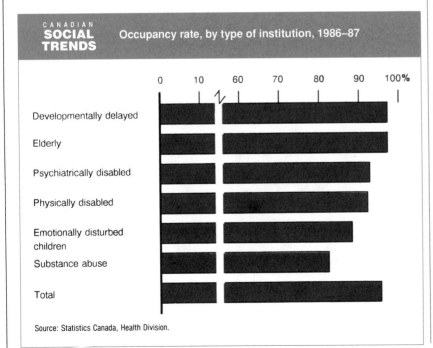

CANADIAN
SOCIAL TRENDS
Proportion of men and women in residential care, by type of institution, 1986–87

Men
Women

Source: Statistics Canada, Health Division.

CANADIAN
SOCIAL TRENDS
Occupancy rate, by type of institution, 1986–87

Source: Statistics Canada, Health Division.

Less private, more public ownership
Most residential care institutions are operated by non-profit organizations such as charities, governments, and religious organizations. In 1986, non-profit organizations ran 64% of residential care facilities, while the remaining 36% were operated for profit.

The proportion of residential care facilities operated by non-profit organizations increased during the 1980s. For example, in 1980, ownership of these institutions was divided roughly equally between profit and non-profit enterprises.

Occupancy rates in the other institutions ranged from 83% in facilities for substance abusers to 93% in facilities for the psychiatrically disabled.

Residential care expenditures

Every day in 1986-87, an estimated $15 million was spent on residential care. In fact, that year, residential care facilities accounted for an estimated 12.5% of all health care expenditures in Canada. Overall, the total estimated annual expenditure on residential care in 1986-87 was $5.5 billion, up from $4.2 billion (in 1986 dollars) in 1979-80.

More than half (56%) of all estimated residential care expenditures in 1986-87 went to facilities for the aged. A further 18% was spent on facilities for the psychiatrically disabled, while 11% and 9%, respectively, went to facilities for developmentally delayed people and emotionally disturbed children. The remaining 7% was divided among other facilities.

The amount spent per patient-day varies considerably by type of institution. Facilities for emotionally disturbed children reported the highest patient-day expenditure at $162. On the other hand, spending per aged patient was relatively low, amounting to just $54 a day.

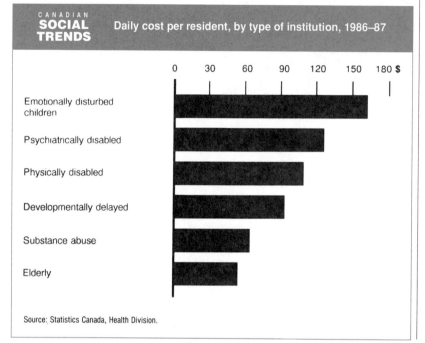

CANADIAN SOCIAL TRENDS

Daily cost per resident, by type of institution, 1986–87

Emotionally disturbed children
Psychiatrically disabled
Physically disabled
Developmentally delayed
Substance abuse
Elderly

Source: Statistics Canada, Health Division.

LIVING ARRANGEMENTS OF CANADA'S "OLDER ELDERLY" POPULATION

by Gordon E. Priest

Amajor change has occurred in the living arrangements of Canada's "older elderly" population (aged 75 and over) since 1971. A higher proportion of these people are living alone or in institutions, while the percentage living with others, primarily family, has declined. And projections to the year 2001 indicate that these trends are likely to continue.

As their living arrangements change, individuals aged 75 and over face a period of adjustment and resettlement. These changes present challenges to the public, private, and volunteer sectors.

Because the 75 and over age group is a fast-growing segment of the population, their living arrangements have implications for policymakers and planners. The next 15 years will likely see a substantial increase in demand for accommodations and services for these seniors.

More older elderly living alone or in institutions

For both men and women aged 75 and over, the number living alone or in institutions increased most rapidly between 1971 and 1986.[1]

Almost a quarter of a million (245,600) older elderly women lived alone in 1986; this was a 147% rise from 99,300 in 1971. Over the same period, the number living in institutions increased 127% from 53,200 to 120,900. These gains far outpaced the 68% increase in the total older elderly female population.

As a result of these rapid growth rates, by 1986, 38% of women aged 75 and over were living alone, up from 26% in 1971. The proportion in institutions also rose from 14% to 19%.

[1] Institutions refer to establishments providing some level of custody or care, as distinct from other collective dwellings such as hotels or rooming houses where no care is provided.

The number of older elderly men living alone or in institutions also grew, although increases were not as pronounced as among women. In 1986, 65,800 men aged 75 and over lived alone, up 78% from 37,000 in 1971. The number in institutions rose at almost the same rate (77%) from 25,700 to 45,300. In comparison, the increase of the total male population in this age range was just 39%.

As a consequence, between 1971 and 1986, the proportion of older elderly men living alone rose from 13% to 17%, and the percentage in institutions increased from 9% to 12%.

A fast-growing group

The number of people aged 75 and over increased 56% from 668,000 in 1971 to 1,040,000 in 1986. By contrast, the population younger than 75 rose just 16% in the same period. As a result, older elderly people constituted 4.1% of the Canadian population in 1986, up from 3.1% in 1971. Projections indicate that by 2001 Canada's older elderly will increase to 1.7 million and will represent more than 6% of the total population.

Women make up the majority of people aged 75 and over. By 1986, 62% of the older elderly were women, up from 58% in 1971. No change is expected by 2001, as the female component of the population aged 75 and over is projected to remain at 62%.

The female majority among older elderly people reflects, in part, women's lower mortality rate. In 1981, a woman aged 75 could expect to live about 12 more years, compared with 9 years for a man of the same age. Also, since women usually marry men older than themselves, their husbands are likely to predecease them. As a result, by age 75, the marital status and living arrangements of women differ sharply from those of men.

Many more older elderly women than men have been widowed. In 1986, about two-thirds of women aged 75 and over were widows, and fewer than one-quarter were married. By contrast, only a quarter of their male contemporaries were widowed, and almost two-thirds were married. Similarly, among those aged 85 and over, about 8 out of 10 women were widowed, compared with 4 out of 10 men.

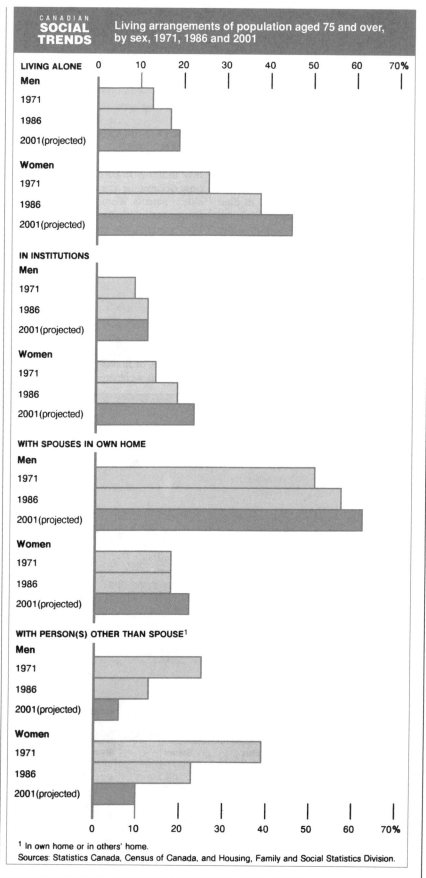

CANADIAN SOCIAL TRENDS

Living arrangements of population aged 75 and over, by sex, 1971, 1986 and 2001

LIVING ALONE
Men — 1971, 1986, 2001(projected)
Women — 1971, 1986, 2001(projected)

IN INSTITUTIONS
Men — 1971, 1986, 2001(projected)
Women — 1971, 1986, 2001(projected)

WITH SPOUSES IN OWN HOME
Men — 1971, 1986, 2001(projected)
Women — 1971, 1986, 2001(projected)

WITH PERSON(S) OTHER THAN SPOUSE[1]
Men — 1971, 1986, 2001(projected)
Women — 1971, 1986, 2001(projected)

[1] In own home or in others' home.

Sources: Statistics Canada, Census of Canada, and Housing, Family and Social Statistics Division.

Proportion of married couples rises

Older elderly men are much more likely than women of the same age to be living with their spouse in their own home. Moreover, the percentage of men in this situation increased from 51% in 1971 to 57% in 1986. By contrast, the proportion of older elderly women living at home with their spouse remained stable at 18%.

Fewer older elderly people living with others

The number and percentage of people aged 75 and over living with someone other than their spouse, either in their own home or in someone else's home, has decreased.[2] By 1986, 146,200 older elderly women without a spouse were living with others, a decline from 152,800 in 1971. At the same time, the number of older elderly men living with others fell from 69,500 to 51,700.

This meant that the proportion of older elderly women who lived with others was 23% in 1986, down from 39% in 1971. Similarly, the proportion of men aged 75 and over living with others was almost halved, dropping from 25% to 13%.

Much of this decline was caused by the falling percentage of older elderly people living in someone else's home. For women, the proportion dropped from 26% to 15%, while for men, the figure fell from 17% to 9%.

The percentage of older elderly people sharing their own home also declined. Among women, the proportion fell from 14% to 8%; the drop among men was from 7% to 4%.

The trend away from living with others may indicate, in part, that fewer adults now occupy the same dwelling as their elderly parents. Women's growing labour force participation has reduced the likelihood that someone will be at home to look after an elderly mother or father. On the other hand, rising incomes among elderly people may have enabled more of them to maintain separate living quarters.

An older group in institutions

People aged 75 and over who lived in institutions in 1986 tended to be older than their counterparts 15 years earlier. In 1986, 25% of all older elderly women in institutions were aged 90 and over; this was up from 15% in 1971. The percentage of older elderly men in institutions who were aged 90 and over also increased from 13% in 1971 to 19% in 1986.

Thus, in just 15 years, not only did the institutionalized elderly population increase sharply, but the age distribution of that population also changed. This shift, however, may not have been driven solely by demographic factors. It is possible that more restrictive admission practices may have screened out younger applicants.

Trends projected to continue

Projections of the living arrangements of older elderly people to the turn of the century indicate that the trend toward living alone or in institutions is likely to continue. At the same time, the proportion living with others is expected to decline even more.

By 2001, a projected 35% of people aged 75 and over will be living alone, up from 30% in 1986. The number of women living alone is likely to nearly double from 245,600 in 1986 to close to half a million in 2001, when they will account for 45% of all older elderly women. Although the number of older elderly men living alone is also expected to nearly double, by 2001 they will still make up just 19% of all men aged 75 and over, compared with 17% in 1986.

In many cases, living alone will necessitate moving to smaller and more manageable accommodations than a large house. Such accommodations may be provided by the current housing market. Alternatively, new housing construction specifically designed for the older elderly or conversions of existing structures could fulfill these requirements. The growing number living alone also has implications for services to this population, which include home care, home security, transportation, and social support, if older elderly people are to maintain some independence and delay the day when they must seek the fuller care of institutions.

The demand for institutional care for the older elderly is also likely to grow. It has been projected that the female population age 75 and over in institutions could reach almost a quarter of a

---

The cost of independence, 1986

A substantial number of people aged 75 and over pay a high percentage of their household income to maintain independent living accommodations. Renters are more likely than homeowners to spend a high proportion of their income on shelter costs. Also, people who live alone, especially women, tend to devote a larger share of their income to shelter than do couples.

In 1986, of older elderly renters who lived alone, 52 out of 100 women and 46 out of 100 men spent at least 30% of their income on shelter; this was also the case for 33 out of 100 older elderly couples who

rented their accommodations. As well, 20 women and 15 men out of every 100 living alone and renting spent more than 50% of their income on shelter expenses; this compared with just 6 in 100 couples.

Shelter costs were a much lighter burden for older elderly homeowners. For instance, the numbers spending at least one-third of their income on housing ranged from 4 in 100 couples to 21 in 100 women living alone. Only a small proportion of older elderly homeowners paid 50% or more of their income for shelter.

Shelter costs as a percentage of household income of older elderly renters and homeowners (1986 spending on 1985 income)

	Number of persons per 100 population paying at least 30% of income on shelter		Number of persons per 100 population paying at least 50% of income on shelter	
	Renters	Owners	Renters	Owners
Women living alone	52	21	20	5
Men living alone	46	15	15	4
Couples (no other household members)	33	4	6	1

Source: Statistics Canada, 1986 Census of Canada.

---

[2] An examination of factors behind decisions about the living arrangements of the elderly is presented in ''The Hypothesis of Age Patterns in Living Arrangement Passages,'' by Leroy O. Stone and Susan Fletcher in *Aging in Canada: Social Perspectives,* edited by Victor W. Marshall, 1987, Fitzhenry and Whiteside.

Projecting the living arrangements of the older elderly population

Projections to 2001 of the population aged 75 and over are based on the publication, *Population Projections for Canada, Provinces and Territories, 1984–2006*. However, some adjustments have been made to these projections. For example, the Census showed that in 1986, the population in the older age groups was not as numerous as had been projected. Therefore, projections to 2001 of the number of people aged 75 and over have been lowered.

Projections of the living arrangements of older elderly people are based heavily on trends since 1971. But obviously, some of these trends will eventually slow and stabilize. For instance, the proportion of people living with others cannot decrease much further at the present rate without reaching zero. Nevertheless, for the next 15-year period, it has been assumed that trends which prevailed in the last 15 years will continue.

Projections of living arrangements could be based on different assumptions, particularly with regard to the institutionalized population. For example, increases in the real income of older elderly people may enable them to purchase services necessary to maintain themselves in their own homes for a longer time. Another possibility is that funding may not be sufficient to expand institutional units at a rate that matches expected demand. Alternatively, governments and the volunteer sector may increase assistance to community-based support services, which would allow older elderly people to continue to live in their own homes.

Advances in medicine and technology could either raise or lower institutionalization rates. Medical technology may keep individuals alive in a disabled state, and thereby increase the numbers requiring institutional care. On the other hand, restorative and rehabilitative medicine could mean a smaller proportion of the population spending their final years in a chronic care setting.

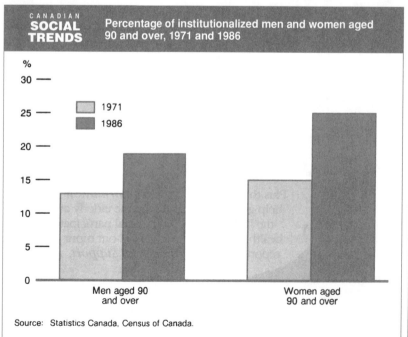

CANADIAN SOCIAL TRENDS Percentage of institutionalized men and women aged 90 and over, 1971 and 1986

1971
1986

Men aged 90 and over

Women aged 90 and over

Source: Statistics Canada, Census of Canada.

Living arrangements of older elderly population, by sex, Canada, 1971 and 1986, and projections for 2001

	1971 Number	1971 %	1986 Number	1986 %	2001 (projected) Number	2001 (projected) %
Men						
Alone	37,000	13	65,800	17	124,500	19
With spouse	142,400	51	221,900	57	407,000	62
With others	69,500	25	51,700	13	43,000	6
In own home	20,700	7	17,000	4	13,500	2
In others' home	48,800	17	34,700	9	29,500	4
Institution	25,700	9	45,300	12	75,500	12
Other	6,600	2	6,700	2	6,500	1
Total	281,100	100	391,300	100	656,500	100
Women						
Alone	99,300	26	245,600	38	474,000	45
With spouse	70,300	18	119,800	18	231,500	22
With others	152,800	39	146,200	23	111,000	10
In own home	52,300	14	49,100	8	32,000	3
In others' home	100,500	26	97,100	15	79,000	8
Institution	53,200	14	120,900	19	242,500	23
Other	11,000	3	15,800	2	5,500	1
Total	386,700	100	648,200	100	1,053,500	100

Sources: Statistics Canada, Census of Canada, and projections from Statistics Canada, Catalogue 91–520 adjusted according to results of 1986 Census.

million in 2001, about double the 1986 figure. The number of men of the same age in institutions is expected to rise from 45,300 to 75,500. As a result, close to 19% of all older elderly people will be living in institutions by 2001, up from 16% in 1986.

At the same time, the proportion of older elderly people living with others is expected to decline sharply. For women, that percentage is projected to fall from 23% in 1986 to 10% in 2001. The corresponding figures for men drop from 13% to 6%. This is an abrupt change from 1971, when living with others was the most common alternative for women (39%) and the second most frequent option for men (25%) in this age range.

The proportion of older elderly people living with their spouse is projected to rise for both sexes. For men aged 75 and over, the percentage living with their spouse will rise from 57% in 1986 to 62% in 2001. For women, an upturn from 18% to 22% is expected.

YOUNG ADULTS LIVING IN THEIR PARENTS' HOMES

by Monica Boyd and Edward T. Pryor

Recent decades have brought unanticipated turns in family composition and living arrangements among both the young and old. More elderly Canadians are living alone, while, until recently, the young have been leaving their parents' homes at increasingly early ages. In Canada, this latter tendency emerged as a growing trend for young adults to establish their own households, thus emptying the parental nest. Between 1971 and 1981, the percentages of unmarried adults who lived at home declined.

However, recent evidence from the Canadian Census has shown a reversal of this trend between 1981 and 1986. The percentage of unmarried young adults who were living with parents rose over the period 1981-1986.

The shift is particularly noteworthy for unmarried people aged 20-29 in respect to the choices they made between living as unattached individuals (that is, alone or with non-relatives) or living in a family household. As of 1986, six out of ten of these women aged 20-24 were living with one or both parents. Seven out of ten men aged 20-24 were still living with parents. Even by their late twenties, over four out of ten unattached or unmarried men and three out of ten women were living at home.

The increasing percentages of young adults in their twenties who are living at home have contributed to an aging of the entire population of children aged 15-34 living at home. In 1971, slightly more than one-quarter of the young women who lived at home and one-third of the young men were aged 20-29. By 1986, nearly 40% of the unmarried women and nearly half of the unmarried men living with parents were aged 20-29. Not only is a higher percentage of the unattached or unmarried young adult population living at home, but they are also more likely to be older than young adults living at home in previous decades.

The reasons for interest in adult children living with parents are manifold, but two aspects are obvious: (1) recent trends in the living arrangements of young adults go against the grain of the previous long-term momentum of the young to make an early departure from their parents' homes, and (2) the underlying question of explaining such a reversal and its consequences for the understanding of contemporary family life.

In part, the reversal of the previous pattern has been masked by other changes in household formation patterns of Canadians such as living alone, the increase in forms of cohabitation not based on a marriage, and increases in family breakdown.

While each has contributed to a proliferation of residential types and patterns, which taken together have tended to reduce average household size, delayed leaving of the family household and subsequent returns to it have apparently emerged as a countervailing tendency, possibly reflecting changes in marriage patterns and the economic conditions facing young adults today.

Factors in leaving or staying in parental homes

Census data provide the overall pattern with respect to delayed marriage. The percentage of Canadians who had been married by a given age declined between 1976 and 1986, indicating a delay in the timing of marriages. Delayed marriage leaves the other residential options of (1) leaving the parental household for other independent living arrangements either alone or with others or (2) remaining in or returning to the parental home during the years that in previous decades might have been spent in a separate household in the married state.

It appears that an increasing number of unmarried young adults have chosen the second option. They remain in their parents' homes at a time in the family life cycle when parents might once have expected to be freed of direct parental responsibilities. The nest may still be emptying, but the process now extends over a longer transitional period.

Many other factors contribute to a decision to leave a parent's home and to establish a new household. Factors associated with the choice between living at home and establishing a separate household are: sex of the adult children, membership in particular ethnic groups, education level attained, labour force participation, and individual income. Some factors are enabling (e.g., high employment income makes household formation feasible, as does higher educational attainment, which often translates into desirable employment), while other factors are retarding (full-time enrolment in higher education).

Compared with people in their twenties living unattached, unmarried persons in their twenties who were living at home in 1981 were more likely to live in a rural area, to have French as the home language, to have lower levels of educational attainment, to be attending school, to be unemployed or not in the labour force, and to have lower incomes. In 1981, nearly one-quarter of the young unmarried men in rural areas were residing with parents, compared with slightly over 11% of unattached men aged 20-29. For young unmarried women living at home, nearly 30% were in settings in which French was the home language, compared with slightly more than 20% of the unattached population. Over one-third of unmarried

people living with parents were attending school, in contrast to the lower school attendance of young adults living alone or with non-relatives. One-quarter of the unmarried-living-at-home population was unemployed or not in the labour force, compared with fewer than 15% of unattached individuals in their twenties. Consistent with the patterns of school attendance and employment, over one-third of the unmarried men and nearly 50% of the unmarried women living with parents had incomes of less than $5,000 in 1980. Approximately two out of ten unattached young women and men had incomes below $5,000.

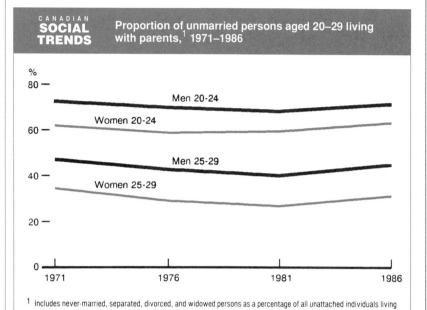

CANADIAN **SOCIAL TRENDS**

Proportion of unmarried persons aged 20–29 living with parents,[1] 1971–1986

[1] Includes never-married, separated, divorced, and widowed persons as a percentage of all unattached individuals living on their own plus unmarried children living at home.
Source: Statistics Canada, Census of Canada.

Unmarried[1] persons aged 15–34 living with parents, by sex and age, as a percentage[2] of unattached individuals and unmarried persons living in families, 1971–1986

	Men					Women				
	1971	1976	1981	1986	Difference 1986-81	1971	1976	1981	1986	Difference 1986-81
					%					
Percentage of unmarried living with parents										
15-19	93.3	92.7	91.9	92.0	0.1	91.5	90.6	90.5	91.4	0.9
20-24	72.4	70.0	68.1	71.2	3.1	62.1	58.9	59.3	63.3	4.0
25-29	46.8	42.8	40.0	44.6	4.6	34.5	29.0	27.2	31.6	4.4
30-34	35.1	32.7	27.8	28.8	1.0	24.7	20.0	17.1	17.7	0.6
Total 15-34	**78.4**	**75.7**	**71.2**	**69.8**	**-1.4**	**74.4**	**70.2**	**66.1**	**63.9**	**-2.2**
Age profile of unmarried population living at home										
15-19	62.2	61.5	57.4	49.1	-8.3	71.9	71.0	66.2	57.5	-8.7
20-24	28.7	28.7	31.0	34.5	3.5	21.6	22.3	25.8	30.9	5.1
25-29	6.6	7.2	8.4	12.0	3.6	4.5	4.7	5.6	8.4	2.8
30-34	2.5	2.6	3.2	4.4	1.2	2.0	2.0	2.4	3.2	0.8
Total 15-34	**100.0**	**100.0**	**100.0**	**100.0**	**-**	**100.0**	**100.0**	**100.0**	**100.0**	**-**

[1] Includes never married, separated, divorced, and widowed.
[2] The population at risk (the denominator) consists of all unattached individuals and unmarried persons in economic families. Married people are excluded.
Source: Statistics Canada, Census of Canada.

The cluttered nest

When all factors are considered together, there was an increased tendency in the mid-1980s for young adults in their twenties who were not currently married to live continuously in their parents' homes or to return to them. The increase occurred largely between 1981 and 1986, a period that encompassed a severe economic recession and increased time spent in pursuing higher education. The percentage of people in the age group 18-24 enrolled full-time in postsecondary education rose gradually from 19.8% in 1976-77 to 24.5% in 1985-86.

Using 1981 Census data, co-residency with parents rather than living as unattached individuals is seen to be related to low educational attainment, having French as a home langauge, being unemployed or not in the labour force, and with having a low income. School attendance was also an important factor. Some young adults may be effectively trapped in their parents' homes because of the high costs of establishing a separate household, particularly in large urban areas where the costs of accommodation are conspicuously higher than average.

What the effects on family life of delayed leaving, willing or unwilling, may ultimately prove to be are unknown. These findings do raise the possibility that contemporary young adults, unlike their predecessors in the late 1970s, will spend more time in a homelife over which they exert less than full control, possibly in the process adopting their parents' behaviour patterns more thoroughly. Whether as a

Characteristics of unmarried[1] persons aged 20–29 living with parent(s) and as unattached individuals,[2] by sex, 1981				
	Unmarried living at home		Unattached individuals	
	Men	Women	Men	Women
		%		
Rural/Urban				
Rural	24.9	20.0	11.2	6.2
Urban	75.1	80.0	88.8	93.8
Total	100.0	100.0	100.0	100.0
Home language				
English	63.8	63.7	77.4	76.9
French	29.7	29.6	20.7	20.6
Other	6.5	6.7	1.9	2.5
Total	100.0	100.0	100.0	100.0
Education				
Less than grade 9	5.9	4.2	3.3	2.2
Grades 9-13	41.6	35.7	35.5	30.6
Non-university certificate or diploma	27.7	30.8	29.4	32.7
University	24.8	29.3	31.8	34.6
Total	100.0	100.0	100.0	100.0
Attending school				
Not attending	66.0	60.9	76.1	71.0
Full-time	25.8	29.3	12.2	12.3
Part-time	8.2	9.7	11.7	16.8
Total	100.0	100.0	100.0	100.0
Employment				
Employed	74.3	72.8	87.3	88.2
Unemployed	13.2	10.6	6.8	5.1
Not in the labour force	12.5	16.6	5.9	6.7
Total	100.0	100.0	100.0	100.0
Income				
Less than $2,500	20.6	29.0	9.2	11.8
$2,500-4,999	16.9	20.3	8.8	12.1
$5,000-7,499	14.5	14.1	10.6	12.9
$7,500-9,999	11.7	12.4	9.8	12.6
$10,000-14,999	20.0	18.0	22.7	28.7
$15,000 and over	16.3	6.2	38.9	21.9
Total	100.0	100.0	100.0	100.0

[1] Includes never married, separated, divorced, and widowed.
[2] Persons living alone or with non-relatives.
Source: Statistics Canada, 1981 Census of Canada.

Population ever married at selected ages, 1976, 1981, 1986			
Age	1976	1981	1986
		%	
19	14	11	8
21	34	29	20
26	75	71	63
31	88	86	82
36	92	91	89

Source: Statistics Canada, Census of Canada.

by-product of pursuing higher education, or because of the relatively low salaries available to the young in the late 1980s, many seem destined to remain in their parents' homes considerably longer than was previously expected. This possibility could indicate a fundamental alteration in the living arrangement patterns of young Canadians relative to previous generations.

But the permanence of this trend is questionable. Continued improvement in economic conditions, were it to be passed on to young adults, might again reverse the growing tendency to stay in one's parents' home; or alternatively, higher levels of enrolment in postsecondary education for longer programs of study could reinforce the existing trend by keeping children at home for even longer periods of time.

WORK, LEISURE, AND SOCIAL PROBLEMS

Christopher by Horst Guilhauman;
oil on canvas, 1984. © Horst Guilhauman.

Work

LABOUR FORCE TRENDS
CANADA AND THE UNITED STATES

by David Gower

A comparison of labour force trends in Canada and the United States puts developments in Canada during the volatile economic times of the 1980s into a broader perspective. The free trade issue, the huge volume of bilateral trade between Canada and the United States, and the large population flows between the two countries all heighten interest in the labour market conditions faced by Canadian and American workers.

Labour force trends over the course of the 1980s have generally been similar in the two countries, although total employment growth was somewhat greater in the United States, and unemployment rates were higher in Canada. However, since 1984, employment has grown more rapidly and unemployment fallen more sharply in Canada.

Employment growth slower in Canada

Employment grew at a somewhat slower rate in Canada than in the United States in the 1980s.[1] Between 1980 and 1987, total employment rose 11.8% in Canada, compared with 13.2% in the United States.

Much of the difference in employment growth occurred because the 1981-1983

recession had a more severe effect on employment in Canada. Total employment in Canada fell 2.3% between 1981 and 1983, whereas it increased slightly (0.4%) in the United States. As well, the post-recession recovery was initially stronger in the United States. In 1984, the number of Americans with jobs grew 4.1%, well above Canada's 2.5% increase.

In recent years, though, employment growth has been faster in Canada. From 1985 through 1987, total employment in Canada rose an average of 2.8% annually, compared with 2.4% in the United States.

Employment rising most rapidly among Canadian women

In both nations, employment increased more rapidly among women than men. Between 1980 and 1987, the number of Canadian women with jobs rose 21.7%, compared with 19.5% for American women. In the same period, total employment among men increased just 5.3% in Canada and 8.6% in the United States.

A smaller percentage of Canadian than American women, however, have jobs. In 1987, 51.3% of Canadian women, compared with 52.5% of those in the United

---

[1] Canadian employment data usually include people aged 15 and over, whereas American coverage starts at age 16. For this analysis, Canadian data were retabulated to include only people aged 16 and over.

States, were employed. As well, this difference was slightly greater than in 1980 when 46.7% of Canadian women and 47.7% of American women had jobs. Despite greater employment growth among Canadian women, this gap widened because the total number of women aged 16 and over rose at an even faster rate in Canada than in the United States.

In both countries, employment growth was particularly rapid among women aged 25-44. Between 1980 and 1987, the percentage of women in this age range with jobs rose from 57.9% to 67.2% in Canada and from 61.2% to 69.3% in the United States.

Increases in the employment of women aged 16-24 and 45 and over were also similar in Canada and the United States, but these gains — around 3 percentage points for the younger women and one percentage point for the older group — were below those of women aged 25-44. As well, while a greater proportion of Canadian than American women aged 16-24 had jobs in 1987, the reverse was true for women aged 45 and over.

Percentage of men with jobs down

There were particularly sharp declines in the percentage of men with jobs in both Canada and the United States during the early 1980s. Between 1980 and 1983, the percentage of Canadian men with jobs fell from 74.3% to 68.4%; in the United States the decline was from 72.0% to 68.8%. Since 1984, the proportion of employed men has gradually increased in both countries, although the percentage of Canadian men with jobs in 1987 was still 3.4 percentage points lower than in 1980. In comparison, the American figure was down only half a percentage point.

Employment rates fell among men of all ages in both countries, but the declines were steeper in Canada. The proportion of Canadian men aged 25-44 with jobs decreased 3.2 percentage points between 1980 and 1987, compared with less than a half percentage-point drop for comparable American men. Among men aged 45 and over, the proportion with jobs fell 6.9 percentage points in Canada and 4.3 points in the United States. As a result, a smaller percentage of Canadian than American men in both these age ranges were employed in 1987, the reverse of the 1980 situation.

The employment rate among 16-24-year-old men also fell more rapidly in Canada than in the United States. However, in 1987, the percentage of Canadian men in this age range with jobs (64.3%) was still above that in the United States (63.1%).

Service sector share of employment growing

Total service sector[2] employment grew substantially in both nations during the 1980s. Between 1980 and 1987, the number of service workers rose 18.1% in Canada and 20.0% in the United States. Meanwhile, there was almost no growth in goods-producing employment in either country. In fact, the total number of Canadians working in the goods-producing sector fell 0.5%; in the United States, total employment in these industries rose, but only 0.2%.

As a result, the proportion of all workers employed in the service sector in both countries rose from just under 66% in 1980 to almost 70% in 1987.

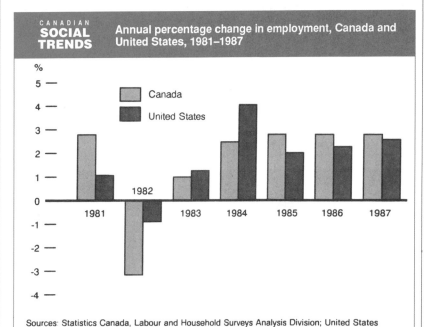

CANADIAN SOCIAL TRENDS Annual percentage change in employment, Canada and United States, 1981–1987

Sources: Statistics Canada, Labour and Household Surveys Analysis Division; United States Department of Labor Statistics, *Employment and Earnings*.

Percentage of men and women employed, by age, 1980 and 1987				
	Canada		United States	
	1980	1987	1980	1987
		%		
Men				
16-24	66.0	64.3	63.5	63.1
25-44	90.6	87.4	89.9	89.6
45 and over	61.9	55.0	59.5	55.2
Total	**74.3**	**70.9**	**72.0**	**71.5**
Women				
16-24	58.0	60.7	53.9	57.1
25-44	57.9	67.2	61.2	69.3
45 and over	29.2	30.2	33.0	34.3
Total	**46.7**	**51.3**	**47.7**	**52.5**

Sources: Statistics Canada, Labour and Household Surveys Analysis Division; United States Department of Labor Statistics, *Employment and Earnings*.

[2] This classification differs from those in regularly published Labour Force Survey series in that "utilities" is included in the goods-producing sector rather than in the service sector. The effect on the data is small, however, since this group represents only about 1% of employment.

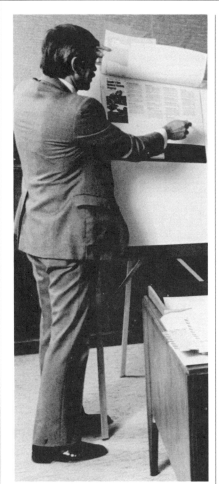

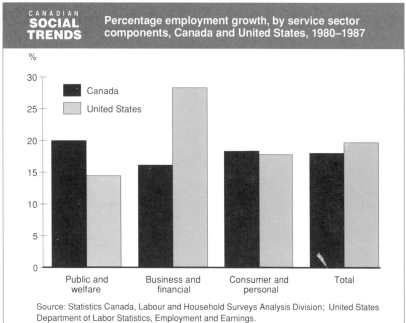

CANADIAN **SOCIAL TRENDS** Percentage employment growth, by service sector components, Canada and United States, 1980–1987

Source: Statistics Canada, Labour and Household Surveys Analysis Division; United States Department of Labor Statistics, Employment and Earnings.

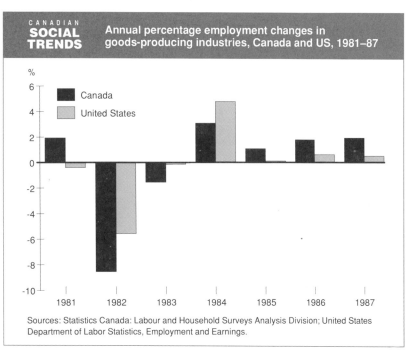

CANADIAN **SOCIAL TRENDS** Annual percentage employment changes in goods-producing industries, Canada and US, 1981–87

Sources: Statistics Canada: Labour and Household Surveys Analysis Division; United States Department of Labor Statistics, Employment and Earnings.

The lack of overall growth in goods-producing employment in both Canada and the United States is largely a result of the 1981-1983 recession. Between 1981 and 1983, total goods-producing employment fell 10.2% in Canada and 5.7% in the United States. While employment in this sector has risen in both countries since the end of the recession, this growth has been only enough to replace losses that occurred during the recession.

Post-recession growth patterns in goods-producing industries differed in the two countries. Employment in Canada's goods-producing sector has grown steadily since 1984, increasing 1-2% each year. By contrast, most of the recovery in goods-producing employment in the United States occurred in 1984; since then, annual growth has been below 1%. In 1987, for example, goods-producing employment rose just 0.6% in the United States, compared with 2.0% in Canada.

Different service industries growing

Growth rates of the different components of the service sector varied in Canada and the United States. In Canada, public and welfare services was the fastest-growing of the three components of the service sector, while business and financial services was the slowest.[3] The opposite occurred in the United States, where business and financial services had the fastest growth rate, and public and welfare services, the slowest. In fact, the American business and financial sector's growth rate (28.3%) was close to double Canada's (16.0%). Growth rates of consumer and personal services were similar in the two countries.

[3] Public and welfare services includes services in the areas of public administration, education, health, justice, and religion, as well as other social services. Business and financial services include transportation, communications, wholesale trade, banking, insurance, real estate, legal, accounting, and computer services, as well as other services to business. Consumer and personal services include retail trade, accommodations, restaurant and recreation services, and other personal and household services. These categories differ from those in regularly published Labour Force Survey series and have been developed for analytical purposes only.

Labour force indicators, Canada and United States, 1980–1987

	1980	1981	1982	1983	1984	1985	1986	1987
Total employment (000s)								
Canada	10,600	10,896	10,549	10,650	10,912	11,214	11,524	11,846
United States	99,303	100,397	99,526	100,834	105,003	107,150	109,597	112,440
Annual % change in employment								
Canada	. .	2.8	-3.2	1.0	2.5	2.8	2.8	2.8
United States	. .	1.1	-0.9	1.3	4.1	2.0	2.3	2.6
Employment — men (000s)								
Canada	6,400	6,497	6,204	6,196	6,320	6,457	6,600	6,737
United States	57,186	57,397	56,271	56,787	59,090	59,891	60,892	62,107
% of men employed								
Canada	74.3	73.9	69.4	68.4	68.9	69.6	70.3	70.9
United States	72.0	71.3	69.0	68.8	70.7	70.9	71.0	71.5
Employment — women (000s)								
Canada	4,199	4,398	4,344	4,454	4,592	4,757	4,924	5,109
United States	42,117	43,000	43,256	44,047	45,915	47,259	48,706	50,334
% of women employed								
Canada	46.7	47.9	46.5	47.0	47.8	48.9	50.1	51.3
United States	47.7	48.0	47.7	48.0	49.5	50.4	51.4	52.5
% employed in service sector								
Canada	65.9	65.6	68.1	68.9	68.7	69.2	69.4	69.7
United States	65.9	66.3	67.9	68.4	68.2	68.8	69.2	69.8
% employed in goods-producing sector								
Canada	34.1	33.8	31.9	31.1	31.3	30.8	30.6	30.3
United States	34.1	33.7	32.1	31.6	31.8	31.2	30.8	30.2
% employed part-time								
Canada	17.8	18.3	19.8	20.8	20.7	20.8	20.7	20.6
United States	16.9	17.1	18.2	18.4	17.6	17.4	17.4	17.3
Unemployment rate (%)								
Canada	7.4	7.5	10.9	11.8	11.2	10.5	9.6	8.8
United States	7.1	7.6	9.7	9.6	7.5	7.2	7.0	6.2
% unemployed six months or more								
Canada	15.3	15.9	20.0	28.2	26.3	25.9	23.8	23.8
United States	10.7	14.1	16.6	23.9	19.1	15.4	14.4	14.0

. . Figures not available.

Sources: Statistics Canada, Labour and Household Surveys Analysis Division; United States Department of Labor Statistics, *Employment and Earnings*.

More part-time work in Canada

A higher percentage of Canadian than American workers are employed part-time.[4] In 1987, 20.6% of Canadian workers were employed part-time compared with 17.3% in the United States. The Canadian figure was up considerably from 17.8% in 1980, whereas there was only a slight increase in the American rate from 16.9%.

Women account for most of the difference between part-time employment rates in the two countries. In 1987, 33.8% of employed Canadian women, compared with 26.1% of their American counterparts, worked part-time. By contrast, part-time employment rates of Canadian (10.6%) and American (10.2%) men were almost the same.

Unemployment higher in Canada

Unemployment trends in Canada and the United States have differed during the 1980s. Before the 1981-1983 recession, unemployment rates in the two countries were roughly similar. But during the recession, the Canadian rate increased much more sharply, peaking at 11.8% in 1983. By comparison, the annual American unemployment rate never exceeded 10% during this period. In addition, unemployment in the immediate post-recession period fell more slowly in Canada.

[4] Refers to those who usually work less than 35 hours per week. Regularly published Canadian data, which include only those who work less than 30 hours weekly, have been retabulated to produce comparable figures.

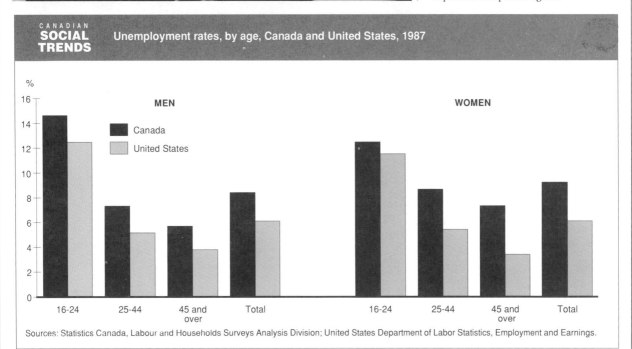

CANADIAN
SOCIAL TRENDS   Unemployment rates, by age, Canada and United States, 1987

Sources: Statistics Canada, Labour and Households Surveys Analysis Division; United States Department of Labor Statistics, Employment and Earnings.

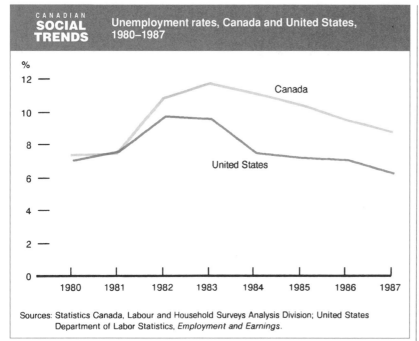

CANADIAN SOCIAL TRENDS
Unemployment rates, Canada and United States, 1980–1987

%
12 —
10 —
8 —
6 —
4 —
2 —
0 —

Canada

United States

1980 1981 1982 1983 1984 1985 1986 1987

Sources: Statistics Canada, Labour and Household Surveys Analysis Division; United States Department of Labor Statistics, *Employment and Earnings*.

Recently, however, unemployment has fallen more rapidly in Canada than in the United States, although in 1987 the Canadian rate was still higher than the American rate. Between 1985 and 1987, Canada's unemployment rate fell 1.7 percentage points from 10.5% to 8.8%, whereas the American rate declined one percentage point to 6.2%.

In both countries, unemployment rates are highest among 16-24-year-olds and decline in successive age groups. For men and women of all ages, unemployment rates are higher in Canada than in the United States.

More long-term unemployed in Canada

Canadians are more likely than Americans to be out of work for long periods. In 1987, almost a quarter (23.8%) of unemployed Canadians, compared with just 14.0% of unemployed Americans, had been out of work for six months or more.

Since the end of the 1981-1983 recession, long-term unemployment has fallen much more slowly in Canada than in the United States. From 1983 to 1987, as a proportion of total unemployment, people unemployed for at least six months fell 9.9 percentage points in the United States, but declined only 4.4 percentage points in Canada.

In both countries, long-term unemployment was highest among men aged 45 and over. Of all unemployed men in this age range in 1987, 38.0% of Canadians and 27.3% of Americans had been looking for work for six months or more.

UNIONIZATION IN CANADA

by Shirley Neill

During the 1970s, the percentage of Canadian workers who were unionized remained remarkably stable. Throughout the years 1970 to 1982, roughly one-third of paid workers belonged to unions. In 1982, for example, 33.3% of paid workers were union members, almost exactly the same percentage as in 1970 (33.1%).

As the size of the total labour force increased, so did the number of Canadians in unions. By 1981, 3.2 million workers were union members, up from 2.3 million in 1970. In 1982, mainly as a result of the overall decline in employment during the recession, total union membership fell to 3.1 million. Union members, however, were less likely than non-members to have lost their jobs in the recessionary period. While the number of employed union members declined 3.3% in 1982, the number of other workers with jobs fell 4.8%.

Canada's unionization trends differ from those in the United States. While the level of unionization in Canada has been stable, union membership has dropped precipitously in the United States. In 1984, just 19% of American workers were unionized, down from close to 30% in 1970.

Union Membership of Men and Women
Overall, the proportion of paid female workers who were union members has increased, while the percentage of unionized paid male workers has declined. The percentage of female workers in unions rose from 21.2% in 1976 to 24.8% in 1982. In the same period, the proportion of unionized male workers fell from 40.5% to 39.2%.

In some ways, comparing unionization rates for women and men understates the growth of female representation in Canadian unions. Between 1970 and 1982, the number of women in unions increased 92%, from just over half a million to just under one million. In the same period, the number of male union members rose only 18%, from 1.8 million to 2.1 million. As a result, in 1982, 32.3% of all union members were women, up from 22.6% in 1970.

Unionization by Industrial Sector
The goods-producing sector of the economy has traditionally had higher unionization rates than the service sector. In 1982, 44.3% of workers in goods-producing industries were unionized, compared with 28.2% of those in services. However, because employment is concentrated in the service sector (72.5% of all paid workers in 1982), the majority of union members are service industry employees. In 1982, 61.5% of union members were working in this sector of the economy.

The level of unionization increased slightly in the service sector between 1973 and 1982 and fell slightly in the goods-producing industries. The percentage of service sector workers who were

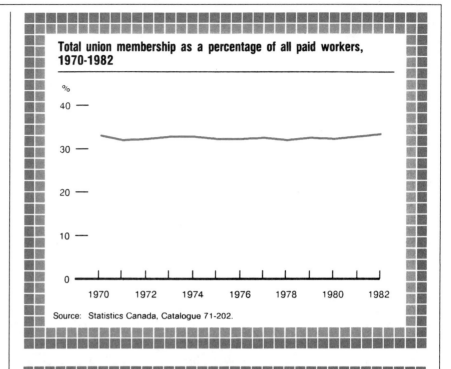

Total union membership as a percentage of all paid workers, 1970-1982

Source: Statistics Canada, Catalogue 71-202.

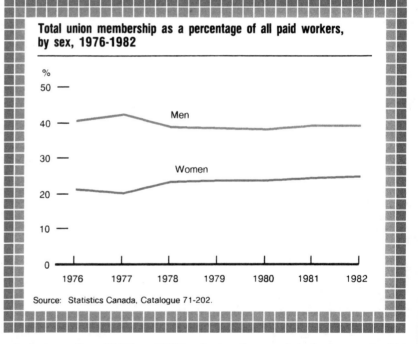

Total union membership as a percentage of all paid workers, by sex, 1976-1982

Source: Statistics Canada, Catalogue 71-202.

unionized rose from 25.7% to 28.2%, while the proportion of unionized workers in goods-producing industries fell from 45.7% to 44.3%.

Unionization in 1985
Between 1982 and 1985, another 225 unions were added to Statistics Canada's union survey – Corporations and Labour Unions Returns Act (C.A.L.U.R.A.). As a result, membership totals after 1982 are not comparable with earlier figures. Nonetheless, 1985 figures provide an in-

teresting snapshot of union membership in the post-recession period.

Results from the updated union survey show that in 1985, 3.5 million Canadian workers, or 34% of all paid workers, were union members.

In 1985, 28% of paid female workers were in unions compared with 38% of paid male workers. Also that year, women made up 36% of all union members.

The 1985 unionization rate was higher in goods-producing industries (37%) than in service industries (33%). However,

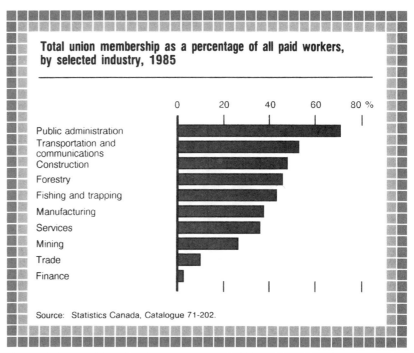

unionization rates among the industries that make up the two industrial sectors varied considerably. In the goods-producing sector, unionization levels ranged from 26% in mining to 48% in construction. Just under 38% of paid workers in manufacturing were unionized.

Variations in unionization rates were even greater in the service sector. Almost three-quarters (71%) of paid workers in public administration and over half (53%) of those in transportation, communications and other utilities were unionized. On the other hand, few workers in either trade (10%) or finance (3%) were union members.

In 1985, Newfoundland and Quebec had the highest percentages of their paid workers in unions, at 40% and 39%, respectively. British Columbia's unionization rate was also high (37%). Alberta (23%) and Prince Edward Island (22%) had the lowest levels of unionization.

Total union membership as a percentage of all paid workers, by selected industry, 1985

Public administration
Transportation and communications
Construction
Forestry
Fishing and trapping
Manufacturing
Services
Mining
Trade
Finance

Source: Statistics Canada, Catalogue 71-202.

Wages of Union and Non-union Workers

Generally, unionized workers' average hourly earnings surpass those of their non-unionized counterparts. This comparison should be interpreted with some care, because differences in occupation, industry, and seniority have not been taken into account. In 1984, average hourly earnings of unionized full-time workers were 34% higher than those of full-time non-unionized workers. Union members averaged $12.27 per hour, while non-union workers made $9.17 per hour.

The earnings gap was even wider among part-time employees. In 1984, the average hourly wages of unionized part-time workers ($10.68) were close to double those of non-unionized part-timers ($5.84).

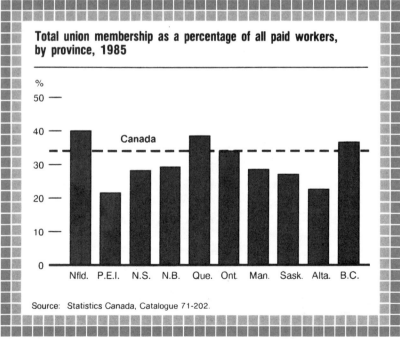

Total union membership as a percentage of all paid workers, by province, 1985

%
50 —
40 —
Canada
30 —
20 —
10 —
0

Nfld. P.E.I. N.S. N.B. Que. Ont. Man. Sask. Alta. B.C.

Source: Statistics Canada, Catalogue 71-202.

SELF-EMPLOYMENT IN CANADA

by Gary L. Cohen

The self-employed[1] make up a vital and growing segment of the labour market in Canada; in fact, the rise in their numbers has been a major component of employment growth over the last decade.

Between 1975 and 1987, the total number of self-employed people in Canada rose 60%, from 1.0 to 1.6 million. In the same period, the number of paid workers rose only 26%, from 8.1 to 10.2 million. Overall, the growth in the number of self-employed persons represented almost a quarter (23%) of total employment growth in this period. As a result, in

[1] The self-employed include primarily those people who own and operate an incorporated or unincorporated business, farm, or professional practice. The self-employed also include some people who do not own a business, for example, independent salespersons and babysitters. On the other hand, a person who owns a business, but does not operate it, is considered to be an investor and not self-employed.

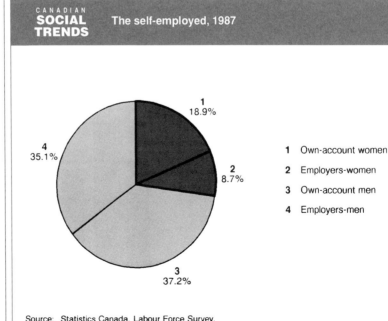

CANADIAN
**SOCIAL
TRENDS**   The self-employed, 1987

1
18.9%

4
35.1%

2
8.7%

3
37.2%

1   Own-account women
2   Employers-women
3   Own-account men
4   Employers-men

Source: Statistics Canada, Labour Force Survey.

1987, almost one out of every seven workers (14%) in Canada was self-employed, up from one in nine (11%) in 1975.

Just over half (54%) of the self-employed are own-account workers, that is, they do not usually employ paid help. The remaining 46% are employers.

However, the number of employers rose somewhat faster than the number of own-account workers in the last decade. From 1975 to 1987, the number of employers increased 73%, compared with a 50% rise among own-account workers.

Industry patterns vary

There is considerable variation in the incidence of self-employment by industry. Self-employment is most prevalent in fishing and trapping industries, where it makes up 66% of employment, and in agriculture, where 56% of workers are self-employed. Self-employment is also a major component of total employment in other services, including amusement and recreational services and personal and household services (34%); construction (28%); and business services (24%). As well, 22% of real estate operators and insurance agents are self-employed. On the other hand, self-employment is much less prevalent in manufacturing (4%); mining (3%); communications (3%); education services (2%); and finance and insurance industries (1%).

However, because total employment differs widely by industry, for example, there are more than two million workers in wholesale and retail trade, but fewer than 40,000 in fishing and trapping industries, the majority of self-employed workers are actually concentrated in just four industries. In 1987, almost two thirds of the self-employed worked in either trade industries (21%), other services (17%), agriculture (16%), or construction (12%).

Men more likely to be self-employed

Men are more likely than women to be self-employed, although the number of self-employed women has increased more rapidly than the number of self-employed men in the last decade. In 1987, 17% of all employed men were self-employed, whereas self-employed women made up only 9% of all employed women.

From 1975 to 1987, however, the number of self-employed women rose more than three times faster than the number of self-employed men. During this period, the number of self-employed women increased 135%, while the

number of self-employed men rose just 42%. As a result, in 1987, women made up 28% of all self-employed workers, up from 19% in 1975.

There are also differences in the type of self-employment of men and women. For example, self-employed men are much more likely to be employers than are self-employed women. In 1987, about half (51%) of self-employed men were employers, compared with only about a third (31%) of self-employed women.

As well, there are differences in the industries in which self-employed men and women are concentrated. Both sexes are strongly represented in the trade industries; in 1987, 21% of both self-employed men and women worked in wholesale or retail trade. However, about 40% of self-employed women worked in other services, mainly personal and household services, whereas more than a third (35%) of self-employed men were in either agriculture or construction.

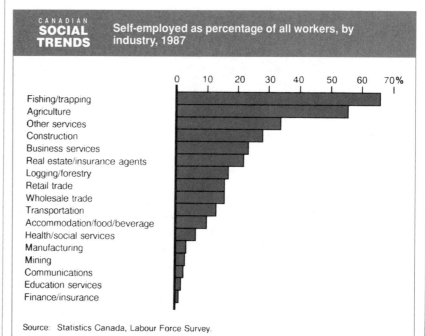

CANADIAN SOCIAL TRENDS
Self-employed as percentage of all workers, by industry, 1987

Source: Statistics Canada, Labour Force Survey.

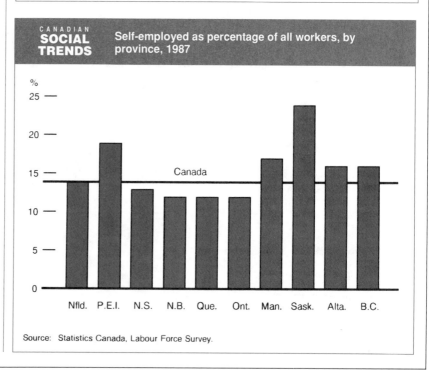

CANADIAN SOCIAL TRENDS
Self-employed as percentage of all workers, by province, 1987

Source: Statistics Canada, Labour Force Survey.

Older workers predominate

Older workers are generally more likely than younger workers to be self-employed. In 1987, nearly half (48%) of all workers aged 65 and over, and 20% of those aged 45-64, were self-employed. In comparison, the figure was 13% for workers aged 25-44 and just 5% for those aged 15-24.

This age pattern likely reflects the fact that the experiences, skills, resources, and opportunities necessary for self-employment are more readily available to older workers. The high incidence of self-employment among older workers also reflects the fact that most paid workers have retired by age 65.

Provinces differ

The proportion of workers who are self-employed varies substantially by province. In 1987, self-employment was most prevalent in Saskatchewan, where 24% of all workers were self-employed. This high rate of self-employment reflects the importance of agriculture in Saskatchewan.

High rates of self-employment also occurred in Prince Edward Island (19%), Manitoba (17%), Alberta (16%), and British Columbia (16%). On the other hand, only about 12% of the work forces in New Brunswick, Quebec, and Ontario were self-employed, while the figure was 13% in Nova Scotia and 14% in Newfoundland.

Urban/rural differences

People who live in metropolitan areas are somewhat less likely to be self-employed than those who live in smaller urban centres or rural areas. In 1987, 11% of workers in metropolitan areas were classified as self-employed, whereas in non-metropolitan areas, 13% of non-agricultural workers and 18% of all workers were self-employed.

Self-employment is relatively more common in smaller urban centres and rural areas because it is most typically associated with small business and farming endeavours, activities that generally form a more prominent part of the labour market in these areas.

Work schedules

For both men and women, employers are more likely than either paid workers or own-account workers to work full-time, that is, to usually work 30 or more hours per week. Among men, in 1987, 98% of employers worked full-time, compared with 92% of paid workers and 88% of own-account workers.

The difference was even more pronounced among women. In 1987, 83% of female employers worked full-time, compared with 76% of paid workers and just 56% of own-account workers.

In addition, among full-time workers, the self-employed put in substantially longer hours than paid workers. In 1987, self-employed full-time workers worked an average of 45.8 hours per week, compared with 36.3 hours for paid workers.

On the other hand, self-employed part-time workers worked fewer average hours per week than paid workers: 11.4 hours compared with 15.2.

Job tenure

Self-employed workers have higher levels of job tenure than paid workers as they generally have been with the same business longer.[2] In 1987, average job tenure was 11.8 years for self-employed men and 6.4 years for self-employed women. By comparison, the average tenure of paid workers was 7.8 years for men and 5.7 years for women.

Multiple jobholding

Self-employment is especially prevalent among people who have two or more jobs or businesses at the same time. In 1987, there were 494,000 multiple jobholders in Canada, nearly half (46%) of whom were self-employed in at least one of their jobs.

[2] Job tenure for paid workers measures the period of time with the same employer, although not necessarily in the same job. Self-employed persons with a business maintain their tenure as long as they consider that their business has not been formally closed, even though it may not currently be active. On the other hand, those own-account workers, such as babysitters, who do not own a business break their "tenure chain" whenever they cease work.

The self-employed sector

In November 1986, 44% of all Canadian workers were in the self-employment sector of the labour market. They included those who were employers, the paid workers they employ, self-employed persons without paid help, and unpaid family workers. The remaining 56% of the work force was made up of paid workers employed by firms with widely-held ownership or in which the owner did not operate the business, and public sector workers, including those in government and in education and health institutions.

CANADIAN
SOCIAL TRENDS   The self-employment sector, November 1986

Self-employed sector

Unpaid family workers - **1%**
Self-employed without paid help - **6%**
Employers - **7%**
Paid workers employed by self-employed - **30%**

Other paid workers **56%**

Source: Statistics Canada, Catalogue 71-535, No.3.

THE LABOUR FORCE PARTICIPATION OF IMMIGRANTS

Adapted from "The Labour Force Participation of Canada's Immigrants" by Nancy McLaughlin; published in *The Labour Force*, Statistics Canada, Catalogue 71-001, September, 1985.

One of the most important questions regarding immigration is how well new arrivals fit into the Canadian labour market. In general, the overall labour force participation rate of persons born outside Canada is roughly similar to that of the Canadian-born population. There are, however, several differences in the labour force composition of immigrants compared with that of the population native to Canada. In particular, the difference between the labour force participation rates of immigrants and non-immigrants is greater among women than among men. In addition, there is considerable variation in the labour force participation rates of particular age groups within the immigrant and Canadian-born populations. Also, the labour force activity of immigrants varies depending on their period of immigration as well as their country of origin.

The comparison of overall participation rates for immigrant and non-immigrant populations, however, is potentially misleading. Immigrants differ from the Canadian-born population in a number of characteristics such as age, education, marital status and the number and age of children, all of which affect labour force participation. It is possible that labour force differences due to these factors may be erroneously attributed to, for example, cultural differences or problems of assimilation into Canadian society. To provide a more accurate picture of the labour force participation of immigrants, differences in labour force activity due to differing age structures, likely the most significant of these characteristics, have been taken into account. Age-adjusted labour force participation rates of immigrants were estimated by calculating what their participation rate would have been if the immigrant population had the same age distribution as the Canadian-born population. These age-adjusted participation rates are presented along with the actual labour force participation rates of immigrants where age structure differences have a major impact.

Overall Labour Force Participation Rates

As of June 1981, the labour force participation rate of immigrant men was almost the same as that for Canadian-born men — 77.9% for immigrant men compared with 78.3% for their Canadian-born counterparts. For women, the gap was slightly larger with 50.6% of immigrant women active in the labour force against 52.1% of Canadian-born women.

When age differences between the immigrant and native-born populations were factored out, however, the labour force participation of male immigrants increased to 79.4% — one percentage point higher than that of the native male population. The change in the age-adjusted participation rate for immigrant women is even greater. While the actual participation rate of immigrant women is 1.5 percentage points below that of native-born women, their estimated 1981 labour force participation rate rises to 55.6% — over three percentage points greater than that of Canadian-born women — if their age distribution had been the same as that of Canadian-born women.

Labour Force Participation Rates of Canadian-born and Immigrant Populations, by Age, 1981

	Men		Women	
	Canadian-born	Immigrants	Canadian-born	Immigrants
	%			
15-24 years	69.9	67.6	61.2	60.6
25-34 years	95.2	95.6	65.1	69.2
35-44 years	94.7	97.0	62.4	70.5
45-54 years	91.3	95.3	54.1	61.9
55-64 years	75.4	84.4	34.3	40.4
65 years and over	17.8	16.2	6.3	5.4
Total	78.3	77.9	52.1	50.6

Source: Statistics Canada, 1981 Census of Canada, unpublished data.

Labour Force Participation by Age Group

Labour force participation rates vary considerably for different age groups of immigrants and the Canadian-born. For both men and women, participation rates of immigrants are higher than those of the Canadian-born for those between the ages of 25 and 64 years, but lower for 15–24 year olds and for those 65 years and over. The gap between the labour force participation rates of male immigrants aged 25–64 and their Canadian-born counterparts increases for successive age groups. The difference among men aged 25–34, for example, was very small (0.4 percentage points) with 95.6% of immigrant men in the labour force compared with 95.2% of Canadian-born men. This difference, however, rises to 2.3 percentage points among men aged 35–44, to 4.0 percentage points for those aged 45–54, and to 9.0 percentage points for the 55–64 age group.

On the other hand, a greater proportion of Canadian-born men aged 15–24, and 65 and over participate in the labour force, although the variation is not large — 2.3 percentage points among the younger cohort and 1.6 percentage points in the oldest group.

Among women, the largest difference between the labour force participation rates of immigrants and the native-born was in the 35–44 age category (8.1 percentage points). The difference declines for each of the two older groups: to 7.8 percentage points among those 45–54, and 6.1 for those aged 55–64. And while there was very little difference in the labour force participation rates of men aged 25–34, for women

the difference was over 4 percentage points — 69.2% for immigrant women in this age group compared with 65.1% for Canadian-born women.

Labour Force Participation by Period of Immigration

Considerable variation is observed when the participation rates of immigrants are examined for the period of immigration. The general trend is for participation rates of men and women to be higher, the longer immigrants have been in Canada, with the exception of those who arrived before 1961.

The labour force participation rate of immigrants increases most rapidly dur-

Labour Force Participation Rates for the Immigrant Population 15 Years and Over, by Period of Immigration, 1981

	Men		Women	
	Actual	Age-adjusted	Actual	Age-adjusted
		%		
Before 1961	70.0	86.8	39.2	60.5
1961-1965	88.9	83.2	62.8	59.5
1966-1970	87.1	79.2	64.3	58.1
1971-1975	86.8	78.6	64.4	56.9
1976	84.5	78.8	58.7	53.2
1977	82.9	77.8	57.6	52.9
1978	81.4	77.5	54.7	51.5
1979	81.2	77.4	54.7	50.9
1980	76.5	72.9	49.3	45.5
1976-1980	81.1	76.6	54.8	50.5
1981	63.4	60.4	35.1	32.7

Source: Statistics Canada, 1981 Census of Canada, unpublished data.

ing their first 2–3 years in Canada. For example, the 1981 labour force participation rate of men arriving that year was 63.4%, while the figure jumped over 12 percentage points to 76.5% for men who arrived in 1980, and it increased a further 4.7 percentage points (to 81.2%) for those who came in 1979.

The relatively low participation rate of those who arrived in Canada before 1961 is explained by the fact that many of these immigrants are older. In 1981, 32% of pre-1961 immigrants were 65 and over compared with 5% of later immigrants and 10% of the total Canadian population. In fact, when the labour force participation rate of pre-1961 immigrants is adjusted to estimate what the rate would be if this group had the same age distribution as the overall Canadian-born population, the participation rate of men increases form 70.0% to 86.8%, while that of women rises from 39.3% to 60.5%. At the same time, the age-adjusted participation rate of all post-1961 immigrant groups declined, with the result that for both men and women, pre-1961 immigrants have the highest age-adjusted participation rates.

Labour Force Participation by Place of Birth

The labour force participation of immigrants also varies considerably by place of birth, although much of the difference is actually accounted for by differences in the age structure of immigrant groups from various origins.

The actual participation rates of men range from a high of 86.2% for those from South Asia to 58.0% for those born in East European nations. The participation rates for women are even more diverse than those of men, ranging from 72.3% for women from the Caribbean to 30.8% for those born in East Europe.

Most of the variation in the participation rates of immigrant men disappears, however, when the figures are adjusted for differences in the age distribution of the various immigrant groups. The range in the adjusted participation rates for men is from a high of 82.1% for immigrants from South Europe to a low of 74.9% for those from East Asia. In addition to immigrant men born in South Europe, those from the United Kingdom, West Europe and Central Europe have high age-adjusted participation rates at 80.5%, 80.4% and 80.4% respec-

1981 Age-adjusted Labour Force Participation Rates of Immigrants, Aged 15 and Over, who Arrived in Canada from 1976–1981, by Place of Birth, 1981

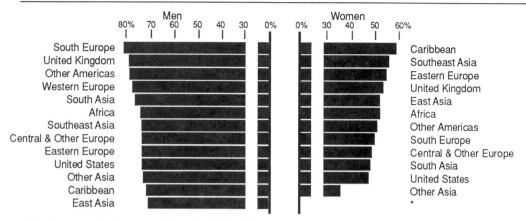

Men		Women
South Europe		Caribbean
United Kingdom		Southeast Asia
Other Americas		Eastern Europe
Western Europe		United Kingdom
South Asia		East Asia
Africa		Africa
Southeast Asia		Other Americas
Central & Other Europe		South Europe
Eastern Europe		Central & Other Europe
United States		South Asia
Other Asia		United States
Caribbean		Other Asia
East Asia		*

* An adjusted participation rate could not be calculated for women from Western Europe (excluding the U.K.) due to an insufficient number of persons in the labour force.

Source: Statistics Canada, 1981 Census of Canada, unpublished data.

tively. Men from the Caribbean, Other Asia, Southeast Asia, East Asia and the United States have age-adjusted participation rates slightly below the rate for Canadian-born men (78.3%).

For women, the highest age-adjusted participation rates are found for those born in the Caribbean (63.5%), followed by immigrants from Southeast Asia, Oceania and Other Regions, and the United Kingdom with rates of 60.1%, 59.0% and 57.9% respectively. Only women born in Other Asia and West Europe have adjusted participation rates below the rate for Canadian-born women (52.1%). The lowest participation rate (44.4%) occurs for women from Other Asia.

When just the most recent immigrants included in this report (those who arrived in Canada between 1976 and 1981) are considered, men from South Europe (81.0%), the United Kingdom (79.2%), and the Other Americas (79.2%) had the highest age-adjusted labour force participation rates, while

those from East Asia (69.7%) and the Caribbean (71.9%) were characterized by the lowest labour force involvement. This picture is somewhat different for women: those from the Caribbean (57.7%) and Southeast Asia (54.5%) had the highest age-adjusted labour force participation rates, while women of Other Asian origins had by far the lowest rate — 34.8%, followed by those from the United States (44.7%).

Immigrants' Countries of Origin

- **West Europe (excluding U.K.):** Eire, Netherlands, Belgium, France
- **Central Europe:** West Germany, East Germany, Switzerland, Austria, Poland, Hungary, Czechoslovakia
- **South Europe:** Portugal, Spain, Italy, Greece, Malta, Yugoslavia
- **East Europe:** U.S.S.R., Romania
- **Other Europe:** Sweden, Denmark, Finland, Norway, Iceland, Liechtenstein, Luxembourg, Andorra,

Monaco, Bulgaria, Gibraltar, Vatican City State, San Marino, Albania

- **South Asia:** India, Pakistan, Sri Lanka, Bangladesh, Nepal, Bhutan, Republic of Maldive
- **Southeast Asia:** Burma, Philippines, Malaysia, Singapore, Brunei, Indonesia, Thailand, Vietnam, Laos, Kampuchea
- **East Asia:** Hong Kong, Republic of South Korea, Taiwan, Japan, Republic of China, Republic of North Korea, Mongolia
- **Other Asia:** Cyprus, Lebanon, Israel, Turkey, Iran, Syria, Jordan, Kuwait, Iraq, Saudi Arabia, United Arab Emirates, Afghanistan, Qatar, Oman, Yemen, Democratic Republic of Yemen, Bahrain
- **Oceania and Other Regions:** Australia, Fiji Islands, New Zealand, Papua New Guinea, New Hebrides, Gilbert Islands, Solomon Islands, Tonga, Tuvalu, West Samoa, New Caledonia, Nauru, Pitcairn, Other.

THE HELP-WANTED INDEX

by Jean-Pierre Maynard and Horst Stiebert

Every day, employers advertise job openings in the classified columns of Canada's newspapers, and unemployed workers or employed workers wanting to change jobs read the ads to find suitable positions. But help-wanted ads can serve a purpose beyond matching workers with employers. Since job advertising is one of the first stages in the hiring process, changes in the level of help-wanted ads have been shown to be indicators of labour market conditions and employment trends.

In periods of economic expansion, when relatively few people are out of work and there are more positions to fill, job advertising is frequent. Also, employers who normally rely on other methods to attract applicants may use newspaper ads.

When demand for labour is slack, the reverse is true. Fewer openings require less advertising. Moreover, a larger labour pool may shorten the time ads appear before jobs are filled – or may eliminate the need to advertise altogether.

The **help-wanted index** provides data on the demand for labour. It indicates labour market conditions by measuring the space devoted to help-wanted advertisements in 18 metropolitan newspapers, relative to a base year (currently 1981), which is given a value of 100.

The help-wanted index is closely tied to economic conditions. For instance, the effect of the energy crisis of the mid-1970s was mirrored in a decline of the index from 109 in the third quarter of 1974 to around 76 in the second, third, and fourth quarters of 1977. The index also varied with the severe recession in the early 1980s and subsequent recovery. From 105 in the second quarter of 1981, the index plummetted to 35 in the fourth quarter of 1982. A steady rise since then, however, brought the index to 138 in the fourth quarter of 1987.

Unemployment

An increase in the help-wanted index frequently precedes a decline in the unemployment rate. For instance, an upturn in the index in the second quarter of 1971 was followed by a drop in unemployment during the third quarter. The same thing happened in the third and fourth quarters of 1978.

On the other hand, quarterly declines in the help-wanted index have usually coincided with rising unemployment rates. For example, as the index fell from the second quarter of 1981 until the first quarter of 1983, unemployment increased. An unbroken rise in the index since then was matched by a decline in unemployment from 12.4% to less than 9%.

Employment/Population Ratio

The help-wanted index and the employment/population ratio both measure the

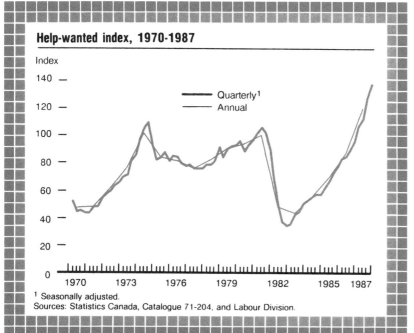

Help-wanted index, 1970-1987

Index

Quarterly[1]
Ann[u]al

[1] Seasonally adjusted.
Sources: Statistics Canada, Catalogue 71-204, and Labour Division.

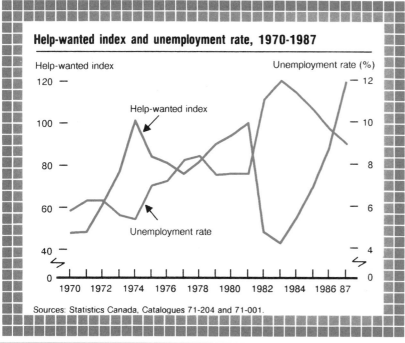

Help-wanted index and unemployment rate, 1970-1987

Help-wanted index   Unemployment rate (%)

Help-wanted index

Unemployment rate

Sources: Statistics Canada, Catalogues 71-204 and 71-001.

The help-wanted index measures space devoted to job advertisements each month in the classified sections of 18 metropolitan newspapers. These papers are: St. John's *Evening Telegram*, Charlottetown *Guardian*, Halifax *Chronicle-Herald*, Saint John *Telegraph-Journal*, Montreal *Gazette*, Montreal *La Presse*, Quebec *Le Soleil*, Sherbrooke *La Tribune*, Ottawa-Hull *Le Droit*, Toronto *Star*, London *Free Press*, Hamilton *Spectator*, Winnipeg *Free Press*, Regina *Leader-Post*, Edmonton *Journal*, Calgary *Herald*, Vancouver *Sun*, and Victoria *Times-Colonist*.

The column space for any given month is compared to the respective average column space in the base year (1981) and then multiplied by the appropriate metropolitan and regional population weights from the Census of Population to obtain national and regional indexes.

labour market from a demand perspective. The employment/population ratio is the number of people employed, expressed as a percent of the working age population. Throughout the seventies and eighties, the two annual measures have paralleled each other. Both indicators increased from 1970 to 1974, dropped to 1977, and rose until 1981. Since then, the sharp economic downturn in the early eighties and the subsequent recovery were reflected in similar movements by both indicators.

Regional Trends

The help-wanted index also reflects varying levels of labour demand in the regions of Canada. This was particularly evident during the years from 1979 to 1987, which spanned the recession and recovery. Overall, the direction of regional trends followed roughly the same pattern, but turning points in the help-wanted indexes and the extent of declines and gains varied.

The space devoted to job ads started to diminish in the Atlantic provinces and Quebec after 1980. Meanwhile, labour demand remained high in Ontario and the West. Between 1981 and 1982, however, all regional indexes declined sharply.

In 1983, the index rose in Quebec and stayed at about the same level in the Atlantic region. Indexes for the other three regions continued to decrease.

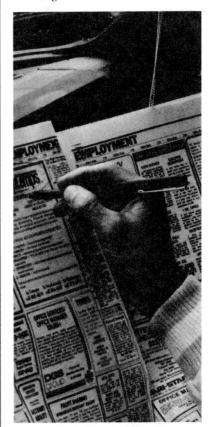

From 1984 on, all regions showed increases. The Atlantic provinces, Quebec, and Ontario had higher help-wanted indexes in 1987 than in 1979. However, levels in the Prairies and British Columbia remained below levels reached in the early eighties.

Conclusion

The help-wanted index is a timely and inexpensive measure of hiring activity which tends to signal turning points in the demand for labour. It has often been an early indicator of a change in labour market trends and closely corresponds to two other indicators of the relationship between workers and jobs, the unemployment rate and the employment/population ratio.

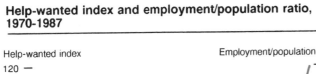

Help-wanted index and employment/population ratio, 1970-1987

Sources: Statistics Canada, Catalogues 71-204 and 71-001.

Help-wanted index, by region, 1979-1987

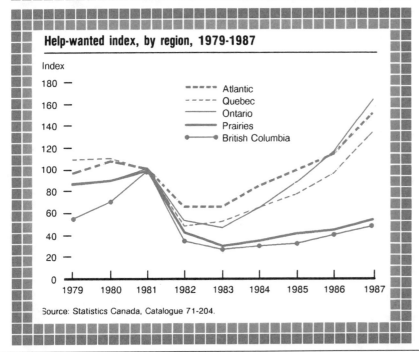

Source: Statistics Canada, Catalogue 71-204.

PART-TIME ADULT TRAINING

by Mary Sue Devereaux and Douglas J. Higgins

In today's rapidly changing work environment, education does not necessarily end once people leave school and settle into a job. For many workers, education is a lifelong process. Because of work or family responsibilities, however, few adults are able to go back to school full-time. As a result, many people seeking to improve job-related skills, increase earnings, or expand employment opportunities enroll in part-time courses. In 1985, 1.3 million Canadians, or more than 8% of the population aged 17-65, participated in such programs.

People who are already relatively well-educated, who are working full-time, or who are employed in a professional or technical occupation are also the most likely to continue their education through part-time training. On the other hand, much smaller proportions of those with little formal education, who work in blue collar jobs, or who are unemployed or not in the labour force enroll in part-time courses.

Wide provincial variations

Participation in part-time training varied across the country. About 11% of people aged 17-65 in Alberta took at least one course in 1986, while the figure was around 9% in British Columbia, Manitoba, and Ontario. Participation rates in the remaining provinces ranged from 7% in Saskatchewan and Quebec to just 3% in Newfoundland.

Training most common at ages 25-44

People aged 25-44 were the most likely to enroll in part-time training courses. In 1985, 12% of 25-34-year-olds and 10% of 35-44-year-olds took at least one such course. Participation in training was much less common among younger and older age groups. For instance, only 6% of people aged 17-24 or 45-54 took a part-time training course, while the figure was just 2% for 55-65-year-olds.

At most ages, men were more likely than women to take a training course. Among 25-34-year-olds, for example, 13% of men and 11% of women took a course, while for those aged 35-44, the participation rate was 11% for men and 9% for women. The exception to this pattern occurred in the 17-24 age group where 8% of women compared with 5% of men took at least one part-time course.

Married men, single women

There was also a contrast between the part-time training activity of men and women depending on their marital status. In 1985, 10% of married men, compared with 7% of separated/divorced men and 6% of those who were single, took a course. The trend for women was just the reverse. Close to 10% of both single and separated/divorced women participated in a training program, compared with only 7% of married women.

These tendencies are related to the fact that married men are more likely than men in other marital categories to be in the labour force, while the opposite is the case for women. Since training, by definition, is undertaken for job-related reasons, training rates are highest among married men and lowest for married women.

Training for the well-educated

People were more likely to enroll in part-time training if they already had a high level of formal education. In 1985, 18% of university graduates and 14% of college graduates took a course, compared with just 5% of those who had not gone beyond high school and fewer than 2% of people with less than Grade 9.

Full-time workers most likely to enroll

Because training is work-related, participation rates were highest among people who were employed, especially those with full-time jobs. In 1985, almost 12% of full-time workers enrolled in a part-time training course. In comparison, the figure dropped to 8% for part-time workers, 6% for the unemployed, and just 2% for those not in the labour force.

A professional activity

Participation in part-time training was also closely related to occupation. People in white collar jobs, especially professional and technical positions, were more likely than other workers to take a course. Professional and technical personnel, however, are also more likely than those in other jobs to have a postsecondary education, which, as noted earlier, is associated with high participation rates in part-time training.

In 1985, 16% of people employed in professional and technical occupations took a part-time training course. This compared with 10% of those in clerical positions, 8% in sales, and 6% of blue collar workers.

Full-time training

In addition to the 1.3 million adults who took part-time training courses in 1985, another 570,000 were enrolled in full-time programs. These courses involved instruction for most of each working day for a month or more.

Most people in full-time programs (79%) attended educational institutions such as universities, community colleges, or trade schools. The others were enrolled in either apprenticeships (12%) or employer-organized programs (9%).

While most people in full-time programs were completing the requirements for a university degree, community college diploma, or trade certificate, about 5% took upgrading or orientation courses in basic skills such as reading and writing, elementary mathematics, or job readiness.

Service sector higher

Training was more common among people employed in the service sector than among those working in goods-producing industries. In 1985, about 10% of service sector workers, compared with 7% of goods-producing employees, enrolled in a part-time training course.

Within the service sector, participation in part-time training was particularly high in non-commercial services such as education, health and welfare, and public administration, each of which has a high concentration of well-educated, professional personnel. In 1985, 14% of workers in these industries took at least one part-time training course. In contrast, only 8% of those employed in commercial services took a course.

Business and commerce courses most popular

The largest proportion of part-time adult training courses were in business and commerce. In 1985, 22% of all courses were in these areas. Technology/trades and data processing each accounted for another 10% of courses, while 8% were in medical/dental subjects, 7% were in each of the humanities and social sciences, 6% were in mathematics/science/engineering, and 5% were in secretarial science.

While business and commerce courses were the first choice of both men and women, there were differences in the other types of training chosen by each sex. While a relatively high percentage of men enrolled in technology/trades (18%), few women were attracted to this field. Alternatively, 10% of women, but virtually no men, took courses in secretarial science. Much of this variation, though, likely reflects differences in the occupational distribution of men and women.

Employers leading providers

A large proportion of part-time training was provided by employers. In 1985, 34% of all those who took a course participated in an employer-sponsored program. Another 21% took community college courses, 17% took university courses, and 11% enrolled in courses given by unions or professional associations. The remaining 17% attended courses at other institutions including vocational, commercial, and private schools.

The likelihood of taking employer-sponsored courses increased with the size of the firm. Of course-takers working in firms with more than 500 employees, close to half (49%) participated in employer-sponsored programs; this

CANADIAN
SOCIAL
TRENDS
Participation rate in part-time adult training, by province, 1985

% of population aged 17-65

- - amount too small to be expressed

Source: Statistics Canada, Education, Culture and Tourism Division, Adult Training Survey, February, 1986.

The Adult Training Survey

The Adult Training Survey was sponsored by Employment and Immigration Canada and conducted by Statistics Canada in February 1986. Because this survey was the first of its kind, comparable time series are not available.

Training was defined as formal educational activity in which participants enrolled for employment-related reasons such as improving job opportunities and skills, increasing earnings, or promoting career development. Educational activities taken out of personal interest or to obtain academic accreditation without any clear job-related purpose were not considered training.

Part-time training included instruction taken daily for most of the working day for less than one month, as well as courses taken a few hours a day, or a few days a week, over any period of time.

compared with just 15% of course-takers employed in firms with fewer than 20 workers.

Paying the price

The majority of part-time training courses, about 70%, required tuition, while the remaining 30% were free. Courses offered by employers were the most likely to be free; just under 70% of these courses entailed no fees. By contrast, 95% or more of all university and community college courses required payment.

For courses which did require tuition, 60% were paid for by the participants, while employers paid for 36%, and the remaining 4% were funded by other sources.

Employers were most likely to finance the training of full-time workers. They paid for 44% of the courses taken by those who worked full-time, compared with only 14% of courses taken by part-time workers. The overwhelming majority (88%) of training participants who were unemployed or not in the labour force paid their own way.

Employer-sponsored courses shorter

The median duration of part-time training courses was 39 hours. The length of courses, though, varied for different providers. Courses sponsored by employers, as well as those supplied by unions and professional associations, had a median duration of 24 hours. University and community college courses tended to be longer, with median durations of 48 and 45 hours, respectively.

The variation in course length is related to the type of training provided by different sponsors. Employers, unions and professional associations usually offer highly job-specific training, whereas many university and community college courses are more theoretical and hence, last longer.

Part-time courses taken by men and women, 1985			
Course	Men	Women	Total
		%	
Business/commerce	23	22	22
Technology/trades	18	2[1]	10
Data processing	11	8	10
Medical/dental	6	11	8
Humanities	6	9	7
Social sciences	5	8	7
Mathematics/science/engineering	7	5	6
Secretarial science	--	10	5
Safety	6	--	3
Upgrading/orientation	2[1]	2[1]	2
Other	12	20	17
Don't know/not stated/not applicable	3	2[1]	3
Total	100	100	100
Total number of participants	**707,000**	**635,000**	**1,342,000**

[1] Data are subject to considerable sampling error and should be used with caution.
-- Data are based on too small a sample to be statistically reliable.
Source: Statistics Canada, Education, Culture and Tourism Division, Adult Training Survey, February 1986.

EMPLOYMENT OF DISABLED CANADIANS

by David Gower

Being disabled remains a substantial impediment to finding and keeping a job in Canada. While a significant proportion of those with disabilities are employed, disabled people are much less likely to be working than their non-disabled peers. As well, gaps between the employment levels of disabled and non-disabled populations exist regardless of sex, age, or educational attainment.

Low level of employment for people with disabilities

In 1984, 42% of disabled Canadians aged 15-64 were employed. In comparison, 67% of the non-disabled population in this age range had jobs. Overall, close to 640,000 disabled people aged 15-64 were working in 1984; they made up about 6% of the total number of Canadians with jobs that year.

Employment levels of those with disabilities declined markedly the more serious the disability.[1] While almost half (48%) of those with a low level of disability were employed in 1984, just 33% of the moderately disabled, and only 17% of those with major disabilities, had jobs.

Of the population with physical and sensory disabilities, those with hearing difficulties were the most likely to be employed, while the sight-impaired had the lowest employment level. People aged 35-64 with mobility and agility difficulties also had relatively low employment rates.

Disabled less often employed at all ages

Excluding full-time students, 59% of disabled men and 47% of disabled women

---

[1] The degree of disability was rated as low, moderate, or major. Those with a low level of disability had some difficulty performing at least one activity; those regarded as moderately disabled were completely unable to perform one or two activities; those with major disabilities were completely unable to perform three or more activities.

The disabled population in Canada

The Canadian Health and Disability Survey defined the disabled as those who had trouble performing one or more of 17 daily living activities, such as walking upstairs, lifting packages, reading ordinary newsprint (with glasses, if usually worn), or hearing what is said in a normal conversation between two people. The disabled also included people with mental handicaps and those limited in the kind or amount of activity they can do because of a long-term physical condition or health problem. People who experienced activity limitation solely due to mental illness, as well as those in institutions, were not included in the disabled population.

Disabled people identified in this study ranged from those who had occasional difficulty performing one activity to those who were completely unable to perform a number of functions.

According to the Canadian Health and Disability Survey, an estimated 2.4 million adult Canadians, 13% of the non-institutionalized population aged 15 and over, had some form of disability in 1983-84. Almost one million of these people were aged 65 and over. The remaining 1.5 million disabled Canadians were aged 15-64; they made up 9% of this population.

The prevalence of disabilities within the population aged 15-64 increased significantly with age. Less than 5% of those aged 15-34, and 10% of those aged 35-54 were disabled in 1984. In comparison, 25% of those aged 55-64 were classified as disabled.

aged 15-34 were employed in 1984. In comparison, 83% of men and 65% of women in this age range without disabilities had jobs.

Differences between employment levels of disabled and non-disabled people were even greater among those aged 35-64. Just 51% of men and 29% of women in this age range with disabilities were working in 1984, compared with 88% of men and 55% of women without disabilities.

Some of the variation between the employment levels of disabled and non-disabled people aged 35-64, however, are the result of differences in the age distribution and family circumstances of these populations. For example, a much higher proportion of disabled people in this age range, compared with the overall population, are aged 55-64, an age group generally characterized by low levels of employment.

When the survey results were standardized (i.e., the employment figures for the disabled population aged 35-64 were recalculated to show what they would have been if the age distribution and family circumstances of this group were the same as that for the non-disabled population) 62% of disabled men and 36% of disabled women were estimated to have been employed. While these figures were closer to those for the non-disabled population than the non-standardized results, most of the gap between the employment levels of disabled and non-disabled people in this age range remained.

Education enhances employment chances

Employment levels for both disabled and non-disabled people increase with rising education; however, the impact of education on employment is greater for those with disabilities. This was especially the case for men.

In 1984, the employment rate (33%) for disabled men aged 15-34 with elementary or no education was less than half that for comparable non-disabled men (71%). In comparison, the employment rate of disabled men in this age range with postsecondary training was only 10 percentage points below that of non-disabled men: 78% compared to 88%.

The pattern was similar for men aged 35-64. There was a difference of 40 percentage points between the employment levels of those with little or no education — for those with postsecondary training the gap was 23 percentage points.

Increased education also had a major impact on the employment of disabled women in that a much higher percentage of those with postsecondary education than those with little or no education were employed. Increased education, however,

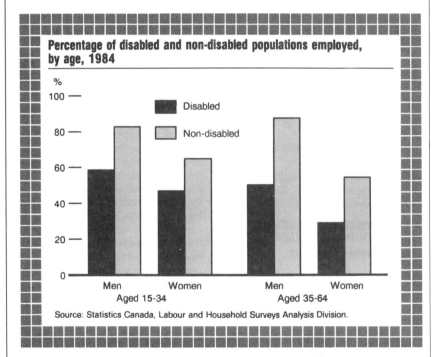

Percentage of disabled and non-disabled populations employed, by age, 1984

Source: Statistics Canada, Labour and Household Surveys Analysis Division.

Percentage of disabled and non-disabled populations employed, by educational attainment, 1984

		Disabled		Non-disabled	
		Elementary or no education	Postsecondary education	Elementary or no education	Postsecondary education
			%		
Aged	Men	33	78	71	88
15-34	Women	28	69	38	77
Aged	Men	42	70	82	93
35-64	Women	18	52	39	68

Source: Statistics Canada, Labour and Household Surveys Analysis Division.

had less effect in reducing employment disparities between disabled and non-disabled women than it did for men, because employment levels of non-disabled women also increased substantially with higher education.

A possible explanation for the particularly large differences between the employment rates of disabled and non-disabled men with low levels of education is that those with little education may be more inclined to seek or hold jobs requiring manual labour. A disability could therefore represent a serious obstacle to the employment of these men.

The actual relationship between education, disability and employment can be complicated. In some cases, the disability will have occurred after the completion of education, and the level of education already attained may affect the ability of a person to adjust to the new situation. In other instances, the type and degree of disability may affect the level of education an individual can attain. This is especially true in the case of the mentally handicapped.

Higher unemployment rates for disabled Canadians

Disabled people have higher unemployment rates than the non-disabled. In 1984, 22% of disabled men aged 15-34 in the labour force and 10% of those aged 35-64 were unemployed. These rates compared with 13% and 6% for men who were not disabled. Among women aged 35-64, 13% of those with disabilities were unemployed

compared with 7% of those without disabilities.

The unemployment rate for women aged 15-34 with a disability (14%) was almost the same as that for the non-disabled (13%).

Many disabled people not in the labour force

Even more significant than differences in unemployment rates is the fact that a far higher proportion of disabled than non-

disabled people are not in the labour force at all; that is, they are neither employed nor looking for work.

In 1984, 24% of disabled men aged 15-34 and 44% of those aged 35-64 were not in the labour force. The comparable figures for non-disabled men were about 5% for both groups.

Among disabled women, 45% of those aged 15-34 and 67% of those aged 35-64 were not in the labour force. These figures compare with 26% for non-disabled women in the younger age range and 40% in the older group.

Questions for the future

Disabled people in Canada are less likely to be employed than non-disabled people regardless of age, sex, or education, although education seems to have some effect in reducing differences in employment levels. Many issues related to the employment of disabled people, however, still must be examined.

- What kinds of jobs do disabled workers have? How many work in jobs specifically designed for those with disabilities?
- Does the low employment rate of disabled people stem from a lack of demand for their services or from factors such as poor transportation or inaccessible buildings and facilities?
- What effects do local labour market conditions have on the employment of disabled people? Are disabled people who live in rural regions at an even greater disadvantage than their urban counterparts?
- How do disabled people fare in terms of income, benefits, and opportunities for career advancement?
- If more disabled people received a higher education, would they achieve the same degree of labour market integration as those who are currently well-educated? Does the type of education make a difference?

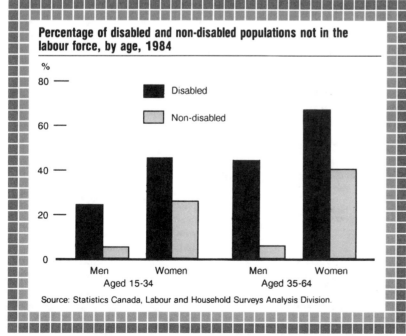

Percentage of disabled and non-disabled populations not in the labour force, by age, 1984

Source: Statistics Canada, Labour and Household Surveys Analysis Division.

LOSING GROUND: WAGES OF YOUNG PEOPLE, 1981-1986

by Ted Wannell

The long-term decline in Canada's birth rate and the aging of the baby boom generation have caused several demographic shifts. One of these is the decrease of the population aged 16-24. Between 1981 and 1986, the number of Canadians in this age group dropped from 4.2 million to 3.8 million. Consequently, the share of the total population accounted for by 16-24-year-olds fell from 17.4% to 15.0%.

It might be expected that reduced labour force competition resulting from a smaller population, combined with rising educational attainment, would tend to increase youth wages. But instead, the inflation-adjusted[1] average hourly wage of young workers was considerably lower in 1986 than in the early part of the decade.

Wages of young workers falling

The average real wage of workers aged 16-24 in 1986 was down almost $1.50 per hour, or 17%, from 1981. In 1986, people in this age bracket earned an average of $7.23 per hour, compared with $8.69 in 1981.

The average hourly wage of 25-34-year-olds was also lower in 1986 than in 1981, although the drop was not as sharp as that for the 16-24 age group. Between 1981 and 1986, the average wage of workers aged 25-34 slipped 5%, from $11.88 to $11.28.

[1] All figures in constant 1986 dollars.

In contrast, average wages for workers aged 35 and over were higher in 1986 than in 1981. The hourly wage of 35-49-year-olds went up almost 6% from $12.62 to $13.33, while the figure for those aged 50-64 rose 8% from $12.03 to $12.97.

Thus, the disparity between the average wage of younger and older workers was wider in 1986 than in 1981. As a result, in 1986, the average hourly wage of workers aged 16-24 was 63% of the national average, compared with 76% in 1981.

Most young workers affected

Average youth wages dropped for both men and women, although the decrease was somewhat greater among men than among women. From 1981 to 1986, the average hourly wage of 16-24-year-old men fell 18% from $9.35 to $7.70, while for women the decline was 15% from $7.83 to $6.67. Consequently, the wage gap between young men and women narrowed slightly. In 1986, the average hourly wage of women aged 16-24 was 87% that of men, compared with 84% in 1981.

Wage rates also declined for young workers at all levels of education. The drop, however, was somewhat smaller among those with postsecondary qualifications. The average wage of postsecondary graduates aged 16-24 fell 15% between 1981 and 1986, while the decline was 19% for those with a high school education, and 17% for those with less than Grade 12.

Youth wages fell in all regions. The largest declines were in Alberta and British Columbia, although wages of young people in these provinces remained the highest in the country. Between 1981 and 1986, the average wages of 16-24-year-old workers dropped 24% in Alberta and 21% in British Columbia. At the same time, young workers' wages fell 17% in Manitoba, Saskatchewan, and the Atlantic provinces, and 14% in Quebec and Ontario.

Part-time work increasing

Some of the drop in youth wages is attributable to the rising incidence of part-time work. In 1986, 15% of all youth employment was part-time, up from 10% in 1981. Because part-time workers are generally paid less than their full-time counterparts, the growth of part-time work tends to reduce overall wage rates. In 1986, for example, part-time workers aged 16-24 averaged $5.83 per hour, compared with $7.47 for full-time workers in this age category.

Industrial restructuring

Changes in the structure of the economy also explain some of the decline in young

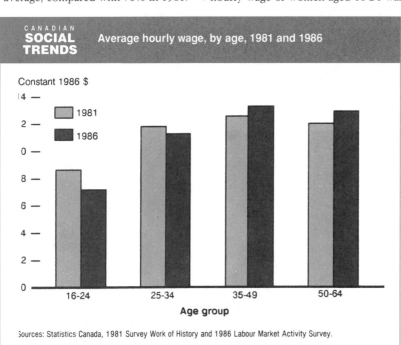

CANADIAN SOCIAL TRENDS

Average hourly wage, by age, 1981 and 1986

Constant 1986 $

■ 1981
■ 1986

Age group

Sources: Statistics Canada, 1981 Survey Work of History and 1986 Labour Market Activity Survey.

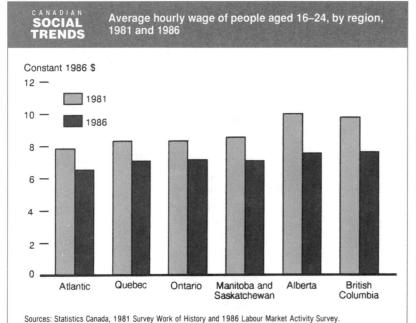

CANADIAN SOCIAL TRENDS

Average hourly wage of people aged 16–24, by region, 1981 and 1986

Constant 1986 $

■ 1981
■ 1986

Atlantic   Quebec   Ontario   Manitoba and Saskatchewan   Alberta   British Columbia

Sources: Statistics Canada, 1981 Survey Work of History and 1986 Labour Market Activity Survey.

The data

The 1981 data are from Statistics Canada's Survey of Work History; the 1986 data are from the Labour Market Activity Survey. Both surveys collected information on the pay and hours worked in all jobs respondents held during the survey year.

The data have been calculated to reflect full-time equivalent jobs. One full-time equivalent job equals 2,080 hours or the number of hours in a 40-hour-per-week job during a year. For example, a 10-hour-per-week job held for a full year was counted as a quarter of a full-time equivalent job, while a 40-hour-per-week job lasting six months was counted as half a full-time job.

workers' wages. In the 1980s, youth employment shifted away from several high-paying industries toward those with lower wages, particularly in the service sector. Perhaps even more important, average youth wages fell in all industries.[2]

Between 1981 and 1986, the proportions of young workers employed in four of the five industries with the highest average wages declined. The share of full-time youth employment[3] in natural resource industries, the highest-paying sector for young people, fell from 9% in 1981 to 6% in 1986. At the same time, the proportion in manufacturing dropped from 19% to 15%. There were also declines of around one percentage point in the proportion of youth employment accounted for by each of distributive and public sector service industries. The exception to this pattern was construction, the third-highest-paying sector for workers aged 16-24, where the share of youth employment rose slightly from 6% to 7%.

At the same time, there was a large increase in the proportion of youth employment in consumer services, the second-lowest-paying sector for young workers. Between 1981 and 1986, consumer services' share of youth employment rose from 26% to 36%.

In all industries, however, youth wages declined. Between 1981 and 1986, the average wage of 16-24-year-olds fell 19% in construction and 18% in natural resource industries. In addition, hourly wages of young workers decreased 15% in both agriculture and consumer services.

Declines in the remaining industries ranged from 12% in manufacturing to 7% in business services.

A legacy of the recession

To some extent, the overall drop in youth wages during the 1980s is also a lingering effect of the 1981-82 recession, which was particularly hard on young workers. For example, in 1983, unemployment among 15-24-year-olds was 22% for men and 17% for women; by contrast, for both men and women aged 25 and over, unemployment that year was just above 9%.

Although the economy subsequently recovered, unemployment remained relatively high among 15-24-year-olds. In 1986, 17% of men and 14% of women in this age range were unemployed. These rates compared with around 8% for both men and women aged 25 and over.

Moreover, the recession was the impetus behind much of the industrial and occupational redistribution of employment that put an increasing proportion of young workers in low-wage sectors. The recession also placed roadblocks in the careers of the baby boom population. In fact, youth wages had started falling in the mid-1970s when this large generation began to crowd the labour market. By slowing their advancement, the recession prolonged the labour market congestion for younger people.

On the other hand, the reduction of youth wages in this period may have helped 16-24-year-olds get jobs more quickly than if wages had not declined. By 1988, youth unemployment in Canada had dropped to pre-recession levels, unlike the situation in some Western European economies, where the wages of young people did not fall.

[2] For more detail on the relative effects of shifts in employment patterns between industries and wage changes within industries, including the methodology used, see Myles, J., Picot, G., and Wannell, T., *Wages and Jobs in the 1980s: Changing Youth Wages and the Declining Middle*, Statistics Canada, Analytic Studies Branch, Research Paper #17.

[3] This section includes only full-time jobs.

Proportion of full-time employment and average hourly wages of people aged 16–24, by industry, 1981 and 1986

	Distribution of full-time jobs		Average hourly wage	
	1981	**1986**	**1981**	**1986**
	%		Constant 1986 $	
Natural resources	9.3	5.6	11.47	9.42
Distributive services	10.2	9.3	9.41	8.54
Construction	6.4	7.3	10.54	8.52
Public sector services	14.7	14.1	9.38	8.33
Manufacturing	19.4	15.2	9.08	7.97
Business services	10.7	9.8	8.45	7.84
Consumer services	26.4	35.7	7.26	6.20
Agriculture	2.8	3.0	6.14	5.22
Total	**100.0**	**100.0**	**8.86**	**7.47**

Sources: Statistics Canada, 1981 Survey of Work History and 1986 Labour Market Activity Survey.

INCOME OF CANADA'S SENIORS

by Colin Lindsay and Shelley Donald

Canada's senior population has grown dramatically in the last two decades. Between 1966 and 1986, the number of Canadians aged 65 and over rose 75% from just over 1.5 million to almost 2.7 million. In comparison, the population under age 65 increased just 22% in the same period. Consequently, people aged 65 and over made up 11% of the total population in 1986, up from 8% in 1966.

Rapid growth of the senior population, which is expected to continue for several more decades, has raised a number of issues. These include concerns about the ability of older people to maintain a satisfactory income and standard of living once they reach retirement age.

The income of people aged 65 and over has improved relative to that of other Canadians since the early 1970s, although it remains well below levels of the rest of the population.

This improvement in the relative income position of older Canadians has resulted from a number of factors, including maturing of the Canada and Quebec Pension Plans (C/QPP), full inflation protection of C/QPP and Old Age Security and Guaranteed Income Supplement (OAS/GIS) benefits, introduction of Provincial Income Supplements, and increased income from sources such as private pensions and investments.

Real incomes of Canadians 65 and over rising

The real income, that is, income adjusted for inflation, of Canadians aged 65 and over has risen faster than that of the population aged 25-64 since the early 1970s.[1] Relative increases in real income were most striking among older unattached individuals — people living alone or in a household with unrelated persons. Between 1971 and 1986, average real incomes rose 61% for unattached women aged 65 and over and 36% for unattached men in this age range. In the same period, the average real income of unattached individuals aged 25-64 increased 28% for women and just 13% for men.

The average real income of elderly husband-wife families also rose more quickly than that of younger families. In the 1971-1986 period, the average real income of elderly families increased 35%, compared with 27% for families headed by men aged 25-64.

Much of the relative increase in the real income of older Canadians occurred during the late 1970s and early 1980s. Largely because of the recession in the early 1980s, the real income of many younger Canadians actually declined in that period. In contrast, the real income of the senior population continued to grow. Between 1979 and 1984, average real incomes rose 18% for unattached women aged 65 and over, 16% for elderly husband-wife families, and 11% for unattached older men. These gains were primarily the result of higher benefits from maturing Canada and Quebec Pension Plans and fully indexed C/QPP and OAS/GIS pensions.

Seniors' income still relatively low

Despite relatively large increases in real income of people aged 65 and over, their average income remains well below that of the rest of the population.

In 1986, elderly husband-wife families had an average income of $28,500, just 63% that of families headed by men aged 25-64; this was up from 59% in 1971.

The average income of unattached men aged 65 and over in 1986 was $13,900, just

[1] This and subsequent conclusions are based on an analysis of money incomes and do not take into account the tax and price advantages and family benefits enjoyed by many seniors; including these might show even further improvement in the economic position of older Canadians relative to the rest of the population. As well, elderly families tend to be smaller than younger families, and therefore, may require less income.

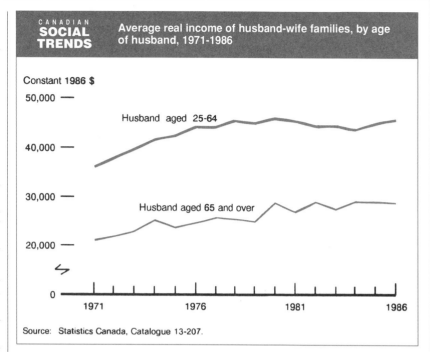

CANADIAN SOCIAL TRENDS

Average real income of husband-wife families, by age of husband, 1971-1986

Constant 1986 $

Source: Statistics Canada, Catalogue 13-207.

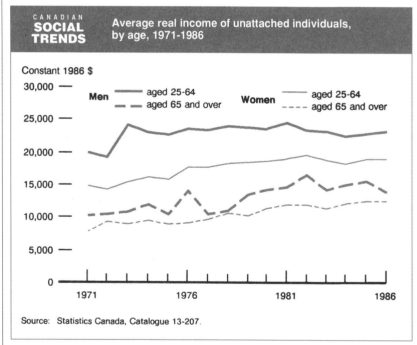

CANADIAN SOCIAL TRENDS

Average real income of unattached individuals, by age, 1971-1986

Constant 1986 $

Source: Statistics Canada, Catalogue 13-207.

60% that of unattached men aged 25-64. At the same time, unattached women aged 65 and over had an average income of $12,600, which was 66% that of comparable women aged 25-64. Both these percentages represent increases from 1971 when the respective figures were 51% and 53%.

Larger increases among older elderly

Increases in the real income of senior Canadians were greater among the older segments of this population. The average real income of families headed by men aged 75 and over rose 47% between 1971 and 1986, compared with 33% for families headed by men aged 65-74. Among unattached individuals, the gain was 46% for men aged 75 and over and 70% for women in this age range. In comparison, average real incomes of those aged 65-74 rose 32% for men and 58% for women.

The income levels of older elderly people, however, remain below those of

65-74-year-olds, although the gap has closed since the early 1970s.

In 1986, the average income of families headed by men aged 75 and over was 79% that of families headed by men aged 65-74; this was up from 72% in 1971.

Among unattached individuals, the average income of men aged 75 and over in 1986 was 87% that of men aged 65-74; this compares with 78% in 1971. For women, those aged 75 and over had an average 1986 income which was 90% that of women aged 65-74, up from 83% in 1971.

Smaller proportion of low-income elderly

One result of the relatively large increases in real income among people aged 65 and over has been a major reduction in the proportion with low incomes. Between 1981 and 1986, the percentage of elderly people with incomes below Statistics Canada's low-income cut-offs[2] fell from 27% to 19%. In contrast, both the percentage of children under age 16 living in low-income families and the proportion of the population aged 16-64 with low incomes increased.

The incidence of low income among older Canadians varies markedly for men and women depending on their family status. For example, unattached people aged 65 and over, particularly women, are among the poorest Canadians. Low-income rates of these groups, however, have fallen sharply since the late 1970s.

In 1986, almost half (46%) of unattached women aged 65 and over had incomes below the low-income cut-offs. This was a substantial improvement from 1979 when almost 70% of older unattached women had low incomes. Levels of low income also declined sharply among older unattached men from 59% in 1979 to 32% in 1986.

The incidence of low income also dropped among elderly husband-wife families. Between 1979 and 1986, the percentage of these families with low incomes fell from 22% to under 10%. As a result, levels of low income among elderly families have been slightly below those for comparable younger families since 1984.

Growing importance of public pensions

The importance of public pensions to the senior population has increased in the last decade and a half. Most of this increase was attributable to growth of the Canada and Quebec Pension Plan. In 1971, when this program was in its infancy, less than 2% of all elderly income came from C/QPP. By 1986, this source provided nearly 14% of the total income of the older population.

The proportion of the income of older Canadians coming from other government transfer payments (other than OAS/GIS) also rose, from 2.2% of the total in 1971 to 3.6% in 1986. On the other hand, the share of the income of older people coming from OAS/GIS has fallen in recent years, from about 40% in 1971 to 34% in 1986.

Nonetheless, together these three public sources accounted for 52% of the total income of Canadians aged 65 and over in 1986, up from 44% in 1971.

While private sources account for a shrinking share of the income of older Canadians, trends for different types of private income varied considerably. The percentage of the total income of seniors coming from private pensions grew from 13% in 1971 to 16% in 1986, and the share resulting from investments rose

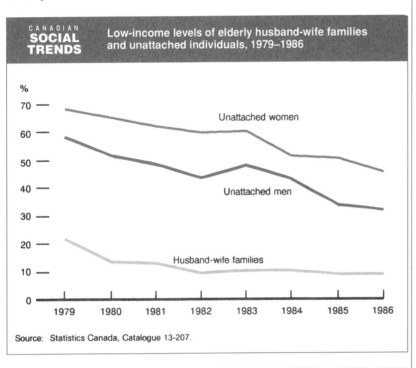

Low-income levels of elderly husband-wife families and unattached individuals, 1979–1986

Source: Statistics Canada, Catalogue 13-207.

Distribution of income sources of men and women, 65 and over, 1971 /1986						
	Men		Women		Total	
	1971	1986	1971	1986	1971	1986
			%			
OAS/GIS	28.1	25.2	59.5	45.3	39.6	34.4
C/QPP	2.1	16.3	1.1	11.0	1.7	13.9
Other government transfers	2.1	3.5	2.4	3.6	2.2	3.6
Investment income	20.2	18.9	19.6	24.1	20.0	21.2
Private pensions	15.8	20.1	8.5	10.5	13.2	15.7
Employment earnings	30.2	14.6	7.2	3.9	21.8	9.8
Other	0.9	1.3	1.3	1.5	1.0	1.4
Total	100.0	100.0	100.0	100.0	100.0	100.0
Total income (constant 1986 $)	12,554	16,760	6,183	10,527	9,122	13,212

Source: Statistics Canada, Household Surveys Division.

[2] The low-income cut-offs define individuals or families as having low incomes if the household unit spends more than 58.5% of income on food, shelter, and clothing.

from 20% to 21%. On the other hand, the proportion of all elderly income coming from employment earnings has fallen from 22% in 1971 to less than 10% in 1986.

Growth of Canada and Quebec Pension Plans

Much of the increased importance of Canada and Quebec Pension Plan benefits to the income of older Canadians is attributable to greater coverage of these programs. In 1971, when C/QPP had been operating for only a few years, just 13% of the senior population received these benefits. By 1986, 1.6 million older Canadians, or 61% of the total, were C/QPP beneficiaries.

Men are generally more likely than women to receive C/QPP benefits. In 1986, 79% of men aged 65 and over, compared with 47% of elderly women, were C/QPP beneficiaries. As a result of this difference, and because average benefits paid to men ($3,500) were higher than those paid to women ($2,500), C/QPP benefits make up a greater share of the income of older men. In 1986, 16% of the income of men aged 65 and over, compared with 11% of that of women, came from C/QPP. This difference should shrink in the future as the rising numbers of women in the labour force build up pension credits under these programs.

OAS/GIS: cornerstone of the income of older Canadians

Old Age Security benefits are paid to all Canadians aged 65 and over who meet minimum residency requirements. As well, approximately half of all seniors receive additional support through Guaranteed Income Supplements, which are based on a means-test and are paid only to pensioners who have little or no income above OAS. GIS payments are reduced by $1 for each $2 of monthly income from sources other than OAS.

The proportion of the senior population receiving GIS benefits, particularly full benefits, has declined sharply. By 1986, half of OAS pensioners received GIS benefits; 11% had no income from other sources and received the maximum benefit. In 1978, 54% had received GIS support, and 19% had received full benefits.

Largely because they tend to have less income from other sources, the groups for whom OAS/GIS benefits are most important are women, the older elderly, and unattached individuals.

In 1986, OAS/GIS benefits made up 45% of the income of older women, compared with 25% of that of men. As well, OAS/GIS pensions accounted for 44% of

the income of people aged 75 and over, compared with 34% for those aged 70-74 and 27% for 65-69-year-olds. Also, 42% of the income of older unattached women and 35% of that of comparable men came from OAS/GIS. In contrast, OAS/GIS accounted for only 25% of the income of elderly husband-wife families.

Private income: different sources for men and women

Private sources[3] remain a major component of the income of older Canadians; however, the relative importance of these sources varies for men and women.

Investment income is especially important for older women. While the actual dollar amount of investment income received by women was less than that for men, this source accounted for 24% of all

income of women aged 65 and over, compared with 19% for older men.

On the other hand, private pensions are more important to older men. In 1986, over 20% of the income of men aged 65 and over, compared with less than 11% of that of women, came from private

pensions. The proportion of both older men and women receiving private pension income, though, has increased. In 1986, 48% of men aged 65 and over, compared with 31% in 1971, reported income from private pensions; for women, the increase was from 11% to 24%.

---

[3] For more information on income from private pension plans and investments, see Oja, G., *Pensions and Incomes of the Elderly in Canada 1971-1985,* Statistics Canada, Catalogue 13-588, No. 2.

Wealth of older Canadians

To some extent, income figures may understate the ability of older Canadians to maintain a comfortable standard of living in that these figures do not include financial holdings and other accumulated assets.

Generally, those aged 65 and over have greater assets than younger people. In 1984, elderly families had an average net worth of $131,000. This compared with just over $100,000 for all families. At the same time, unattached individuals aged 65 and over had an average net worth of $52,000, compared with $38,000 for all unattached individuals.

Net financial assets and home equity constitute most of the wealth of older Canadians. In 1984, each of these sources made up over 35% of the net worth of elderly families and over 40% of that of unattached older individuals.

As well, 80% of families headed by someone aged 65 or over owned their own homes, compared with 71% of all families. In addition, 91% of elderly families owning homes did not have a mortgage, compared with just 48% of all home-owning families.

Again, the gap between the importance of private pensions to the retirement income of men and women is expected to close in the future as the full impact of women's increased labour force participation is felt.

While the contribution of employment earnings to total income declined for both older men and women, the drop was greater among men. Between 1971 and 1986, earnings as a proportion of the income of older men fell from 30% to 15%. In the same period, the share of older women's income from this source declined from 7% to 4%.

Leisure

TELEVISION VIEWING

By Anthony Young

Canadians spend a considerable amount of time each day watching television. In fact, television viewing accounts for, on average, about one in five of people's waking hours. As a result, much of the information Canadians receive about their society and the world comes from this medium.

Overall, in 1987, Canadians watched an average of 3.4 hours of television a day. This figure has changed very little in the 1980s, although it is up slightly from the mid-1970s. For example, in 1976, daily viewing averaged 3.2 hours.

There is considerable diversity, though, in the amount of time people spend watching television and in the types of programs they enjoy. Generally, women watch more than men, and the elderly watch more than younger people. The amount of time people spend watching television, however, is high for all groups, including children and teenagers.

Women, older people watch more

Women generally watch more television than men. In 1987, women aged 18 and over watched an average of 3.8 hours a day, compared with 3.2 hours for men.

For both men and women, average viewing time increases with age. Women over age 60, for example, watched 5.1 hours a day in 1987, the most for any age group of either sex. Among men, those aged 60 and over also watched the most television, 4.5 hours a day.

Children aged 2-11 and young people aged 12-17 do not watch as much televison as most adults; however, they do spend a substantial part of their days in front of a television set. In 1987, children watched 3.1 hours of television a day, while the figure was 2.7 hours for those aged 12-17.

Drama and news most watched programs

The largest share of Canadians' television viewing time is devoted to dramas. These programs accounted for about one-third of all viewing in 1987. News and public affairs made up another 20%, while comedy and variety/game shows represented 13% and 12%, respectively, and sports, 6%.

Not surprisingly, there are differences in the program preferences of men and women. Men spend about twice as much of their viewing time as women on sports programs, whereas dramas account for a greater share of women's viewing.

There are also differences in the program choices of adults and young people. Most significantly, the proportions of children's and teenager's viewing time devoted to news and public affairs are less than half that of adults. In 1987, news and public affairs programs represented only 7% of the viewing time of children and 10% of that of teenagers; this compared with 22% for adults. On the other hand, greater shares of the viewing time of children and teenagers were devoted to dramas and comedies.

Foreign programs popular

Most of the television programs Canadians watch come from outside the country. In 1987, foreign programming accounted for 64% of all viewing time.

The distribution of viewing time between programs from foreign and domestic sources, though, varies considerably depending on the type of program. Almost all the dramas and comedies Canadians watch are imported, whereas most news and public affairs, along with the majority of sports programs, are Canadian in origin.

During 1987, 98% of comedies and 87% of dramas watched came from foreign sources, while 87% of news and public affairs and 78% of sports programs were Canadian.

More viewing in the east

People in Quebec and the Atlantic provinces other than Prince Edward Island watch more television than those in

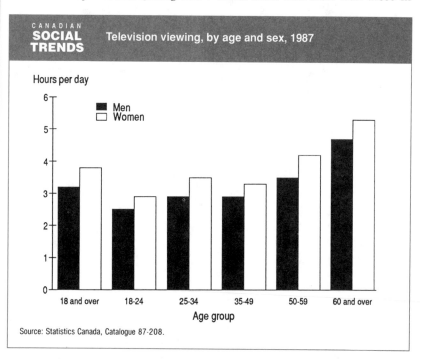

CANADIAN SOCIAL TRENDS — Television viewing, by age and sex, 1987

Hours per day

Source: Statistics Canada, Catalogue 87-208.

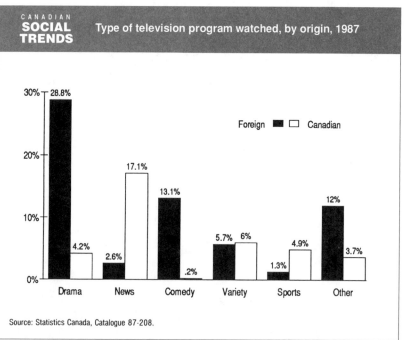

CANADIAN SOCIAL TRENDS — Type of television program watched, by origin, 1987

Source: Statistics Canada, Catalogue 87-208.

Ontario and the Western provinces. Residents of Quebec, Newfoundland, Nova Scotia, and New Brunswick watched an average of around 4 hours a day during 1987, compared with just over 3 hours a day in the other provinces.

CANADIAN SOCIAL TRENDS

Television viewing, by province, 1987

Hours per day

Province	Nfld.	P.E.I.	N.S	N.B.	Que.	Ont.	Man.	Sask.	Alta.	B.C.

Canada

Source: Statistics Canada, Catalogue 87-208.

EATING OUT

By Linda Robbins

Whether it's a candlelit dinner in a gourmet restaurant or a hamburger from a fast-food outlet, meals eaten or purchased away from home are increasingly popular with Canadians. In fact, according to a 1988 Gallup survey,[1] about seven out of ten adults had eaten out within the last week, and only 5% said that they never eat out at all.

As a result, eating out expenditures, including meals in table-service restaurants, fast-food establishments, and cafeterias, make up a rising proportion of food spending. In 1986, the average household spent more than a quarter of its total food budget on such meals, a substantial rise over 1969, when eating out accounted for 15% of the food dollar.

Trends in both household formation and labour force participation have contributed to the growing frequency of eating out. Two-income couples and one-person households often lack the time or the desire to prepare meals at home, preferring instead to dine in a restaurant or buy take-out/delivery items.

Some population groups are more likely than others to have meals away from home. Affluent people, for example, eat out more often and spend a larger share of their food budget on these meals than do people in lower-income households. Similarly, households in which the wife is employed full-time, married couples without children, and people living alone are the most likely to patronize foodservice establishments.

Most Canadians eat out

The vast majority of Canadians eat out at least occasionally, and most do so regularly.

The 1988 Gallup survey reported that 69% of adults had been restaurant patrons during the previous week; of these, 46% had eaten out within the past three days.

A further 18% had eaten a restaurant meal one to four weeks earlier, while 7% had done so more than a month before. Only 5% of all adults said that they never eat out.

The likelihood of eating out is strongly associated with income. Whereas 59% of people whose household income exceeded $40,000 had eaten out in the previous three days, the figure was just 31% for those in the less-than-$20,000 category.

Young people were particularly likely to have eaten out recently. Close to two-thirds (63%) of 18-24-year-olds had eaten out within the last three days. This proportion fell in older age groups to just over a quarter (27%) of people aged 65 and over.

[1] Gallup Canada, Inc., and Canadian Restaurant and Foodservice Association, *Gallup on Eating Out*, September 1988, Vol. 2, No. 1.

Higher levels of education were also associated with the likelihood of eating out. Sixty-four percent of people with a university education had been to a restaurant in the last three days, compared with 44% of those with high school, and 30% who had not gone beyond public school.

Who spends the most?

Meals away from home accounted for 27% of the total food budget of Canadian households in 1986, up from 15% in 1969. Expenditures on eating out, however, vary for different groups.

Eating out makes up a particularly large proportion of food expenditures in high-income households. Meals away from home represented 35% of the food spending of households with incomes above $60,000, but just 21% for those in the less-than-$10,000 bracket.

Childless families spend proportionally more on eating out than do families with children. Fully 30% of the food expenditures of childless couples in 1986 were on meals away from home, compared with 22% for families with children. Somewhat surprisingly, the proportion of the food budget devoted to eating out was almost the same for lone-parent families and husband-wife families with children.

As well, in households where the wife had a full-time job, 30% of the food dollar was spent on meals away from home. If she worked part-time, eating out accounted for 25% of the household's food budget, and for households in which the wife was not employed, the proportion was just 20%.

As might be expected, single people spent considerably more of their food dollar on meals away from home than did families. In 1986, eating out represented half of the food expenditures of single men and 30% of those of single women. By contrast, the corresponding figure for families with children was 22%.

However, singles' spending on food away from home fell at older ages. While single men under age 45 spent 56% of their food dollar on restaurant meals (the highest percentage of any group), the corresponding figure for single men over age 65 was 27%. For single women, comparable shares were 45% and 17%, respectively.

Meals away from home also make up a much larger proportion of the food budget of city households than of those in rural areas. Eating out accounted for 29% of the food expenditures of households in large cities (population 500,000 and over), compared with 21% for rural households.

The percentage of food expenditures allocated to eating out varies in different provinces, with proportionate spending generally higher in Ontario and the west than in Quebec and the Atlantic region. Ontario and Alberta households spent the greatest share of their food dollar on meals away from home (29%), while the figure was 28% in Saskatchewan, and 27% in both British Columbia and Manitoba. Percentages in the other provinces were below the national average (27%): Quebec (25%), Prince Edward Island (23%), New Brunswick (22%), and Nova Scotia (20%). Newfoundland households spent just 13% of their food dollar on eating out, the smallest share in any province.

Where we eat

In 1987, there were almost 35,000 food-service establishments in Canada, with total receipts of more than $12.0 billion. This compared with around 32,000 establishments in 1981, with receipts of

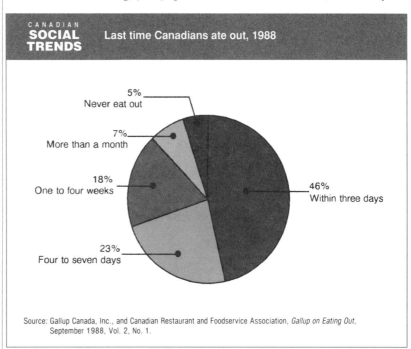

CANADIAN SOCIAL TRENDS — Last time Canadians ate out, 1988

- 5% Never eat out
- 7% More than a month
- 18% One to four weeks
- 23% Four to seven days
- 46% Within three days

Source: Gallup Canada, Inc., and Canadian Restaurant and Foodservice Association, *Gallup on Eating Out*, September 1988, Vol. 2, No. 1.

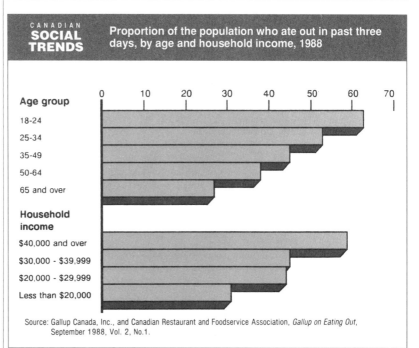

CANADIAN SOCIAL TRENDS — Proportion of the population who ate out in past three days, by age and household income, 1988

Age group: 18-24, 25-34, 35-49, 50-64, 65 and over

Household income: $40,000 and over, $30,000 - $39,999, $20,000 - $29,999, Less than $20,000

Source: Gallup Canada, Inc., and Canadian Restaurant and Foodservice Association, *Gallup on Eating Out*, September 1988, Vol. 2, No.1.

$10.7 billion (constant 1987 dollars).

The largest share of Canadians' eating out expenditures — 58% in 1986 — was in table-service restaurants. Fast-food restaurants received another 25% of the away-from-home food dollar, with take-out/delivery outlets and eat-in/drive-in restaurants accounting for 13% and 12%, respectively. Another 10% of spending on meals away from home was in cafeterias, and the remaining 7% was in other kinds of restaurants.

Something different

During 1988, about 80% of Canadian adults tried at least one restaurant where they had never eaten before. This proportion included 39% who had been to 1-3 new places, 17% who had tried 4-6, and 24% who had eaten at 7 or more.

The most common reason for trying a new restaurant, mentioned by 34% of patrons, was curiosity about the food. Recommendations prompted another 28% to try a new place.

Type of meal

Overall, dinner accounted for about half of all expenditures on meals away from home, and lunch, about a third. Another 7% of eating out spending was for breakfast, while the remaining 11% was spent between meals.

Microwave ovens

Eating out is the ultimate solution for people who do not want to be bothered with time-consuming meal preparation. The next best thing, however, may be a microwave oven. In fact, the number of Canadian households with microwave ovens has risen steeply during the 1980s. By 1988, 54% of all households were equipped with these appliances, up from 8% in 1981, and just 1% in 1975.

Vending machines

In 1986, Canadians spent over $285 million buying beverages and food from almost 137,000 vending machines. Beverages, mostly coffee and soft drinks, accounted for about two-thirds of these sales. The food purchased from vending machines tended to be snack items such as chocolate bars, candies, and potato chips.

More than half (53%) of all vending machines were located in industrial plants or business offices. Another 10% were in institutions such as hospitals, universities, and schools, and almost as many (9%) were in hotels, motels, restaurants, and taverns. The rest were in a variety of outlets such as service stations, theatres, and bowling alleys.

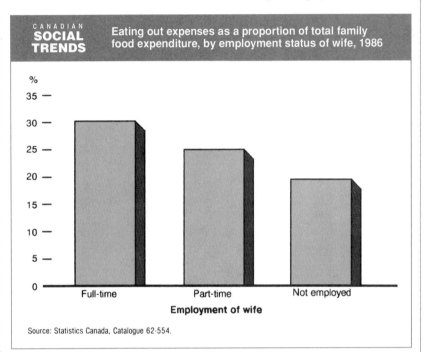

CANADIAN SOCIAL TRENDS

Eating out expenses as a proportion of total family food expenditure, by employment status of wife, 1986

Employment of wife

Source: Statistics Canada, Catalogue 62-554.

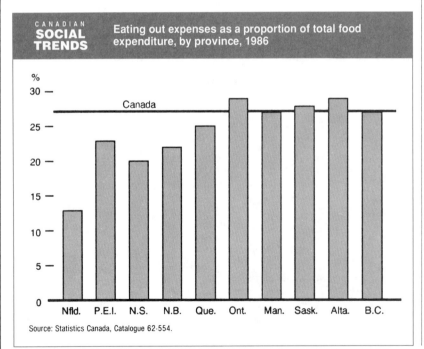

CANADIAN SOCIAL TRENDS

Eating out expenses as a proportion of total food expenditure, by province, 1986

Source: Statistics Canada, Catalogue 62-554.

LOTTERIES IN CANADA

by Mary Blickstead

Playing lotteries has become commonplace in Canada since their legalization in 1969. Surveys indicate that almost every Canadian has bought tickets at least once. And opportunities to make such purchases have multiplied. By 1985, five government-sponsored lottery corporations were offering three nationwide games and a variety of regional lotteries. Thousands of retailers across the country sell tickets in outlets ranging from booths in malls to large chain stores. But while the annual amount spent on government-run lotteries now adds up to billions of dollars, as a proportion of individual family expenditures, lotteries are minimal, representing less than half of one percent.

Ticket sales rise

The chance of winning millions has led to steady increases in sales of lottery tickets. In 1985, Canadians spent $2.7 billion on government lotteries. Adjusting for inflation this was close to a threefold increase from 1976. However, during the 1981-1983 recession, spending on lotteries (in constant 1985 dollars) declined, indicating that, to some extent, ticket purchases are tied to the overall state of the economy.

In 1985, expenditures on lotteries were highest in Ontario, where for the first time, sales topped $1 billion. Quebec ranked next at $883 million, followed by British Columbia ($330 million), the Western region ($318 million), and the Atlantic region ($153 million).

Family spending on lotteries

In 1986, 70% of Canadian households reported buying tickets for government-run lotteries, up from 65% in 1982. The average annual reported expenditure per family in 1986 was $146.[1] This was an increase from 1982, when ticket purchases for government lotteries amounted to $108 (in constant 1986 dollars) per family.

Spending on lotteries accounted for only a very small proportion of total family expenditures. In 1986, tickets for government-run lotteries represented 0.42% of average family expenditures.

[1] Reported expenditures on government lottery tickets may be underestimated. In fact, total personal expenditures on lotteries recorded in the National Accounts are more than double the amount reported by individual families. Some of the discrepancy can be attributed to purchases by non-residents, but separate estimates of such purchases are not available.

Lottery corporation	1976	1977	1978	1979	1980	1981	1982	1983	1984	1985
					current $ 000s					
Atlantic Lottery Corporation	11,579	40,602	43,618	41,096	52,557	66,750	78,635	109,162	134,987	152,734
Loto Québec	183,341	202,897	253,652	347,816	436,466	479,652	541,411	662,177	741,102	883,121
Ontario Lottery Corporation[1]	218,793	240,431	235,105	323,786	490,300	506,900	550,100	661,800	811,974	1,007,830
Western Lottery Corporation	71,273	74,058	129,826	156,305	200,225	210,567	237,425	350,477	483,476	317,858
British Columbia Lottery Corporation	. . .	. . .	. . .	. . .	. . .	. . .	. . .	. . .	. . .	330,061
Total	484,986	557,988	662,201	869,003	1,179,548	1,263,869	1,407,571	1,783,616	2,171,539	2,691,604

Interprovincial Lottery Corporation ticket sales, by lottery corporation, 1976 to 1985

[1] Includes value of free tickets.
. . . not applicable.
Source: Regional Lottery Corporations.

Nonetheless, this was up from 0.33% in 1982.

Quebec residents were the most likely to buy government lottery tickets: almost eight out of 10 (78%) families reported such purchases in 1986. The proportions were close to the national average (70%) in New Brunswick, Ontario, Alberta, and British Columbia. For residents of Manitoba, Saskatchewan, and Nova Scotia, the percentage ranged from 60% to 65%. On the other hand, fewer than half of families in Newfoundland and Prince Edward Island purchased lottery tickets.

Quebec families also spent the largest amounts of money on government lotteries. In 1986, families in Quebec paid an average of $187 for such lottery tickets. This was well above levels in the next highest provinces: Alberta ($142), Ontario ($139), and British Columbia ($137). Spending on lotteries was lowest in Newfoundland ($58) and Prince Edward Island ($67).

Family income

Both the proportion of families reporting expenditures on government lotteries and the amount they spend tend to rise with family income. In 1986, just under half (49%) of families with incomes below $10,000 bought lottery tickets, and the average expenditure for these families was $49. By contrast, 81% of families with annual incomes between $50,000 and $60,000 bought tickets and spent an average of $238. The likelihood of buying a ticket (76%) and the amount spent ($207) declined somewhat for families with incomes of $60,000 and over.

Low-income families, however, spend a higher percentage of their total income on lotteries than do families at high-income levels. For instance, 1986 lottery spending amounted to 0.65% of the before-tax income of families receiving less than $10,000; the corresponding figure for families at the $60,000 and over income level was just 0.25%.

The players

A survey conducted by the Western Canada Lottery Corporation[2] and a poll undertaken for Loto Québec[3] show that men and women are equally likely to be players, and that lottery players are somewhat younger than the population as a whole.

The Western survey indicated that 25- to 34-year-olds were over-represented among lottery players. This age group made up more than 30% of all lottery players, but just 26% of the population aged 18 and older in that region. People aged 35-54 were also slightly over-represented among ticket buyers. At older ages, lottery playing dropped off. Just 2% of sales were to people aged 75 and older, whereas this group accounted for nearly 6% of the region's population aged 18 and over.

The Quebec survey showed the same pattern among people who played the province's three most popular lotteries. That is, the 25-34 age group was somewhat over-represented among players, while older people were under-represented.

According to the Quebec survey, the majority of lottery players (67%) made both individual and group purchases. Another 30% bought tickets only on an individual basis, and 3% participated only in group purchases.

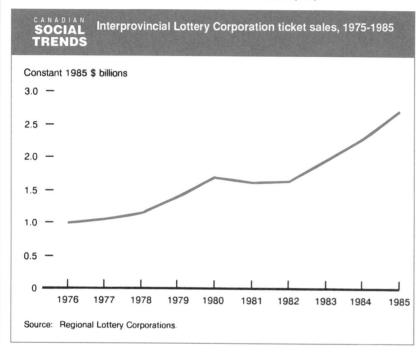

CANADIAN SOCIAL TRENDS — Interprovincial Lottery Corporation ticket sales, 1975-1985

Constant 1985 $ billions

Source: Regional Lottery Corporations.

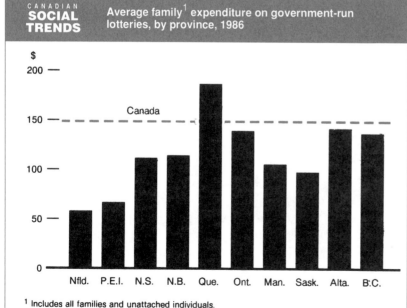

CANADIAN SOCIAL TRENDS — Average family[1] expenditure on government-run lotteries, by province, 1986

1 Includes all families and unattached individuals.
Source. Statistics Canada, Household Surveys Division.

2 Western Canada Lottery Corporation, *Annual Report, 1985/86*, p. 9.
3 Groupe conseil Coopers & Lybrand, *Characteristics of Lottery Players*, Loto Québec, 1986.

Winning

The cost of lottery tickets ranges from 50 cents to $10. The odds of winning go from about one in three to one in 14 million. Odds, of course, are related to prizes, which include everything from a free ticket to millions of dollars. Chances of winning a major prize ($100,000 or more) in the three national lotteries start at one in 500,000.

During 1985, lottery prizes totalled almost $1.3 billion. Most of these winnings were in the $2, $5, and $10 categories, but many millions of dollars were paid out on prizes of $50, $100, and $1,000. As well, each year a small number

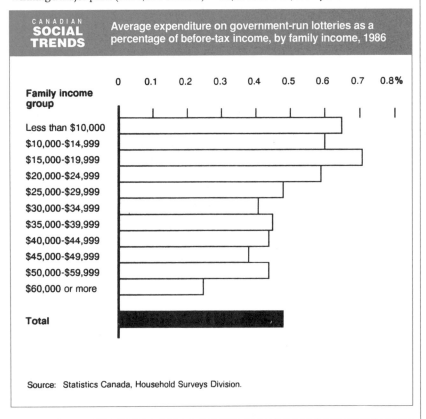

CANADIAN SOCIAL TRENDS

Average expenditure on government-run lotteries as a percentage of before-tax income, by family income, 1986

Source: Statistics Canada, Household Surveys Division.

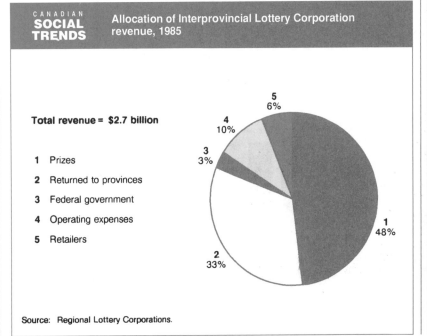

CANADIAN SOCIAL TRENDS

Allocation of Interprovincial Lottery Corporation revenue, 1985

Total revenue = $2.7 billion

1 Prizes
2 Returned to provinces
3 Federal government
4 Operating expenses
5 Retailers

1 48%
2 33%
3 3%
4 10%
5 6%

Source: Regional Lottery Corporations.

of players beat the odds and became lottery millionaires. For example, in 1985, around 100 prizes of $1 million or more were awarded.

Surveys of major winners in Ontario[4] and the Western provinces[5] showed that most of them handled their winnings conservatively. Nearly three-quarters (73%) reported banking some of the money; 15% paid off their mortgage; 7% invested in bonds; and 6% invested in real estate.[6] About a quarter (26%) did some travelling, while nearly the same proportion (23%) bought a new vehicle. In addition, four out of 10 winners (44%) shared their prize with family. Only a minority, for example, 3% in Ontario and 11% in the Western provinces, reported problems with solicitations for money.

Most major winners continued to buy lottery tickets. In the West, for instance, 78% of major winners bought the same number of tickets, and 20% bought more. Just 1% lost interest in playing lotteries after their win.

Where does the money go?

Almost half (48%) of the total revenue from lottery sales is returned to the players as prize money. Operating expenses account for another 10% of total revenue, while an additional 6% goes to the 32,000 retailers across the country. As well, about 3% of the proceeds are paid to the federal government. The remaining funds, a third of total sales, are returned to the regional corporations. These funds are used to support a variety of activities in the provinces, including sports and recreation, cultural events, heritage and citizenship, health care, medical and scientific research, education, and social and charitable organizations.

[4] Ontario Lottery Corporation, *Annual Report, 1985/86,* p. 4.
[5] Western Canada Lottery Corporation, *Annual Report, 1985/86,* p. 11.
[6] Survey respondents could indicate more than one use for their lottery winnings.

PRIVATE TRANSPORTATION

by Mary Sue Devereaux

I n 1987, Canadians owned more than 13 million private vehicles, about one for every two people in the country. Automobiles, vans, and trucks have become an integral part of the majority of households. Many Canadians, for example, depend on their vehicles for transportation to work, shopping, running errands, and vacation travel.

Currently, about eight out of ten households have at least one car, truck, or van. As well, recent years have seen particularly rapid growth in the proportion of households with more than one vehicle. Consequently, close to 40% of all households now have two or more.

But while cars, vans, and trucks are almost taken for granted as a necessary part of modern life, they are also associated with a set of problems. These include impaired driving, environmental degradation, urban congestion, and the need for public investment in road construction and maintenance.

Ownership rising

In 1987, the vast majority of Canadian households (83%) owned at least one vehicle. This was a considerable change from the early 1950s, when just over half of households had a vehicle.

Most of the increase in vehicle ownership took place in the 1950s and 1960s. Between 1953 and 1970, the percentage of households owning a vehicle rose from 52% to 78%. By contrast, the rise in ownership rates since 1970 has been much more gradual. Between 1970 and 1987, the proportion of households with a vehicle rose only five percentage points, from 78% to 83%.

On the other hand, ownership of more than one vehicle has risen sharply in recent years. In 1987, 39% of all households had two or more vehicles. This was up from 4% in 1953 and 17% in 1970.

Part of the recent growth in vehicle ownership rates is attributable to an increase in the proportion of households with vans and trucks. By 1987, 23% of households owned at least one of these vehicles, a rise from 20% in 1984, the first year for which this information was collected.

Provincial variations

Vehicle ownership rates vary somewhat across the country. In 1987, the proportion of households owning at least one vehicle ranged from 79% in both Newfoundland and Quebec to around 90% in Alberta (90%) and Prince Edward Island (88%). Ownership rates were also above the national average (83%) in British Columbia (87%), Saskatchewan (87%), Manitoba (85%), and New Brunswick (85%). Figures were close to the national level in Nova Scotia (82%) and Ontario (82%).

Provincial variation in the proportion of households with at least two vehicles was more pronounced. In 1987, more than half (53%) of all households in Alberta and Saskatchewan had more than one vehicle. On the other hand, just 29% of those in Newfoundland and Quebec were so equipped.

Provincial differences in the ownership of vans and trucks were also substantial. A relatively large proportion (43%) of Saskatchewan households had vans or trucks, possibly because these vehicles tend to be associated with agriculture, which is a major part of that province's economy. Van and truck ownership rates were also high in Alberta (40%) and Manitoba (32%). By contrast, comparatively few Ontario (18%) and Quebec (14%) households had these vehicles.

Vehicles more common in rural areas

Perhaps because of factors such as distance, relative isolation, and the lack of public transportation, as well as involvement in agriculture, rural households are more likely than those in large metropolitan areas to own vehicles. In 1987, 92% of rural households had a vehicle of some sort, compared with 80% in big cities.

Multiple-vehicle households were also more common in rural areas; over half (54%) of rural households had at least two vehicles, while the corresponding figure was just 35% in metropolitan areas.

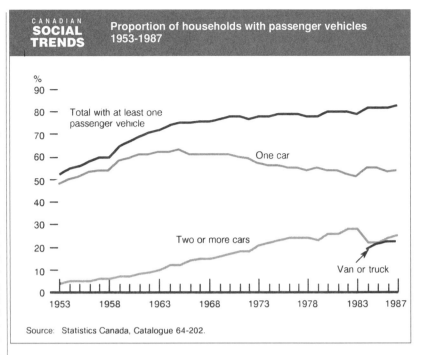

Proportion of households with passenger vehicles 1953-1987

Source: Statistics Canada, Catalogue 64-202.

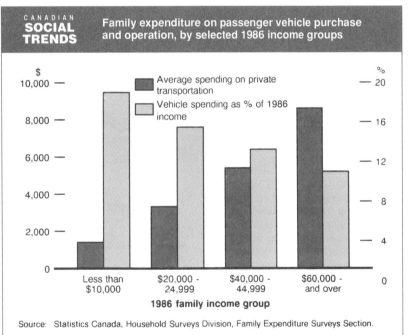

Family expenditure on passenger vehicle purchase and operation, by selected 1986 income groups

Source: Statistics Canada, Household Surveys Division, Family Expenditure Surveys Section.

Ownership high for traditional families

Almost all husband-wife families, especially those with children, own vehicles. Fully 95% of husband-wife families with children under age 18 owned at least one vehicle in 1987, and the majority (57%) had two or more.

Vehicle ownership rates were considerably lower among lone-parent families and people who lived alone. For example, 63% of lone-parent families had a vehicle in 1987, while the proportion was 59% for one-person households. Elderly people who lived alone were the least likely to own a vehicle (39%).

Not unexpectedly, vehicle ownership is strongly associated with household income. In 1987, almost all (96%) households with incomes of $55,000 and over had at least one vehicle, and the majority (71%) had two or more. By contrast, fewer than half (46%) of households with incomes below $10,000 had a vehicle.

Spending on private transportation

The amount of money Canadians spend on motor vehicles is substantial. In fact, spending on private transportation, including the costs of buying vehicles, plus expenditures on parts, repairs, and operation, amounted to 11.7% of all personal expenditure in 1986.

Spending on private transportation, however, varies with household income. In 1986, for example, households with incomes over $60,000 that operated vehicles spent an average of almost $8,700 on them, about six times more than the $1,400 spent by comparable households with incomes less than $10,000.

Most of this difference is attributable to the fact that well-to-do households are much more likely than less affluent ones to have purchased a vehicle. Whereas 43% of households with incomes exceeding $60,000 bought a vehicle in 1986, the comparable proportion was just 6% for those with incomes under $10,000.

Nonetheless, vehicle purchase and operation expenditures represented a much larger share of the income of families whose incomes were relatively low than of families at higher income levels. While buying and operating vehicles amounted to 19% of the before-tax income of families in the less-than-$10,000 range, the proportion was only about 10% for families in the $60,000 and over bracket.

A new car

Currently, about one million new cars are purchased in Canada each year. The annual number sold, however, has fluctuated during the 1980s. Sales slumped drastically during the recession in the early years of the decade, dropping from more than a million in 1979 to 713,000 in 1982. A strong rebound in the immediate post-recession period brought total sales to a record 1,137,000 in 1985. In the next two years, though, sales declined, falling to 1,065,000 in 1987.

A growing proportion of automobiles purchased by Canadians are foreign.[1] In 1987, 34% of new cars sold in Canada were imported, up from 19% in 1973. About two-thirds of these foreign cars were from Japan.

As well, buyers paid more for new foreign cars in 1987 than they did for those built in North America. By 1987, the average price paid for North American cars was $14,300, compared with $14,700 for cars from Japan and $17,800 for those built in other foreign countries. This was a change from the early 1970s, when

CANADIAN SOCIAL TRENDS

Average price of new cars, by place of manufacture, 1973-1987

Constant 1987 $ 000s

Other foreign countries

North America

Japan

Source: Statistics Canada, Catalogue 63-007.

th American cars were more costly 1 imports.

In 1984 and 1985, the average price of cars imported from countries other than Japan dropped sharply. This decline reflected sales of relatively inexpensive cars from the Republic of Korea. As sales of these Korean vehicles tapered off, the average price of foreign cars increased.

Overall, the average 1987 selling price of a new car was $14,800. In constant 1987 dollars, this was up 18% from 1980.

A spring thing

New-car buying in Canada tends to be seasonal, with people most likely to make a purchase in the spring. In 1987, more than 100,000 new cars were sold each month from March to June; the highest figure (121,000) was reported in April.

By contrast, the number of new cars sold each month from December 1986 to February 1987 did not surpass 70,000. Sales were lowest in January at just 56,500.

[1] The origin of vehicles is determined by the countries where they are manufactured, not by the company that makes them. Thus, cars made in North America by a foreign company are considered North American, and cars made overseas for a North American manufacturer are considered foreign.

PASSENGER TRAFFIC ON COMMERCIAL AIR SERVICES

Canada is a highly mobile society. Data on air passenger traffic demonstrate that this is so, as more and more Canadians take advantage of the availability of affordable air travel. Long distances separating family members have been shortened. Work schedules often involve commuting between distant urban centres. For many, air travel has made possible a mid-winter escape from the harsh Canadian climate.

A growing number of Canadians now find air travel within their reach, as air carriers vie with each other for the travel dollar. Increased competition, brought about by changes in regulations, has allowed the carriers to introduce (and withdraw) services more freely. Consequently, despite a downturn during the recession of the early eighties, by 1985 passengers on scheduled flights and charters numbered about 27 million. This was up from 1975 when the total was around 21 million.

Traffic on scheduled flights, whether within Canada or to international destinations, far exceeds the number of passengers flying on charters. Since 1980, however, charter traffic has grown much faster than scheduled traffic.

Travel within Canada is heavily dominated by scheduled flights, with charters accounting for only a small fraction (3%) of all passengers. The situation for international air travel is somewhat different: while the scheduled market continues to be much larger than the charter market, charters make up a growing share. In 1985, charters accounted for 26% of all international air passengers, a rise from 20% in 1975.

SCHEDULED SERVICES

Domestic Scheduled Services

From 1975 to 1980, the number of passengers travelling on domestic scheduled services increased from 10.4 million to 13.9 million, a rise of 34%. During the recession, numbers dropped to a low of 11.2 million in 1983. The end of the recession did not mean the recouping of all lost passengers. In 1985, the total was 11.9 million, still 14% below the 1980 high.

Toronto dominated the domestic

Top ten city-pairs for domestic scheduled flights, 1975, 1980-1985

1985 rank	City-pair	1975	1980	1981	1982	1983	1984	1985
					Passengers - 000s			
1	Montreal-Toronto	963	1,127	1,115	988	972	1,085	1,198
2	Ottawa-Toronto	496	575	559	571	557	624	633
3	Toronto-Vancouver	302	532	547	459	469	495	458
4	Calgary-Vancouver	291	455	472	470	440	437	430
5	Calgary-Toronto	174	397	433	420	388	396	400
6	Calgary-Edmonton	413	723	690	487	389	362	351
7	Edmonton-Vancouver	254	377	378	373	352	353	349
8	Toronto-Winnipeg	238	316	301	305	299	305	322
9	Edmonton-Toronto	139	298	307	301	265	274	270
10	Halifax-Toronto	168	220	228	237	204	245	260
	Others	6,924	8,959	8,498	7,532	6,908	7,308	7,251
	Total	**10,360**	**13,920**	**13,525**	**12,141**	**11,242**	**11,884**	**11,919**

Source: Statistics Canada, Catalogue 51-501E.

Top ten city-pairs for scheduled Canada-United States flights, 1975, 1980-85

1985 rank	City-pair	1975	1980	1981	1982	1983	1984	1985
					Passengers - 000s			
1	Toronto-New York	488	683	623	559	560	624	637
2	Montreal-New York	331	354	320	305	284	330	410
3	Toronto-Chicago	172	210	202	190	197	222	228
4	Vancouver-Los Angeles	123	197	187	156	175	176	184
5	Toronto-Boston	87	137	136	140	160	173	171
6	Montreal-Miami	172	240	230	199	157	161	166
7	Toronto-Los Angeles	105	188	178	143	161	148	162
8	Toronto-Miami	115	157	158	159	130	137	134
9	Vancouver-San Francisco	120	145	139	119	126	129	133
10	Montreal-Boston	110	134	131	124	124	133	129
	Others	3,502	5,205	5,108	4,516	4,264	4,630	4,485
	Total	**5,324**	**7,650**	**7,411**	**6,609**	**6,339**	**6,865**	**6,839**

Source: Statistics Canada, Catalogue 51-501E.

scheduled sector, serving as a focal point for much of the air traffic flow throughout the country. In 1985, seven of the top ten city-pairs involved Toronto.

Throughout the 1975-1985 period, Toronto-Montreal ranked as the number one city-pair. In 1985, for example, Toronto-Montreal accounted for 10% of all domestic scheduled flights. Ottawa-Toronto was the second most travelled route, except in 1980 and 1981, when it was surpassed by Calgary-Edmonton.

Scheduled air traffic between all top ten city-pairs declined during the recession. By 1985, half of them had regained the traffic lost in that period. Those that had not recovered involved western cities. The hardest-hit city-pair was Calgary-Edmonton, notable not only because 1985 traffic was below the pre-recession high, but also because numbers had declined steadily to less than the 1975 level.

International Scheduled Services

From 1975 to 1985, the international scheduled market grew faster than the domestic scheduled market. The number of international scheduled air passengers increased by over 31%, from 8.3 million in 1975 to 10.9 million in 1985. This compared with a 15% rise in the number of domestic scheduled air passengers.

As with domestic flights, international traffic rose between 1975 and 1980 and then declined during the recession. A peak occurred in 1980, when volume reached 11.3 million passengers. Numbers dropped in the next three years, but started to rise again in 1984. Yet by 1985, total volume was still about 4% below the 1980 high.

While the number of international scheduled passengers has fluctuated, their choice of destinations has been quite stable, with the United States standing first, followed by Europe, southern destinations, and others.

From 1975 to 1985, Canada's prime international market remained the continental United States. Although there have been minor variations, at least 60% of all international scheduled passengers went to the United States.

As is the case for domestic scheduled services, Toronto once again occupied a key position: it was the Canadian half of five of the top ten transborder city-pairs. The two leading city-pairs were Toronto-New York and Montreal-New York, ranking first and second, respectively, in every year from 1975 to 1985.

Europe stood second as a destination for international scheduled flights, accounting for 21% of traffic in 1985. The southern market (Bermuda, the Bahamas, the Caribbean Islands, Mexico, Central

1985 rank	City-pair	1980	1981	1982	1983	1984	1985
		Passengers - 000s					
1	Toronto-Vancouver	50	61	110	152	121	163
2	Calgary-Toronto	14	57	70	73	61	58
3	Edmonton-Toronto	6	15	24	48	40	55
4	Halifax-Toronto	-	-	-	19	11	10
5	Toronto-Winnipeg	3	2	2	7	18	7
	Others	48	57	35	40	59	68
	Total	**120**	**193**	**242**	**338**	**310**	**360**

Top five city-pairs for chartered domestic flights, 1980-1985

− Nil or zero.
Source: Statistics Canada, Catalogue 51-501E.

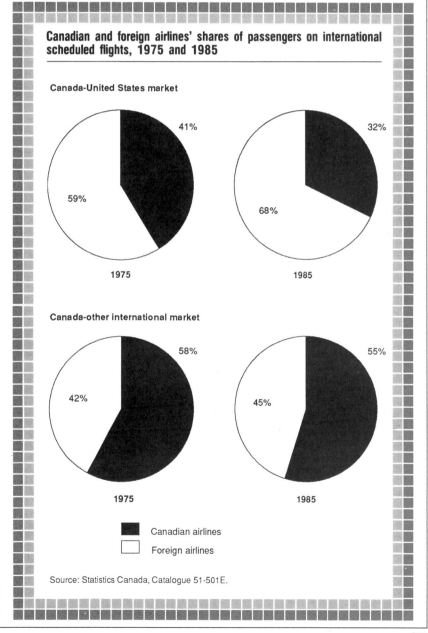

Canadian and foreign airlines' shares of passengers on international scheduled flights, 1975 and 1985

Canada-United States market

1975: 41% / 59%
1985: 32% / 68%

Canada-other international market

1975: 58% / 42%
1985: 55% / 45%

■ Canadian airlines
□ Foreign airlines

Source: Statistics Canada, Catalogue 51-501E.

America, and South America) made up another 8% of all international scheduled services.

Remaining market shares were small. Asia, accounting for about 6% in 1985, had grown from around 3% in 1975. Africa and the Pacific region each hovered close to the 1% mark.

In 1985, Canadian airlines carried 41% of all international scheduled passengers, a decline from 46% in 1975. Approximately 32% of passengers in the Canada-United States market were flown by Canadian carriers in 1985, down from 41% in 1975. Canadian carriers' share of the Canada-other international market also dropped, falling from 58% to 55%.

CHARTER SERVICES

Domestic Charter Services

From 1980 to 1985, the number of passengers travelling in Canada on advance booking charters tripled from 120,000 to

Top ten city-pairs for chartered Canada-U.S. flights, 1975, 1980-1985

1985 rank	City-pair	1975	1980	1981	1982	1983	1984	1985
				Passengers - 000s				
1	Montreal-Fort Lauderdale	15	37	133	183	147	150	137
2	Toronto-Fort Lauderdale	26	49	56	87	101	123	135
3	Toronto-Tampa	8	110	132	115	124	112	135
4	Toronto-Las Vegas	22	15	35	45	42	52	117
5	Vancouver-Honolulu	39	126	111	165	128	98	110
6	Toronto-Orlando	1	82	102	94	108	98	108
7	Toronto-Clearwater/ St. Petersburg	49	70	80	81	96	96	103
8	Vancouver-Reno	15	86	101	105	102	103	92
9	Edmonton-Honolulu	42	67	50	56	53	60	56
10	Calgary-Honolulu	16	68	49	61	53	54	54
	Others	223	626	627	641	620	617	699
	Total	**458**	**1,334**	**1,478**	**1,634**	**1,574**	**1,562**	**1,746**

Source: Statistics Canada, Catalogue 51-501E.

Top five city-pairs for chartered Canada-Europe flights, 1975, 1980-1985

1985 rank	City-pair	1975	1980	1981	1982	1983	1984	1985
				Passengers - 000s				
1	Toronto-London (England)	243	131	112	131	156	148	182
2	Montreal-Paris (France)	37	21	20	40	38	60	108
3	Toronto-Manchester (England)	57	73	76	77	83	79	77
4	Toronto-Glasgow (Scotland)	64	79	75	88	75	77	75
5	Vancouver-London (England)	88	55	55	52	85	62	65
	Others	471	404	427	489	480	521	556
	Total	**961**	**763**	**765**	**877**	**916**	**947**	**1,062**

Source: Statistics Canada, Catalogue 51-501E.

Top five city-pairs for chartered Canada-South flights, 1975, 1980-1985

1985 rank	City-pair	1975	1980	1981	1982	1983	1984	1985
				Passengers - 000s				
1	Toronto-Acapulco (Mexico)	38	32	32	40	93	90	73
2	Toronto-Bridgetown (Barbados)	58	46	39	47	47	61	61
3	Montreal-Acapulco (Mexico)	22	50	34	26	61	82	61
4	Toronto-Montego Bay (Jamaica)	19	22	19	54	43	41	50
5	Toronto-Puerto Vallarta (Mexico)	2	12	11	15	36	43	39
	Others	482	268	226	210	330	429	633
	Total	**621**	**430**	**361**	**393**	**610**	**746**	**917**

Source: Statistics Canada, Catalogue 51-501E.

360,000. Nonetheless, this was relatively insignificant compared with the 11.9 million domestic travellers who used scheduled services in 1985.

Primarily, domestic charters are long-haul. In 1985, five city-pairs accounted for over 80% of all passengers on domestic charters. Each of these city-pairs involved Toronto, and four of the five other cities were at least 1,500 kilometres away (Vancouver, Edmonton, Calgary, and Winnipeg). Halifax, at 1,287 kilometres, was the exception.

Safety

An aviation accident occurs when a passenger or crew member sustains a serious flight-related injury or when damage to an aircraft requires major repairs. From 1970 to 1984, the number of accidents per 100,000 hours flown for all commercial aviation decreased from 13.6 to 6.6. Not only did the accident rate decline, but so did the absolute number of accidents, which fell from 219 in 1970 to 151 in 1984. Technological advances, both in the air and on the ground, have meant a better safety record despite increases in the number of hours flown.

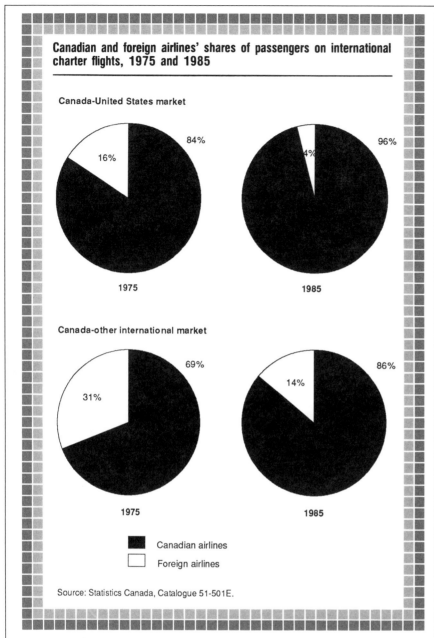

Canadian and foreign airlines' shares of passengers on international charter flights, 1975 and 1985

Canada-United States market

1975 — 84% / 16%

1985 — 96% / 4%

Canada-other international market

1975 — 69% / 31%

1985 — 86% / 14%

■ Canadian airlines
□ Foreign airlines

Source: Statistics Canada, Catalogue 51-501E.

International Charter Services

Unlike international scheduled traffic, the number of international charter passengers rose steadily throughout the eighties, and by 1985 totalled 3.8 million. This was almost double the 2 million who had flown on international charters in 1975.

There was also a shift in the most popular destinations. In 1985, nearly half (47%) of passengers on international charters were bound for the United States; another 28% went to Europe; and 24% to southern destinations. This was a marked change from 1975, when Europe accounted for 47% of all passengers, followed by the south (30%), and the United States (22%).

Charter traffic to the United States rose from 458,000 in 1975 to 1.63 million in 1982. Declines in the next two years brought the 1984 figure down to 1.56 million, but an upturn in 1985 resulted in an all-time high of 1.75 million.

Most Canadians flying in the Canada-United States charter market go to warm weather vacation spots. In 1985, of the top ten city-pairs, eight involved either Florida or Hawaii. The respective destinations of eastern and western Canadians are also evident. In the east, they tend to go to Florida; in the west, to Hawaii.

If on the other hand, Canadians are travelling to Europe, the leading market is the United Kingdom. Of the top five city-pairs in 1985, four involved the United Kingdom. Travel to Europe did not decline

during the recession of the early eighties; numbers rose steadily to an all-time high of more than one million in 1985.

The Canada-South market, however, was affected by the economic downturn. Passenger traffic to southern destinations fell 16% from 430,000 in 1980 to 361,000 in 1981. Sustained growth in the following years brought the 1985 total to 917,000.

Unlike international scheduled services, Canadian carriers increased their share of traffic on international charters. In 1985, they transported 96% of all Canada-United States charter passengers, up from 84% in 1975. Comparable figures for the Canada-other international market were 86% and 69%.

Discount Fares

In the late 1970s, when domestic charters were granted the right to compete with scheduled services, discount excursion fares became common. Before then, the range of air fares was limited. Apart from scheduled first class fares and economy class, there were a small number of excursion fares, but these were available only during off-peak seasons.

The change in Canadian fare structures was also prompted by the passage of American legislation in 1978, which introduced a whole new range of price levels and fare types to the United States market. The proximity of American airports to Canada's largest population centres forced the Canadian industry to follow suit or risk losing business to cheaper carriers south of the border.

By 1985, 53% of all domestic passengers travelled on discount fares, up from 45% in 1983.

Distance is an important factor in discount fare utilization. In 1985, discount carriage on long-haul (800 kilometres or more) services represented 64% of passenger volume, compared with 46% for short-haul (less than 800 kilometres).

Based on *Aviation in Canada*, Chapter II, Part II, Statistics Canada, Catalogue 51-501E

TRAVEL WITHIN CANADA

by Laurie McDougall

igures from the Canadian Travel Survey[1] indicate that we are, indeed, a nation of travellers. In 1986, for example, Canadians made an average of almost four overnight trips[2] per person to destinations within the country.

The amount of domestic travel by Canadians, however, dipped sharply in the early 1980s, largely as a result of the recession. Between 1979 and 1984, the annual number of overnight trips fell 13%, from 77 million to 67 million. The level of domestic travel recovered somewhat by 1986, when Canadians went on more than 75 million trips. This, however, was still 2% below the number of trips taken in 1979.

The difference in levels of domestic travel between 1979 and 1986 is even greater when considered on a per capita basis. The annual number of trips per person aged 15 and over declined 12%, from 4.3 in 1979 to 3.8 in 1986. The 1986 figure, however, was up from a low of 3.5 in 1984.

Westerners most likely to travel

The likelihood of travelling varied considerably for residents of different provinces,[3] with people from the Prairie region, by far, the most likely to travel. In 1986, Saskatchewan residents made an

[1] This survey is carried out by Statistics Canada on behalf of Tourism Canada. Data were collected in 1979, 1980, 1982, 1984 and 1986.
[2] A domestic trip was defined as an overnight trip within Canada with a one-way distance of at least 80 km.
[3] Prince Edward Island has not been included in most of the provincial comparisons. Because the definition of domestic travel refers only to trips with a one-way distance of 80 km, few trips within this province would be far enough to qualify.

average of 6.0 overnight trips per person within Canada, while the figure was 5.7 for Alberta residents and 4.9 for those living in Manitoba.

Residents of Newfoundland, on the other hand, were the least likely to travel. People from this province made just over 2 trips per person in 1986. In the remaining provinces, the average number of trips per person ranged between 3 and 4.

Interprovincial travel

Most domestic trips take place within the traveller's own province. During the 1979-1986 period, in-province trips accounted for 80% or more of all domestic travel. Still, in 1986, about one in five domestic trips (over 14 million in total) were to another province.

Travellers from New Brunswick, Nova Scotia and the Prairie region were the most likely to set out on interprovincial journeys. In 1986, 36% of all domestic overnight trips taken by residents of New Brunswick and 28% of those by Nova Scotians were to another province. At the same time, more than a quarter of domestic trips taken by people from Manitoba (27%), Saskatchewan (26%), and Alberta (26%) also were to other provinces.

Quebec, Ontario, and British Columbia, on the other hand, were characterized by below-average levels of interprovincial travel. Fewer than 17% of trips taken by people from these provinces in 1986 involved crossing a provincial boundary.

Newfoundland, perhaps because of its relative isolation, had the lowest level of out-of-province travel of any province. Just 12% of domestic trips taken by Newfoundlanders were to other parts of Canada.

The destination of travellers who leave their own province is usually an adjacent province. This is especially true for travellers from Quebec and Ontario. In 1986, for example, 58% of out-of-province travellers from Ontario went to Quebec, while 82% of those from Quebec went to Ontario.

There was also a substantial exchange of travellers between Alberta and British Columbia. In 1986, each was the destination of about 60% of the other's out-of-province traffic.

The pattern was similar in the Maritimes where 79% of out-of-province travellers from Prince Edward Island and more than half of those from both Nova Scotia and New Brunswick went to another Maritime province.

More business travel

There has been a particularly large increase in the amount of business travel in Canada

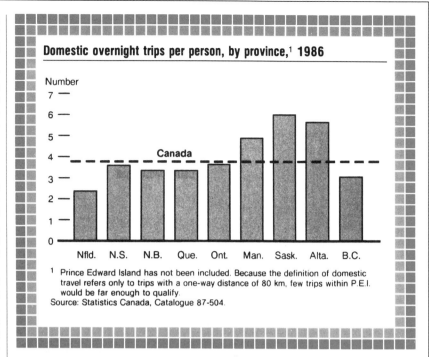

Domestic overnight trips per person, by province,[1] 1986

[1] Prince Edward Island has not been included. Because the definition of domestic travel refers only to trips with a one-way distance of 80 km, few trips within P.E.I. would be far enough to qualify.
Source: Statistics Canada, Catalogue 87-504.

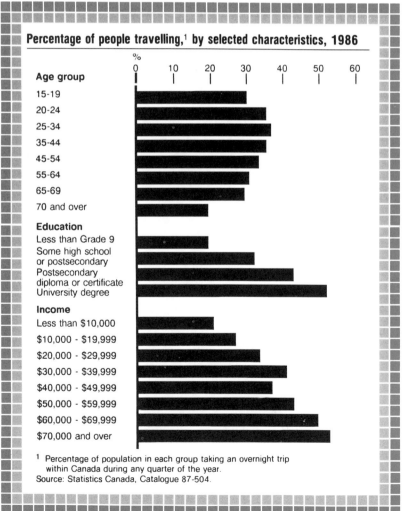

Percentage of people travelling,[1] by selected characteristics, 1986

[1] Percentage of population in each group taking an overnight trip within Canada during any quarter of the year.
Source: Statistics Canada, Catalogue 87-504.

in recent years. While the number of non-business trips declined 6% between 1979 and 1986, the number of business trips increased 26% in the same period. As a result, business trips accounted for 15% of all domestic travel in 1986, up from 11% in 1979.

A relatively high proportion of business travel is interprovincial. In 1986, about 30% of business trips compared with 17% of other domestic trips were from one province to another.

The growth of business travel has contributed to several other changes in domestic travel patterns including more weekday trips, more flying, and greater hotel usage.

Vacations and visits
Roughly 80% of all trips within Canada in the 1980s were either pleasure trips or visits to friends or relatives. The distribution of the overall share of domestic travel between these types of travel, however, shifted somewhat during this period. Pleasure trips made up 45% of all travel in 1980, but only 39% in 1986. In the same period, the proportion of trips taken to visit friends or relatives increased from 36% to 40%.

Home away from home
Because of the high percentage of trips that are visits, a large proportion of all travel nights are spent with friends or relatives. In both 1979 and 1986, over half (51%) of all overnight stays in which the type of accommodations was known were with family or friends.

Hotels and motels account for a growing share of overnight stays. In 1986, 23% of all travel nights were spent in these types of accommodations; this was up from 18% in 1979. All of this increase was due to growth in hotel usage. Between 1979 and 1986, the number of overnight stays in hotels rose 60%, while the number of motel stays dropped 6%.

Most of the remaining travel nights are spent in either cottages or campgrounds. While the proportion of overnight stays in cottages remained relatively stable at around 18% in the 1980s, the share accounted for by campground usage declined from 10% in 1979 to 7% in 1986.

In the summer, on the weekend . . .
Not surprisingly, summer is the most popular season for travel in Canada. Just over a third of all domestic travel takes place in July, August or September. Another quarter of trips occur during the spring, while winter and fall each account for roughly a fifth of all travel.

Most trips, approximately six out of ten, are taken on the weekend. The proportion of weekend trips, however, slipped from 66% in 1984 to 60% in 1986. The growth of business travel was partly responsible for this trend.

Who travels?
Except for people aged 70 and over, a large percentage of Canadians in all age groups travel. In each quarter of 1986, around 35% of people aged 20-54 made at least one domestic trip. The travel rate was somewhat lower for those aged 15-19 and 55-69; still, an average of around 30% of people in these age ranges travelled each quarter.

Canadians aged 70 and over, on the other hand, were less likely to travel than younger people. In 1986, only 18% of people in this age range travelled each quarter.

High levels of education and income were also associated with high rates of travel. In 1986, over half of university graduates (52%) travelled within Canada each quarter. This was three times greater than the rate for people with only elementary education (18%). Similarly, the travel rate for people with incomes of $70,000 and over was 53%, compared with 20% for those with annual incomes of less than $10,000.

THE FILM INDUSTRY IN CANADA

by Carol Strike

The introduction of television in the 1950s, and the growth in popularity of home entertainment innovations such as VCRs and pay television in more recent years have had a profound impact on the movie industry in Canada. Movie attendance has dropped substantially, and there has been a major reduction in the number of motion picture theatres in Canada. As well, ownership of movie theatres is becoming increasingly concentrated. At the same time, the vast majority of feature films shown in this country are foreign.

Going to the movies: a declining pastime
Perhaps the most striking trend related to the film industry has been the sharp decline in movie attendance in Canada. In the early 1950s, close to 250 million movie tickets were sold each year; in 1985, there were just under 75 million paid admissions to movie theatres.

Most of the decline in movie attendance occurred during the 1950s. The annual number of paid admissions to theatres had fallen below the 100 million mark by 1961; then throughout the 1960s, 1970s, and early

1980s, total movie attendance ranged between 80 and 90 million.

The decline in movie attendance is even more dramatic when expressed in per capita terms. In 1985, Canadians went to the movies an average of fewer than 3 times per person. In comparison, in the early 1950s, they had attended an annual average of around 17 movies per person. Again, most of this decline took place in the 1950s. Average movie attendance has continued to decline in recent years, falling from 3.7 movies per person in 1980 to 2.9 in 1985.

Attendance at drive-in theatres has also fallen, although the trend followed a somewhat different pattern than that for regular movie theatres. Drive-in attendance did not peak until 1976 when these theatres attracted a total of 13 million viewers. Attendance at drive-ins, however, declined substantially in the subsequent decade, such that by 1985, total paid admissions to these theatres had fallen below 6 million.

Theatre attendance statistics no longer represent the number of movies that Canadians actually see each year. Movies are common fare on regular television, while VCR ownership and subscriptions to pay television continue to increase. In 1986, virtually all Canadian homes (99%) had televisions, and two-thirds (65%) were hooked up to cable. At the same time, more than a third (35%) of all homes had VCRs, and 10% subscribed to pay television.

Theatres and drive-ins closing
The drop-off in movie attendance has resulted in the closure of hundreds of theatres. The number of regular motion picture theatres declined from a peak of 1,950 in 1955 to 788 in 1985; the number of drive-in theatres has also fallen, from a high of 315 in 1975 to 219 in 1985.

While the overall number of movie theatres has declined, the number of screens has increased. This is because of the growing number of multi-screened theatres. In 1985, there were 1,450 screens in Canada, about 1.8 per theatre. This was up from fewer than 1,200 screens in 1972. The trend toward multi-screened theatres also occurred at drive-ins, although the overall number of drive-in screens fell from 328 in 1979 to 279 in 1985.

Concentration of theatre ownership increasing
A growing proportion of movie theatres are operated by chains. In 1985, theatre chains owned an estimated 64% of all regular motion picture theatres and made 88% of all operating revenues. These proportions were up from 61% ownership and 86% of revenues in 1980.

A somewhat different trend is emerging for drive-in theatres. Chains owned 54% of all drive-ins and made 77% of operating revenue in 1985. These figures were down from 1980 when chains owned 63% of all drive-ins and generated 80% of revenues.

Few Canadian films
Only a small proportion of feature films shown in Canada are of Canadian origin. In 1983, Canadian productions made up just 14% of all new features shown that year. This figure, however, represents an increase from the 1972-1982 period when domestic productions made up only 4% of all new features released in Canada during this period.

Most new films released in Canada are from the United States. Over the past quarter century, between a third and half of all new features came from the United States each year; in 1983, 54% were American.

Most of the remaining new movies that have been shown in Canada originated in France or Italy. Between 1972 and 1983, 19% of new releases were from France, while 9% were made in Italy.

The number of new feature films (75 minutes or more) shown in Canada has dropped sharply in recent years. Between 1979 and 1983, the number of new releases fell from 970 to 474. In fact, the 1983 total was the smallest annual number of new releases in the past 25 years.

The film production industry
There were over 500 film production companies in Canada in 1985. Only 11% of

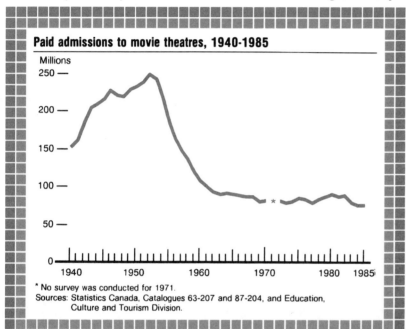

Paid admissions to movie theatres, 1940-1985

Millions

* No survey was conducted for 1971.
Sources: Statistics Canada, Catalogues 63-207 and 87-204, and Education, Culture and Tourism Division.

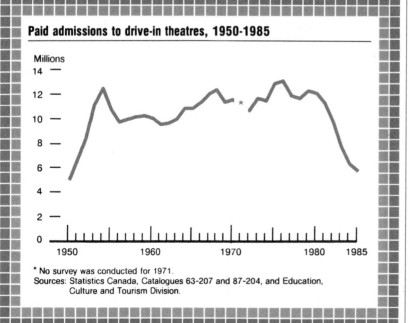

Paid admissions to drive-in theatres, 1950-1985

Millions

* No survey was conducted for 1971.
Sources: Statistics Canada, Catalogues 63-207 and 87-204, and Education, Culture and Tourism Division.

Movie going varies widely by province

Albertans were Canada's most avid movie-goers in 1985, averaging a total of over four paid admissions per person to theatres and drive-ins. Residents of Ontario and British Columbia followed with close to four admissions per person. On the other hand, residents of New Brunswick, Newfoundland and Prince Edward Island, and Quebec were relatively infrequent movie-goers, averaging only about two admissions per person.

Total paid admissions per person to movie and drive-in theatres, by province, 1985

Source: Statistics Canada, Education, Culture and Tourism Division.

these producers, however, specialized in feature films and theatrical shorts. The largest proportion of film producers in Canada, over 40%, made industrial and educational films, while 31% specialized in television programs and commercials. The other 17% of producers either did not have, or did not report, a specialization.

Television programs and commercials generated the greatest share of film production revenue. While fewer than a third of film producers specialized in these areas in 1985, they made 62% of all operating revenue. There has been a shift, however, in the distribution of revenue generated by television programs and commercials. The share of all film production revenue coming from commercials fell from 49% in 1980 to 34% in 1985; in the same period, revenue from TV programs increased from 19% of the total to 28%.

Of the remaining film revenue in 1985, 22% came from the production of industrial and educational films, 8% came from feature films, and 3% came from theatrical shorts. The final 5% came from other sources.

NEW NECESSITIES
POPULAR HOUSEHOLD APPLIANCES

by Mary Sue Devereaux

A number of recently introduced household appliances have had such wide appeal and gained acceptance so rapidly that they have almost become "necessities". Videocassette recorders (VCRs) and microwave ovens are examples of popular technological innovations that have entered the inventory of a substantial proportion of Canadian households. Cable television, freezers, dishwashers, and air conditioners could also be included among today's new necessities, while home computers and pay-TV may be the necessities of tomorrow.

Four in ten with VCRs or microwave ovens

VCRs and microwave ovens have been the growth appliances of the 1980s. In 1983, just 6% of Canadian households had videocassette recorders; by 1987, the proportion had risen to 45%. Acquisition of microwave ovens was almost as fast. From 5% in 1979, the percentage of homes with microwave ovens increased to 43% in 1987.

Freezers in more than half of households

A number of other household appliances have been around longer, but ownership

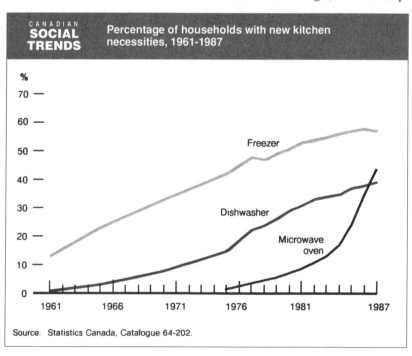

CANADIAN SOCIAL TRENDS

Percentage of households with new kitchen necessities, 1961-1987

Source: Statistics Canada, Catalogue 64-202.

continues to grow. For instance, by 1987, 57% of homes had freezers, up from 51% in 1980 and just 13% in 1961. Growth potential for freezers may be limited by the fact that one-third of Canadian households are in apartments or flats, where a lack of space may make freezers impractical. Also, improvements in the effectiveness and size of refrigerator freezer compartments may have reduced the need for a separate appliance.

Tuning in

Cable television is one of the most prevalent new necessities. The proportion of Canadian homes with a cable connection was 67% in 1987, having risen steadily from 40% in 1975. Pay-TV is much less common, with just 10% of Canadian households subscribing in 1986. Cable- and pay-TV are not available in all areas; however, as the accessibility of these services increases, it is likely that they will become part of a growing proportion of households.

Washing up/cooling down

Although dishwashers and air conditioning (central or window-type) have been available for over 25 years, widespread acceptance as standard household equipment has been relatively slow. In the early 1960s, fewer than 3% of Canadian homes had either appliance. By 1980, close to 30% of households had dishwashers, while 17% had air conditioning. A slow rise in the 1980s brought the proportion of dishwasher-equipped homes to almost 40% in 1987 and the percentage with air conditioning to 20%.

More than one

While telephones and television sets are now "necessities" in nearly all of Canada's households, they are not "new". The saturation level (90%) for both was reached in the mid-1960s, and by 1987, 98% of Canadian homes were equipped with these appliances.

Increasingly, however, Canadians are finding it desirable to have more than one telephone or television. In 1961, just 8% of households had two or more telephones; by 1987, that proportion had risen to 57%. Similarly, the percentage of homes with at least two television sets rose from 4% in 1961 to 47% in 1987. In fact, by 1987, 28% of Canadian households had two or more colour TVs.

Data processing at home

The next generation of necessities may include home computers. In 1986, just 10% of homes had a computer.

Ownership rises with income

Not surprisingly, the higher the household income, the more likely the household is to be equipped with the new necessities. For instance, 65% of households with annual incomes of $55,000 and over had microwave ovens in 1987; at the less-than-$10,000 income level, the proportion was only 18%. Similarly, while 69% of households in the $55,000-and-over bracket had VCRs, the percentage was just 17% in the less-than-$10,000 income range. The corresponding proportions for dishwashers were 69% at the top of the income scale and 13% at the bottom.

The same trend is apparent with freezers. At the high income level, 70% of households had freezers compared with just 33% of households with incomes less than $10,000. This discrepancy may, in part, reflect the kind of dwellings in which the two groups lived. Whereas 78% of households in the high-income category occupied a single detached house, the majority (61%) of low-income households were in apartments, flats, or mobile homes.

A cable-TV connection was also associated with household income. At the $55,000-and-over level, almost eight in 10 households (78%) had a cable hook-up. Although the proportion was smaller in low-income households, more than half (53%) of these homes were cable subscribers.

From novelty to necessity

Many items that were considered luxuries when they first came on the market are now standard household fixtures. Virtually all Canadian homes are equipped with refrigerators, radios, television sets, and telephones. In fact, these appliances have long ceased to be novelties, having reached the saturation point (90% of households) at least 20 years ago. For example, only three out of ten households (29%) were equipped with refrigerators in 1948. By 1954, the proportion had more than doubled to seven in ten (70%), and the 90% mark came in 1960.

Radio and television reached the saturation level in a relatively short time. Even in 1941, radios could be found in the majority (78%) of Canadian households; by 1947, the percentage was 90%. Similarly, it took only about a decade for most households to acquire a television set. The proportion of homes with TVs rose from 10% in 1953 to 90% in 1963.

Telephones came to Canadian households at a slightly slower pace. In 1941, just 40% of homes had a telephone, and in 1947, the proportion was only 50%. The saturation point was not reached until 1966.

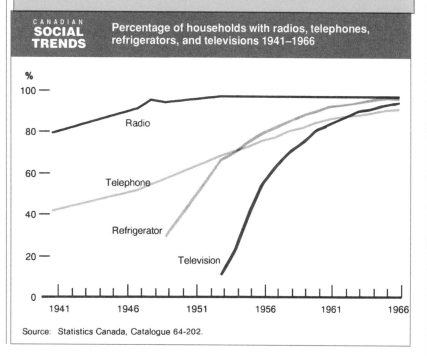

CANADIAN SOCIAL TRENDS

Percentage of households with radios, telephones, refrigerators, and televisions 1941–1966

Source: Statistics Canada, Catalogue 64-202.

Husband-wife families with children best equipped

In addition to income, the likelihood that a household will have the new necessities is associated with family type. As an example, relatively high proportions of husband-wife families with children under age 18 had freezers (75%), VCRs (65%), microwave ovens (56%), and dishwashers (56%). Also, the annual income of this type of household was well above the 1986 average ($44,400 as opposed to $35,700), and 73% of these families lived in single detached houses in 1987.

By contrast, while lone-parent families with children under age 18 may have had the same needs and desires as two-parent families, low income (an average of $19,100 in 1986) seems to have blocked acquisition of many goods for a large number of lone-parent households. One-third of these households had microwave ovens compared with more than half of husband-wife households with children under age 18. The proportions of lone-parent families with VCRs (38%), dishwashers (29%), and freezers (43%) were at least 25 percentage points lower than the corresponding figures for two-parent families with children under age 18.

Married couples without children at home were generally more likely than lone-parent families with children under age 18 to have the new necessities, but they were much less likely to have them than were other households with children. Married couples, however, were not a homogeneous group, in that the category ranges from newlyweds just becoming established to empty-nesters who have retired and may have considerable discretionary income.

The new necessities were least likely to be found in one-person households. While all ownership rates were low, the age of the person had some bearing on the items that he or she would have. People aged 65 and over who lived alone were more likely than their younger counterparts to have freezers (37% versus 23%) and air conditioning (20% versus 16%). On the other hand, the younger group was more likely to have VCRs (27% versus 8%), microwave ovens (25% versus 18%), pay-TV (9% versus 3%), and home computers (5% versus 1%).

One new necessity that had very little relationship to household type was cable television. About two-thirds of households (whether one-person, lone-parent, or husband-wife with and without young children) had cable hook-ups.

City/country

City or country living made little difference to ownership of some of the new necessities, while others were more common in rural areas than in cities. Still other items and services were more likely to be found in city than in country households.

VCR ownership rates were almost identical for large cities and rural regions. In 1987, 46% of households in urban areas with 100,000 or more population had VCRs; the proportion in rural areas was 42%. Similarly, 40% of city households had dishwashers compared with 39% in the country.

On the other hand, freezers were much more prevalent in rural than in city homes. More than eight out of 10 (81%) rural households had freezers, in contrast to fewer than half (48%) of households in large cities. This difference no doubt reflects, to some extent, the small number of apartment-dwellers in rural areas.

Microwave ovens were also more common in country (49%) than in city households (40%), but compared with freezers, the difference was not large.

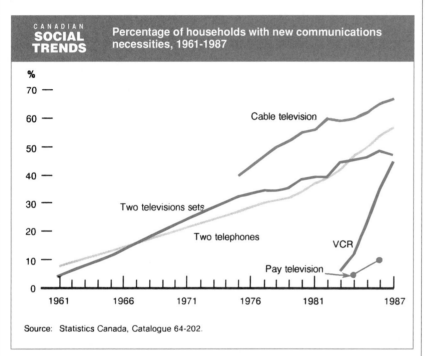

CANADIAN SOCIAL TRENDS

Percentage of households with new communications necessities, 1961-1987

Source: Statistics Canada, Catalogue 64-202.

Percentage of households with new necessities, by selected 1986 income groups, 1987

New necessity	1986 income group			Average 1986 income of households possessing item/service
	Less than $10,000	More than $55,000	Total	
	%			$
Cable-TV	53	78	67	38,300
Freezer	33	70	57	39,800
VCR	17	69	45	44,700
Microwave oven	18	65	43	43,800
Dishwasher	13	69	39	47,100
Air conditioning	11	30	20	43,900
Home computer*	2	20	10	46,900
Pay-TV*	4	15	10	43,300

* 1985 income data.
Source: Statistics Canada, Catalogue 13-218.

Percentage of households with new necessities, by province, 1987

New necessity	New-found-land	Prince Edward Island	Nova Scotia	New Bruns-wick	Quebec	Ontario	Manitoba	Saskat-chewan	Alberta	British Columbia	Canada
					%						
Cable television	61	46	60	59	58	73	67	48	67	84	67
Freezer	71	60	61	66	45	58	68	77	66	60	57
Two or more telephones	49	47	53	51	53	61	58	48	63	54	57
Two or more TVs	52	42	50	50	51	46	50	47	48	40	47
VCR	45	35	45	43	44	46	47	40	48	44	45
Microwave oven	22	33	35	33	37	44	53	57	56	45	43
Dishwasher	15	23	24	25	42	36	39	43	53	45	39
Air conditioning	--	--	3	4	13	32	38	25	9	7	20
Pay television*	4	--	7	6	7	13	3	6	11	9	10
Home computer*	10	--	12	10	9	12	9	9	12	10	10
					000s						
Total households	**9,556**	**168**	**43**	**313**	**246**	**2,530**	**3,451**	**405**	**378**	**872**	**1,149**

-- Amount too small to be expressed. * 1986 data.
Source: Statistics Canada, Catalogue 64-202.

Some items and services were more typical of city than of rural homes. The proportion of city households with air conditioning (23%) was double that for rural households (11%). And probably reflecting the availability of service, city households were much more likely than those in rural areas to have cable- and pay-TV connections. In 1987, 77% of homes in large urban areas had cable television; the proportion in the country was just 20%. Similarly, while 12% of city households had pay-TV, only 2% of rural households were subscribers.

Wide provincial variations

The provinces varied widely in ownership rates of the new necessities. For example, while 22% of Newfoundland homes had microwave ovens, the proportion was more than two and a half times higher (57%) in Saskatchewan. The percentage of households with VCRs ranged from 35% in Prince Edward Island to 48% in Alberta.

Alberta also had the highest proportion of households with dishwashers (53%); Newfoundland had the lowest (15%). Freezers were most common in Saskatchewan households (77%), but least likely to be found in Quebec homes (45%).

British Columbia stood first for cable-TV connections (84%) and Prince Edward Island ranked last (46%), probably indicating the availability of service in the two provinces. Ontario residents were most likely to be pay-TV subscribers (13%); Manitoba residents, least likely (3%). The highest proportion of homes with more than one television set was in Newfoundland (52%).

The percentage of homes with air-conditioning was less than 5% in the Atlantic provinces, but 38% in Manitoba, not surprising given the climatic differences in the two areas.

Ontario, Alberta, and Nova Scotia shared the lead for home computer ownership: 12% of households in these provinces were outfitted with computers.

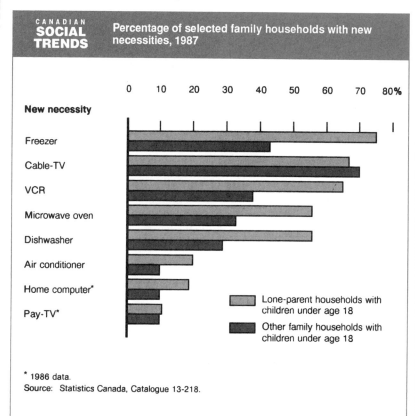

CANADIAN SOCIAL TRENDS
Percentage of selected family households with new necessities, 1987

New necessity:
Freezer
Cable-TV
VCR
Microwave oven
Dishwasher
Air conditioner
Home computer*
Pay-TV*

Lone-parent households with children under age 18
Other family households with children under age 18

* 1986 data.
Source: Statistics Canada, Catalogue 13-218.

Social Problems

ILLEGAL DRUG USE IN CANADA

by Holly Johnson

The level of illegal drug activity known to police has risen substantially in Canada since the early 1960s. Most of this increase, however, occurred during the 1960s and 1970s; in fact, the overall level of drug crime in 1987 was actually below the level in 1980. The one drug for which there has been a substantial increase in the number of offences in recent years, though, is cocaine.

Trends in drug offences

There were major increases in the incidence of drug offences in Canada throughout the 1960s and 1970s. The number of drug crimes recorded by the police rose from just 5 per 100,000 population in 1962 to over 309 in 1980.

In contrast, the incidence of drug crime known to the police declined in the 1980s. Between 1980 and 1986, the number of drug offences per 100,000 population fell 29% from 309 to 220. This downward trend was followed by a 10% increase in 1987, when the drug crime rate rose to 241. This figure, though, was still 22% below the rate in 1980.

Drug offences make up only a small proportion of criminal activity known to police in Canada. The 62,000 drug offences recorded by the police in 1987 represented less than 2% of all recorded offences that year. As well, this figure was down slightly from 1980, when drug offences made up 3% of all offences.

Cannabis offences falling, cocaine rising

Cannabis offences make up the vast majority of all illegal drug activity known to police. There has, however, been a marked decline in the incidence of these offences in the 1980s. Between 1980 and 1987, the number of cannabis offences declined 34% from 65,000 to 43,000. Still, offences involving cannabis made up 70% of all drug offences in 1987, although this was down from 87% in 1980 and 90% in 1976.

The incidence of cocaine offences, on the other hand, has increased dramatically in recent years. The number of cocaine offences known to police rose almost 400% between 1980 and 1987, from 1,700 to 8,200. This includes a 22%

increase in 1987 alone. As a result of this growth, cocaine offences made up 13% of all drug offences in 1987, compared with 2% in 1980.

Only a small proportion of drug offences, just 1% in 1987, involve heroin. The incidence of these cases has remained stable at around 3 per 100,000 population since 1980.

The remaining drug offences involve other narcotics such as codeine, morphine, and methadone, as well as controlled and restricted drugs.[1] Overall, the incidence of other narcotic offences has increased in recent years while the rate for controlled and restricted drugs has fallen.

Between 1980 and 1987, the number of other narcotic offences rose 183% and their share of all drug offences climbed from 3% to 10%. In the same period, police recorded 32% fewer controlled or restricted drug offences. As a result, the share of all drug crime accounted for by these offences fell from 6% to 5%.

There has also been a decline in the amount of drugs either lost in transit or stolen. The Bureau of Dangerous Drugs at Health and Welfare Canada reported that 3,200 quantities of drugs were either lost in transit or stolen in 1985; this compared with 5,400 such incidents in 1981. Three-quarters of all these losses were from pharmacies, while the remainder were from hospitals, licensed dealers, such as pharmaceutic companies and manufacturers, and medical practitioners.

Most drug offences for possession
The majority of drug offences in Canada are for possession, although a significant proportion involve the more serious charge of trafficking.[2] In 1987, 67% of all drug offences were for possession, while 30% were for trafficking. The remaining drug offences involved either cultivation or importing.

The type of offence, though, varies depending on the drug. For example, most cannabis offences are for possession, while the largest proportions of cocaine and heroin offences involve trafficking.

In 1987, 72% of all cannabis offences were for possession, 25% were for trafficking, and the remainder were for

[1] Controlled drugs include speed, amphetamines, and barbituates; they are available through prescription but are illegal to sell. Restricted drugs include LSD, MDA, and psilocybin and are illegal both to possess and sell.
[2] Includes possession for the purpose of trafficking.

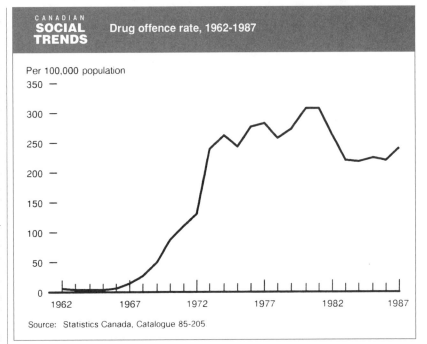

CANADIAN SOCIAL TRENDS — Drug offence rate, 1962-1987

Per 100,000 population

Source: Statistics Canada, Catalogue 85-205.

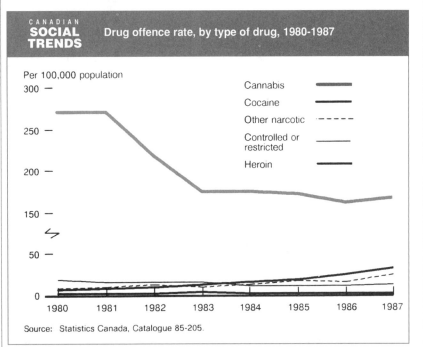

CANADIAN SOCIAL TRENDS — Drug offence rate, by type of drug, 1980-1987

Per 100,000 population

Cannabis
Cocaine
Other narcotic
Controlled or restricted
Heroin

Source: Statistics Canada, Catalogue 85-205.

Drug usage declining
There is some evidence, in addition to police statistics, which indicates that overall drug usage has declined in the 1980s. According to the Ontario Addiction Research Foundation, the percentage of Ontario high school students using cannabis fell sharply from 32% in 1979 to 16% in 1987. The proportion using stimulants such as speed also declined from 12% in 1981 to 8% in 1987. At the same time, use of these drugs by adults remained constant.

The proportion of Ontario adults who have ever used cocaine, however, doubled in recent years from 3% in 1984 to 6% in 1987. In the same period, the proportion of students who have ever used cocaine remained stable at about 4%, although regular use of cocaine was higher among students than adults.

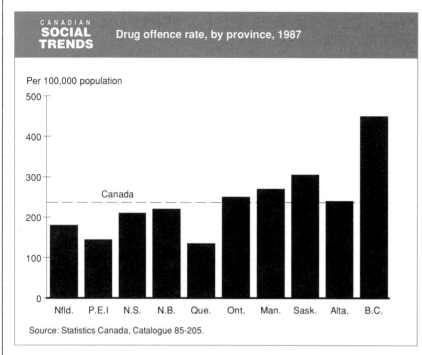

CANADIAN SOCIAL TRENDS

Drug offence rate, by province, 1987

Per 100,000 population

Canada

Nfld.　P.E.I　N.S.　N.B.　Que.　Ont.　Man.　Sask.　Alta.　B.C.

Source: Statistics Canada, Catalogue 85-205.

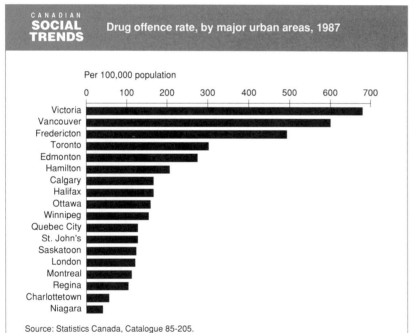

CANADIAN SOCIAL TRENDS

Drug offence rate, by major urban areas, 1987

Per 100,000 population

0　100　200　300　400　500　600　700

Victoria
Vancouver
Fredericton
Toronto
Edmonton
Hamilton
Calgary
Halifax
Ottawa
Winnipeg
Quebec City
St. John's
Saskatoon
London
Montreal
Regina
Charlottetown
Niagara

Source: Statistics Canada, Catalogue 85-205.

offence rates in Alberta, Nova Scotia and Prince Edward Island. At the same time, there were much smaller declines in Ontario, New Brunswick, Newfoundland, and Saskatchewan, while rates actually rose 9% in Quebec, 8% in Manitoba, and 6% in British Columbia.

Urban drug offence rates

The east-west pattern in the incidence of drug crime also holds for major metropolitan areas, although there are some exceptions. Victoria, with 676 offences per 100,000 population, and Vancouver, with 598, had the highest rates of illegal drug activity of any cities in Canada in 1987. The next highest rates, though, occurred in Fredericton (491) and Toronto (301).

Statistics on drug crime

Some caution must be used in interpreting trends in official drug crime statistics. Drug offences usually involve consenting parties and so are less likely than other types of crime to be reported to the police. Consequently, drug offences that come to the attention of police are, for the most part, those that they detect on their own. Because of this, variations in the number of drug offences recorded by the police in different jurisdictions, as well as changes in drug rates over time, may reflect changing priorities of police departments as they relate to the detection of these and other offences.

In addition, official drug crime statistics as measured by the Uniform Crime Reporting Survey do not represent a full count of the actual number of offences. As stated above, many such crimes are either not detected or not reported to police. As well, only the most serious offence is counted in incidents involving several violations of the law. For example, drug offences which occur in conjunction with more serious violent or property crimes will not be counted. In addition, when more than one drug offence occurs in the same incident, for example, trafficking in one drug and possession of another, only the most serious, in this case trafficking, will be recorded. Lastly, when one type of offence is committed more than once at the same time, for example, selling drugs to a number of different people, it is counted as only one incident.

cultivation and importing. In comparison, around half of all cocaine (51%) and heroin (47%) offences were for trafficking, while only 45% of cocaine and 40% of heroin offences were for possession. In addition, 12% of heroin offences and 4% of those involving cocaine were for importing.

Drug offence rates highest in the west

Levels of illegal drug activity known to police are generally higher in the western provinces than in central or eastern Canada. In 1987, there were 447 drug offences for every 100,000 people in British Columbia, 307 in Saskatchewan, 284 in Manitoba, and 244 in Alberta. In comparison, drug offence rates in the other provinces ranged from a low of 132 per 100,000 population in Quebec to a high of 247 in Ontario.

The incidence of drug offences fell in most provinces in the 1980-1987 period. There were particularly large declines, between 55% and 60%, in the drug

On the other hand, the lowest urban drug crime rates in 1987 were reported in Niagara (41) and Charlottetown (57). The next lowest rate, though, occurred in Regina (106), which had a rate just below that in Montreal (112).

Generally, the larger the urban area, the higher the drug offence rate. In 1987, cities with more than 250,000 people had an average of 249 drug offences per 100,000 population; this compared with rates of 211 in cities between 50,000 and 250,000 people, 192 in cities between 10,000 and 50,000 people, and 203 in communities with less than 10,000 residents.

Dealing with drug offenders

Not surprisingly, given the overall decline in illegal drug activity known to police in the 1980s, the number of charges and convictions for drug offences also declined.

Between 1980 and 1987, the number of people charged with drug offences fell 30%, from a total of 62,000 to 43,000. Compared with other types of crime,

though, a large proportion of drug offences result in charges. In 1987, charges were laid in three-quarters of all drug offence cases, whereas only about 45% of violent offences and around 20% of all other Criminal Code offences resulted in charges.

There has also been a significant decline in the number of convictions for drug offences.[3] In 1985, there were a total of 28,000 drug convictions, 43% less than in 1981.

The majority of drug convictions result in fines. In 1985, 58% of guilty charges for these offences resulted in fines. Another 23% resulted in jail sentences, while 19% either resulted in probation or were discharged.

The likelihood of being sent to jail varies for different drugs. In 1985, three-quarters of heroin convictions resulted in incarceration, as did 42% of those involving cocaine, 40% of those for controlled or restricted drugs, and 30% of those for other narcotics. On the other hand, just 20% of convictions for cannabis offences

The costs of drug abuse

The social and economic dimensions of drug abuse extend beyond the criminal justice system. The costs of drug abuse include lost productivity, accidental injuries and death, disruption to families and communities, and public expenditure needed to maintain health care and social systems.

In 1983, there were over 72,000 admissions to residential facilities in Canada for treatment of alcohol and drug problems. The same year, over 5,000 hospitalizations in psychiatric and general hospitals were for drug psychoses, drug dependence, or nondependent drug abuse. As well, these figures do not include the majority of drug abusers who receive treatment through outpatient services or who cause physical harm to themselves or others as a consequence of drug impairment.

resulted in jail terms. Most cannabis convictions, about 60%, resulted in fines.

Overall, about 6% of all inmates in federal penitentiaries in 1987 were incarcerated for drug offences. At the same time, roughly 4% of all admissions to provincial jails involved these offences.

[3] Court statistics on convictions from the Bureau of Dangerous Drugs cannot be linked directly to police statistics on the number of offences. Court statistics measure the number of charges coming before the court, while police statistics count incidents which may involve more than one offence and result in more than one charge. In addition, offences known to the police may not result in a court appearance until the following calendar year.

Drug charges in Canada and the United States

Levels of illegal drug activity are much higher in the United States than in Canada. As well, while rates have fallen in Canada in the 1980s, they have risen sharply in the United States.

In 1987, there were 385 drug crime arrests for every 100,000 people in

the United States. This was more than double the comparable Canadian figure of 169 people charged with drug offences for every 100,000 people in this country. As well, while the American figure rose 49% between 1980 and 1987, the Canadian rate declined 34%.

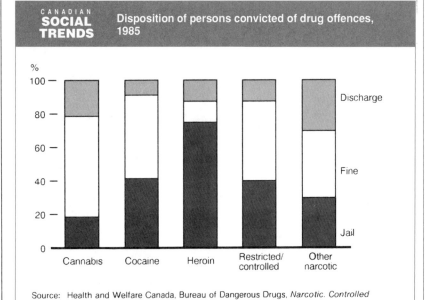

CANADIAN **SOCIAL TRENDS**

Disposition of persons convicted of drug offences, 1985

Source: Health and Welfare Canada, Bureau of Dangerous Drugs, *Narcotic. Controlled and Restricted Drug Statistics, 1985.*

IMPAIRED DRIVING OFFENCES

by Holly Johnson

There has been a major decline in the incidence of impaired driving offences in Canada in the 1980s.[1] In fact, the number of people charged with impaired driving offences in 1987 was the lowest total since data were first collected in 1974.

The recent decline in the incidence of impaired driving offences mirrors increased efforts by police, community groups, and government to curb this problem over the course of the last decade. According to police statistics, programs like roadside breathalyzers, and groups such as Mothers Against Drunk Driving, Students Against Drunk Driving, and Citizens Against Impaired Driving seem to have had the desired impact on the attitudes and behaviour of Canadians with respect to drinking and driving.

Despite the decline in the number of people charged with impaired driving in the 1980s, drinking and driving remains widespread, and continues to be a major cause of accident, injury, and death on the nation's roadways.

On the basis of roadside surveys, the Road Safety Directorate of Transport Canada estimates that one in four drivers on a typical weekend evening has been drinking, and that one in 20-25 is legally impaired by the effects of alcohol. The Traffic Injury Research Foundation estimates that 25-30% of all drivers injured in motor vehicle accidents are impaired and that almost half of all traffic fatalities involve someone who has been drinking.

The costs of impaired driving, though, go well beyond the health risks to those who drink and drive. For those charged and convicted with impaired driving offences, additional costs may include the loss of income and employment, strain on families, and loss of status in the community. For victims of traffic accidents involving impaired drivers, the consequences may include lost productivity, emotional trauma, and sometimes serious injury and even death. For society as a whole, the consequences of impaired driving include the costs incurred by the criminal justice and health care systems,

as well as rising insurance premiums for other drivers.

Impaired driving offences declining
The incidence of impaired driving declined for the fourth consecutive year in 1987. That year, just over 128,000 people were charged by police with impaired driving offences. This was down about 1% from 1986, and 21% from 1981, when a high of 162,000 persons were charged with these offences.

The decline in the incidence of impaired driving in the 1980s is even sharper when expressed on a per capita basis. In 1987, there were 500 people charged with impaired driving offences for every 100,000 Canadians, a decrease of 2% from 1986, and a drop of 25% from 1981.

The number of people charged with impaired driving as a proportion of all criminal offenders has also declined. In 1987, those charged with impaired driving offences made up 18% of all persons charged under the Criminal Code, down from 24% in 1981.

The decline in impaired driving charges in the 1980s represents a change from the previous decade when there was a slight increase in the incidence of these offences. Between 1974 and 1981, for example, the number of people charged with impaired driving offences increased from 631 per 100,000 population to 666, a rise of 6%.

The large majority of impaired driving charges are for operating a motor vehicle either while impaired or with more than 80 mgs. of alcohol in the blood. In 1987, 91% of all people charged with impaired driving were charged with these offences. Failing or refusing to provide a breath sample was the second most common impaired driving offence, accounting for 7% of all persons charged. On the other hand, people charged with impaired driving causing death or bodily harm, or

[1] The data in this article describing impaired driving offences refer only to those incidents of impaired driving known to police.

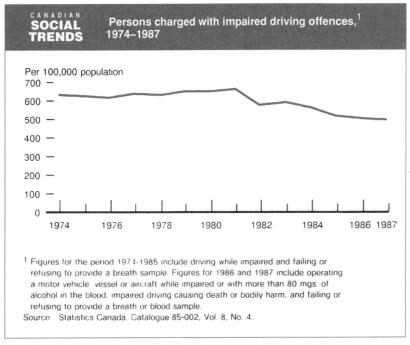

CANADIAN SOCIAL TRENDS
Persons charged with impaired driving offences,[1] 1974–1987

Per 100,000 population

[1] Figures for the period 1974-1985 include driving while impaired and failing or refusing to provide a breath sample. Figures for 1986 and 1987 include operating a motor vehicle, vessel or aircraft while impaired or with more than 80 mgs. of alcohol in the blood; impaired driving causing death or bodily harm; and failing or refusing to provide a breath or blood sample.
Source: Statistics Canada, Catalogue 85-002, Vol. 8, No. 4.

CANADIAN SOCIAL TRENDS
Persons charged with impaired driving, by type of offence, 1987

Fail/refuse to provide breath sample - **7.2%**

Cause bodily harm - **1.0%**
Fail/refuse to provide blood sample - **0.3%**
Operation of vessel or aircraft - **0.3%**
Cause death - **0.1%**
} **1.7%**

Impaired operation of motor vehicle - **91.1%**

Source: Statistics Canada, Catalogue 85-002, Vol. 8, No. 4

failing to provide a blood sample, made up only small proportions of those charged with impaired driving offences.

Provincial rates vary

There is wide variation in the incidence of impaired driving offences across the country. In 1987, the provinces with the highest number of people charged with impaired driving offences per 100,000 residents were Alberta (830), Saskatchewan (821), and Prince Edward Island (765). The figure was also above the national average (500) in New Brunswick (659), Manitoba (600), Nova Scotia (577), and Newfoundland (538), while rates were considerably lower in British Columbia (489), Ontario (412), and Quebec (397). In fact, Quebec and Ontario have consistently reported the lowest impaired driving rates since 1974.

The incidence of impaired driving offences declined in all provinces between 1981 and 1987. The largest decrease

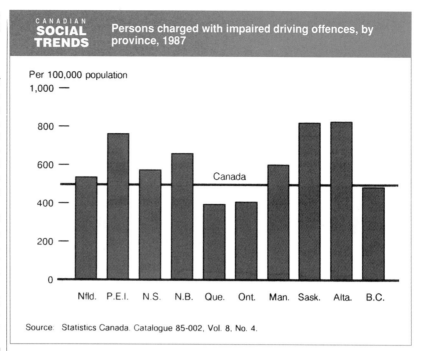

CANADIAN SOCIAL TRENDS

Persons charged with impaired driving offences, by province, 1987

Source: Statistics Canada. Catalogue 85-002, Vol. 8, No. 4.

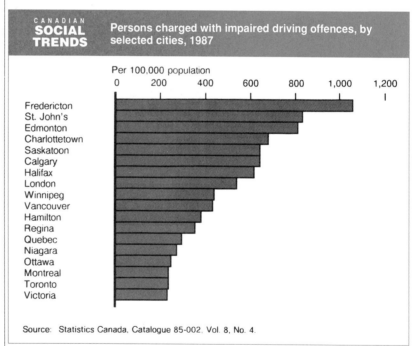

CANADIAN SOCIAL TRENDS

Persons charged with impaired driving offences, by selected cities, 1987

Source: Statistics Canada. Catalogue 85-002, Vol. 8, No. 4.

The law on impaired driving

As of 1985, impaired driving offences include operating a motor vehicle, vessel, or aircraft while impaired or with more than 80 mgs. of alcohol in the blood; impaired driving causing death or bodily harm; and failing or refusing to provide a breath or blood sample.

Penalties for driving either while impaired or with more than 80 mgs. of alcohol in the blood, or for failing to provide a breath or blood sample include a minimum $300 fine and 3-month driving prohibition for the first offence; a minimum 14-day prison term and 6-month driving prohibition for the second offence; and a minimum 90-day prison term and 1-year driving prohibition for subsequent offences. The court may require the offender to undergo treatment for alcohol dependency in place of any of the above penalties.

For impaired driving causing bodily harm, the penalties include a maximum 10-year prison term, 10-year driving prohibition, and fine of any amount. Impaired driving causing death brings a maximum penalty of 14 years in prison, a 10-year driving prohibition, and a fine of any amount.

In 1987, approximately 20,000 persons were sentenced to serve time in jail as a result of impaired driving.

occurred in British Columbia where the number of persons charged per 100,000 population fell 46%. There were also large declines in Prince Edward Island (31%), Saskatchewan (28%), Alberta (25%), Newfoundland (25%), Ontario (24%), and Nova Scotia (23%). In comparison, the rate declined 14% in both Quebec and Manitoba and just 6% in New Brunswick.

There were, however, increases in the rate of impaired driving in five of the ten provinces between 1986 and 1987. There was a particularly large increase of 20% in Newfoundland, while there were increases of 4% or less in Prince Edward Island, Nova Scotia, Quebec, and Saskatchewan.

Urban rates differ

As with the provinces, there is considerable variation in the incidence of impaired driving offences among major urban areas. In 1987, there were particularly large numbers of people charged with impaired driving offences per

100,000 population in Fredericton (1,061), St. John's (835), and Edmonton (814). In contrast, there were fewer than 300 persons charged with these offences per 100,000 people in Quebec City, Montreal, Niagara, Ottawa, Toronto, and Victoria.

Who drinks and drives

A significant proportion of Canadians drive after drinking. A 1985 survey conducted by Health and Welfare Canada estimated that 16% of all adults had driven after consuming alcohol at least once in the previous month.

Men are far more likely than women to drive while impaired. The Health and Welfare Canada survey estimated that 25% of men, compared with 8% of women, drove after drinking at least once the previous month. Not surprisingly, men make up the vast majority of people charged with impaired driving. In 1987, for example, 92% of all those charged were male.

Men between the ages of 25 and 44 are the most likely people to drink and drive. In 1985, 35% of men in this age range reported driving after drinking at least once the previous month. In comparison, the figure was around 20% for men aged 15-24 and aged 45-54; 17% for men aged 55-64; and 5% for men aged 65 and over.

Among women, those aged 35-44 were the most likely to drink and drive. In 1985, 11% of these women drove after drinking at least once the previous month, while the figure was 9% for those aged 15-34, and 7% for those aged 45-54.

A large proportion of all impaired driving incidents are accounted for by a small proportion of chronic offenders. In the 1985 Health and Welfare Canada survey, more than half of all drinking and driving incidents were accounted for by less than 3% of adults. These individuals reported driving while impaired on at least five occasions. Specific attention to this group may be a critical step in further reducing the incidence of this offence.

JOB DISPLACEMENT

This article has been adapted from the G. Picot and T. Wannell report *Workers Experiencing Permanent Job Loss*

Plant closures and relocations, workload and shift reductions, and the failure of businesses of the self-employed meant that almost half a million long-term workers lost their jobs during the years 1981 to 1984. This period included the 1981-82 recession, which undoubtedly contributed to the lay-offs. By 1986, about two-thirds (63%) of these displaced workers had new jobs. However, 17% had left the labour force, and 20% were unemployed, some of whom had not worked since their initial job loss. Those who were re-employed had spent, on average, half a year looking for work and generally earned less than on their old jobs.

Reason for Job Loss

For the 469,000 workers displaced during the 1981-1984 period, the most frequent reason for losing their jobs was plant closure or relocation (44%). Reductions in workload accounted for a further 34%, while elimination of a position or shift displaced another 9%. Business failures among the self-employed caused 2% of job losses, and other reasons made up the remainder.

Characteristics of Displaced Workers

A "hazard ratio" is used to assess which groups were most likely to be displaced. It is calculated by dividing the percentage of displaced workers with certain characteristics by the percentage of the labour force with the same characteristics in January 1986. A hazard ratio of 1.0 for any group means that its incidence of job loss equalled the national average. A value above 1.0 indicates a group with a higher-than-average chance of job loss, while the opposite holds for values below 1.0.

Among the provinces, Alberta and British Columbia had the highest hazard

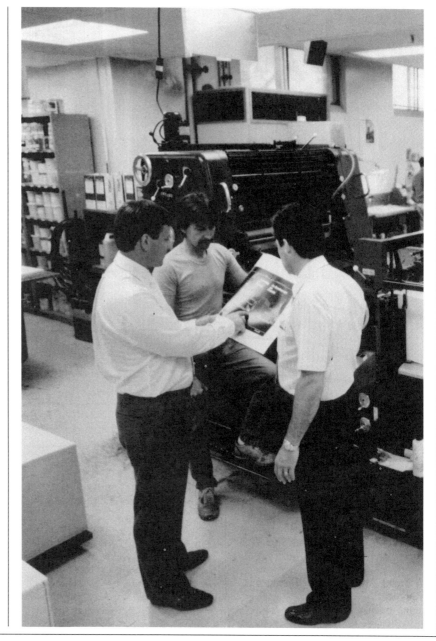

ratios: 1.4 and 1.3, respectively. Two other provinces, Quebec and Newfoundland, also had high ratios (both 1.2). Saskatchewan's ratio was lowest at just 0.6.

Men were slightly more likely than women to be laid off. The male hazard ratio was 1.1 compared with 0.8 for women. Much of the discrepancy resulted from the different occupations and industries in which men and women were employed. Industries with a largely male workforce, such as construction and manufacturing, were hardest hit during the recession.

The 25-34 age group had the highest hazard ratio – 1.3. On the other hand, slightly older workers in the 35-44 age range were least likely to lose their jobs, with a hazard ratio of just 0.8.

Education tended to reduce the risk of job loss. Postsecondary graduates were about half as likely to be displaced as people who had not finished high school (0.6 versus 1.2). In fact, hazard ratios were higher than average for all levels of education below postsecondary graduation.

With a hazard ratio of 2.7, workers in the construction industry had the greatest

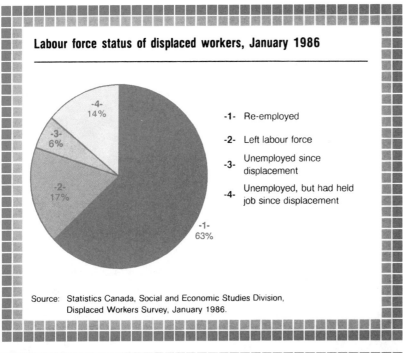

Labour force status of displaced workers, January 1986

-1- Re-employed
-2- Left labour force
-3- Unemployed since displacement
-4- Unemployed, but had held job since displacement

-4- 14%
-3- 6%
-2- 17%
-1- 63%

Source: Statistics Canada, Social and Economic Studies Division, Displaced Workers Survey, January 1986.

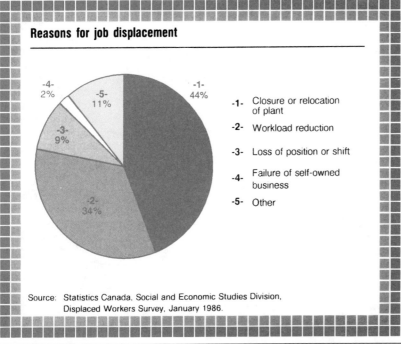

Reasons for job displacement

-4- 2%
-5- 11%
-3- 9%
-1- 44%
-2- 34%

-1- Closure or relocation of plant
-2- Workload reduction
-3- Loss of position or shift
-4- Failure of self-owned business
-5- Other

Source: Statistics Canada, Social and Economic Studies Division, Displaced Workers Survey, January 1986.

Displacement hazard ratios, by selected characteristics

Characteristics	Hazard ratio[1]
Total	**1.0**
Sex	
Men	1.1
Women	0.8
Age group	
20-24	1.0
25-34	1.3
35-44	0.8
45-54	0.9
55 and over	1.0
Education	
Less than high school	1.3
Some high school	1.2
High school graduate	1.1
Some postsecondary	1.2
Postsecondary graduate	0.6
Industry	
Construction	2.7
Manufacturing	1.8
Trade and finance	1.0
Agriculture and primary	0.9
Transportation, communications, utilities	0.6
Public administration, services	0.5
Occupation	
Blue collar	1.4
White collar	0.8
Managerial/professional	0.8
Job tenure	
3 years	3.2
4-5 years	1.4
6-10 years	0.8
More than 10 years	0.5
Province	
Newfoundland	1.2
Prince Edward Island	0.7
Nova Scotia	0.8
New Brunswick	1.0
Quebec	1.2
Ontario	0.8
Manitoba	0.7
Saskatchewan	0.6
Alberta	1.4
British Columbia	1.3

[1] A hazard ratio greater than 1.0 indicates higher-than-average probability of displacement, while the opposite holds for hazard ratios less than 1.0.

Source: Statistics Canada, Social and Economic Studies Division, Displaced Workers Survey, January 1986.

chance of job loss. Manufacturing workers, at 1.8, were next most likely to be displaced. The ratio dropped to 1.0 in trade and financial industries, 0.9 in agriculture and primary industries, and 0.6 in transportation, communications and utilities. Least likely to lose their jobs were workers in public administration and in services,[1] whose hazard ratio was just 0.5.

Chances of displacement were higher in blue collar occupations than in managerial/professional or white collar jobs. The hazard ratio for blue collar workers was 1.4, compared with 0.8 for both the managerial/professional and white collar categories (clerical, sales, and services).

The less time workers had been with their employer, the greater were their chances of displacement. The hazard ratio for workers with three years' service was 3.2. As length of service increased, the ratio fell steadily, bottoming out at 0.5 among workers with more than ten years.

Retraining

Only a minority of workers, 70,000 or 15%, undertook some form of retraining after they were laid off. Over half of them participated in part-time as opposed to full-time programs.

Displaced male and female workers were about equally likely to retrain – 15% of men and 16% of women.

The incidence of retraining was highest in younger age groups. Almost 22% of displaced workers under age 25 enrolled in some kind of program, but at age 55 and over, the participation rate was just 5%.

Higher levels of education appear to predispose displaced workers to retrain. More than one-quarter (28%) who were postsecondary graduates enrolled in a program. The participation rate dropped

[1] Education and related services, health and welfare services, consumer services, services to business management, and miscellaneous services.

For the purposes of this article, occupations are grouped into three categories: managerial/professional, white collar, and blue collar.

The managerial/professional category covers: management and administration; natural sciences, engineering and mathematics; social sciences; religion; teaching; medicine and health; artistic, literary and performing arts fields; and sport and recreation.

White collar occupations are those in clerical, sales, and service fields.

The blue collar category is comprised of occupations in: primary industries such as farming, fishing, forestry and mining; processing; product fabricating, assembling and repairing; construction; and equipment operating.

to 18% for those with some postsecondary education and to 15% for workers with a high school diploma. Just 4% of displaced workers with less than high school graduation retrained.

Workers displaced from manufacturing and agriculture and primary industries had the highest training participation rate: 19%. About 16% of transport workers and 15% of service industry and construction workers enrolled. Those who lost jobs in the communications/utilities and trade/financial industries had the lowest participation rate: 11%.

Participation in retraining did not vary substantially among the three main occupational groups. About 17% of managers/professionals retrained, very close to the figure of 16% for blue collar and white collar workers.

Moving to Look for Work

The number of displaced workers who moved to find employment was even smaller than the number who retrained. After losing their jobs, 66,000 or 14% of workers moved to find new ones.

Men were about three times more likely than women to move. Just 6% of female displaced workers moved to search for a job, compared with 18% of men.

Age was also an important factor, with younger workers showing a greater tendency to move. Nearly one in five displaced workers under age 35 (19%) moved to look for work. The percentage of movers dropped to 14% among 35-44-year-olds; to 10% for those aged 45-54; and to 7% among displaced workers aged 55 and over.

Education was not as closely associated with the likelihood of moving as were workers' age and sex, although postsecondary graduates were more mobile than some less educated workers. Movers accounted for 18% of displaced postsecondary graduates, compared with 10% of the group with less than a high school education. However, 17% of those with some high school education moved.

Leaving the Labour Force

About 80,000 displaced workers (17% of the total) had left the labour force by January 1986.

Age appears to have been the primary factor in the decision, as 44% of displaced workers over age 54 left the labour force. Those under age 25 were the next most likely to drop out, but just 19% did so. Workers in the 25-54 age range were least likely to be leavers (12%).

Other groups with above-average proportions leaving the labour force were women, people with comparatively little education, white collar workers, and residents of the Atlantic region and British Columbia.

Long-term Unemployed

In January 1986, 94,000 displaced workers were unemployed; about 30,000 of them, or 6% of the total, had not worked since their original job loss. Groups markedly overrepresented among these long-term unemployed included people aged 45 and over, those with only an elementary school education, former service workers, and Quebec residents.

Re-employed Displaced Workers

Although the majority of displaced workers (63%) had found jobs by 1986, the percentage re-employed varied considerably in different regions. About 73% of displaced workers in Ontario and the three Prairie provinces had new jobs. By contrast, in the Atlantic region, Quebec, and British Columbia, the proportions re-employed were in the 52% to 55% range.

Men were more likely than women to be re-employed, and workers aged 25-44 had more success in the job market than those who were younger or older. The re-employed also tended to be better-educated than workers who had left the labour force or were unemployed. By occupation, people displaced from managerial/professional positions were the most likely to find new jobs, followed by blue collar and then white collar workers.

Duration of Job Search

Displaced workers who found new jobs had searched for an average of 27 weeks. However, close to four out of ten (38%) looked for 6 months to a year, and an

Retraining and moving after job loss, by sex, age and education

Characteristic	Retrained after job loss	Moved after job loss	Total number of displaced workers
	%		000s
Total	15	14	469
Sex			
Men	15	18	322
Women	16	6*	147
Age group			
20-24	22*	18*	27
25-34	18	19	174
35-44	15*	14*	113
45-54	15*	10*	86
55 and over	5*	7	69
Education			
Less than high school	4*	10*	78
Some high school	12*	17	118
High school graduate	15	14	142
Some postsecondary	18*	12*	44
Postsecondary graduate	28	18*	87

* Data are subject to considerable sampling variability and should be used with caution.
Source: Statistics Canada, Social and Economic Studies Division, Displaced Workers Survey, January 1986. *

The Displaced Workers Survey was a supplement to Statistics Canada's Labour Force Survey in January 1986. Although 1.5 million workers who had lost jobs from 1981 to 1985 were identified, only those with at least three years' service with the same employer were the subject of analysis. Workers who were displaced in 1985 were also excluded, as not enough time had passed to consider the job loss permanent. This definition left a group of displaced workers numbering nearly half a million.

additional 12% required more than a year. On the other hand, for some the search was relatively brief; 26% found work in 3 weeks or less.

Workers in the Atlantic region had the longest average job searches (35 weeks), while those in Manitoba and Saskatchewan looked for a relatively short time (19 weeks). The number of weeks seeking employment was also above average in Quebec (31) and British Columbia (29), but somewhat below average in Alberta (23) and Ontario (24).

Job searches were slightly longer for men than for women, averaging 28 weeks and 25 weeks, respectively. Older workers generally needed more time than younger ones. Average job searches ranged from 21 weeks for those under age 25, to 34 weeks for the 55 and over age group.

Workers with the least education had the longest job searches. Those with less than high school looked an average of 35 weeks, compared with 28 weeks for high school graduates, and 21 weeks for workers with at least some education past high school.

Blue collar workers generally searched longer than those displaced from managerial/professional or white collar occupations. Blue collar workers took an average of 31 weeks to find new jobs, compared with 23 weeks for the managerial/professional category and 24 weeks for white collar workers.

Redistribution among Industries and Occupations

Job displacement and re-employment substantially shifted the industrial and occupational distribution of these workers, with the majority changing either industry or occupation. This redistribution can be roughly assessed by calculating net gains and losses, that is, the number of displaced workers who found new jobs in a specific industry or occupation minus the number originally displaced from the same industry or occupation.

Manufacturing industries lost the largest number of employees through displacement: a net loss of 47,000. The construction industry was also a net loser, but at 4,000 workers, the loss was much smaller.

On the other hand, services posted the largest net gain of displaced workers: 23,000. Public administration also absorbed a considerable number, gaining 16,000. The transportation/communications/utilities and trade/financial industries also gained, together employing 11,000

more displaced workers than had been laid off from those industries over the 1981-1984 period. In the agriculture and primary industries category, lay-offs almost equalled the number of displaced workers who found new jobs.

Displaced workers tended to shift into white collar occupations at the expense of the blue collar and managerial/professional categories. The number employed in white collar jobs increased by 21,000, while the number in managerial/professional positions fell by 11,000, and in blue collar fields, by 10,000.

Salary Changes between Lost and New Job[2]

A majority (56%) of re-employed workers reported that their new job paid less than their old one. Their average loss was $152 (-36%) a week. For those (44%) whose salaries increased, the mean gain was $61 (18%) a week. The differences average out to a net weekly loss of $58 (-16%), the equivalent of about $3,000 a year. Wage increases among the minority who found higher-paying positions could not compensate for the sharp cuts suffered by the larger number who accepted lower-paying jobs.

Almost equal proportions of men and women took a drop in pay between the old and new jobs: 57% and 54%, respectively. The frequency of pay loss varied more with age. The proportion of losers was highest among workers aged 45 and over (more than 60%); people in the 35-44 age group were least likely to be losers (53%).

Education proved to be somewhat of a buffer against pay losses. Just 40% of postsecondary graduates were in jobs paying less than their lost jobs, compared with 59% of high school graduates, and 65% of workers who had not attended high school. But as a group, not even postsecondary graduates had an overall gain in pay.

In general, the likelihood of a salary decline increased with the length of service on the lost job. The proportion reporting lower salaries rose from 50% for workers with four or five years' service to 62% for those with more than ten years. The proportion of workers with three years' service who had a salary loss was also relatively high (56%).

Displaced workers with long intervals between jobs generally settled for lower-paying positions than did those who found work quickly. Just 38% of workers who found jobs in three weeks or less took a pay cut, compared with 73% of those who spent more than a year out

of work.

Workers displaced from part-time jobs were the only large group with substantial pay increases. This was because more than three-quarters of those who were re-employed switched to full-time jobs. The result was 83% earning more on their new jobs.

On the other hand, about 16% of people re-employed from full-time jobs were working part-time, and more than three-quarters of them were earning less than on their lost jobs.

Conclusion

While fortunes varied greatly among individual displaced workers, as a whole, they fared poorly. A large number left the labour force. Those who found new jobs took an average of half a year to secure them and were likely to earn less than on their old jobs. Only a minority retrained or moved after they were laid off.

As well as contributing to these lay-offs, the 1981-82 recession affected displaced workers' chances of finding new positions by forcing them into the job market during a period of very high unemployment.

The displacement process had some effect on the distribution of employment, as workers shifted from manufacturing, primary, and construction industries into services and public administration.

---

[2] Salary changes do not account for the effects of inflation over the four years during which workers were displaced and re-employed.

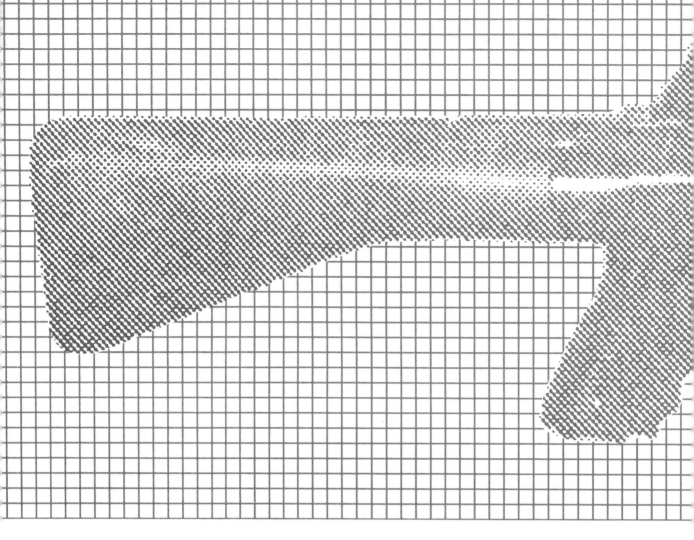

VIOLENT CRIME

by Holly Johnson

Several sources indicate that many Canadians are apprehensive about crime. In 1981, 40% of respondents to the Canadian Urban Victimization Survey said they felt unsafe walking alone in their own neighbourhood at night. The highest levels of fear were reported by elderly people and women: 59% of those aged 65 and older and 56% of women felt unsafe walking alone at night. In comparison, 37% of those under 65 and just 18% of men expressed this fear.

A 1984 Decima Quarterly Report *poll found a similar level of concern among Canadians. More than 4 in 10 (44%) of those surveyed agreed with the statement: "I don't feel safe when I go out alone at night in my neighborhood." Again, people aged 65 and over (58%) and women (57%) were more likely to express this fear than were those under age 65 (44%) or men (32%).*

has risen in Canada. Growth in the incidence of this type of criminal activity, however, has been similar to increases in other types of crime, and violent offences continue to account for only a small proportion of all crime.

In addition, less serious offences, such as simple assaults, make up the majority of all violent crime. Few violent offences involve a weapon or result in bodily harm to the victim. As well, increases in the less serious violent offences have accounted for most of the overall growth in violent crime, particularly in recent years. In fact, incidence rates for more serious offences, such as homicide, attempted murder, aggravated sexual assault, and robbery, have either fallen or been stable in the last several years.

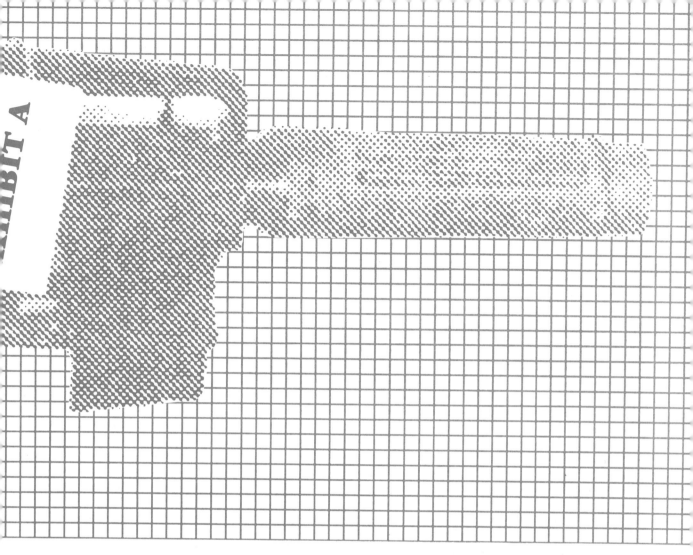

Violent crime[1] rate rising

The incidence of violent crime has increased substantially in Canada. Between 1962 and 1986, the number of crimes of violence recorded by the police rose from 221 per 100,000 population to 801, a 264% increase. This increase, however, was similar to that for other types of crime. The property crime rate, for example, rose 194% in the same period.

Trends for violent and property crime, though, differed in recent years. Rates for both increased by just over 200% between 1962 and 1982; however, between 1982 and 1986, the violent crime rate continued to increase, rising 17%, while the property crime rate fell 3%.

Violent offences include homicide (murder, manslaughter, and infanticide), attempted murder, sexual assault, assault, and robbery.

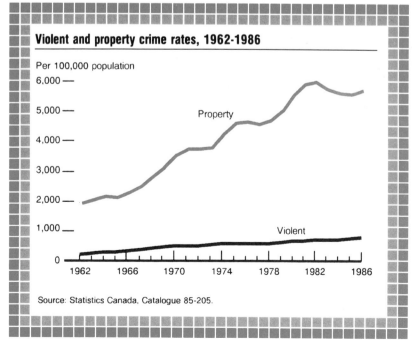

Violent and property crime rates, 1962-1986

Per 100,000 population

Source: Statistics Canada, Catalogue 85-205.

Crime statistics

Official statistics on crime in Canada are obtained from the Uniform Crime Reporting system which counts all criminal incidents recorded by the police. However, because many crimes are never reported to the police, official statistics represent only a portion of all crimes committed. The Canadian Urban Victimization Survey estimated, for example, that in 1981, only 34% of violent crimes were reported to the police. Victims tend not to report violent incidents because they feel the offence is minor, the police likely can't do anything about it, reporting would be inconvenient, or the offence is a personal matter and of no concern to the police. Fear of revenge from the offender, and a concern with the attitudes of criminal justice workers toward this type of incident are additional reasons why victims of sexual assault often do not involve the police.

Official crime statistics underrepresent even the actual occurrence of criminal activity reported to police. This is because when an incident involves several separate offences, only the most serious is recorded. If, for example, an incident involves sexual assault, break and enter, and wilfull damage to property, only sexual assault, the most serious offence, is recorded.

The way police record violent and property crimes also differs. For violent crimes, one offence is recorded for every victim in each incident. For property crimes, though, one offence is recorded for every separate incident.

Still, violent crime accounts for only a small proportion of all crime in Canada. In 1986, violent crimes made up just 9% of all Criminal Code offences, a figure similar to that recorded throughout the period since 1962.

The majority of violent crimes are non-aggravated assaults. Assaults made up three-quarters (76%) of all violent crime in 1986 and most were the least serious type of assault. In 1986, close to 70% of assaults were simple assaults, while just 20% involved bodily harm or the presence of a weapon, and only 2% were aggravated assaults. The remainder were evenly split between assaults involving a peace officer and other types.

Most of the remaining violent crimes in 1986 were either sexual offences (12%) or robberies (11%). Homicides and attempted murders made up less than 1% of all violent offences that year.

As with assaults, the majority of sexual offences were the least serious type. In 1986, over 90% of all sexual assaults did not involve a weapon or result in injury to the victim.

Long-term trends for different types of violent crime have varied, with both assault and sexual assault characterized by particularly large increases. The number of non-sexual assaults per 100,000 population, for example, increased 290% between 1962 and 1986.

The incidence of rape also increased substantially. The number of rapes recorded by the police rose from 3.1 per 100,000 population in 1962 to 10.3 in 1982, an increase of 233%. In the same period, the incidence of indecent assaults, most of which are committed against women, also increased, though not as sharply as the rate for rape. Between 1962 and 1982, the indecent assault rate rose 62%, from 21 per 100,000 population to 34.

Legislation on sexual offences was changed in 1983. Rape and indecent assault were replaced in the Criminal Code with three levels of sexual assault: aggravated sexual assault, which involves endangering the

Victims of violent crime

One of the ironies of crime in Canada is that those who express the greatest fear of crime are often the least victimized. While women and elderly people are the most likely to fear for their personal safety, they are not the groups at highest risk of victimization. In 1981, men were twice as likely as women to be victims of violent crime, and for both sexes, victimization rates were highest, by far, for young adults.

Despite a lower overall risk of victimization, women and the elderly may feel greater vulnerability to violent criminal activity because they are less able to resist an attack, and are more likely to be injured. Women experience the added danger of sexual assault, a threat uncommon to most men.

Violent crimes are most likely to occur in public places such as pubs or bars, other commercial establishments, and streets or parking lots. In 1981, 44% of sexual assaults, 50% of robberies, and 52% of assaults took place in one of these locations.

There were marked differences, though, in the circumstances surrounding assaults on men and women. While public places were the most common location for assaults on both, women were more likely than men to be assaulted in their own homes or in the home of someone else. In 1981, 23% of assaults against women, compared to 5% of those against men, occurred in their own home; another 14% of assaults on women and 10% of those against men occurred in the home of someone else. Women were also more likely than men to be assaulted by relatives: 12% of female victims compared to just 2% of men were assaulted by a family member.

Violent crime lower in Canada than in the United States

Levels of violent crime in Canada are well below those in the United States. The incidence of the most serious types of violent crime* in the United States, for example, was more than five times the rate for Canada in 1985. That year, there were well over 500 such crimes per 100,000 population in the United States compared with just over 100 in Canada.

As well, the incidence of the most serious violent crimes has been rising in the United States in recent years, while the rate has been falling in Canada. Between 1983 and 1985, the serious violent crime rate rose 3% in the United States, but fell 10% in Canada.

* These figures refer only to serious violent crimes, whereas the data in the rest of the article include all violent offences. The Canadian rate includes homicide, attempted murder, rape and aggravated sexual assault, wounding and aggravated assault, and robbery. The U.S. rate includes murder, forcible rape, aggravated assault, and robbery.

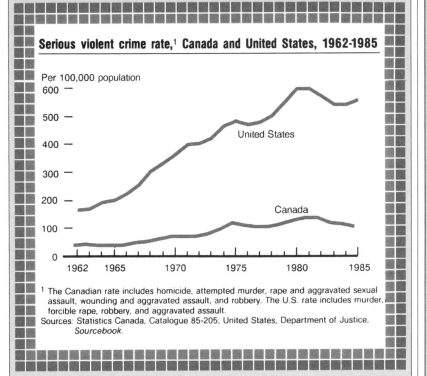

Serious violent crime rate,[1] Canada and United States, 1962-1985

Per 100,000 population

[1] The Canadian rate includes homicide, attempted murder, rape and aggravated sexual assault, wounding and aggravated assault, and robbery. The U.S. rate includes murder, forcible rape, robbery, and aggravated assault.
Sources: Statistics Canada, Catalogue 85-205; United States, Department of Justice, *Sourcebook.*

life of, or maiming or disfiguring the victim; sexual assault causing bodily harm, or using or threatening to use a weapon; and simple sexual assault. Because of these changes data collected on sexual offences after 1982 are not comparable with earlier data.

The incidence of sexual offences as defined in the revised legislation has increased. Between 1983 and 1986, the number of reported sexual offences rose from 48 per 100,000 population to 80. Most of this increase, however, was accounted for by growth in the incidence of simple sexual assaults. These increased from 42 incidents per 100,000 population in 1983 to 75 in 1986.

On the other hand, the incidence of the more serious forms of sexual assault changed little in the 1983-1986 period. There were about 2 aggravated sexual assaults per 100,000 population throughout this period, while the rate for sexual assaults involving a weapon or causing bodily harm increased slightly, from 3 to 4 incidents per 100,000 population.

Overall rates for homicide, attempted murder, and robbery also increased significantly since 1962; however, the incidence of these offences has been falling in recent years.

The number of homicides rose from 1.4 per 100,000 population in 1962 to 3.1 by 1977. This rate remained fairly stable at around 2.8 between 1978 and 1985, and then dropped to 2.2 in 1986, the lowest it has been since 1971.

Rates for attempted murder increased from a low of 0.4 per 100,000 population in 1962 to a high of 3.8 in 1982, but then fell to 3.4 in 1985 and 1986.

The incidence of robbery, which involves violence or the threat of violence to steal from another person, followed a similar pattern. The number of robberies per 100,000 population rose from 27 in 1962 to 111 in 1982. Between 1982 and 1986, though, the robbery rate fell to 91.

The incidence of robberies involving guns has also declined in recent years. Between 1981 and 1986, the number of robberies using guns fell from 37 per 100,000 population to 26. In comparison, the rate for robberies involving other weapons rose slightly, from 22 to 24, in the same period.

Violent crime higher in western Canada

Rates of violent crime are generally higher in the western provinces than in central or eastern Canada. In 1986, British Columbia had the highest violent crime rate of any province, with 1,254 violent offences per 100,000 population. Manitoba (1,035), Alberta (918), and Saskatchewan (878) also had relatively high violent crime rates.

Prince Edward Island and Quebec had the lowest violent crime rates with just 499 and 550 offences per 100,000 population, respectively. In the other Atlantic provinces, the violent crime rate was just over 600, while the rate in Ontario (791) was just under the national level (801).

This pattern varies, however, for some types of violent crime. Perhaps the most interesting example is that Quebec, with the second lowest overall violent crime rate, had the highest robbery rate of any province. As well, the number of robberies using

guns per 100,000 population in Quebec was more than three times greater than in the province with the next highest rate.

Violent crime in cities and towns

The generally higher incidence of violent crime in the west also appears when major metropolitan areas are compared, although there are some exceptions. While Victoria, Vancouver, and Edmonton reported the highest violent crime rates in 1986, Calgary had the lowest rate of any major Canadian city. On the other hand, Montreal had the

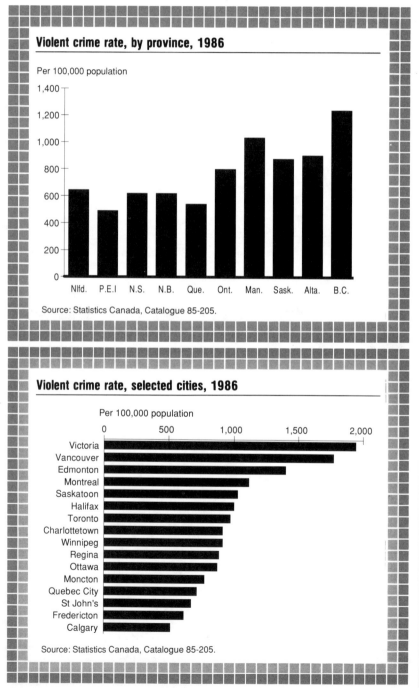

Violent crime rate, by province, 1986

Per 100,000 population

Source: Statistics Canada, Catalogue 85-205.

Violent crime rate, selected cities, 1986

Per 100,000 population

Source: Statistics Canada, Catalogue 85-205.

fourth highest urban violent crime rate, and Halifax, Toronto and Charlottetown all had higher rates than Winnipeg and Regina.

Violent crime rates are generally higher in large urban areas than in small cities or towns, although the incidence of violent crime generally increased more rapidly in smaller centres in the last decade.

In 1986, cities with a population of 250,000 or more had an average of 933 violent crimes per 100,000 population. This compared with rates of 822 in cities with a population between 50,000 and 250,000, 769 in cities with 10,000 to 50,000 people, and 729 in centres with a population of between 750 and 10,000.

Between 1977 and 1986, the violent crime rate in towns with less than 10,000 population increased 48%, compared with 44% for cities with 10,000 to 50,000 people, 42% in cities with population between 50,000 and 250,000, and 38% in the largest urban areas.

Police solve most violent crimes

The police generally solve, or clear, about three-quarters of reported violent crimes. In 1986, 44% of all violent offences were cleared by charge, while another 29% were cleared otherwise.[2]

There is some variation, though, in the percentage of the different types of violent offences that are cleared by charge. In 1986, 76% of homicides and 77% of attempted murders resulted in charges. At the same time, only about half of assaults (56%) and sexual assaults (47%) were cleared by charge, while the figure was just 29% for robberies.

Most violent offenders are men. In 1986, 76% of those charged with violent crimes were men, while 8% were women and 16% were young offenders.

[2] Offences can be cleared by charge or cleared otherwise. Offences are cleared by charge when an arrest is made, a summons to appear is issued, or a warrant to apprehend is laid against at least one person. An offence is cleared otherwise when the offender has been identified and enough is known to issue a warrant, yet, there is a reason outside of police control that prevents charging. Clearance rates for homicide are from *Homicide in Canada*, Statistics Canada, Catalogue 85-209. Rates for other crimes are from *Canadian Crime Statistics*, Statistics Canada, Catalogue 85-205.

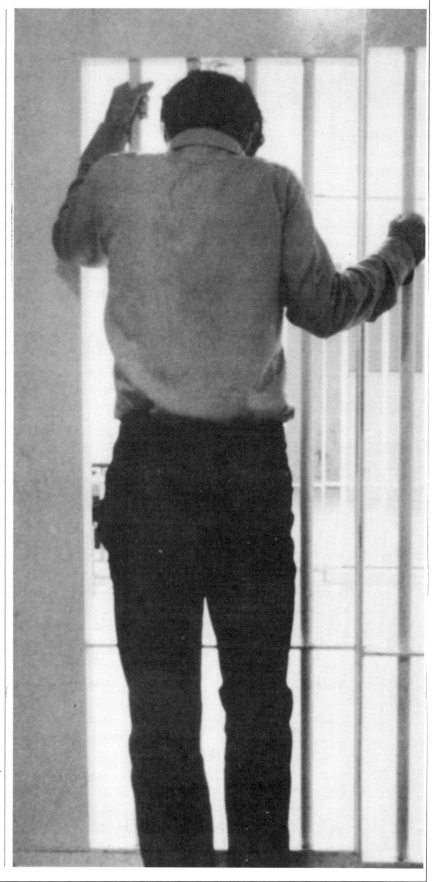

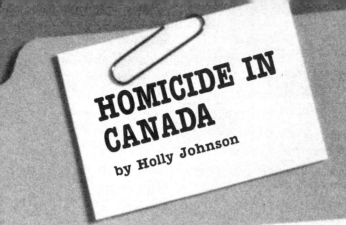

HOMICIDE IN CANADA

by Holly Johnson

The homicide rate in Canada has gone through several distinct phases in the past twenty-five years. Between 1962 and 1977, the number of homicides per 100,000 population increased steadily from 1.4 to 3.1. In the period 1978-1985, however, the homicide rate was relatively stable, fluctuating between 2.5 and 2.8. Then, in 1986, the rate dropped sharply to 2.2, the lowest level since 1971.

The actual number of homicides followed a similar pattern. Between 1962 and 1977, the number of homicides almost tripled, increasing from 265 to 711. Then, in the period 1978-1984, the number of homicides stabilized, ranging from a high of 682 in 1983 to a low of 593 in 1980. In 1985, there were 704 homicides in Canada, but the number fell sharply to just 561 in 1986.

Although homicides attract a great deal of publicity, they make up only a small proportion of all reported violent crimes. Between 1962 and 1985, homicides ranged between 0.4% and 0.6% of all reported violent crimes. In 1986, this figure dropped even lower to 0.3%.

The incidence of homicide is also relatively low compared with other forms of non-natural death. In 1985, there were 2.8 homicides per 100,000 population; the same year, there were 16.2 deaths per 100,000 population as a result of traffic accidents, 14.9 as a result of other accidents, and 12.9 suicides.

Homicide Rates Increase from East to West

As with other violent offences, homicide rates in Canada are generally highest in the western provinces and lowest in the Atlantic region. In 1986, Manitoba had the highest provincial homicide rate, with 4.4 homicides for every 100,000 residents. British Columbia (3.1) and Alberta (2.7) were also characterized by relatively high homicide rates. On the other hand, there were no homicides in Prince Edward Island in 1986, and just 0.7 per 100,000 residents in Newfoundland.

The Northwest and Yukon Territories both had homicide rates far in excess of the national rate. In 1986, there were 27.5 homicides per 100,000 residents in the Northwest Territories, while in the Yukon Territory, the rate was 13.1.

Firearms and Other Methods of Homicide

From 1976 to 1978, about 38% of homicides annually involved firearms. In 1979, the year after gun control legislation came into force, the proportion declined to 33%. Since then, the proportion remained at about that level, except for 1982, when the figure climbed to 37%. In 1986, 31% of homicides were the result of shooting. The proportion of homicides involving handguns, though, remained relatively stable. Throughout the 1976-1985 period, about 10% of homicides involved handguns each year. In 1986, however, the proportion fell to 7%.

Between 1976 and 1986, the percentage of all homicides caused by stabbing increased from 20% to 29%, while the percentage due to beatings remained at 22%.

Homicides Committed during Another Crime

In 1986, 17% of all homicides occurred during the commission of another crime. This figure, however, fluctuated somewhat in the last decade. It rose from 13% in 1976 to about 20% in 1981 and 1982, and then fell back to 14% in 1984.

Robbery, theft, and break and enter were the criminal acts that most often resulted in homicide. Homicides that took place during the commission of one of these offences increased from 8% of all homicides in 1976 to 13% in 1985, but dropped to 11% in 1986. Homicides committed during a sexual assault made up 2% of all homicides in 1976, 6% in 1981, and 4% in 1986.

The types of crimes resulting in homicide differ according to the sex of the victim. The most common type of offence resulting in the death of a woman was sexual assault, while for men the most common were robbery, theft, and break and enter.

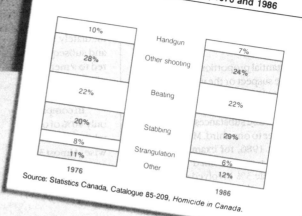

Methods Used to Commit Homicide, 1976 and 1986

Method	1976	1986
Handgun	10%	7%
Other shooting	28%	24%
Beating	22%	22%
Stabbing	20%	29%
Strangulation	8%	6%
Other	11%	12%

Source: Statistics Canada, Catalogue 85-209, Homicide in Canada.

Homicides and Alcohol and Drug Consumption

In a substantial proportion of homicides, either the suspect or the victim had consumed alcohol or drugs. Between 1976 and 1986, the proportion of homicides involving these substances ranged from one-quarter to one-third. Most involved alcohol. In 1986, for example, 22% of homicides were classified as alcohol-related, while 3% involved drug usage.

A High Proportion of Homicides Solved

Relative to other crimes, the police solve a high proportion of homicides. In 1986, 76% of homicides resulted in charges

being laid against an accused. In another 9% of cases, a suspect was identified but not charged. In most of these cases the suspect either committed suicide immediately after the incident, confessed and subsequently died, or was committed to a mental hospital. Fifteen percent of homicides committed in 1986 were unsolved.

In comparison, police laid charges in only 40% of other violent crimes in 1986, while another 30% were cleared otherwise. Almost 30% of violent crimes other than homicide were not solved.

Homicide Suspects

The majority of homicide suspects are young men. In 1986, 57% of all homicide suspects were men aged 29 or under. Overall, men made up 85% of homicide suspects that year. The age and sex profile of homicide suspects remained relatively constant over the last decade.

Between 1976 and 1986, the annual percentage of homicide suspects of native origin fluctuated between 18% and 23%. In 1986, 20% of homicide suspects were native, a proportion considerably higher than the 3% representa-

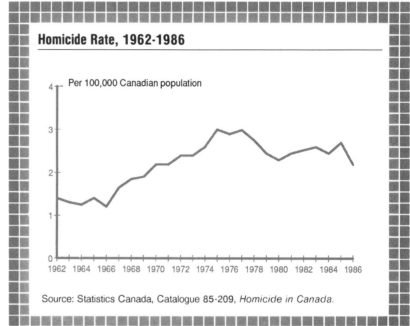

Homicide Rate, 1962-1986

Per 100,000 Canadian population

Source: Statistics Canada, Catalogue 85-209, *Homicide in Canada*.

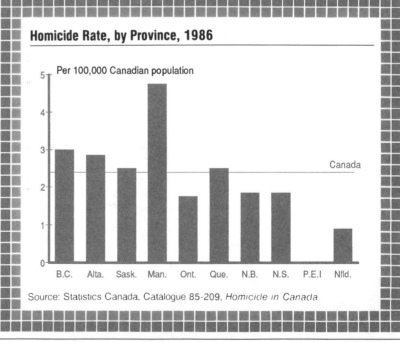

Homicide Rate, by Province, 1986

Per 100,000 Canadian population

Source: Statistics Canada, Catalogue 85-209, *Homicide in Canada*.

Homicide and the Criminal Code

Homicide currently includes three categories: murder, manslaughter and infanticide. According to police records, most homicides, about 91% annually, are murders. Another 8% are classified as manslaughter, while fewer than 1% are infanticides.

Murder is further broken down into first- and second-degree murder. First-degree murder includes planned and deliberate murder; murder of a police or custodial officer killed in the line of duty; murder committed in the course of certain other criminal acts such as hijacking, kidnapping or sexual offences; and murder committed by someone previously convicted of either first- or second-degree murder. All other murder is considered second degree.

The penalty for both first- and second-degree murder is life imprisonment. Persons convicted of first-degree murder are eligible for parole after 25 years; those convicted of second-degree murder must serve at least 10 years before they are eligible for parole.

Manslaughter generally is the killing of someone without intent. The maximum sentence for manslaughter is life. Infanticide is the killing of a newborn child by its mother; it carries a maximum sentence of five years imprisonment.

Historically, Canada's homicide rate has been between one-third and one-quarter of that in the United States. In 1986, the homicide rate in Canada was 2.2 compared with 8.6 in the U.S.

Relative to other countries with comparable measures of homicide, the 1985 Canadian homicide rate of 2.8 was higher than in Scotland (1.1), England and Wales (1.2), and Sweden (1.5), but lower than in Italy (4.4) and France (4.6).

Homicide Rates in Canada and the United States, 1962-1986

Sources: Statistics Canada, Catalogue 85-209, *Homicide in Canada;* U.S. Department of Justice, *Crime in the United States.*

tion of native people in the general population.

Homicide Victims

Historically, just over one-third of homicide victims have been women and about two-thirds men. In 1986, 36% were female and 64% male. About half of all victims have been between the ages of 18 and 39.

The percentage of homicide victims who were of native origin fluctuated during the last decade, ranging from a low of 12% to a high of 19%. In 1986, 14% of homicide victims were of native origin.

Victim-Suspect Relationship and Location of Homicide

A popular image of homicide is that of a stranger-to-stranger attack in a park or dark alley. While such incidents do occur, the majority of homicides involved people who knew each other, and most took place in a home setting.

In 40% of homicides solved in 1986, suspects and victims were domestically related, while another 35% involved social or business acquaintances. In only 25% of cases did the victim and suspect not know each other.

Domestic homicides were predomi-

nantly those in which victims and suspects were immediate marital or common-law family members: 37% involved wives killed by husbands; 29% were children killed by parents; 10% were parents killed by children; 10% were husbands killed by wives; and 4% involved siblings. Other family relationships such as grandparent, uncle, aunt or cousin made up the remaining 9% of domestic homicides.

The largest proportion of homicides occurred in the victim's home. In 1986, 47% of all homicides took place in the home of the victim, which may also have been the suspect's home. Another 9% occurred in the suspect's residence.

·Only 17% of homicides happened in a public place. An additional 10% occurred in a private place, such as another residence, while 2% took place in a correctional institution, and 5% in other locations. The actual location of 9% of homicides was not known.

Homicides in the victim's home are most likely to involve people who share a domestic relationship. Over half (53%) of homicides in the victim's home in 1986 involved relatives, while 17% involved acquaintances. A substantial proportion (12%), however, occurred during the commission of another crime and involved non-relatives. An additional 4% of offenders were unknown to the victims and 14% of cases were unsolved.

The nature and circumstances of homicides vary depending on the sex of the victims. Women are more likely than men to be killed in their own homes, and at the hands of someone domestically related to them. In 1986, 61% of female homicide victims were killed in their homes compared with 40% of male victims. At the same time, 62% of female homicide victims compared with 27% of male victims were killed by someone related to them through kinship, marriage or common-law union. As well, the overwhelming majority (79%) of victims of spousal homicide were women.

Police and Correctional Officers Murdered

The number of police officers reported murdered while on duty in Canada each year has not changed substantially over the past twenty-five years. Between 1962 and 1986, a total of 92 police officers, or about 4 per year, were murdered. The annual number ranged from a low of 1 to a high of 11. Four officers were murdered in 1986.

Between 1962 and 1986, 16 staff members of correctional institutions were killed in the line of duty. The highest annual number of such homicides in a year was 3 in 1975, 1978, and 1982. In 1986, no correctional staff members were murdered.